D0791517

INSIGHT GUIDE

NORTHERN ITALY

APA PUBLICATIONS

Part of the Langenscheidt Publishing Group

INSIGHT GUIDE
NORTHERN Italy

ABOUT THIS BOOK

Editorial

Editor
Dorothy Stannard
Editorial Director
Brian Bell

Distribution

UK & Ireland
GeoCenter International Ltd
The Viables Centre , Harrow Way
Basingstoke, Hants RG22 4BJ
Fax: (44) 1256-817988

United States
Langenscheidt Publishers, Inc.
46–35 54th Road, Maspeth, NY 11378
Fax: (718) 784-0640

Canada
Prologue Inc.
1650 Lionel Bertrand Blvd., Boisbriand
Québec, Canada J7H 1N7
Tel: (450) 434-0306. Fax: (450) 434-2627

Australia & New Zealand
Hema Maps Pty. Ltd.
24 Allgas Street, Slacks Creek 4127
Brisbane, Australia
Tel: (61) 7 3290 0322. Fax: (61) 7 3290 0478

Worldwide
**Apa Publications GmbH & Co.
Verlag KG (Singapore branch)**
38 Joo Koon Road, Singapore 628990
Tel: (65) 865-1600. Fax: (65) 861-6438

Printing

Insight Print Services (Pte) Ltd
38 Joo Koon Road, Singapore 628990
Tel: (65) 865-1600. Fax: (65) 861-6438

©1999 Apa Publications GmbH & Co.
Verlag KG (Singapore branch)
All Rights Reserved
First Edition 1999

CONTACTING THE EDITORS
Although every effort is made to
provide accurate information, we
live in a fast-changing world and
would appreciate it if readers
would call our attention to any
errors or outdated information
that may occur by writing to:
**Insight Guides, P.O. Box 7910,
London SE1 1WE, England.
Fax: (44 171) 403-0290.**
e-mail:
insight@apaguide.demon.co.uk

This guidebook combines the
interests and enthusiasms of
two of the world's best known
information providers: Insight
Guides, whose titles have set the
standard for visual travel guides
since 1970, and the Discovery
Channel, the world's premier
source of nonfiction television pro-
gramming.

Insight Guides' editors provide
practical advice and general
understanding about a place's
history, culture, and people. Discovery Channel and its extensive
web site, www.discovery.com,
help millions of viewers explore
their world from the comfort of their
home and also encourage them to
explore it firsthand.

How to use this book

Insight Guide: Northern Italy has
been carefully structured to convey an understanding of the
region and its culture, and to
guide readers through its sights
and attractions:

◆ The Features section, with a
yellow colour bar, covers the
country's history and culture in

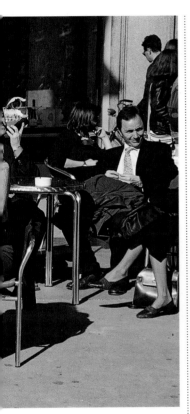

lively authoritative essays written by specialists.

◆ The Places section, with a blue bar, provides full details of all the sights and areas worth seeing. The chief places of interest are coordinated by number with the maps.

◆ The Travel Tips section, with an orange bar, at the back of the book offers a convenient point of reference for information on travel, accommodation, restaurants, and other practical aspects of the country.

◆ The Photographs are chosen not only to illustrate the beauty and variety of the cities and landscapes but also to convey an impression of the everyday lives of the Northern Italians.

The contributors

Long-standing Italophile **Lisa Gerard-Sharp**, a writer and broadcaster who wrote the majority of this book, aims to convey the contemporary flavour of life in the north – from its guise as a café society and fashion showcase to its seminal role as an economic powerhouse and hot-bed of regionalism.

Roger Williams, journalist, novelist and Insight Guide veteran, whose acclaimed novel *Lunch With Elizabeth David* was partly set in Italy, was a leading contributor to the book. He paints a refreshingly new picture of Turin, Piedmont, Valle d'Aosta, Friuli and Trieste. The other key member of the writing team was **Jonathan Keates**, an Italian expert and author of the wrily perceptive *Italian Journeys*, as well as being a regular contributor to the literary pages of the British press. Here, Keates turns his critical eye to the history section, as well as writing the chapter on art and architecture.

The Travel Tips were compiled by **Sibylle Geier** and **Nicky Swallow**. The principal photography was provided by **Bill Wassmann**, **John Heseltine** and **Michael Jenner**. Picture research was by **Hilary Genin**, with maps created by **Zoë Goodwin**. Editing was completed by **Pam Barrett**, Roger Williams and **Dorothy Stannard**, and the book was proofread and indexed by **Laura Hicks**.

Map Legend

▄ ▪ ▪	International Boundary
– – – –	Region Boundary
– •–	National Park/Reserve
– – – –	Ferry Route
Ⓜ	Metro
✈ ✈	Airport: International/Regional
🚌	Bus Station
🅟	Parking
ⓘ	Tourist Information
✉	Post Office
🏛 † ✝	Church/Ruins
†	Monastery
☾	Mosque
✡	Synagogue
🏰	Castle/Ruins
∴	Archaeological Site
⋒	Cave
1	Statue/Monument
★	Place of Interest

The main places of interest in the Places section are coordinated by number with a full-colour map (e.g. ❶), and a symbol at the top of every right-hand page tells you where to find the map.

INSIGHT GUIDE
NORTHERN ITALY

CONTENTS

Maps

Introduction

People

History

Features

The Certosa
di Pavia,
Lombardy

THIS RESONANT REGION

Diverse landscapes, a wealth of cultural sites and a proud
people make Northern Italy a distinctive region

Northern Italy has previously been ill-served by guidebooks, with a plethora of books on selected cities, notably Venice and Milan, yet a dearth of readable writing on the distinctiveness of northern society, complemented by its rural hinterland and historic cities. Apart from conveying the charm of the scenery, from country villas and gardens to national parks, this book hopes to redress the balance by highlighting the "minor" art cities, from Mantua to Trento, as well as covering the complex social scene. In this, as in all aspects of society, regional rivalry is an Italian characteristic writ large, taking the form of pride in local opera and architecture, dialects and dishes, festivals and football teams.

Moreover, even in standard tourist terms, few comparable regions can match northern Italy for sheer variety of scenery and linked leisure pursuits, from hiking along the Ligurian coast or lounging on the brash Adriatic beaches to sailing on the melancholic northern lakes, wallowing in the sybaritic spas of the Euganean hills, or simply skiing or dog-sledding in the prestigious Dolomite mountain resorts.

Since the boundaries of northern Italy are disputed by the Italians themselves, we have arbitrarily decided to draw the line beneath Emilia Romagna. This resonantly artistic region was too rich to leave in the notional no-man's land of "central Italy". However, we rightly excluded Florence, Tuscany, Umbria and areas south, since these places are well served in their own right by other Insight Guides. ❏

PRECEDING PAGES: a Venetian gondolier; classic ingredients in the culinary heart of Europe; murals in the South Tyrol; the alpine pastures of Trentino.
LEFT: Ciao! Greetings from Portofino.

THE NORTHERN ITALIANS

"Italians are baffled by their own behaviour. The only people who have no doubt...
are foreigners who streak through it in a few days" — Luigi Barzini

In northern Italy, geography is destiny, to a greater degree than elsewhere, simply because a citizen born in the wealthy north sees little need to move from the confines of his cosy world. Still less does the average citizen desire to shape his destiny in any but the most obvious economic ways. Why stray when one's status is already assured at home, when there is a ready-made support system to help one through the complex bureaucracy operated by a heartless state?

The price of peace

If the Faustian pact weighs inner life, exploration and stimulation against the safety and comfort of a known world, there is no contest. Which northerner does not want to eat decent food, stock home-made wine in a small cellar, dress smartly, drive an acceptable car, do up his home, and live in a small town unscarred by urban blight. This is a conservative society that half believes in the old saying *"Moglie e buoi dei paesi tuoi."* (Choose your wife and your cattle from your own backyard.) As the English writer Jonathan Keates says of the complacent citizens of Modena: "There is little anguish or doubt or stress because the *piccolo mondo moderno* they inhabit is so full of certainties."

When parochialism becomes self-perpetuating, regional differences remain as pronounced as ever. Mobility may have increased but the Italian mindset tends to stay behind, comparing the new place unfavourably with the cherished home town. As the novelist Tim Parks says astutely: "When an Italian leaves a place it is almost always with the intention of returning victorious and vindicated."

According to the historian Valerio Lintner, the so-called northern Italian character emerged during the time of the medieval city-states, creating "the relaxed, friendly and congenial atmosphere which we now associate with many Italian cities". Compared with the more feudal

south, the north fostered the development of communities run with relative autonomy and respect for the rule of law, cities imbued with a sense of civic responsibility. The importance of commerce, finance and social mobility distinguished the north from the autocratic, land-owning southern societies. The abiding

northern values are regional pride and attachment to one's roots, compounded by complacency, conservatism and consumerism. A Christian work ethic justifies the pursuit of wealth and the passionate defence of the interests of the tribe. In case this all seems too cosy, the mixture is stirred with resentment of Roman bureaucracy and racist slurs on other regions, particularly with regard to perceived southern fecklessness.

Despite certain shared values, the regions have preserved their cultural distinctiveness. Even the Milanese metropolis is less cosmopolitan than comparable European capitals. Italians delight in the game of regional and city

LEFT AND RIGHT: the silly and the sober – different faces of Bologna.

stereotyping: they are suspicious of the cool, secretive, contradictory Venetians but secretly admiring of the materialistic, prosaic, joyless Milanese; the aloof, melancholic, patrician Piedmontese are compared with the mean, enterprising, independent Genoese, heirs to an equally noble tradition, and the bluff, hardy Trentini are the more Italianate neighbours of the Germanic South Tyroleans. Further south, the rough, rebellious Romagnoli are distinguished from the greedy, pampered, sensuous Emilians and

> **STYLISH BIRTHRIGHT**
>
> "It helps to have been born in Milan: it's a graphic city, dedicated to good design, but also deeply surrealistic."
> – Fashion guru Anna Piaggi.

port to social mobility and conventional success. More than any other region, rich Lombardy feels treated as the milch cow for bloated southern bureaucracy. An entrepreneurial ethos is shared by immigrants and incomers drawn to Milan's economic success. Milan has long been a melting pot, a magnet for ambitious Italians from poorer regions. The Milanese pride themselves on their glamorous image as creative, stylish movers and shakers. Yet any journey on the city metro will reveal the myth

the smugly bourgeois Bolognese who run the regional capital. Only when describing southerners does the northern vocabulary suddenly shrink to a few choice insults.

Materialistic Milan

Milanese citizens see themselves as running the real capital of Italy, at odds with slothful and incompetent Rome. Even Cardinal Biffi of Bologna, mooted as a candidate for the Papacy, sees no shame in declaring: "As a Milanese, I would be deeply unhappy if I had to go and live in Rome." The character of the Milanese is calibrated on their antipathy to Rome, and on a commitment to money-making, the sole pass-

of the Milanese as fashion plates. The city of silk suits is restricted to certain quarters and certain classes. In many ways Silvio Berlusconi, the brash media magnate, is the quintessential Milanese, a powerful, self-made man with a perma-tan and televisual blue suits; if he were a perfume, it would be Essence of Milan, a potent parvenu, packaged elegantly but swiftly passé.

Milan is often dismissed as a "prose capital", its citizens as rational and unromantic as the neon signs that light up the grey city centre. Yet the actress Veronica Pivetti is eager to dispel such notions: "As a real Milanese, I even love the fog and the drizzle on those sad November days." Socially, the Milanese Catholic hinterland can be as conformist as anywhere in southern Italy. Irene Pivetti, the actress's politician sister, is a high-profile product of such conservatism, with intransigent public views on such social issues as contraception and divorce.

Indeed, beyond the northern capital, Lombardy remains economically progressive but socially conservative. The Milanese metropolis, dedicated to shiny materialism, is no myth, but sophisticated Milan is shackled by its straitlaced hinterland and the dreary industrial foothills of the Alps. Despite an early and influential socialist movement, a countercurrent of who propounds a truculent racism in public but is a smoother operator in private. Marco Formentini, former Mayor of Milan, represents a slightly less brutish strand of northern federalism: "We believe in a united Europe of 50 regions like Lombardy, Bavaria or Wales – and not in the Europe of 12 nations."

Secretive Turin

The Milanese dismiss Turin as *grigio*: a grey, dead city. First impressions may confirm Turin as a severe city populated by taciturn, reserved, hard-working Piedmontese. However, the citizens can be seen in a softer light during their

Catholic paternalism still colours the regional character today, swelling the ranks of the northern separatist movement.

Scraping the glittering Latin surface of Lombardy reveals Longobard bluffness and the brutality of the Teutonic tribes who colonised the fat, rich plains in the 6th century. The loud, unsophisticated temperament lives on in Umberto Bossi, leader of the separatist Northern League (Lega Nord). As a born-again Lombard, he is a zealous demagogue

LEFT: Umberto Bossi, leader of the Lombard separatists, the Lega Nord.
ABOVE: quintessential Milan man, Silvio Berlusconi.

festivals devoted to general gluttony, or in their cult of café life and *stuzzichini*, Turin *tapas*. Under the city arcades, moneyed *Torino-bene* (respectable citizens) sip coffee and nibble on *gianduiotti*, the city's hazelnut-studded chocolates. They possess the languid composure and sophistication sought by Ferrero Rocher, the Piedmontese chocolate firm.

Turin is perceived as melancholic, old-fashioned and prey to provincialism, a view belied by the city's aristocratic past and industrial present. The historian Denis Mack Smith notes: "The aristocracy of Turin belonged to a closed society in which pigtails and powdered wigs survived longer than elsewhere, where serfs and feudal prisons could be found." Today the old guard still maintains a snooty, almost French *sang-froid*, a haughtiness bred of rigid, stoical Piedmontese society with its blue-blooded lineage. Amadeo di Savoia, Duke of Aosta, is the last remaining emblem of monarchism in the Italian Republic. The monarchy was abolished by a referendum in 1946, and male descendants are still banned from permanently settling in Italy.

The spirit of public service is part of the Piedmontese ethos, one embodied by Count

> **FEED THE REVOLUTION**
>
> In 1860, after plotting the Risorgimento (Italian unification) in Turin's Il Cambio restaurant, Cavour said: "Today we've made history, now let's have dinner."

capitalism, and his plans to halt privatisation and abolish Nato. Emma Bonino, who was born north of Turin, is, like the classic Piedmontese politician, both an outsider and an insider. Her controversial role as Fisheries Commissioner in Brussels caused her to be dubbed "the Eva Peron of the halibut". Unlike most faceless Brussels bureaucrats, she is a forthright liberal and also an approachable, unpompous member of the Radical Party.

The Archbishop of Milan, Cardinal Martini,

Camillo di Cavour (1810–61), the aristocratic patriot and prime minister. In dutifully rising to the challenge, Cavour was industrious, moderate, reasonable, tolerant: a typical Piedmontese of the old school. Yet he was equally Piedmontese in his political pragmatism and his forthright appreciation of good food.

This sense of duty and (restaurant) service is shared by a number of individualistic contemporary politicians. Fausto Bertinotti, the dedicated but disruptive leader of the Marxist Communist Party, is partial to chic suits and urban café life. Bertinotti, who grew up in a hotbed of trade unionism in Turin, continues to rattle the establishment with his suspicion of

is a Piedmontese candidate for the papacy and a spokesman for Milanese liberalism. Although a pillar of the establishment, he is also a modernist. However, his attitude to celibacy in the priesthood ("It will remain in force, but local adjustments may be made.") can be seen as either sheer sophistry or a masterpiece of Piedmontese diplomacy.

Tyrolean twist

Trentino-Alto Adige has a split personality, with Austrian and Italian influences reflecting a dual cultural heritage. Germanic traits are evident in the citizens' law-abiding nature and environmentally aware approach to the lakes and mountains. As befits such a rugged region, the South Tyrol is proud of producing some of Italy's hardiest sportspeople, including Reinhold Meisner, a world-famous climber, and Alberto Tomba, the country's most famous alpine skier. Francesco Moser, a politician and former cycling world champion, is typical of hearty, Italianate Trentino folk: a bluff wine-lover who cultivates his vineyards of luscious red Marzemino wines.

The German-speaking community in Bolzano (Bozen) claims Lili Gruber, a celebrity television journalist. She was no Latin siren but a cool, direct interviewer who won popularity

canny, cosmopolitan and conservative but concealing a sinister heart. The Republic was respected but not much loved, while widespread fear was engendered by its skilful spies. Yet there is a lighter side to the Venetians: a pronounced aesthetic sense, poetic sensibility and a playful nature sustained by pageantry, a pleasure-seeking image once matched by morals as slippery as the lagoon itself.

According to the historian Valerio Lintner, Marco Polo (1254–1324) best represents the Venetian character of old, "adventurous and daring in pursuit of profit, whilst financially conservative and prudent". The Venetians are

for her un-Italian toughness and journalistic professionalism.

Venetian subtlety

The Venetians are naturally courteous and tolerant, as befits a cosmopolitan people who have come to terms with the loss of empire. Their philosophical detachment is often mistaken for aloofness, with their calm and sanguine air likened to Anglo-Saxon aplomb. Still, the lingering image is of a cool and closed people,

LEFT: South Tyrol has a distinctly Austrian character – from its law-abiding citizens to its wooden chalets.
ABOVE: café society in sophisticated Portofino.

also noted for their curiosity and spirit of intellectual enquiry, a disposition that led to empire-building. Yet this lofty outlook is tempered by a profound indifference to matters beyond the lagoon. It is a view personified by Marco Polo, who remained a home-town boy despite his exploits. "Every time I describe a city, I am saying something about Venice," he wrote.

Genoese adventurers

As befits a former maritime state, Genoa is cosmopolitan, raffish and commercial in equal measures. The mercantile character of the city, and the citizens' skill at money-lending, have given the Genoese an undeserved reputation for meanness, much like the Jews elsewhere. However, as befits an erstwhile republic that pioneered such modern devices as bills of credit, cheques and insurance, Genoese banking and business skills are held in high regard. The people are reputed to be rugged individualists, shrewd, calculating, enterprising and independent. The great seafarer Christopher Columbus (1451–1506) is naturally the city's most famous son. Giuseppe Mazzini (1805–72) was a romantic adventurer of the old school: the "father of the Italian nation" succeeded in putting a united Italy on the political agenda.

Renzo Piano, one of the world's most celebrated architects and urban planners, is as enterprising, cosmopolitan and chameleon as Genoa, his native city. Apart from designing the Pompidou Centre in Paris with Richard Rogers, the Potsdamerplatz in Berlin and Kansai airport in Osaka, he has also left his mark on northern Italy. Piano remodelled part of the historic Fiat Lingotto works in Turin, designed a new aquarium and congress centre in Genoa, and conceived a high-tech wind tunnel for the Ferrari test track at Maranello. He approaches every new challenge with typical Genoese pragmatism: "My rule is that if I have to build a monastery, then I become a bit of a friar, and if

THE NORTH-SOUTH DIVIDE

The north-south divide is as elusive yet definite as the Italian character itself. Racist northerners often joke that Garibaldi did not unify Italy but dismembered Africa. Angelo Maraini, an activist in the secessionist Northern League, declares: "Thank goodness we in the north were invaded by the Austrians, and the Habsburgs left good traces in our blood." Lombardy and the Veneto are Italy's richest regions, and 80 per cent of the country's personal taxation comes from the north, which has some of the highest productivity rates in the European Union. In this culture of economic dependence, the financial burden is shouldered by the north, while the south receives the subsidies.

Commentators increasingly wonder whether the glue of national solidarity can continue to support a rich north and a poor south. The argument for fostering closer ties with regions north of the Alps has a clear appeal for northerners. After all, Milan is closer to Munich than to Messina, and Brescia does more business with Bavaria than with Bari. In federalist eyes, the banding together of the northern Italian regions would be a triumph, embracing the industrial triangle of Turin, Milan and Genoa as well as the wealth of small businesses in Emilia. This seductive logic has won many sympathisers. A federalist Europe represents the best hope for dissatisfied northern Italians.

I have to work for Ferrari, then I'm a mechanic."

The Ligurians of the Genoese hinterland are considered a proud, stubborn people with the ingenuity to make the most of humble resources. Liguria has long been a land of fishermen-sailors and merchant-wayfarers, although, with the development of such renowned resorts as Portofino, the population has looked for more profitable activities. Alfonso Scanio, a Green MP, even accuses the Ligurians of "going in for disposable tourism: the belief that if they ruin one thing, something else will come along".

> **MARRIAGE VOWS**
>
> "He might leave home for a plate of spaghetti, but for a woman, never." – Pavarotti's wife on first hearing the (accurate) rumours that the singer was about to leave her for his secretary.

Greedy Emilians

Given their superb cuisine and love of the good life, citizens of Emilia Romagna are routinely envied. In the eyes of fellow Italians, the Emilians are a soft, sensual, pampered people with a cosmopolitan outlook. Yet they are secretly admired for their pragmatism and public honesty, and for the smooth efficiency with which they run the prosperous cities of Italy's political "red belt". Luciano Pavarotti, the ultimate figure of a tenor, personifies the generosity, gregariousness and greed of Emilians. In the rarefied world of opera, Pavarotti is as earthy and pampered as his home town, Modena.

The Bolognese are considered the intellectual bourgeoisie personified: progressive, sociable, affable and open. The common criticism of these model citizens is that they are smugly superior, prescriptive about the world's wrongs, while dabbling in daring social experiments. As the capital of the former Papal States, Bologna became virulently anticlerical and still maintains a wary relationship with the church. Pope John Paul II even condemned the region as the most degenerate in Italy, given its record divorce and abortion rates.

Liberals, however, praise such qualities as civic maturity and tolerant attitudes to sex and drugs. Yet Luciano Pignotti, a long-term city resident, finds the fabled Bolognese openness skin-deep, a form of conformity: "The Bolognese pride themselves on being open-minded

so everyone else has to be open-minded, too."

Writers and film directors from Emilia Romagna are extraordinarily attuned to aesthetic concerns. Federico Fellini (*see page 349*) may be the god of the Emilian cinematic pantheon, but Antonioni and Bertolucci are also venerable names. When asked why his films always look so lush, Bernardo Bertolucci pointed to his upbringing in Parma: "Growing up in such a beautiful city is a kind of *dolce condanna*, a sweet prison sentence. Look at our

local painter, Parmigiano, he was the most decorative of all the Mannerists, the least tortured. I think beauty is in my DNA."

Michelangelo Antonioni, the veteran film director, has always looked to his native Ferrara for inspiration. As an artist who deals in lush surface beauties, he lingers over shadowy encounters in Renaissance palaces, soft mists that rise over the Po Valley. His film *Beyond the Clouds* (1998) focused on unfulfilled erotic encounters in his secretive city, the black-magic capital of Italy. If planning any form of social, erotic or gastronomic encounters with northerners, one would do well to begin with the Emilians. ❑

LEFT: Luciano Pavarotti with his new young wife Nicoletta Mantovani.

RIGHT: Sophia Loren and Federico Fellini.

Decisive Dates

1000–800 BC "Villanova" culture flourishes.
500 BC Etruscans rule Po valley from Bologna.
219 BC Carthaginian army under Hannibal crosses the Alps.
27 BC–AD 14 Reign of Emperor Augustus.
307–337 Reign of Emperor Constantine. Christians no longer persecuted in the empire.
374 Saint Ambrose becomes Bishop of Milan.
410 Rome falls to the Goths.
489 Theodoric, King of the Ostrogoths, makes Verona his capital.

535 Ravenna becomes the chief city of Byzantine Italy.
568 The Longobards, led by Alboin, overrun northern Italy.
697 Paoluccio Anafesto elected first Doge of the Venetian Republic.
773 Invited by the Pope, Charlemagne seizes the Longobard domains.
1088 Foundation of Bologna University.
1176 Lombard League, formed to challenge Holy Roman Emperor Frederick Barbarossa, defeats his forces at Legnano.
1202–04 Fourth Crusade. The sack of Constantinople provides Venice with a springboard for a Mediterranean trading empire.

1320 The Visconti family rises to power in Milan.
1321 Death of Dante Alighieri, poet and author of *The Divine Comedy*, in exile at Ravenna.
1347 The Black Death begins to ravage northern Italy.
1381 Venice wins the so-called War of Chioggia against its trade rival Genoa.
1402 Death of Gian Galeazzo Visconti.
1405 The Venetians conquer Verona and Padua.
1480 Ludovico Sforza seizes power in Milan.
1485 Birth of Titian (Tiziano Vecellio), who becomes Europe's most admired painter in the 16th century.
1499 French army, led by Louis XII, attacks Milan and overthrows the Sforza dynasty.
1530 Charles V crowned Holy Roman Emperor at Bologna by Pope Clement VII. Lombardy becomes part of the Empire.
1545 Pier Luigi Farnese created first Duke of Parma and Piacenza by Pope Paul III. The First Council of Trent opens.
1556 Milan and Lombardy pass to Charles V's son Philip II, King of Spain.
1570 Venice loses Cyprus to the Turks. A decisive Venetian naval victory over the Turks at Lepanto the following year fails to halt the collapse of the trading empire.
1598 The Duchy of Ferrara, ruled for more than a century by the d'Este family, passes to the Papacy for lack of an heir. Illegitimate Cesare d'Este becomes first Duke of Modena.
1607 Claudio Monteverdi's *La Favola d'Orfeo* opens in Mantua and creates vogue for opera in northern Italy.
1627 Death of Vincenzo Gonzaga, Duke of Mantua, whose famous picture collection is sold to Charles I of England.
1630 Mantua sacked by the Imperial army during the Thirty Years War.
1683 Victor Amadeus II seizes power as Duke of Savoy.
1693 Birth of Giambattista Tiepolo, Venice's last great painter.
1713 Treaty of Utrecht. Austria becomes ruler of Lombardy and Mantua. Victor Amadeus II recognised as King of Piedmont and Sardinia.
1718 Venice surrenders the Peloponnese to the Turks.
1745 Popular uprising against an occupying Austrian army by the Genoese offers the earliest symbol of Italian dreams of unification.
1796 French forces invade Italy.
1797 Terrified by the French invasion, the Ven-

etian Republic, Europe's oldest independent state, votes for its own abolition.

1800 Napoleon decisively defeats the Austrian army at Marengo.

1813 Napoleon defeated at Leipzig. Italian states, except Genoa and Venice, restored to their former rulers.

1831 Ciro Menotti's abortive revolt in Modena. Giuseppe Mazzini founds Young Italy movement in Genoa.

1840 Alessandro Manzoni publishes the definitive version of his novel *I Promessi Sposi*.

1848 Revolutions in all Italian states. Venice expels Austrian garrison. King Carlo Alberto of

1880–1900 Widespread social unrest in Italian cities. Rioting and street battles in Milan.

1904 Giovanni Giolitti becomes prime minister.

1912 Giovanni Agnelli begins mass production of Fiat automobiles in Turin.

1915 Italy enters World War I as ally of Britain and France.

1922 Fascists under Benito Mussolini seize power in Italy.

1938 Racial laws strike at Italy's Jewish communities.

1940 Italy enters World War II as ally of Nazi Germany.

1943 After Italy surrenders to the Allies, Mus-

Piedmont declares war on Austria.

1849 Failure of revolutions and defeat of Carlo Alberto. Austria re-establishes dominance in northern Italy.

1850 Giuseppe Verdi's *Rigoletto* first performed in La Fenice, Venice

1859 Franco-Austrian war in northern Italy. French victories at Magenta and Solferino begin the process of unification under Victor Emmanuel II of Piedmont. In 1866 Austria cedes Venice and all of the Veneto to Italy.

PRECEDING PAGES: historical map of Italy.
LEFT: Isabella d'Este (1474–1539) by Caroto.
ABOVE: the Battle of Solferino, 1859.

solini flees to Salo, and German armies occupy the north. Beginning of the Partisan movement.

1945 Mussolini captured by Italians and executed in Milan.

1948–92 Parliamentary democracy introduced, dominated by Christian Democrats, though Lombardy and Emilia Romagna remain Communist.

1951 Italy joins the EEC as founder member.

1992–94 Elections see the rise of Umberto Bossi's Lega Nord (Northern League) and Silvio Berlusconi's Forza Italia as important political forces in northern Italy.

Late 1990s Extensive privatisation gets underway as part of Italy's preparation for European Monetary Union. ❑

VIRGILIVS POETARVM EXCELENTISSIMVS

VLTIMA CVMEI IAM VENIT CARMINIS ETA
MAGNVS AB ETERNO SANCTORVM NASCITVR ORDO

CULTURAL CORRIDORS

The early tribes wandered in and out of the region, and though Rome long held sway, others, such as the Longobards, also had a lasting effect

The earliest northern Italian about whom we know anything turned up as late as 1992, when his 5,000-year-old corpse, perfectly preserved, was discovered by German tourists in the Tyrol. This body of a man in his early 30s, lying where presumably he had fallen while seeking shelter in a mountain storm, retained everything from blue tattoo marks to the traces of a last meal, a quiverful of arrows carried for hunting and a cloak of woven grass, useless in the end against the bitter cold of the high peaks. Though found close to the Austrian frontier, "the Ice Man", whose organic remains, the oldest known in Europe, continue to intrigue and puzzle the scientists, was finally judged to have been of Italian origin.

Two thousand years later his descendants began leaving the mountains for the great plains below, in those days a terrain of forests and marshes between rivers such as the Po and the Ticino. Almost nothing is known of the people who scratched primitive hunting scenes and human figures on the surface of rocks in Val-camonica, north of Brescia. Settlers further south, however, known today as Villanovans (from a village in the Apennine foothills where their traces were first identified), left bronze weapons, jewellery and clay urns in the graves of their dead.

Arrival of the Etruscans

The biggest Villanovan settlement was based on the site of modern Bologna, the place chosen for their capital by the Etruscans, who swept northwards in the 5th century BC to claim the area as an outpost of a realm which included Tuscany and Lazio and stretched as far as Italy's eastern seaboard. Feline, as the Etruscan town was called, fell eventually to the Celtic tribes swarming across the Alps during the 4th century, but it was the Romans, triumphant after Hannibal's defeat in 202 BC, who finally

became masters of the land they named Cis-alpine Gaul (modern France being known as Transalpine Gaul).

Clearing the fertile river plains for farming, they laid their dead-straight roads between newly-built towns such as Piacenza, Cremona and Modena, whose historic city centres even

today preserve the classic Roman grid pattern and traces of ramparts, baths, theatres or are-nas. Prosperous and generally well-governed, Cisalpine Gaul benefited also from good schools, which fostered a lively literary culture. Some of the foremost Latin writers were native north Italians. The poet Gaius Valerius Catullus came from Verona and divided most of his short life (*circa* 84–54 BC) between Rome and a villa at Sirmione on Lake Garda. His verse, written in a racy, colloquial style, mingles scenes from daily life, letters to friends and satirical hits at well-known political figures with poems chart-ing the course of a disastrous love affair with the aristocrat Clodia Metella. From nearby

LEFT: Virgil, author of *The Aeneid*, was born in Mantua.
RIGHT: Noah sends out the dove; 13th-century mosaic at St Mark's Cathedral, Venice.

Padua (Patavium) came the historian Livy (Titus Livius), who began his huge *Story of Rome from its Foundation* in 29 BC; issued in instalments, it achieved instant classic status and had a profound influence on later European historiography. Legends of pre-Roman Italy meanwhile inspired Virgil (Publius Virgilius Maro), born near Mantua, to write *The Aeneid*, which was unfinished at his death in 19 BC.

The decline of Rome

Racked by internal tensions between the army and successive emperors, as well as facing increased unrest along its frontiers, the Roman Empire, around the end of the 3rd century AD, began entering a slow spiral of decline. Interested watchers of this protracted imperial collapse included the Germanic people known as the Goths, scattered over a wide area around the basin of the River Danube. Seizing his moment, their king, Alaric, led them westwards into Greece and Italy, and Rome itself was finally surrounded and sacked in 410. Though Roman generals drove the Goths back across the Alps, the seat of imperial rule had already shifted to the eastern city of Byzantium, or Constantinople, and fresh barbarian hordes, including the Huns under their leader Attila,

м 5809 Verona - Arena

swept into northern Italy. By the beginning of the 6th century almost all of Italy lay under the sway of the Gothic warlord Theodoric, with the city of Verona as his capital.

When Theodoric died in 526 the Byzantine Emperor Justinian, a Bulgarian peasant's son, possessed of an iron resolve to snatch back the lost Roman dominions, invaded Italy and began a process of reconquest lasting nearly 30 years. While Justinian continued to govern from Constantinople, the Italian provinces were administered by his proconsul, known as the *exarch*, from the coastal city of Ravenna. Once the headquarters of Rome's Adriatic fleet, this was the spot Theodoric had marked for his burial place with an impressive domed mausoleum. The Byzantine presence in Ravenna renewed the tradition, so strikingly established here a century earlier in Empress Galla Placidia's memorial chapel, of pictorial mosaic decoration in the city's churches.

Settlement of the Longobards

Northern Italy was not allowed to remain at peace for long. In 568, only a few years after the last Goths had been driven out, another barbarian people began the march southwards. Within a decade the Longobards, leaving their tribal homeland of north Germany, had

racy eventually gave the name "Lombardia" to the whole region between the northern lakes and the River Po.

An uneasy balance of forces now existed between the Byzantine Empire, clinging to what remained of the exarchate around Ravenna, and the Longobards, determined to gain full control of Italy. In 751 Ravenna yielded to the Longobard King Aistulf, and it seemed as if Rome itself would fall to the victorious northerners. Three years later, having secured a promise of help from King Pepin of the Franks, Pope Stephen II accorded him the honour of an official anointing ceremony

RIGHT: Charlemagne, first Holy Roman Emperor.

THE LOMBARD LEGACY

The Longobards may have disappeared into the history books and museums, but their presence lives on in the northern Italian plains across which they spurred their horses. The pattern of countless farms and small villages retains the character of their ancient tribal settlements, the *casali*, in which the big arcaded barns around a courtyard are incorporated into a dwelling house in such a way as to create an easily defensible stronghold. Their Germanic language became an integral part of modern Italian; many words connected with war (*guerra*), like *scudo* (shield), *elmo* (helmet) and *spada* (sword), are Longobard, as well as equestrian terms such as *staffa* (stirrup) and *briglia* (bridle). Even such everyday words as *casalinga* (housewife) and *guinzaglio* (dog-lead) betray a Longobard origin, and so, too, do the hundreds of place-names ending in -ago, -ara or -engo – Asiago, Martellago, Novara, Lendinara, Marengo, Offanengo. To a hot-blooded Neapolitan or Sicilian, the sober, hardworking character of the northern Italians is the ultimate legacy of this ancient German descent.

achieved almost complete mastery over the Po valley and the northeastern area between the Dolomites and the Adriatic coast, known as Friuli. As their chief cities they chose Pavia, southwest of Milan, and Brescia, which had been an important trading centre under the Romans. Though the Longobards soon embraced Christianity and accepted the surviving imperial forms of law and civil administration, they never lost their pride in their ancient north European ancestry and warlike ancestral traditions. This powerful warrior aristoc-

in return for direct military action against the Longobards.

Under Pepin's successor, Charlemagne, who was crowned as the first Holy Roman Emperor by Pope Leo III on Christmas Day 800, the last Longobard king of northern Italy, Desiderius, was deposed. Pavia, for a time the provincial capital of the new imperial domain before being overtaken by Milan and Verona, became a leading centre for training civil servants and lawyers as well as the earliest of Italy's university towns, While successive emperors, especially Otto III (983–1002), did their best to establish a bulwark of secular power in the north against the Longobard legacy, popes

LEFT: an old postcard of Verona's Roman amphitheatre.
RIGHT: Charlemagne, first Holy Roman Emperor.

showed themselves more than prepared to assert the Church's rights and privileges.

Charlemagne had been ready to countenance the breathtaking piece of forgery known as the Donation of Constantine, whereby a so-called territorial grant from the Emperor Constantine to Pope Silvester guaranteed sovereignty over an area which became an independent papal state and remained one until 1870. In more positive ways the Church contributed forcefully to stability and continuity throughout Italy during the most unstable periods of early medieval history.

In the north, landscape and society both underwent serious changes as a result of the introduction of monasticism by the Benedictine order during the 7th and 8th centuries. By the year 1200 the Lombard plain, the foothills of the northern Apennines and the Emilian region were dotted with monasteries and convents large and small, incorporating extensive farm buildings and dedicated to forest clearances and irrigation schemes as well as the daily round of church services.

First wave of Romanesque

The inspiration for many to join the monastic orders was initially offered not so much by Italians as by wandering monks from Ireland, who travelled south across France and Germany along pilgrim routes to Rome. One such was St Columbanus, whose abbey of Bobbio near Piacenza, founded in 612, became one of the most widely respected centres of learning in Europe during the early Middle Ages.

Irish monks also helped to found the monastery at Nonantola, east of Modena, whose distinctive architecture and sculpture were influential in creating the first wave of the Romanesque style, which dominated church architecture from Scotland to Spain during the 12th century.

It was the bishops of the various cities, however, who did most to earn respect for the Church among the ordinary men and women of northern Italy in the troubled centuries following the Roman imperial collapse. Towns such as Parma, Reggio and Cremona all relied on their respective bishops as the ultimate representatives of authority, whether spiritual or secular, and such figures were expected, when necessary, to put on armour, carry weapons and ride horses into battle. Many were canonised after their deaths and proved redoubtable protectors of their cities through miraculous intervention at times of crisis.

When the Hungarians threatened Modena in the early 10th century, for example, prayers were directed to St Geminianus, who had been the town's first bishop 600 years earlier. He had driven away marauding Huns by blanketing the city with a dense fog, and now his timely intercession brought about the same result with the Hungarians. The fact that the Emilian plain on which Modena stands has always been notorious for its thick fogs may also have helped. ❏

LEFT: the Doge, like the Pope, was elected for life.
RIGHT: a 17th-century view of Venice's Rialto bridge.

CITY STATES AND DYNASTIES

Street fights, power battles, clan allegiance, courage and cunning shaped the
communities as they grew into powerful, independent city states

As the towns of northern Italy grew more prosperous during the 11th and 12th centuries, so they became increasingly unwilling to accept the authority of emperors, popes or bishops. Instead, the most powerful citizens began to reach out towards gaining control over the surrounding countryside, the *contado* as it was called, reducing the local barons to submission, revising outworn tax systems and introducing ambitious schemes for improving agriculture. Within the cities themselves the old warrior aristocracy gave way to a bourgeois nobility, unembarrassed for the time being by its associations with trade and always able to boost its numbers by granting titles and honours to families whose fortunes had risen through shrewd business dealings.

For this very reason, thought the German Bishop Otto of Freising, the towns of northern Italy "greatly exceed the other cities of the world in wealth and power". The prosperity of these *comuni,* as they were known – Milan, Bologna, Cremona and others – based largely on trade in textiles and dyestuffs, secured a deep sense of collective loyalty among their inhabitants. Even today an Italian's first allegiance is to his home town, to his *campanile,* the bell tower which punctuates the skyline on the plains of Lombardy and Emilia. In everything from politics to football *campanilismo* is a vital influence, just as it was 900 years ago.

Birth of the Lombard League

The rising power of the communes met its match in 1152, when the German prince Frederick Barbarossa was named Holy Roman Emperor. Determined to assert what he believed was his God-given authority, he demanded control of everything from tax-gathering to the appointment of magistrates. The infuriated communes, led by Milan, united as the Lombard League and began a 20-year

struggle against imperial dominance, which only ended when Frederick conceded full sovereign rights to each city in return for its recognition of him as overall ruler. The Lombard League soon became a symbol of Italian unity, and the story of the conflict was eventually to inspire the leaders of the Risorgimento, the

19th-century struggle for nationhood. In 1848 Giuseppe Verdi chose the League's signal victory at Legnano as the theme of the patriotic opera *Aida.*

The growth of elites and aristocracies among the citizens of the communes led at length to major power struggles between individual families jostling for leadership and, ultimately, for outright domination of the town and its surrounding *contado.* The strife between Montagues and Capulets forming the background to Shakespeare's *Romeo and Juliet* has its foundation in the history of 14th-century Verona, where members of the Montecchi and Capuleti families, aided by their households and

LEFT: German prince Frederick Barbarossa being crowned Holy Roman Emperor.
RIGHT: Malatesta, 15th-century ruler of Rimini.

hangers-on, fought running battles in the city streets. Here and elsewhere the richer clans had started to build themselves fortified palaces which could be used both as storehouses for merchandise and as symbols of pride and defiance in the teeth of their rivals.

Street battle for power

Mantua's story during the 13th and 14th centuries provides a typical example. From about 1260 onwards the commune became increasingly dominated by the Buonaccorsi family. In 1272 Pinamonte Buonaccorsi, combining an immense fortune with personal courage and

political skills, became the city's effective ruler from his grimly imposing crenellated *palazzo* in Piazza Sordello.

For more than 50 years the Buonaccorsi held sway in Mantua until, in 1328, Luigi Gonzaga, head of a peasant clan from the village of Polirone, who had made a series of shrewd land deals with local monasteries and bought up city property, carried out a spectacular *coup d'état*. In a ferocious street battle on a moonlit August night, Rinaldo Buonaccorsi was severely wounded but managed to escape to his palace, where he died on the threshold after slipping in his own blood and hitting his head against

one of the great gates which he had earlier ordered his servants to close behind him.

The rise of the Gonzagas to more or less royal status – Holy Roman Emperor Sigismund in 1433 allowed them to display the imperial eagle on their coat of arms – is typical of what was happening elsewhere in an Italy increasingly dominated by powerful clans seeking ever more blatant affirmations of their aristocratic significance. Certain northern Italian cities, on the other hand, saw an implicit menace in such overwhelming predominance among members of a single family.

The republic of Venice made the most deliberate effort of all to limit the power of individual

GENOA, LA SUPERBA

Genoa was so successful as a commune that it soon became a fully independent state. It drew its wealth from a rapidly expanding trade and maritime empire, knocking out the rival republics of Pisa and Amalfi before shifting its attention to Venice, its main competitor in the East during the 12th–13th-century crusades. Genoa maintained trading centres in the Greek Islands, the Black Sea, Tunisia and Egypt, and acquired such riches that the city became known as "La Superba". Money was almost the only unifying force in a commune notorious for political unrest among its merchant aristocracy. The Genoese retain a reputation in Italy for being cynical, mercenary and mean.

citizens by creating a political mentality which focused on the state rather than on the fulfilment of personal ambition. Since the early Middle Ages its ruler had been an elected Doge, chosen from among a limited number of senators, themselves members of the so-called Grand Council whose composition was restricted to families whose names were inscribed in *The Golden Book of the Republic*. A system of committees, the Ten, the Thirty and so on, acted as checks and balances on one another's

NO FUN BEING A DOGE

Of Venice's first 25 Doges, three were murdered, one was executed, three were judicially blinded, four deposed, one exiled, four abdicated, one killed by pirates and one made a saint.

Europe. The Fourth Crusade in 1204 had brought the Republic spectacular gains in the Eastern Mediterranean through its shrewd exploitation of the crusaders' greed and internal dissensions, which led to the sack of Constantinople. The Venetians had lost the War of Chioggia (1378–81) against the Genoese, but it was Genoa, its resources worn thin by the struggle, which suffered more, while Venice, as a result of forced loans efficiently raised among its loyal citizenry, made a remark-

power, and an impressive range of sumptuary laws, controlling everything from the height and style of buildings to the colour and sleeve-length of official robes, reminded everyone that the state and the rule of law came before everything else.

Venice's success was based both on this deep sense of corporate identity and on the skill with which its merchants learned to seize on whatever commercial advantages came their way from other states, both in Italy and in the rest of

LEFT: a sea battle in the War of Chioggia (1378–81) fought between the Genoese and the Venetians.
ABOVE: the Lion of St Mark, symbol of Venetian power.

ably swift recovery. One by one the mainland towns of Padua, Verona, Bergamo and Treviso fell into Venetian hands, and by the middle of the 15th century the territory controlled by the Republic stretched almost to the gates of Milan. Venice itself meanwhile had become Europe's fastest-growing and most prosperous city, the centre of a trade network stretching as far as China, Russia and Africa, and commanding a Mediterranean empire which included the Ionian islands, Crete and Cyprus.

Even a natural disaster on the scale of the Black Death, sweeping across northern Italy during the 14th century, had no long-lasting effect on the mounting affluence in town and country. Drainage and land clearance projects improved productivity on the Lombard plain, where the planting of rice was introduced, making *risotto* a characteristic regional dish. Mulberry trees, planted on the slopes of the Alpine foothills, fostered a thriving silk industry, and the pasturing of large cattle herds in the fields around Parma and Reggio encouraged the production of *grana*, the hard cheese known to us as Parmesan.

RISOTTO FROM SPAIN

The first rice in Italy was planted at Pisa in 1468 by the Spaniards, who had been introduced to the crop by the Arabs.

The growth of northern towns echoed this prosperity, nowhere more so than Milan, where

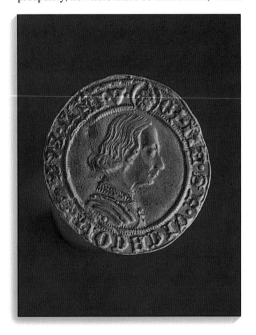

the Visconti family had gradually risen to power in the 14th century's closing decades. On 5 September 1395 the imperial legate ceremonially invested Gian Galeazzo as duke, and the new ruler immediately set out to challenge the might of neighbouring states such as Savoy, Ferrara and Venice. It looked, indeed, as if the whole of Italy were in danger, especially when Gian Galeazzo moved south into Tuscany to take possession of Pisa and Siena, and wrested control of Bologna from the Pope. When he died unexpectedly in 1402 the various potentates struck back swiftly at his successor Filippo Maria, who was filled with the same territorial ambitions but was not nearly as effi-

cient a soldier as his father. In the ensuing, prolonged war, Filippo Maria saw his son-in-law Sforza change sides and join the enemy alliance formed by Florence, Venice and the Pope.

Sforza was the son of a *condottiere*, a soldier of fortune, one of that ruthless mercenary breed which hired out its services to Italian rulers in need of a competent military leader. The great Renaissance sculptors Donatello and Verrocchio left us memorable bronze statues of two of them, astride their warhorses, in Padua and Venice respectively.

On Filippo Maria Visconti's death in 1447, Francesco Sforza took possession of Milan after a long siege and began embellishing his city fine churches, hospitals and new fortifications. Resolved to turn Milan into a capital appropriate to a state which could rival Florence or Naples as a major player on the Italian political stage, he gathered around him artists, musicians, technocrats and humanist scholars in what soon became one of the most brilliant of all Renaissance courts.

Leonardo in Milan

Milan's cultural life attained its utmost splendour under Francesco's nephew, Ludovico il Moro ("the black"), who succeeded him in 1480. The inspired Tuscan architect Bramante arrived to stage elaborate masques and pageants for the court and to design the ducal mausoleum and Santa Maria delle Grazie. In the same convent church Leonardo da Vinci painted his *Last Supper*. Summoned from Florence, he became Ludovico's scientific and technological adviser.

The envy of rival states at length brought the Sforzas to their knees. In 1499 Milan fell to a combined force of Venetians and Swiss, joined by King Louis XII of France, which drove Ludovico into exile. Even if the French and Spanish governors of Milan continued to employ Sforza princes and their agents in governing Lombardy, the city became a pawn in the power games of alien monarchs. The rest of Italy might have taken warning from the fact that in the first 30 years of the 16th century the Milanese changed rulers 11 times. ❏

LEFT: head of Filippo Maria Visconti (1392–1447) on a Milanese gold ducat coin.
RIGHT: Bianca Maria Sforza (1472–1510).

HEYDAY OF THE VENETIAN REPUBLIC

At its zenith, the Venetian Republic was a political heavyweight, queen of the Adriatic and an effective power player in world affairs

"Many a subject land looked at the winged lion's marble piles, where Venice sat in state, throned on her hundred isles," wrote Lord Byron as he reflected on the glory that was La Serenissima. He was writing of the Venetian heyday, between the 14th and 16th centuries, the age of empire, a golden age of conquest abroad and patriotic display at home. Citizens declared themselves "Venetians first, Christians afterwards", implying a greater duty to State and empire than to God. "Redeem us, O Christ," sang the choir in St Mark's, to which the response was distinctly unorthodox: "To the Most Serene and Excellent Doge, Health, Honour and Victory Perpetual." Paradoxically, the Republic's strength lay in its perceived weakness, in the belief that Venice was always alone in the world, forced to fend for itself and shun the shifting sands of political allegiances. In turn, rivals envied the Venetians' autonomous approach and the mercantile spirit of a great trading empire – not to mention their shrewd mastery of foreign affairs and good governance of the Republic at home.

OSTENTATION AND PURITANISM

La Serenissima's role as a Mediterranean power was perfectly captured by Venetian artists, for both patrons and posterity. The Republic was fed on a diet of pomp, with sumptuous receptions and lay and religious feasts; some of these are celebrated in the paintings of Bellini and Carpaccio. However, the Venetian taste for portraying pageantry went beyond the dictates of patrons. Moreover, despite a reputation for extravagance, the Republic harboured a puritanical streak. The prominence of black costumes in 16th-century Venice led a modern historian to liken the scene to "a Swiss Sunday". Yet in this authoritarian, regimented and censorious city, some nobles lived so lavishly that the State imposed laws governing dress codes and the gilding of gondolas.

▷ AWARDS FOR THE FAVOURED
On special occasions, the Doge would distribute medals, such as this 17th-century silver *osella*, to the Gran Consiglio, the council of nobles which had elected him.

△ SEALED LIPS
Secret denunciations could be posted in a *bocca di leone* ("lion's mouth" letter box). The boxes were placed in various locations across the city.

▷ WEDDED TO THE SEA
The Bucintoro, the Doge's barge, was lavishly decorated with gilded carvings and used for important state visits. On Ascension Day it carried the Doge to the Lido, where he would perform the ceremony of Venice's Marriage with the Sea, a famous city tradition captured on canvas by Canaletto (1657–1768).

△ SEAT OF THE SENATE
An 18th-century painting by by Gabriele Bella shows the room where the Doge would consult his 200 senators.

▽ ENDURING BEAUTY
Visitors to the Doge's Palace can still admire Tintoretto's decoration of the Sala del Senato, dating from 1574.

OUTPOSTS OF EMPIRE

Military towers, citadels and lighthouses on the Croatian coast, Cyprus and Crete *(above)* attest to the reach of the Venetian empire. Such imperial power was born of patriotism, geography and trading supremacy. Venice bordered two worlds, the Byzantine and Muslim East and the Latin-Germanic West. As gateway to the East, the city traded incense, precious metals, slaves, silks and spices for northern staples, including salt and wheat. The purpose of Venetian imperialistic ambitions was to preserve trade routes and consolidate commercial opportunities. As a result, Venice became a melting pot for "Jews, Turks, Armenians, Persians, Moors, Greeks and Slavs... negotiating in this great emporium, which is always crowded with strangers" (John Evelyn).

The conquest of Croatia was achieved in the 10th century, and Venice soon developed trading posts in the Aegean, Black Sea and Syria. In 1204 The Sack of Constantinople gave Venice "one quarter and half a quarter" of the Roman Empire. Valour was expected in the name of glory: blind Doge Dandolo stormed Constantinople at the age of 90.

◁ **NAVAL POWER**
Venetian naval power was second to none. Here Holy Roman Emperor Frederick Barbarossa, who was in conflict with the Pope and the Lombard League, surrenders to Doge Ziani in 1176.

▽ **DOGE'S FINERY**
Doges wore distinctive hats, made of embroidered silk and adorned with precious stones, such as this *corno* worn by Doge Barbarigo (1485–1501).

NOBLE COURTS TO NATIONHOOD

As the city states grew rich, they became prey to the big powers. Finally, the French Revolution showed them how they could become free

Always attractive to invaders from elsewhere in Europe, Italy in the 16th century lay at the mercy of the armies of France and Spain, both eager to gain control of its rich resources, human and material. Louis XII's invasion, successful to begin with, involved him eventually in the League of Cambrai, an alliance formed by Pope Julius II and designed to curb the overweening territorial ambitions and political self-confidence of the Venetian Republic. In 1509 Venice was severely defeated at the Battle of Agnadello, but it managed to hang on to most of its lands. As a result the Pope was lured away from the league, but he kept Spain as an ally. Louis now found himself facing a new confederation, the so-called Holy League of all the Italian states, whose battle-cry "Out with the barbarians!" both echoed an ancient hatred of French invaders and anticipated the spirit of the 19th-century Risorgimento.

Emperor Charles dominates Italy

Louis's successor, François I, attempted a further bid for mastery in northern Italy, but his disastrous defeat at Pavia in 1521 at the hands of Holy Roman Emperor Charles V (Charles I of Spain) was the prelude to a complete overturning of the established order throughout the Italian peninsula. In 1527 Rome was sacked and humiliated by imperial troops, and only in 1529 was peace concluded, effectively making Charles master of Italy. Though a member of the Sforza family was given the duchy of Milan, this was a mere gesture of dynastic politeness. The Genoese, shrewd as ever, saw which way the wind was blowing and committed their entire fleet, led by the great admiral Andrea Doria, to the Emperor's service.

Charles V, half Spanish and half Habsburg, was now the most powerful man in Europe – or, as he had good reason to believe, in the entire

world. He boasted that the sun never set on his empire, which stretched halfway round the world. In Italy, however, he had to reckon with a resurgent Papacy, determined to recover international prestige and moral authority. In 1545 Pope Paul III, on behalf of his son Pier Luigi Farnese, persuaded Charles to create an independent duchy from the cities of Parma and Piacenza and their surrounding territories. Another small but important north Italian state was created in 1598 on the death of Alfonso d'Este, Duke of Ferrara. Pope Clement VIII claimed the duchy as a papal fiefdom, since there were no legitimate heirs. In compensation, Alfonso's bastard son Cesare was allowed to move the Ferrarese court to the city of Modena, where he became a sovereign duke.

The papal annexation of Ferrara ended one of the most enlightened of the smaller Renaissance states. The d'Este family were enthusiastic patrons of art, literature and music. In 1516 the poet Ludovico Ariosto had published

---

LEFT: Princess Maria Louisa di Parma (1751–1819), mother of King Charles V of Spain.
RIGHT: Venetians drinking chocolate.

his stupendous epic fantasy of love and chivalry *Orlando Furioso*, composed in Ferrara and very loosely based on d'Este history. This in turn inspired Torquato Tasso, another Ferrarese protégé, to write a more serious, loftier epic, *Gerusalemme Liberata*, a tale of the First Crusade. Both poems were among the most widely imitated and admired in 16th-century Europe.

Painters and musicians

In Mantua meanwhile the Gonzaga dukes had prospered through a series of marriages among illustrious families, not just in Italy but also

Monteverdi whose opera *Orfeo* received its first performance at Mantua in 1607.

Opera, the fashionable new art form in early 17th-century Italy, found its keenest audiences in Venice. The state, for all its skilful diplomacy, had never fully recovered from its defeat at Agnadello and from the sacrifice to the Turks in 1570 of one of its prized imperial possessions, the island of Cyprus. Still more serious had been the loss of its Eastern spice markets to Portugal and Spain. The decline was at first barely perceptible, and until the close of the 17th century, when a costly war with Turkey and trade competition with France weakened it

within the Valois and Habsburg dynasties of France and Austria. Splendid buildings such as the Palazzo del Te, adorned with frescoes by Giulio Romano, and the stately domed church of Sant 'Andrea, designed by Leon Battista Alberti, had proclaimed the exalted ambitions of the Gonzaga dynasty.

Like the d'Este, with whom there were marriage links, the family used its wealth to patronise painters and composers. Under Vincenzo I, who succeeded to the dukedom in 1587, a splendid picture collection was gathered together, including works by the young Peter Paul Rubens, who visited the court in person. Here, too, came musicians, led by Claudio

beyond recovery, Venice was still regarded with awe, envy and curiosity by travellers visiting its domains from other parts of Europe. The Republic's ancient system of government by committee was closely studied among political theorists, especially in England and Holland. Attempts within the state to make the administration more democratic were resisted by its aristocracy, though a mounting financial crisis meant that by 1700 several *nouveau riche* families had been able to buy their way into the prestigious *Golden Book*.

As the 17th century progressed, northern Italy fell an increasing prey to the great-power manoeuvres of Austria, France and Spain.

While a duchy like Modena prospered owing to the shrewd operations of its d'Este rulers (one princess, Maria Beatrice, became Queen of England in 1685 as the wife of King James II), Mantua was less fortunate, losing practically all its assets though the diplomatic miscalculations of the last Gonzaga heirs. The most abiding success among the older ruling dynasties was that of the house of Savoy, based on its capital at Turin. The dukes played the game of alliances so skilfully that they raised their state to the

TRAVEL BUGS

Travel during the days of the Grand Tour lacked the comforts of even the cheapest expedition today. To describe a hotel as "lousy" had a vivid meaning.

century saw the start of improved roads and waterways and the building of handsome villas surrounded by parks and formal gardens. The transfer of power in Lombardy from Spain to Austria in 1714 brought new life to Milan, and during the reigns of Maria Theresa and Joseph II the city entered fully into the spirit of the European Enlightenment, with a vigorous intellectual life encouraged by a benign Habsburg government. Milan became a favourite haunt of foreign visitors on the Grand Tour, while Venice entered

dignity of a kingdom, known as Piedmont, or as Sardinia from the island they acquired through the Treaty of Utrecht.

Sites for the Grand Tour

Even if ancestral feudalism prevailed in the countryside, the nobility in Venice's mainland possessions, in the territories of Parma and Modena, and above all in Lombardy, were beginning to take their rural estates more seriously as sources of investment. The early 18th

LEFT: portrait of Barbara Gonzaga, daughter of Ludovico, by Mantegna (circa 1431–1506).
ABOVE: an operatic recital in 17th-century Venice.

on a new, if not surprising, final phase of its existence as an independent capital. The once powerful and dignified Serenissima became the favorite pleasure resort of those in search of non-stop entertainment and sexual adventure, whether in the legendary carnival, the licensed gambling dens, the opera houses or even certain of the convents. No wonder a disgruntled political reformer among the Republic's senators referred to it as "a boxful of puppets".

Most of the Italian states were taken wholly by surprise when the French Revolution, from its outbreak in 1789, began sending sinister ripples across the Alps. The thriving bourgeoisie in cities of mainland Venice such as Brescia,

Verona and Padua welcomed the new doctrines of political liberty and equality, and Genoa, by now thoroughly decadent, leaped at the chance of overturning the Doge and senators and devising a revolutionary government for itself. This gesture had been inspired largely by the French invasion of Lombardy in 1797, led by Napoleon Bonaparte, then a young general, whose ancestors were Tuscans settled in Corsica. When he seized outright power in France, Napoleon took it upon himself to reorganise Italian affairs, making his

THE SPOILS OF WAR

Many works of art in the Louvre in Paris are spoils of war taken by Napoleon. The French destroyed churches and dissolved monasteries, seizing their riches.

brother-in-law Eugène de Beauharnais viceroy of Milan and Venice.

Napoleonic government in northern Italy was not an unmixed blessing. The French were often seen as arrogant and patronising, but the regime planted the seed of a united Italian state in which justice and taxation could be administered with universal fairness. Young men of bourgeois families could entertain ambitious career prospects, and children of both sexes gained access to a decent secular education. When Napoleon and his armies were beaten at Waterloo in 1815, and the old rulers returned to their various states under the watchful eye of Austria (to whose Habsburg dynasty most

were related), these freedoms were not forgotten. In the years immediately following the Napoleonic wars, Milan, with an enlightened nobility and bourgeoisie, became the natural flashpoint for the earliest stirrings of what historians call "Il Risorgimento", the movement towards natural unity among the eight sovereign states of which Italy now consisted.

In 1821 a revolution was attempted by Milanese members of the secret society known as the Carbonari and, although the ringleaders were executed or exiled by the Austrians, their example was an inspiration to other fledgling "patriotic" movements. Ten years later it was Modena's turn to rebel, when the factory-owner Ciro Menotti tried to overthrow the harsh regime of the hated Duke Francesco IV and was executed by firing squad.

Like its neighbouring duchy of Parma, Modena was a satellite of the Austrian Empire, whose province of Venetia-Lombardy was run by combining well-intentioned efficiency with the ruthless surveillance of an extensive spy network. Only in 1848 did the first cracks start to appear in the reactionary Habsburg government apparatus. The two dukes of Parma and Modena were driven out by their subjects, Milan's citizens revolted against Austrian troops and, most heroic of all, Venice expelled its civil and military governors, resumed its ancient republican charter and kept imperial troops at bay in a siege lasting nearly a year.

Piedmont holds the key

Each of those revolutions had looked towards the strong, well-drilled army of the kingdom of Piedmont for its ultimate guarantee of success. With King Charles Albert at its head, the Piedmont force which invaded Lombardy in 1848 seemed to bring dreams of unification closer than ever to reality. Charles Albert's decision-making unfortunately failed to catch his best ideals (he became known as *il re tentenna*, "King Ditherer"), and his defeat by the Austrians at Custoza was the result of fatal hes-

LEFT: the French in Italy; illustration from Paris's *Le Petit Journal*, 13 May 1893.
RIGHT: combined French and Piedmonte forces routed the Austrians at the battle of Solferino in 1859.

itations. A further debacle at Novara in 1849 drove him into exile.

It was his son Victor Emmanuel II who set out to rally international support for a united Italy under Piedmontese rule, with the help of his astute prime minister Camillo di Cavour. Though all the 1848 revolutions had failed, "the Italian question" was now a European issue, and Austria could no longer sustain its image as the bringer of peace and good order to northern Italy. In 1858 Cavour's skilful negotiations with Napoleon III of France persuaded the latter to declare war on Austria, and the Austrian Emperor Franz Josef II saw his armies defeated at the bloody battles of Solferino and Magenta. The combined French and Piedmontese campaign was assisted by the great freedom-fighter Giuseppe Garibaldi (*see below*).

The treaty which Austria was finally forced to make at Villafranca in 1859 surrendered the whole of Lombardy, including Milan, together with the ducal territories of Parma and Modena, to Piedmont, which now became the Kingdom of Italy under Victor Emmanuel II. Only in 1866, when Austria was worsted in a war with Prussia, did the Veneto and Friuli join the kingdom, foreshadowing the complete unification for which so many had fought for half a century. ❏

CAVOUR AND GARIBALDI

Count Camillo di Cavour (1810–61) was one of Italy's greatest statesmen. Originally a successful and progressive agriculturalist and industrialist, he gradually came to believe in the need for Italian unity and independence, which he felt was best achieved through the leadership of Piedmont, the strongest Italian state. To raise support for the Italian cause he travelled to England and France, and he also contributed Piedmontese troops to the Crimean War, thus winning a place at the peace conference, where he brought the Italian question to the attention of Europe.

The key to Cavour's eventual success was his alliance with Giuseppe Garibaldi. Garibaldi had honed his fighting skills as a mercenary in South America, where he had been exiled for his part in a republican plot in Genoa in 1834. It was in South America that Garibaldi first formed his famous Red Shirts. He returned to Italy in order to fight in the revolutions of 1848; his bravery and determination quickly made him a popular hero and caught the attention of Cavour. After helping defeat the Austrians in northern Italy, Garibaldi went south to capture Sicily and Naples.

Cavour was appointed Italy's first prime minister in 1861, under the new king, Victor Emmanuel, but he died only four months later and never saw the complete unification of Italy, which was not achieved until 1870.

THE TUMULTUOUS 20TH CENTURY

Finally united, Italy was nearly torn apart again when Benito Mussolini took the country into a disastrous alliance with the Third Reich

Italy became a fully unified nation on 20 September 1870, when the army of King Victor Emmanuel II entered Rome, till then capital of the independent Papal States. Nothing could have prepared the many thousands of Italians who had actively engaged in the Risorgimento for the problems nationhood now brought in its wake. The alienation of ordinary people from an over-centralised government was made worse by an obsessive bureaucracy, a failure by the authorities to deal with various forms of corruption and a sense that the king and his ministers, eager to modernise the new state and place it on an equal footing with the great European powers, really did not understand the concerns of the people they rules.

Northern Italy had the advantage over the southern provinces of possessing an improved road system, railway links between several of the principal towns and some light industry, mostly in Lombardy and the Veneto. After 1870 a deliberate attempt was made to create a state rail network, and cities such as Turin, Milan and Bologna soon became the focus of a steady drift of migrant workers from the old country estates. The bitter memory of a peasant life in which there was seldom enough to eat, and nothing belonged to the farmer beyond his clothes and household furniture, has burned deep into the national psyche, and most Italians would always rather live in a town. Hence the decidedly utilitarian look of much of the agricultural landscape in the Po valley, a countryside inhabited for profit rather than pleasure.

Boulevards and parks planned

During the 19th century's closing decades the character of larger towns underwent important changes. The ramparts with which most of them had been surrounded were pulled down, the citadels and barracks often demolished at the same time, and tree-lined boulevards, parks

and gardens were laid out instead. Certain of the old princely residences were adapted for alternative uses: the Duke of Modena's palace became a military academy and at Colorno near Parma the ducal summer retreat was turned into a lunatic asylum. On the outskirts of Genoa heavy industry sprang up to sustain Italy's new

W HITLER   PACE CIVILTA ANNO LAVORO   W MVSSOLINI

shipbuilding drive, designed to modernise the merchant fleet and to produce iron-clad battleships which by 1890 made the Italian navy the world's third largest.

The gradual sophistication of the northern industrial base brought with it an inevitable tension between the growing urban labour force and its employers. Anarchism became popular among workers in the towns of Emilia and Romagna, and Italy's first big industrial strikes broke out in the textile factories of the Piedmontese town of Biella. An independent workers' party developed in Lombardy during the 1880s, dedicated to union activism and concentrating on attempts to mobilise peasant

---

LEFT: Fascist congress at Modena, 1934.
RIGHT: Mussolini's various pacts with Hitler cemented the bond between the fascist states.

labourers. In 1884 demonstrations broke out in the villages around Mantua, spreading quickly to other parts of Italy where unemployment and high prices had severely hit the farming community. To act as a counterweight to this new politicisation, priests in the Catholic church were urged by their bishops to spend more time addressing social question and finding ways to reconcile the workers and their employers.

Poverty and prosperity

In the countryside life seemed to slide from bad to worse and malnutrition and disease threatened the poorest in parts of Emilia and the

Bava Beccaris, the city's army commandant, suspicious of activities involving a group of beggars gathered outside a Capuchin monastery, rallied troops and stormed the building. When hostile crowds took to the streets, forming barricades, the General panicked, ordering his men to charge the demonstrators, and 50 people were killed. The response of King Umberto was to award Bava Beccaris a hero's welcome in Rome and a medal. This clear indications of the monarch's sympathies brought him a violent end two years later at the hands of the anarchist assassin Gaetano Bresci.

Events like these forced social change on a

Veneto. The two largest cities, Milan and Turin, continued to grow and prosper. The modern urban profiles of each, with tall apartment buildings on the Parisian model, broad suburban avenues, grandiose railway stations, tramlines, department stores and mass circulation newspapers, were largely created during these closing 19th-century years. Venice, on the other hand, reconciled to its destiny as an art capital, began encouraging tourism as a serious investment, with new hotels and regular steamboat services up and down the Grand Canal.

In the very centre of Milan during May 1898, there was an incident which, for many, sums up the failure of post-Risorgimento Italy. General

country preparing to enter a remarkable period of prosperity, marking the fastest growth-rate of any European country in the years immediately before the Great War. Under its prime minister, the skilful, unscrupulous fixer Giovanni Giolitti, the nation courted diplomatic approval among great powers, while setting itself up as their commercial competitor. Turin began to rival Milan as a centre for new industries, chief among them the Fiat automobile firm, founded by a group of young, speed-obsessed aristocrats and cavalry officers led by Giovanni Agnelli. Following a tour of USA car plants, Agnelli started producing cheap Fiat models on an assembly line, while the factory also built aeroplanes and engines for submarines. Other north Italian businesses achieved similar success in the early 1900s as international brand names, including Pirelli tyres and Olivetti typewriters.

The *belle époque* in Italy was an era when the flourishing bourgeoisie could enjoy lavish cinema epics made in increasingly busy film studios, operas like Puccini's *Tosca* or *Madam Butterfly*, outrageous art events organised by the young iconoclasts of the Futurist movement and the poetry of that

DISASTER STRIKES

The great disaster of World War I was the battle of Caporetto in 1917. Austria took almost 300,000 prisoners, and there was a bout of strikes and protests.

the country's northeastern corner, where disputed territory in the Tyrol, Istria and around Trieste offered a suitable pretext for attacking the Austrians, still viewed with suspicion only half a century after their expulsion from the rest of Italy. Unfortunately the handling of military operations by General Cadorna and his staff revealed the army's unreadiness for battle, and after the disastrous Battle of Caporetto in 1917 the nation faced the possibility of upheaval from within through strikes, peace protests and the

unblushing self-publicist Gabriele D'Annunzio (*see page 287*), who later built himself a gloomy retreat on the shores of Lake Garda. Further pleasures included motor racing and seaside holidays, the latter becoming an almost religious institution during July and August.

Italy remained neutral in the World War I until in May 1915 when popular demonstrations urged the government to join in the conflict on the side of Britain and France. The major theatre of war for the Italian army lay in

overall weakness of the government. Even when, with the help of Allied contingents from Britain and the USA, Italian troops avenged their earlier defeat by a second battle at Caporetto, the ensuing peace brought a sense of disillusionment and betrayal of expectations among ordinary Italians.

Mussolini steps in

Someone who seized his opportunity to capitalise on the atmosphere of political tension prevailing after the war was a footloose young journalist from the Romagnolo village Predappio named Benito Mussolini. Mobilising support among various disaffected social groups,

LEFT: the early 1900s saw Italian companies from Martini to Marconi making headway in world markets.
ABOVE: Puccini's *Madam Butterfly* was a sensation.

he secured valuable backing from landowners, industrialists and police chiefs for his new movement, known as Fascism, using icons and symbols from Italy's Roman past to project its dynamic image. By 1925 he had more of less gained control of the government, and though Italy was still nominally a constitutional monarchy under Victor Emmanuel III Mussolini became effectively its overall dictator.

As "Il Duce", a title based on the same Roman word for leader which the Venetian and Genoese had accorded to their elected heads of government, Mussolini played the role of world-class politician, conducting a savage attitude towards Italy's Jewish population. It was never a large community, and since unification, several Jews had played an important role in public life, from which religious prejudice had earlier barred them in the various sovereign states. There was no strong tradition of anti-semitism in Italy however, and in places such as Venice, Genoa and Ferrara Jews were seen as pillars of society. The racial laws passed in 1938, depriving them of various civil rights, marked a further step towards total submission to Germany's behests which led to Mussolini's declaration of war in 1940.

Italy was hopelessly unprepared for war, and

colonial war in Ethiopia and sending squadrons to Spain to fight for Franco's nationalists in the civil war. Northern Italy initially welcomed the new Fascist order, viewing it as a guarantee of stability, though certain areas, notably in Emilia, remained sceptical and unreceptive despite the incessant waves of propaganda.

Racial laws

Personal vanity as much as anything else drew Mussolini closer to Germany's Nazi regime, where he saw Adolf Hitler as a pupil. Growing dependence on Germany for raw materials made the Duce readier to accept Hitler's demands, which included the need for a tougher an attempted invasion of Greece was only sustained with the help of heavy German reinforcements. British and American forces crushed the Italian armies in Northern Africa and began a series of devastating air attacks on major industrial centres. The mood in Italy was one of widespread disillusion with the massive fraudulence of Fascist propaganda and of a deepening sense of shame at the country's involvement in a war it seemed to be losing. In 1943, as the Allies landed in the south, Mussolini tendered his resignation to the King. General Badoglio took charge of the government and offered Italy's surrender.

Disaster now struck civilian Italy as a new

phase of the war began when the Germans invaded, seizing control of the north and installing Mussolini as leader of a puppet Fascist state ruled from the resort town of Salò on Lake Garda. Mussolini installed his mistress, Claretta Petacci, here and became little more than a blustering figurehead, incapable of controlling the thuggish extremists who joined him. The Germans matched this brutality with their own, rounding up Jews to be sent to concentration camps and punishing those who maintained links with the various partisan groups now mobilising in the north.

TERRIBLE REPRISALS

The worst German reprisal was in the winter of 1944 when the entire population of almost 2,000 living in and around the village of Marzabotto near Bologna was massacred by firing squads.

Wehrmacht patrols. Greatest credit of all belongs to the partisans, whose role in weakening the German hold on Italy was played down or else shamefully undermined by British and American generals and politicians fearful of Communist influence. In April 1945, a few days after Mussolini and Claretta were captured, shot and hung upside down in Milan's Piazzale Loreto, peace was declared and Italy's process of rapid recovery began. By the end of the 1950s Milan had become the nation's eco-

Heroic resistance

Ordinary Italians now fought with honour and courage against the Germans throughout the north. The annals of 1943–45 are full of moving episodes in which everyone from farmers' wives and schoolteachers to priests and small children helped to save lives, hide prisoners and refugees, carry secret messages or bamboozle

LEFT: Axis allies – Mussolini and Hitler.
ABOVE: a guard of honour greets Hitler's arrival for talks with Mussolini at Italy's Brenner Pass in 1940.

nomic capital, as opposed to Rome, associated with a sequence of rapidly changing governments all involving the right-wing Christian Democrat party and carefully excluding the Communists for whom most northerners, especially in Emilia Romagna, tended to vote.

The end of the Cold War during the early 1990s led to new political alignments in the north, with the media tycoon Silvio Berlusconi forming a conservative grouping, Forza Italia, alongside the neo-fascist Alleanza Nazionale. Growing impatience with government from Rome led to a breakaway movement, led by Umberto Bossi, aiming at the creation of a separate north Italian state known as Padania. ❑

THE CONTEMPORARY SCENE

*Consumerism and conviviality, conformity, chaos and clannishness
are the keynotes of northern society*

The light-hearted *"terrazza* law" is often cited as an explanation for the cheery resilience of Italian life. According to café society logic, because the sun shines and people can dine *alfresco*, all troubles will eventually evaporate. Although the southern mindset readily indulges in *carpe diem*, the northern approach is more rooted in reality: seize the day and sun oneself, but also sacrifice inner life and leisure to making and spending money or shoring up one's image. Life beyond the sunny café terrace tends to remain a shadowy web of petty provincialism, stifling convention and rampant consumerism, underpinned by a clannish network of interest groups and the extended family.

Civic-minded northerners usually admire the perceived order and incorruptibility of public life north of the Alps. Compared with Italy, these are countries in which dealing with the authorities, setting up a company, lying in a hospital bed, paying bills or posting letters all seem fairly simple procedures. South of the Alps, however, the state is either feared or flouted.

Paradise postponed

The American writer Gore Vidal commented that while the genius of America was to separate the state from religion, the genius of Italy was to separate the state from the people. As Matt Frei, a BBC foreign correspondent, remarked, if the country could only re-invent the relationship between the individual and the state, "it would shorten queues in banks, deliver letters on time, open museums, improve the traffic and the health system. If it could do that, Italy, with its culture, weather, beauty, humanity, humour, industry, inventiveness, unselfconscious eccentricity and delicious food,

would surely be the closest thing to paradise on earth."

In the meantime, contemporary society is a paradoxical mixture of creativity, conformity and chaos. "In Italy there are neither angels nor devils, only average sinners," was the witticism of Giulio Andreotti, seven times premier. With

its culture of patronage and corruption, the Italian democratic system defies most rules of a democracy. In response, the average tax-dodging northerner dedicates considerable energy and inventiveness to foiling the system, a complex bureaucracy whose wheels are oiled by *galoppini*, unofficial facilitators skilled in speeding up procedures by fair means and foul. In a recent abuse of benefits, thousands of supposedly blind pensioners were found to hold driving licences, while star footballers were receiving disability pensions.

Such irregularities seep into every area of life. A landing at Milan's Malpensa airport may be marred by thoughts of the billions of illicit

---

PRECEDING PAGES: a summer's day by the lake; an *espresso* in Verona.
LEFT: Prince Victor Emmanuel of Savoy, with his fiancée, Alejandra di Andia.
RIGHT: mail men in Venice.

lire mixed into the fresh cement. Even the taste of a *cappuccino* in Verona is soured by the *tangente,* the bribe that was necessary to produce the processing plant. Subversion of regulations is an ancient pastime, with cunning (*furbizia*) praised over probity. Indeed, after Trieste was ceded to Italy from the old Austro-Hungarian empire in 1918, taxes were promptly doubled on the assumption that people never paid more than 50 per cent of their dues. If guile fails, Catholic society still offers the path of confession, contrition and absolution.

In the recent past, the north has been content to leave politics to southerners and to concentrate on making money. However, northerners have been politically radicalised by the protest movements of the 1990s and by the increasing appeal of federalism as a solution to their grievances. In the late 1990s, the region positioned itself as the new Italy, turning its back on a baroque political structure steeped in *clientelismo* (nepotism). Yet the region remains deeply old-fashioned, despite its faddism. It is a paradox that, although priding themselves on their free-spirited nature, the people live in a conservative, over-regulated society. As Matt Frei says: "From the formal greeting to the social ritual of the *passeggiata*, the life of the

URBAN MYTHS: ONE

Italians are resolutely urban, drawn to the cosy ideal of living in a small or medium-sized town. The classic northern town is self-contained, self-sufficient and inward-looking. It may well be on a hill-top with modern culture grafted onto a medieval settlement. Such traditional towns regularly top European surveys for superb quality of life. For the northerners provincial life represents security, modernity, comfort and conviviality while the countryside tends to represent the past, with its primitive conditions and poverty.

Large towns such as Modena, Padua and Verona can be seen as smaller versions of the successful provincial town at which Italians in the north excel. Not that smaller towns have a monopoly on beauty and quality of life. For all its inconvenience, Venice is praised as a deeply liveable city, while Bologna is regularly voted the place with the best quality of life in Italy. Even unsung cities such as Milan have their passionate fans, praising secret courtyards and hidden gardens. In the wintry elegance of 18th-century Turin, present-day citizens can cast their eyes along the dark streets and see glittering temples of consumerism basking in the luminosity of the Alps.

Turin and Detroit may both be noted for their car industries, but the Italians are certain that their city has a better quality of life.

average Italian is defined by a set of rules as complex as those of a secret monastic sect."

Northerners are not by nature law-abiding, perceiving the long arm of the law as yet another infringement on personal liberty. Paying taxes, parking in designated places and queuing are seen as similar unnecessary constraints. In a country where civic awareness is undeveloped, there is an assumption of lawlessness in most dealings with the state. Whether it is struggling against the telephone company or the tax office, battles with the authorities absorb a great deal of energy. Yet the law is only one of the arms which the indi-

own in five years' time; a healthy, middle-aged couple may plan where to be buried in the family vault. Commenting on the cloying social packaging of northern life, Tim Parks, the Verona-based novelist, says: "*Cappuccino* until 10, then *espresso*; *aperitivo* after 12; your pasta, your meat, your *dolce* in bright packaging; light white wine, strong red wine, *prosecco*; baptism, first communion, marriage, funeral."

Unshakeable conservatism

At heart is "the extraordinary power of convention, the thorough-going, unshakeable conservatism of a people whose favourite delu-

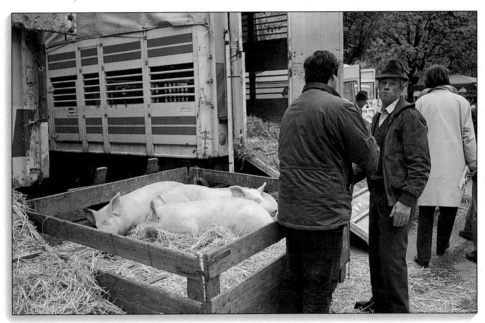

vidual uses in his essentially lawless struggle. In state schools, rebellion for the sake of rebelling is par for the course, as are strikes against educational reforms.

In truth, citizens are torn between tradition and rebellion, conformity and individuality. Despite a sense of chaos, social life is neatly ordered, underpinned by excessive planning. A young couple may decide to marry in exactly three years' time, or move into a house of their

LEFT: catching up on today's news in Parma.
ABOVE: to market in Alto Adige. Despite Northern Italy's dominant industrial base, it still clings to a strong rural tradition.

sion is that they are not bound by delusion". The writer Jonathan Keates would concur with the Italian correspondent John Hooper, who sees the rituals underlying the specious modishness of life: "A lot of what is Italian that is presented to the outside world is hyper-modern or hyper-vogueish, be it Ferrari cars, Versace ties, dried tomatoes or balsamic vinegar. Yet Italy remains profoundly old-fashioned and hidebound, not only by bureaucratic inefficiency but also by practices intended to limit competition and protect this or that interest group."

This archipelago of interest groups is at the heart of society. Even family companies are often organised in such a way as to minimise taxes and employers' contributions. Bizarrely, according to tax returns, employees seem to earn more than their employers while professional people and specialised craftsmen can claim subsistence levels despite running several homes or boats. Italians have always taken refuge in tribalism, a complex system of extended loyalties whose survival validates virtually any course of action. "Me and my clan, my family, my shop, we'll manage – and all the rest can go to hell" is the crudest version of this philosophy, as expressed by Hans Magnus Enzenberger, an observer of Italian society.

URBAN MYTHS: TWO

Small towns continue to flourish in northern Italy because the people like to feel the embracing comfort of a life contained. At the simplest level, citizens create a cosy little world of "their" baker, dressmaker, ironing-lady or picture-framer, conveying the social status of a patron rather than of a mere consumer. Personal recommendation here is everything: *Il mio falegname di fiducia* (my trusted carpenter), often a moonlighting civil servant, could not work for anyone of indiscriminating taste. In its attachment to provincialism and small-town values, Italian society combines cosiness and pride in equal measure, making urban life stultifyingly narrow yet also deeply pleasurable.

Family ties

It is a cliché that Italy is not a country but a mosaic made up of ten million families. As the cornerstone of a conservative society, *la famiglia* is a sophisticated network of patronage and power. Marriage is still seen as a contract for life, and not necessarily severed by marital infidelity. Belonging to a northern family is still a cradle-to-the-grave commitment, with children treated as miniature adults, sons cosseted and daughters trained to be competent but generally more docile. (For a woman, faking subservience is a small price to pay for power in the family.)

Miraculously, the family seems impregnable, despite the rise in social mobility and divorce, the constraints of small apartments, the caprices of domineering parents, the lowest birthrate in Europe, and the virtual absence of state child support. Even so, the population has become the first in the world to possess more pensioners than teenagers and young children. By 2050 the ratio will rise to three to one if this resolutely consumerist society continues to eschew *bambini* in favour of beautiful houses and holidays in Bali.

In the meantime, however, nearly 60 per cent of pampered Italians under 34 still live at home. *Mammismo*, an unhealthy attachment to one's mother, tends to afflict sons, who are termed *mammoni*, mummies' boys. For all offspring, parents are looking for a state of *lo starbene*: a steady job, preferably in the family business or as a civil servant (*statale*). Parents tend to buy or build their children houses so money can be spent on consumer durables rather than rent.

The cloying but comforting rituals of family life are revealed in the saying "*Natale con i tuoi, Pasqua con chi vuoi*" (Spend Christmas with your family, but Easter with whoever you wish). Yet, given the overweening importance of the family, friends (and lovers) come a distant second, with soulmates spurned in favour of a network of useful acquaintances for whom the game of gifts and favours is second nature. Jonathan Keates is scathing about the superficiality of social chit-chat and of society's shared fear of solitude: "The tyranny of family life proscribes individualism, annihilates outline and perspective. Without secrets, without worlds apart, without moments of determined solitariness, the grain and colour of personality are rubbed away." Even the Italian concept of *individualismo* is more "me-firstism" than genuine originality.

Fortunately, there are compensations for the complacency, smugness and patently money-making ethos of northern life. Convention and consumerism may be part of the social warp and weft but conviviality is the real religion. On a good day, the forfeiture of liberty seems a small price to pay for the inbred gregariousness of Italians.

Luigi Barzini condemned his fellow-countrymen for their "eternal search for shallow pleasures and distractions," but the sociologist Luciano Gallino presents the case for the other

On average, compared with Britain, a similar country in terms of wealth, Italy possesses three times the number of retail outlets, and twice the number of cafés. Tellingly, "foodie" or "privacy" are not familiar terms in the local lexicon. An appreciation of good food is the prerogative of all, while privacy is the preserve of none. The emphasis is on the everyday values of sociability, simplicity and pleasure. *Allegria* is a blend of bubbly *joie de vivre* with copious sunshine, good company and collective high spirits. *Allegria* is infectious, as are sybaritic living and a communal way of life. Its much rarer counterpart is a fleeting melancholy

side: "However ridiculous it may seem, Italian food and sociability are important elements in a civilisation." Conviviality is inextricably bound up with eating well, which is one of the highest aims of Italian existence.

The Slow Food Movement

As gourmets delight in pointing out, Italy is the only country in the world where the marketing strategy of McDonalds has been hampered by the birth of the Slow Food Movement.

LEFT: *benvenuti!*
ABOVE: a warm welcome from the vendor at a street snack bar.

induced by solitude, abysmal autumn weather and seasonal tax rises.

Jonathan Keates muses on the certainties of middle-class life in quiet-living, consumerist Middle Italy: "The shops will always bulge with acquisitive lures and promises, the appalling television channels will be there to offer the bromide and novocaine of endless game shows, and the news magazines will order their graver thoughts on matters a little more global than the thousand different ways of preparing a risotto or the chances for Juve and Samp in the league championships." On a sunny day, even this cynical appraisal of a soulless *dolce vita* has considerable appeal. ❏

REGIONALISM RULES

"We have made Italy, now we must make the Italians," declared Massimo d'Azeglio (1798–1866), prime minister of Piedmont, after the creation of the Kingdom of Italy

Before 1945, says the cookery writer Claudia Roden, "you could divide Italy according to cooking fats: there was butter in the north, pork fat in the centre and olive oil in the south. The Italy of polenta and rice was the north, and the Italy of pizza and dry pasta was in the south." Now, she thinks, the borders have been blurred, and pizza and pasta have triumphed. However, regional flavours survive in rich sauces and robust attitudes; national uniformity is only notional, even in politics, language and culture. As Massimo d'Azeglio, a shrewd architect of national unity, declared: "To make Italy out of Italians, one must not be in a hurry".

Identity crisis

If regionalism is a religion in northern Italy, then Italian-ness is a mere cult. In 1815 Metternich, the Habsburg prime minister, famously dismissed Italy as a "geographical expression". The country is a collection of peoples, with the disparate regions remaining diverse. Nationalism remains an elusive concept in a country not noted for its symbols of unity, communality of purpose or common institutions that command respect. National sentiment is restricted to sport, be it the resurgence of Ferrari or the mixed fortunes of the national football team.

Local loyalties cast a long historical shadow over the contemporary scene: distinctive regional identity was a factor in keeping Italy disunited. This was compounded by the fragmented nature of the city states, duchies, republics and Papal States, each with its own allegiances and cultural traditions. Until 1861 the regions were separate, independent, even rival states who submitted to different rulers, and were protected by sovereign armies. The people's common refrain was: *"Franza o Spagna, purché si manga."* (France or Spain, it matters little as long as we get fed.)

LEFT: Alto Adige has a distinctly Austrian flavour.
RIGHT: Bolzano is the bilingual capital of Alto Adige, with both Italian and German being spoken.

Turin, sandwiched between the great powers of France and Austria-Hungary, was frequently overrun and has retained a foreign flavour. Indeed, Count Cavour saw Turin as the nodal point between "German and Latin races", with the Piedmontese alone possessing the better qualities of Latins and Germans. In Piedmont,

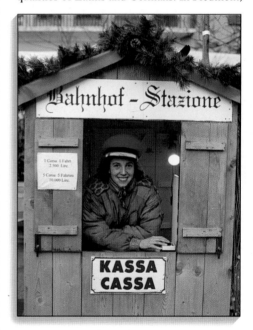

the pervasive French influence is reflected in the region's penchant for fussy French cuisine, at odds with filling Italian country fare. The Austro-Hungarian influence in Lombardy, Friuli-Venezia Giulia and the Veneto helped to instil a tradition of sound administration and fair taxation. In the case of Venice, Austrian pragmatism overlays an exotic eastern heritage, the republic's role as the hub of a trading empire with Africa and the Levant.

Whether living in famous cities or in one-horse towns, citizens generally carry their home town around for life, like a standard. Just as exile from home is the greatest fear, so "local boy made good" is the classic communal myth.

Deeply engrained regionalism also dictates fierce rivalry, just as civic pride implies competition. Such warped local patriotism is predicated on the belief that Italy would be paradise without *"gli altri"*, fellow Italians from rival regions and cities.

Borderlands

For a country that superficially seems so clear and culturally distinct, Italy abounds in borderlands. The country's frontiers were only definitively fixed in 1954, when Italy's dispute with what was then Yugoslavia was settled. Yet even within northern regions that are undeni-

ably Italian there are alien pockets, places on the edge little stirred by a national consciousness. One such anomaly is Trieste; as a splinter in the Habsburg empire, Trieste gave *Mitteleuropa* its only access to the Mediterranean. In 1963 Friuli-Venezia Giulia was also accorded special status because of its Slovene-speaking population in the Trieste hinterland.

In the north it is hard to find Italy pure and undiluted. The region has its share of mini-states, including Campione d'Italia, a slice of Italy in Swiss territory. The world's oldest republic, San Marino, has a seat in the United Nations but lives on pageantry and postage stamps. Seborga, an enterprising principality behind the Italian Riviera, unilaterally declared its independence in 1995 but has yet to be officially recognised.

The Italian Constitution granted a measure of autonomy to French-speaking Valle d'Aosta and Italian-German-speaking Trentino-Alto Adige. Known as Südtirol in German, Alto Adige is the most complex case, a region spiritually Austrian but legally Italian. In 1919 the dismantling of the Austro-Hungarian Empire resulted in the Tyrol being divided, with South Tyrol awarded to Italy and eventually swallowed up by the new region of Trentino-Alto Adige in 1948. The Italian state gerrymandering ensured an Italian-speaking majority but, until recently, left the German-speaking population dissatisfied. Culturally, Bolzano (Bozen), the German and Italian-speaking capital of Alto Adige, still feels like an Austrian city, with its mountain chalets, brass bands, neat window boxes, and its banks built with a most un-Italian disregard for security.

Northern Italy abounds in linguistic differ-

OLD MIGRANTS AND NEW IMMIGRANTS

Since 1945 more than 6 million southerners have migrated to the northern industrial heartlands, but in more recent years the influx of non-European Union immigrants has resulted in new ethnic communities, who currently comprise 2 percent of the population, with a burgeoning underclass of illegal immigrants. In major northern cities, such as Milan and Genoa, the social strain of immigration has been increasingly felt, particularly with the arrival of boatloads of North and West Africans, Albanians and citizens from the former Yugoslavia. (Non-European Union immigrants now comprise a quarter of the prison population.) Their presence has played into the hands of

the instinctive racist tendencies shared by many northern Italians, and swelled the ranks of the secessionist movements. In critical northern eyes, today's immigrant could be an Eastern European prostitute in Milan, an Albanian cleaner in Turin, or a North African trader in Genoa.

While acceptance and integration look remote, the humanity of Italians ensures that many illegal immigrants are treated with tolerance, at least on a personal level. Moreover, Italians are gradually adjusting to the phenomenon of African-Italians speaking the language fairly fluently. Even so, mixed marriages or friendship across the racial divide are still taboo.

ences past and present. Piedmont shares more than a frontier with France: French was the court language until the mid 19th-century, and the local dialects reflect French and old Tuscan influences. Count Cavour was as much Swiss and French as Piedmontese because his mother was from Switzerland and his grandmother from Savoy. As prime minister, Cavour still spoke better French than Italian, never travelled south of Florence, and was more familiar with the culture and history north

LINGUA FRANCA

French was the language of the court in Piedmont until the mid-19th century, when only a tiny minority of the country spoke standard Italian. King Vittorio Emmanuel never mastered it.

elementary schools in certain regions, and permitted the street names Italianised by Mussolini to revert to their original forms. (In the area around Trieste, place names were already written in Italian and Slovene, with Italian and German used in Alto Adige). The promotion of minority languages was both a genuine admission of cultural diversity and a sop to regionalist separatist sentiments. As a result, Ladin, the Latin-based language spoken by a minority in Trentino-Alto Adige, was given

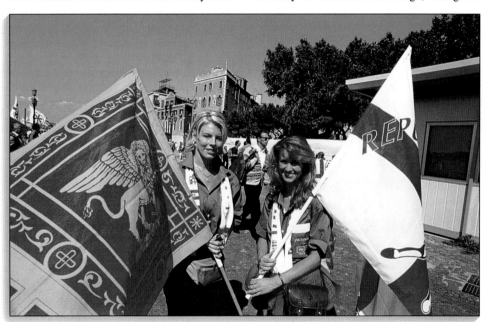

of the Alps. Today citizens still delight in pointing out "incomprehensible" dialects, from guttural *bergamasco* in Bergamo to the Provençal French of Valle d'Aosta or the Frenchified dialects of the alpine Piedmontese hinterland.

Regional dialects and languages

Although the advent of television led to greater linguistic homogeneity, regional dialects and even languages survive. In the 1990s the state approved the teaching of minority languages at

special status. Languages granted similar recognition included German (in Alto Adige), Slovene (around Trieste), Friulano (in the north-east), Provençal French (in Valle d'Aosta and Turin) and Occitano (in Turin and Cosenza). As well as asserting their differences in dialects, cuisine and folklore, the regions have become hotbeds of political debate. Northerners express their political and economic differences in their attachment to parties with radical aspirations, from the left-wing efficiency of Emilia to the secessionist movements that flourish in Lombardy and the Veneto. These leagues combine protest against political corruption with a more ancient rebellion

LEFT: a souvenir vendor, one of the new generation of African-Italians, on the Riviera.
ABOVE: "regionalism first, nationalism second".

against the capital. The state is perceived as siphoning off northern taxes and diluting northern identity. To staunch federalists, however, even Italian unification was a historical error.

Lombardy, the Veneto and Piedmont spearhead the federalist movement. The political goals range from a desire for more regional autonomy to outright secession from the Italian state. Although the Lombards have been the dominant force since the creation of the first modern league in 1982, the equally prosperous

> **ARRIVISTE CELTS**
>
> "The Lombards were upstarts and newcomers descended from the Celts and only arrived on the Italian peninsula in the 9th century." – The Venetian League.

citizens of the Veneto are challenging their leadership. The Movimento Nordest (Northeast Movement), based on the Catalan model, aims to make northern Italy autonomous.

Protection of profits

On one level, the federalist movement is fuelled by fierce regional pride and by resentment against poorer regions and the "thieving" state. Supporters of the leagues complain of their taxes being squandered in the south by the state machine. Certainly, autonomy would free the regions from the dead hand of bureaucracy, but for self-righteous northerners the primary aim is the protection of homegrown profits. Yet such

grievances are underpinned by a sense of history as a living inspiration, from glorious ceremonials to a commemoration of valiant causes. South of Milan the nondescript town of Pontida regularly re-enacts the 1176 Battle of Legnano, a victory of the Lombard League over imperial forces. The pageant represents a rejection of the modern state and an indictment of Italian unity. The glue of national solidarity runs very thinly.

The questioning of the nation state is not restricted to contemporary Italy, but it has assumed a distinctly local character. Even if the leagues ultimately fail to find a leading role in the national democracy, they have succeeded in rousing regional passions. With Italy desperate to flaunt its European credentials, passions run high on both sides of the political divide, with supporters of unity equally vehement. Cardinal Martini, the Piedmontese Archbishop of Milan, denigrates what he sees as selfish parochialism, including the secessionist parties' attempts to make capital out of regional greed and materialism.

Although his influence may be on the wane, Umberto Bossi, leader of the Northern League (Lega Nord), is the rabble-rousing mouthpiece of working-class anger with a rallying cry: "*C'è l'ho duro!* (I've got a hard on)." Yet guile is also part of his armoury: when speaking to a hardline audience in Bergamo, Signor Bossi is a separatist; when speaking to the Venetian League, he is a regionalist; when in Rome, he is a federalist, and when in Sicily, he becomes pro-autonomy. In 1996 his Northern League created the surreal and self-styled country of Padania, complete with passports and currency.

Despite all disclaimers, northerners like being Italian, provided that it is graced with a local dimension in politics, food and wine. Thanks to regional prosperity and an instinct for compromise and consensus, the north remains one of Italy's success stories. Northern confidence is not dented by its cultural and social diversity, or the controversies surrounding separatism. In the words of the Italian playwright Ennio Flaiano, "Things are tragic but not serious." ❏

LEFT: the separatist Northern League's self-styled country of Padania even has its own currency.

Football Fever

Football, like opera, is a national obsession and a source of patriotic pride. The pre-match atmosphere in Milan's San Siro stadium is a festival of explosions, pounding drums and chore-ographed clapping, with stands decked in banners, dapper fans embracing fur-clad companions, and families devouring mounds of *porchetta*-filled *panini*, fresh ham rolls; only *caffè borghetti*, strong, sweet coffee, fuels the competition. Even so, the rivalry between the two Milanese sides explodes in a post-match finale in which the winning fans parade a coffin draped in the losers' colours.

The game thrives on classic regional and city rivalries: the major northern teams include Juven-tus, AC Milan, Inter Milan, Sampdoria (one of two Genoa teams) and Parma. Milan proclaims itself the capital of European soccer while Juventus, one of the world's richest clubs, prides itself on tac-tics, stamina and strength. Milan and Rome have two teams apiece, and Berlusconi's AC Milan is a rival to Fiat and Agnelli's Juventus at Turin.

The major Italian clubs are envious of the lucra-tive sponsorship and merchandising deals that can be struck by foreign rivals. Instead of rushing to the souvenir stands for replica shirts, more than 2,000 Juventus fans show their loyalty by taking skiing holidays on the Valle d'Aosta slopes where the team retreats for winter training. Refined Italian fashion sense precludes the wearing of football strips as leisure-wear: the major sides must be content with merchandising exquisite packages of wine, olive oil and *panettone* Christmas cake in club colours.

Nonetheless, Italian imports have enriched for-eign football, despite their reputation as precious individualists rather than team players. In turn, Inter Milan and AC Milan have sides studded with foreign players. According to Gianluca Vialli, for-mer Juventus star and manager of Chelsea: "In Italy, foreign footballers are idols, we treat them like kings." However, Berlusconi has complained that there is no spirit to his all-star Milanese side and called for more home-grown players.The cur-rent decline in standards has also been attributed to the lack of investment in youth training, accen-tuated by a marked preference for buying ready-made foreign players. Even Vicenza, a first-division club with a reputation for nurturing young players, recently abandoned its youth programme.

Known as the Azzurri, the Blues, the national side has had mixed fortunes. Just as Mussolini launched the 1934 World Cup as a celebration of the Fascist state, so Italia 90 was staged as a showcase for state-of-the-art stadia and "*la nuova ricca Italia*", the newly wealthy, corruption-free country. In the end, the 1990 World Cup was bet-ter remembered as a quagmire of kickbacks and political mismanagement. Italy, three times world champions, followed this with a disappointing per-formance in the 1998 World Cup. In that year Ital-ian football was struck by doping scandals which

cast a shadow over Serie A, the world's premier football league, sullying the reputations of such lofty sides as Parma, Bologna and Juventus. Critics aired their suspicions that the sudden develop-ment of muscle mass in star players owed much to steroid abuse.

The future for Italian football may lie in its fam-ily atmosphere and superb stadia, and in the bur-geoning immigrant community of Africans and former Yugoslavs. As the journalist Vittorio Zucconi says: "If we want to save the national team, let's build football pitches next to refugee camps and open up our public parks to the sons of immigrants who never give up the ball for fear that someone might steal it." ❑

RIGHT: Juventus striker Alessandro del Piero, playing for his country in the 1998 World Cup.

PRINCES OF INDUSTRY

"The dynamism of Italian enterprise contrasts strongly with the inertia of the institutions." – Charles Richards in "The New Italians"

There is nothing incestuous about Benetton, says Luciano Benetton of his family business worth several billion pounds to his children: "We stick together and decisions are made quickly." As a "typical" family firm, albeit one on a grand scale, Benetton reflects the region's traditional strengths: the firm is heir to an ancient crafts and textiles tradition, and is imbued with a belief in design skills and functional beauty. Although industrial giants such as Benetton and Fiat are not wholly representative of the region's success, they share a family ethos and an almost Protestant work ethic. Linked to a belief in the redemptive powers of paternalism, this is sober-suited capitalism with a social conscience.

Northern Italy is the powerhouse of the Italian economy, driven by an entrepeneurial spirit and a paternalist past. Compared with its competitors, the north cannot compete on price, economies of scale or research and development. High labour costs also mean an undue concentration on the luxury end of the market. Instead, the region plays to its strengths, foremost of which is an exceptional concentration of successful family-run companies. With a dense web of small and medium-sized companies, the north is the model for Italian capitalism, producing a range of specialist goods. Flexibility, follow-up, a reliable network of suppliers and a commitment to quality and detail also characterise the northern model. (A thriving black economy also accounts for about a quarter of Italy's GDP.)

Commercial continuity

Even though northern Italy only industrialised itself in the 1950s, commerce and merchant capitalism flourished as far back as the middle ages. In a medieval version of the postwar "economic miracle", cities such as Milan, Genoa, Cremona, Pavia and Piacenza led the

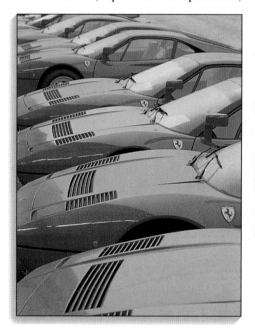

way, trading in textiles and crafts. In many cases a tradition of making similar things for centuries has given the region the edge in confident styling. Unlike the French and British service economies, the Italians are still fully engaged in making things: from white goods to red Ferraris; spectacles to sportswear; pullovers to Parmesan cheese. Wool and silk are transformed into fabrics and fine clothes, felt into hats, leather into shoes; metal turns into arms, helicopters, cars and carriages; wheat becomes pasta; fruits of the forest and cured meats are sold as specialised foodstuffs.

In modern times, Turin and Milan have driven the economic engine of northern industrialisation, with Olivetti, Montedison and Pirelli coming to prominence in the 1920s. The economic boom of the 1950s transformed Italy from an impoverished country into one of the wealthiest in the world. The AGIP petroleum company also redrew the industrial map of postwar Italy; Enrico Mattei exploited the discovery of

LEFT: Gianni Agnelli, head of Fiat.
RIGHT: Italian stallions – a clutch of Ferraris at the company's factory in Modena.

The Fiat Family

Avvocato Gianni Agnelli, the patriarch of the Fiat dynasty, famously said that, in order to run a successful Italian company: "You need an uneven number of directors; and two is too many." Such autocratic attitudes have helped make Fiat the force that it is.

As Italy's largest industrial group, Fiat is worth over £35 billion and is the world's fifth largest car producer, second only to Volkswagen among European manufacturers. In passing, Fiat has swallowed up Alfa Romeo, Ferrari, Lancia and Piaggio

motorbikes. The company also controls banks and insurance companies, and has concerns in the construction, aerospace and defence industries, not to mention fashion, food, publishing, the media and sport, including Juventus, Italy's most prestigious football club.

As a family affair, Fiat ensures that it is not just another car company but part of the Italian social fabric. With a management noted for its shrewdness and political connections, Fiat has never been afraid to face down governments. The Agnelli family exerted discreet pressure on Mussolini to prevent Ford from entering the domestic market in the 1920s. Fiat has since been helped by the fact that Italy is one of the most protected markets in

Europe. (High tariffs on imported cars remained in place until 1961.) Moreover, Susanna Agnelli's spell as Italian foreign minister in the 1990s conveniently coincided with lucrative new South American contracts for the family firm. As for the press, Fiat owns *La Stampa*, the influential Turin daily, and the company's influence across the media still guarantees acts of editorial self-censorship in the company's favour.

The Agnelli, from Piedmontese landowning stock, founded Fabbrica Italiana Automobili Torino (Fiat) in 1899, and in the process made modern Turin. In 1912 Giovanni Agnelli travelled to the United States to study Henry Ford's methods and production lines. The Agnelli formula was to fuse American-style production techniques, management and devotion to profit with old-fashioned northern Italian philanthropism and stylishness.

Fiat produced the first car in Turin in 1899, building the brutalist Lingotto factory, praised by Le Corbusier as "one of industry's most exciting spectacles", in 1923. Here the Topolino model moved up the production line from floor to floor until emerging on the rooftop test track. The company later abandoned Lingotto to move to the Mirafiori complex in the city suburbs. However, the revamped Lingotto plant remains a testament to the industrial giant, a hotel and conference centre complete with the surreal rooftop test track.

Fiat rode the economic boom of the 1950s, providing most ordinary families with their first small car. The company prospered during the 1950s and by the 1970s had 15,000 workers in Turin, rising to 150,000 by 1980. Fiat was swept up in the corruption scandals of the early 1990s, with Romiti and other top executives arrested for paying bribes to win a contract on the Milan metro. At the height of the scandals, "VIP" came to mean *visti in prigione*, or spotted in prison.

By the 1990s, turnover was between five and seven per cent of Italian GDP, with more than two million workers dependent on Fiat-related companies. However, aggressive marketing from foreign competitors has pushed Fiat's recent share of the domestic car market below 50 per cent. Hitherto the company's industrial strategy has been to diversify but to remain a family firm and resist mergers. Ironically, the fate of the Agnelli's company stake may now depend on what Fiat's new, non-family chairman does for the share price. ❑

LEFT: Alfa Romeo, once a competitor, is now part of the £35 billion Fiat empire.

methane gas in the Po Valley to build an enormous empire embracing petrochemicals, roads, engineering, textiles and nuclear power. Turin was transformed from being the capital of the kingdom of Savoy to the car capital, a new industrial giant within a united Italy.

Fiat, to an outsider, is Turin. Yet according to sociologist Luciano Gallino: "They could close Fiat tomorrow and Turin would survive." The city is no longer simply Fiat but an engineering, electronic and computing centre. The Piedmontese are practical

CAR CITY

"Visitors think Turin is industrial, a car manufacturing city like Detroit; but Turin is not Detroit." – local resident Giuseppe Galimi.

Biella Valley is the loom of the Italian textile and clothing industry (*see page 83*). Even the unemployed are largely involved in the thriving *economia sommersa*, the black economy.

Milan's banking infrastructure and role as the hub of the media and service industries has made it Italy's de facto capital in commercial affairs. The city's role as fashion and design capital and ability to reinvent itself has brought it prestige and people. Milan has always been a magnet for hard-working migrants from the south, such as the late

people with a gift for mechanics and engineering, as well as some of the best technical institutes in Italy. But Turin is not a typical motor manufacturing city. With superior coffee and a negligible crime rate, Turin and its hinterland are devoted to the good life: Piedmont produces vermouths, including the famous brands of Martini and Cinzano, owned by the Agnelli dynasty, as well as magnificent wines. As for fashion, Alessandria is the city of Borsalino hats, famed as the world's finest, while the

ABOVE: drivers on Ferrari's Formula One motor racing team, including Michael Schumacher (second from right).

Gianni Versace, and it also draws commuters from the Lombardy hinterland, notably Brescia, which acts as a New Jersey to Milan's Manhattan. Lombardy, the Milanese hinterland, is the richest and most populous region in Italy, producing a quarter of GNP and a third of all Italian exports. With an average income double that of the south, Lombardy has few rivals. Only the Veneto, Italy's fastest-growing economy, could conceivably outstrip it, given the success of small and medium-sized companies in sectors as diverse as fashion and furniture. Benetton is merely the Veneto's shop window for related family firms which provide shared services and a pool of skilled labour.

Family fortunes

Northern Italians are at ease with the concept of a firm as a family empire, whatever its size. Fiat may be a car company, but the major shareholder is the Agnelli family, and control passes dynastically. As for the fashion and textile industry, family groups are the norm, from Benetton to Missoni, Ferragamo to Ermenegildo Zegna.

Being an orphan or a self-made man is no impediment to founding a family firm: Milanese Leonardo del Vecchio was both, and has made Luxottica, a world leader in designer spectacles, a company to pass to his offspring.

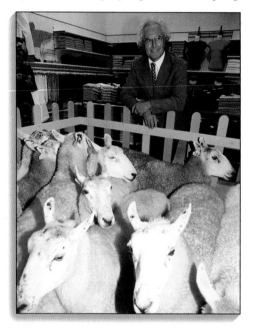

The north has an illustrious pedigree of paternalist benefactors, mostly from sober Piedmontese stock. The classic case was Camillo Olivetti, who founded the typewriter firm that became a computer and telecommunications giant. In building workers' model villages in Ivrea, near Turin, he was motivated by a sense of community and social duty. This corner of Piedmont has a tradition of industrial patronage dating back to the 1840s.

Ermenegildo Zegna, the textile tycoon, founded Centro Zegna in Trivero, a socially enlightened project complete with hospital, school, shops and sports centre. He also created and substantially funded road-building and reafforestation projects, blasting tunnels through rocks to create a superb nature reserve. The same spirit of enlightened paternalism has always been part of the Fiat philosophy, with social housing in the industrial flatlands around Turin intended to accommodate the influx of southern migrants in the 1950s.

Fame and shame

The princes of Italian industry include the pantheon of golden names, from Agnelli to Armani, Benetton to Ferragamo. Then there are the falling stars such as Silvio Berlusconi; the lost souls, such as Carlo de Benedetti; and the tragic victims of the corruption scandals, such as Raul Gardini. The Agnellis, founders of Fiat, the country's most successful company, dominate the industrial establishment's *salotto buono* (high society) – *see page 72.*

Silvio Berlusconi still clings to his media empire despite being found guilty of financial corruption. During his brief spell as premier in 1994, he exploited his brand name, running the country as a corporation, and promoting the association between football and politics; he even called his cabinet the Azzurri, a term normally reserved for the national squad. Despite his falling star, Berlusconi possesses a magnificent villa, near Milan, with Renaissance masters and a family mausoleum, modelled on an Etruscan necropolis.

Carlo de Benedetti, formerly head of Olivetti, was jailed during the corruption scandals of the 1990s. When running the computer giant, de Benedetti admitted to paying bribes, which he presented as an unavoidable evil of the murky system, with its absence of a free market. "We Italians dislike genuine competition amongst ourselves." (Olivetti, based near Turin, has since been restructured as a telecommunications company.) Raul Gardini, former head of the Ferruzzi agro-industrial empire and the country's paymaster of bribes, committed suicide in his Venetian palazzo in 1993 rather than face the consequences.

United colours

By contrast, Luciano Benetton's star is in the ascendant. To outsiders he may simply be the prince of pullovers, but in the Veneto this taciturn entrepreneur is a major employer, a political force and a family figure writ large. Although the Benetton group is the world's largest buyer of wool, it is still run like the family knitwear firm it was in the 1950s. At the age of 20, Luciano Benetton sold his accordion to finance the knitting machine his sister needed to launch the family business.

However, despite 7,000 shops in 120 countries, the high-profile clothing company is only the tip of the iceberg. The family conglomerate embraces banking, motor racing, sportswear and food, forming the 16th biggest group in Italy. Set amongst orchards and vineyards near Treviso, the headquarters are modelled around a corporate village and the family's Palladian villa. The cosy atmosphere

marketing with a social crusade. Toscani's pet project is Fabrica, a Benetton-financed "centre of creativity" and the family's bid for immortality. Housed near Treviso, this hubristic venture is described as an "electronic Bauhaus", but as a concept it seems as woolly as a Benetton pullover.

According to Toscani: "Companies are the new churches; it is only through them that problems can be solved." Certainly, the fervour attached to company life is matched only by the region's economic success. In 1987 Italy won a coveted place on the table of the G7, largely thanks to the performance of the northern econ-

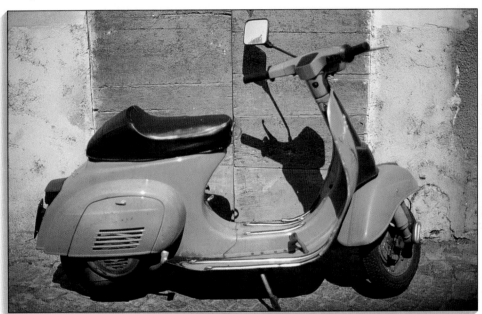

is maintained at mealtimes: the Benetton clan dines together, while the canteen serves workers with fresh produce from the family's kitchen gardens.

Benetton's talent was to reshape the traditional small-scale structure of the Italian textiles industry as an organisation capable of competing on world markets. Yet it is the provocative marketing campaigns that have made Benetton's name. Oliviero Toscani is the creative supremo and showman responsible for combining slick

LEFT: Luciano Benetton surveys his flock.
ABOVE: a perennial design classic, Piaggio's Vespa motorscooter was introduced in 1946.

omy. By the late 1980s export boom, "made in Italy" had become an international hallmark of style and quality.

Although the recession and corruption scandals of the 1990s rocked confidence in Italy's business empire, the region's strengths enabled the world's fifth-largest economy to bounce back. The current challenge is to combat "spaghettiphobia"; this is the fear that many foreign companies have of investing their money in Italy. On present performance, the appeal of quality consumer goods made with Italian style and attention to detail should outweigh any sober-suited scruples about corruption and bureaucracy. ❏

A SENSE OF STYLE

For the cognoscenti, Italy is a design showcase, excelling at ineffable chic and the art of understatement

A character in Tim Parks's *Mimi's Ghost* accuses the Italians of considering beauty "more as a consumer product than as something of spiritual value, a question of owning a particular shirt and tie, a particular style in furnishing". Certainly, the practised materialism of the contemporary northerner implies having an eye for the right Ferrari, floor tiles or Fendi fur coat rather than relishing the intricacies of restoring Leonardo's *Last Supper.*

Milan may be the design showcase, but most northern cities are citadels of good taste, with smart shops and shiny people committed to sophisticated consumerism. A northern city is also a stage set designed for preening and posturing, a place *fare bella figura*, to cut a fine figure.

Appearance is all

Yet conspicuous consumption is only part of the public picture. Although Milan remains the focus for fashion and creative innovation, a sense of style is in the Italian genes. Insolent chic and the flaunting of wealth are allied to a deep aesthetic sense, insouciant grace, and a gift for understanding the spirit of a treasured place or object. People have an innate pride in making things beautiful, *fatta ad arte*, although not necessarily built to last. Linked to a sense of beauty is the belief that visual awareness is a birthright for all: a life lived in public ensures a stylish parade, from polished symbols of success and staturs to design flair bound by social conventions.

In this baroque society, appearances are everything, with every age and caste possessing its uniform, usually a model of good taste. The Carabinieri, along with all Italian police forces, take pride in their decorative dress code: Armani was naturally commissioned to design their lightweight summer costume. The criminal fraternity are equally slavish followers of

fashion: the successful *mafioso* tends to team an Armani suit with a Moschino waistcoat and Pollini shoes; even in prison, privileged *mafiosi* insist on wearing Fila and Tacchini sportswear. The uniform Italian look has been successfully marketed abroad: the England football team, for example, is just one of many squads that

feel more stylish playing in Umbro, part of the Ferragamo empire.

To pass the appraising gaze of a Milanese requires a crash course in cultural one-upmanship. A certain nonchalance, cool conservatism, understated chic and the correct brand of sunglasses send the right messages. Not that style is simply a question of conspicuous consumption: a pullover slung jauntily around one's shoulders can say more than a designer label. If in doubt, the look of deluxe anonymity is the safe sartorial badge of modern Italy. To convey social status, it helps to have an entourage and to avoid public transport.

While the northerners are rarely philistine in

PRECEDING PAGES: a boutique in trendy Genoa.
LEFT: Carla Bruni on the catwalk.
RIGHT: Milanese chic for sale.

fashion, conformity triumphs over originality. Although city slickers pride themselves on their individuality, dressing appropriately for the season and occasion is considered more important than dressing to please oneself or one's mood. To be accidentally over-dressed for, say, a visit to a park or pizzeria can be a cardinal sin; equally well, a mere "stroll" can be taken to mean parading in all one's finery. As for beach etiquette, dress codes are often enforced on the Ligurian Riviera. A few years ago the mayor of Diano Marina, an inconsequential Ligurian resort, caused a sensation by banning ugly women from his beaches.

POLITICALLY CORRECT DRESSERS

Off-duty, a young right-winger favours a Barbour jacket and Timberland boots while his left-wing counterpart chooses a checked shirt, jeans, a long pullover and a Loden coat. Gianfranco Fini, leader of the Fascist party, reassures putative followers with his conservatively cut grey suits and rimless glasses. On the other hand, Fausto Bertinotti, leader of the die-hard Marxist Rifondazione party, has given Communism a safely capitalist image with his preference for Burberry trench coats and English tweed. The dyed-in-the-(designer)-wool revolutionary is often called the best-dressed man in Parliament, the propounder of champagne Communism.

The fashion map

Despite the internationalism of the fashion world, northern design houses pride themselves on their deep regional roots. Milan is the undisputed fashion capital while Lombardy and Emilia Romagna have the greatest concentration of *alta moda* (haute couture) houses (*see page 219*). Missoni, the colourful knitwear label, is based in Lombardy, while Emilia dominates the leather industry, from shoes to bags, belts and accessories. Patrick Cox, the Italian-based shoe designer, praises local manufacturers for excelling at choice, availability, delivery and sheer quality. The region also has La Perla, the sexy lingerie company, and Mandarina Duck, the chic luggage firm; few professional women would be without their supple Duck handbags. North of Turin, Piedmont's Biella Valley is the centre of the textile industry, and home to the exclusive Ermenegildo Zegna fabric and menswear firm. Benetton, based in the Veneto, is one of Europe's most profitable production lines (*see page 75*).

Milan's reputation for fashion has not developed by chance but by design. An innovative industrial culture, sound mass-production techniques and a role as a melting pot set the city on a successful course. The prestigious Prada and Gucci labels are part of the Italian fashion renaissance, a reminder that the battle between Gucci kitten heels and Prada mules is as crucial to the economy as the changing fortunes of Fiat. The contribution of fashion to Italy's balance of payments is second only to tourism's – and the bottom line counts more than the hemline.

As a result, the Milan-based fashion industry has the strength to transcend corruption, recession or the Asian meltdown. The 1980s, the archetypal designer decade, witnessed the triumph of Italian taste, a strong trend that continues despite the corruption scandals of the 1990s. These implicated a roll-call of top designers, with luminaries such as Armani, Ferre, Krizia and Versace admitting to paying bribes to the tax authorities.

The north has always been a magnet for the most talented designers, with stars such as Versace coming from the poor south to the heady heights of Milan. Most of the top Milanese-based designers are deeply traditional, serving a resolutely bourgeois clientele. Innovation might be elsewhere, but the northerners know how to treat fashion as opera while delivering collections of sleek sophistication.

Unlike the London fashion scene, Milanese designers are not besotted with youth or creativity; and unlike the Parisians, the Milanese are prepared to put profit before prestige, wearability before exclusivity. The essence of the Italian look is timeless classicism, no cultural fusion but a clear statement of identity. Since functional simplicity is increasingly dominating the catwalks, the Milanese designers look set to be a main influence in the next decade,

FELLOW TRAVELLERS

City buses are the preserve of the poor: nuns, students, tourists and the self-consciously left-wing.

ing native talent to style American furniture, Japanese cameras, German limousines and French family cars. In styling, foreign status symbols are often products of *la linea italiana*, Italian style.

Umberto Eco, best-selling novelist and questing culture-surfer, sees design in elevated Italian terms: "Design does not mean that I am commissioned by a more or less interesting industrial firm to bestow a form upon a more or less stupid product." Instead, it means to have carte blanche to reinvent the world through a single object.

A basic philosophy

In a country that worships visual display, competitiveness and creativity are inevitable. Style is also an emblem of high seriousness, with great attention accorded the simple purchase of a picture or a place mat. Design is no mere styling but a philosophy involving creative alchemy and a crafts-based aesthetic, brainstorming and problem-solving skills, allied to a talent for interpreting mass culture. Fortunately, the world remains in thrall to Italian taste, invit-

These are always seductive consumerist objects made with grace, style and the design flair imprinted in the Italian genes.

In 1946, the Italian architect Ernesto Nathan Rogers stated that design should be all-embracing, "from the spoon to the city". Italian designers have dutifully filled our world with vintage Vespa scooters and Olivetti typewriters; black Anglepoise lamps and sexy red Alfa Romeos; sleek Alessi kettles and Artemide lighting; Achille Castiglioni cutlery and rustic terracotta tiles. Among the everyday objects cast in sinuous sculptural forms are sleek chrome kitchen appliances and twirly pasta quills. In turn, Giandomenico Belotti's Spaghetti Chair was

LEFT: Giorgio Armani is one of the most successful fashion designers in the world.

ABOVE: Murano glass perfume flasks – or works of art?

literally inspired by squiggly pasta. As a result of such diversity, the inimitable character of *la linea italiana*, or Italian style, has a continuing impact on international taste.

The north is known for its smooth, streamlined objects, from washing machines to motorbikes. Creatively, however, designs can be functional or futuristic, elitist or democratic. Northern design has depended on the creative cross-fertilisation between crafts, art and architecture. Giú Ponti, the 20th century's greatest Modernist, believed that Italy had been created half by God and half by architects. He detested the superfluous and favoured practical, perfect

forms such as his Superleggera, the consummate chair, a sculpted lightweight piece. Indeed, Italian chairs, desks and lamps have often been designed by major architects, which explains the rationality and rigour of the finished products.

The irrepressible spirit of Italian design taps into avant-garde movements in politics and the arts. Above all, design is still treated as an artistic impulse, with practitioners often possessing a background in art or architecture. Gaetano Pesce's flamboyant foam chairs are gorgeous iconic objects that wittily evoke both traditions: Sunset in New York (1980) is a sofa with skyscrapers reflected on glass

flooring. Italian products are a synthesis of both form and function.

Northern design remains a noisy, chaotic, unbureaucratic world, with "radical" studios and colourful personalities. Foremost among the design studios are the Milanese Alchymia (1976) and Memphis (1981). Founded by Ettore Sottsass, Memphis changed the domestic landscape, rejecting cosy domesticity and derivative designs, along with the notion that "form follows function": these objects were stars in their own right.

As the best-known of designers, Sottsass shocked bourgeois Italy with surface decoration and gaudy colours. Yet, at the start of the electronic age, the eclectic designer was so intimidated by his brief for Olivetti computers that he created "a big, eerie aluminium object, completely impenetrable". Memphis, which designs furniture, household objects and fabrics, has now reverted to classic styles.

Technical versatility

Star designers happily turn their hands to the humdrum – a vase, pen, poster, knife, canopener or doorknob. Eclectic designers switch fields with considerable flair and confidence, from interior to industrial or graphic design. As a result, northern technical design skills are often under-rated; yet in the early 1960s the country styled the first transistor radio and the first portable television. Nor should the avant-garde nature of Italian design be overlooked: in the same decade, native designers shattered the consensus on lighting; henceforth a lamp could look like a paper pyramid or a spaceship.

Italy has a talent for transforming the mundane and everyday into the beautiful. At best, northern style marries form and function, accessibility and aesthetics. Yet the design spectrum has room for divergent views, particularly regarding the importance of practicality. Anna Piaggi, fashion guru, daring stylist and an editor of Italian *Vogue*, declares: "Originality is of little use without practicality."

At the other end of the scale, Alessi kettles are design icons rather than kitchen implements. "I prefer it if they work," concedes Alberto Alessi, "but I don't think people buy an Alessi kettle to boil water." Indeed not: a fashion statement is its own *raison d'être*. ❏

LEFT: fine footwear – Italian leather shoes.

Textile Valley

Armani, Valentino and Versace represent only the most glamorous tip of the Italian fashion industry. Paris, Milan and London may be great fashion centres, noted for style and marketing, but Piedmont's unprepossessing valleys remain Europe's main textile manufacturing centre. Most European designers source their fabrics in northern Italy, from Chanel and Hugo Boss to Paul Smith to Marks and Spencer, who say: "It is simply a matter of going to where the best skills are. One of our manufacturers goes back five generations; and there is a lot of investment in fabrics and new technology."

Even American designers such as Ralph Lauren and Calvin Klein recognise the superior quality and creativity of the Italian manufacturers and prefer to have their top range of clothes sewn in Italy. As for the French, although most of the *prêt-à-porter* collection is sourced in Italy, patriotic designers such as Hermès are loth to admit that they use the northern Italian Loro Piana mill.

The Biella Valley, nestling in the alpine foothills of Piedmont, is home to more than 200 textile mills which produce luxury cashmere, mohair and worsted fabrics, as well as innovative man-made textiles. The valley was once the poor cousin of France's Lyon, Britain's Bradford or Italy's Como but is now the country's foremost textile centre. Biella is without equal as a wool-spinning centre, spinning the thread ever thinner, softer and finer. The mills process superb merino wool from Australia, raw silk from China, and untreated cashmere from Inner Mongolia. (It takes the entire working life of a single goat to make one luxury cashmere sweater.)

Although Biella has been a textile centre for several centuries, it more than doubled its share of the international market between 1980 and 2000. According to the fashion editor Gianni Bertasso: "The Italians unashamedly stole ideas from the British and the French, but their real merit was to invest money in innovation in the 1970s, when the rest of the global market assumed that the textile industry had reached its peak."

With well-paid skilled workers, the Biella Valley is at the forefront of research and development. Microtene 10,000, produced in Trivero, is an imper-

RIGHT: Piedmont produces some of the finest fabrics in the world.

meable polyester so light that 9,000 metres weigh under 0.4g. Not that tradition is ever forgotten. Ludovico Barbera, a local designer, says: "Working with cloth is like making a good wine: the longer it is left to mature, the better the product."

Biella has a tradition of industrial patronage dating back to the 1840s, when Ermenegildo Zegna, an enlightened benefactor, built schools, hospitals and a nature reserve. This menswear giant from the village of Trivero in the Biella Valley produces the cloth used in more than 30 per cent of the world's luxury menswear market and supplies such labels as Gucci, Romeo Gigli, Valentino and Jil Sander. As Anna Zegna, marketing manager of the

sober Piedmontese Zegna family firm, points out: "The valley's production system stretches from the raw fibre to the finished product." The company's austere 19th-century mill produces 21st-century fabrics with a mixture of laser technology and old-fashioned techniques. Teasels, which still grow wild in southern Italy, are used to raise a napped surface on fine woollen cloth

At the other end of the scale is Zegna's High Performance suit, described as the nearest fashion will get to a Ferrari. Made of thread finer than a human hair, the garment keeps the wearer warm in winter and pleasantly cool in summer, and ensures that an executive can step off a plane in a perfect, crease-free suit. ❑

ART AND ARCHITECTURE

*Some of Europe's finest Romanesque and Renaissance art
can be found in the towns and villages of northern Italy*

Comparatively little survives to remind us that northern Italy was one of the most affluent and sophisticated areas of the Roman empire. A few of the largest structures have endured, however, as symbols of imperial grandeur. The arena at Verona, for example, one of the largest ever to have been built, is still in use, though gladiatorial contests and wild-beast fights have been replaced by colourful performances of operas by Verdi and Puccini.

Equally impressive is the triumphal arch of Emperor Augustus at Aosta, in the Piedmontese Alps, erected in 24 BC to commemorate the defeat of a local Celtic tribe. A bastardised version of the Roman architectural grand manner is to be found at Ravenna, where the mausoleum of Theodoric the Goth overawes us with ponderous masonry and a domed roof.

Unrivalled early Christian art

Ravenna is more famous for its outstanding examples of late Roman and Byzantine mosaic art. The 5th-century tomb of Empress Galla Placidia is adorned with panels showing Christ as a shepherd amid apostles and evangelists, all against a rich blue ground. At Aquileia the vast basilica's mosaic floor is full of Biblical imagery. This traditional Roman art form was renewed under the Byzantine emperors, and in other Ravenna churches, such as Sant' Apollinare in Classe, as well as in the cathedral baptistry, the sheer sumptuousness and scale of the mosaic design are unrivalled in early Christian art. As the church established itself as a significant force in medieval Italian society, so a wave of cathedral building began in the larger cities, intended to create both a spiritual focus for the townsfolk and a symbol of civic pride for the commune. Parma led the way in 1058, followed by Modena in 1099 and Ferrara 40 years later. The first two cathedrals are noted for their outstanding sculptural detail, by some of the earliest named artists in Europe. In the

baptistry at Parma, Benedetto Antelami designed a striking sequence of scriptural panels and representations of the calendar months with their zodiacal signs and respective labours. At Modena, Wiligelmo was keener on extravagant fantasy carvings, though over the north door he placed the earliest known image of

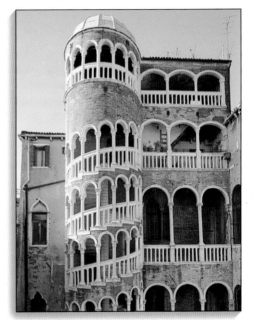

King Arthur, Guinevere and the Knights of the Round Table.

Romanesque art of the 11th and 12th centuries flourished most notably at Verona, where the church of San Zeno Maggiore was decorated on its main doors with vigorous bronze reliefs showing Biblical episodes, and in Venice, where the basilica of San Marco most obviously reflected a synthesis between native styles and those of Venice's trading partner, and rival, Byzantium.

The basilica contains exquisite mosaic work, especially in the Capella di Sant' Isidoro, but perhaps the most hauntingly beautiful examples of this in the Venetian lagoon are to be

LEFT: the byzantine Basilica San Vitale, Ravenna.
RIGHT: staircase, Palazzo Contarini del Bovolo, Venice.

found in the cathedral on the island of Torcello.

The high Middle Ages of the 13th and 14th centuries brought the Gothic style to northern Italy, and its features, such as pointed arches and ballflower moulding, are to be found in Bologna's great church of San Petronio, begun in 1390, in the design of heavily gilded panel paintings intended to hang above altars and shrines. Giotto, the leading Tuscan painter of the 14th century, paid a visit to Padua, and his frescoes for the Scrovegni chapel (1303–05) were a seminal influence on Italian art.

The ultimate medieval flourish was provided by Milan Cathedral, for which the Visconti

incredible lavishness in its stone carving, iron work, stained glass and marquetry contrasts tellingly with the simple life led by the monks in their cells.

The Renaissance painters

While the Certosa was being built, during the 15th century, the earliest major painters of northern Italy were developing their individual styles. Andrea Mantegna (1431–1506) turned a typically Renaissance passion for the classical past into a uniquely personal, romantic distillation of Greek and Roman themes. His brother-in-law Giovanni Bellini (1435–1516)

family in 1386 presented an entire marble quarry. So powerful was the impact of its pinnacles and buttresses that 16th-century architects working on its completion made no attempt to overwhelm the general Gothic effect with more than a few details of Renaissance classicism.

Unquestionably the most brilliant fusion of Gothic and Renaissance occurs in the Certosa di Pavia, one of Italy's loveliest buildings but among the least visited by foreign travellers. Begun in 1396, it is still the church of a Carthusian monastery, but contains enough to remind us that it was also a princely mausoleum for the Visconti and Sforza families. An almost

became one of the most admired and influential artists of his time, noted above all for the radiance and delicacy of his altarpieces, featuring the Virgin and Child attended by groups of saints. Bellini worked mainly in the various towns belonging to the Venetian Republic, and Mantegna's major achievement, the frescoed Camera degli Sposi, is in Mantua, where he built himself a house.

Ferrara meanwhile was evolving its own important school of painters under the patronage of the d'Este dukes. Cosimo Tura, appointed court painter in 1458, led the way with his highly idiosyncratic style, using grotesque landscape backgrounds and angular, dramatically posed figures. His pupil Francesco Cossa (1438–81) left the exuberantly allegorical frescoes of the months of the years adorning Ferrara's Palazzo Schifanoia.

The accumulated wealth of Venice made it a focus for aspiring young painters from the surrounding provinces, several of whom became Giovanni Bellini's pupils. Lyrical and profound, Giorgio da Castelfranco, known as Giorgione, born around 1478, was a classic example of youthful genius stifled

COUNTRY STYLE

Andrea Palladio (1508–1580) was one of the most influential architects of the Veneto, where the farming estates of the aristocracy mattered as much as their palaces on the Grand Canal (*see Palladian Style, page 121*).

in grandly-conceived canvases and fresco cycles, while Jacopo Robusti, called Tintoretto (1560–1635), made dramatic experiments with light and composition during a highly prolific career.

Further west, in the region of Emilia, a lively and original tradition of painting had developed, beginning with the significant figure of Antonio Allegri, known as Correggio, from the town near Reggio Emilia where he was born in 1489.

by premature death, at 32. From the Alpine region of Cadore, Titian (Tiziano Vecellio) was one of the longest-lived of all Renaissance painters, an incomparable colourist whose style had made several fascinating experimental shifts by the time he died in 1576 aged 91.

The rising generation of Venetian artists who learned from Titian included two painters with markedly differing styles. Paolo Caliari, called Veronese from his home town of Verona, expressed the sheer visual excitement of his era

LEFT: the ornate cupola of St Mark's, Venice.
ABOVE: frescoes at Villa Barbaro, Maser, by Paolo Veronese.

Baroque

During the latter half of the 16th century the wealthy city of Bologna became the art capital of Italy, its sensuous, poetic idiom nurtured by Annibale Carracci (born 1560) and his cousin Ludovico. The early Baroque artists who followed in their wake, notably Domenichino and Guido Reni, found fame not only in Italy but also throughout northern Europe, and collectors such as King Charles I of England and the Swedish Queen Christina paid high prices for their work. Perhaps the most successful of all the Emilian Baroque painters came from the little town of Cento near Modena. Giovanni Francesco Barbieri (1591–1666) was known as

Guercino, "little squint-eyes", a nickname which soon brought him fame as a painter of rapturous saints and erotically charged biblical scenes. The fanciful and excessive aspects of the Baroque style which typified architecture and decorative arts in South Germany, Sicily and Spain left northern Italy relatively untouched. The rulers of the various states were generally too preoccupied with diplomacy to spend much time on adorning their palaces, though the charming little summer residence of the

COURT PAINTERS

In the 18th century there was a great diaspora of Italian painters who became travelling artists among the courts of Europe, carrying their skills as far afield as Lisbon and St Petersburg.

Stupinigi, a sort of Torinese Versailles. Beginning with such panache, the 18th century saw an exciting renewal of painting, especially in the towns of the Veneto, which had not forgotten their Renaissance heritage. The art of the portrait was revived in the city of Bergamo by the slightly eccentric and always memorable Vittorio Ghislandi, known as Fra Galgario (1655–1743), while in Venice itself Sebastiano Ricci (1659–1734) made a deliberate study of the grand manner of Veronese and

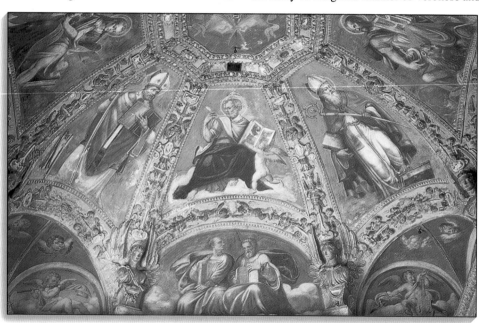

dukes of Modena at Sassuolo, created during the mid-17th century and recently restored, is an exception.

Eighteenth-century townscapes

Towns and cities, meanwhile, were left largely unaltered, apart from Turin, which was carefully re-planned by Duke Charles Emmanuel II (died 1675) and his successors. When the duchy of Savoy became a kingdom in 1720, the newly-enriched Victor Amadeus II built a splendid basilica at Superga in appreciation for his victories in the Spanish War of Succession. Its designer was Filippo Juvarra, who also created the grandiose royal summer palace of

Titian, paving the way for other travelling artists among the courts of Europe.

The most triumphant reassertion of Venetian art as a mixture of brio, fantasy and vivid colouring, with notes of worldliness and humanity enlivening even the most solemn spiritual moments, came from the brush of Giambattista Tiepolo (1696–1770). He started out as the creator of impressionistic altarpieces for Venice's churches, and had soon mastered the art of fresco painting, devising such daring effects on ceilings and walls (Vicenza's Villa Valmarana, Udine's episcopal palace) that he began to receive major commissions from elsewhere in Europe; it was during a visit to Madrid that he died. Tiepolo's artist contemporaries were much patronized by British travellers on the Grand Tour, none more so than Antonio Canal, "Canaletto" (1697–1768), whose views of Venice furnished classic images of the city in its closing decades as an independent capital. Canaletto had started his career as apprentice to his father, who was a theatrical scene painter.

Trend-setting Milan

Milan, under Napoleonic rule 1800–15, led the way as a centre of new fashions and fresh ideas, and it was here that Italy's greatest 19th-century painter, Francesco Hayez (1791–1882),

cityscape was Ippolito Caffi (1806–66), destined to die in a naval battle against the Austrians. Venetian art schools had been heavily influenced, meanwhile, by the lonely genius of Antonio Canova (1757–1822), the great sculptor of his age. Though he spent much of his working life in Rome, Canova was determined to return to his birthplace at Possagno, near Asolo, north of Venice, where he built himself an austerely lovely *tempietto* (little temple) as a mausoleum.

Sculpture in northern Italy found another remarkable practitioner at the close of the 19th century. Medardo Rosso, working in Paris as

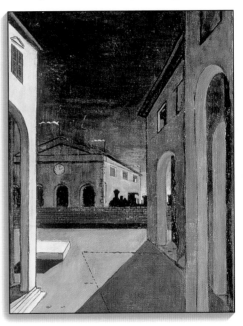

chose to work after an apprenticeship in Venice. Hayez aspired to fame as the creator of exalted historical themes based on meticulous studies of costume and decor, but his true gift lay in portrait painting, and his images of his contemporaries, Milanese aristocrats, poets, musicians or fellow artists, are some of the most intense from the turbulent Risorgimento age.

Venice went on inspiring painters, however, and the last and best among many who sought to revive Canaletto's tradition of the *veduta* or

LEFT: the Sant'Aquilino chapel, San Lorenzo Maggiore, Milan. **ABOVE:** a sculpture by futurist Umberto Boccioni. **RIGHT:** de Chirico's *Turin Melancholy* (1915).

well as Milan and Turin, devised forms which both evoked realistic situations from urban life and sought to reproduce, through bronze, clay or wax, the fluidity of living movement.

His world, that of the newly-industrialised northern cities, was what in 1908 inspired the Futurists, led by the poet Marinetti and artists such as Umberto Boccioni and Giacomo Balla, to begin their deliberately eccentric revolution against the classic traditions of Italian art. Their strident gospel of modernism, obsessed with speed, power and aggression, contributed to a national state of mind which, only a decade later, would accept the ideology of Mussolini and his Fascist cohorts. ❏

VENETIAN ARTISTS

The most impressive and influential painters of northern Italy found patronage from the wealthy Republic

The Venetian school embodies a poetic, painterly sensibility at odds with the rational, monumental and sculptural Florentine style. The lagoon artists were painters of colour, light, texture and space, reflecting the ambiguity of their shimmering, watery world. Paradoxically, the inclusiveness of the Venetian

vision and the varied sources of patronage meant that Venetian art was less formulaic than other schools, with the greatest painters free to form their own inimitable personal styles.

With his sweeet sensibility and expressiveness, Bellini freed Venetian painting from Byzantine stiffness. Carpaccio captured the texture of everyday Venetian life, with his pink-hued palaces, curious chimneys and canal-side crowds. Tintoretto brought religious fervour, while Titian, the complete Renaissance man, elevated Venetian art to universal grandeur with his ineffable technique and monumentality. Tiepolo, the Rococo "poet of light" who brought the great era to a dramatic close,

delighted in a palette of pastel tones, matched by ethereal scenes of Olympian grandeur.

Giovanni Bellini (circa 1430–1516) is often considered the founder of the Venetian school and one of the best-loved Venetian painters. He worked in Padua, Ferrara and Verona but has left many masterpieces in his home city. A number are known as *sacre conversazioni* ("holy conversations") because of the rapt stillness of mood. These are not all limpid, idealised Madonnas: in his poignant *Pietà* in the Accademia, the suffering Virgin cradles her son in her arms, her careworn face a testament to Bellini's expressive powers; the city of Vicenza looms in the background, showing the painter's love of landscape and his skill at opening out a canvas. The church of the Frari is home to another Bellini masterpiece: the *Madonna and Saints* is a subtle and luminous triptych of the Virgin flanked by saints and cherubic angels, one trilling on a flute, the other strumming a mandolin. The musical motif recurs in Bellini's work, reinforcing the notion of music as a symbol of order and harmony. The charming church of San Zaccaria displays a superb Bellini altarpiece noted for its beguiling interplay of colour and light in a rich blend of reds, golds and blues. This soft and lyrical work embodies the inner harmony implicit in the finest works of Quattrocento and High Renaissance art. Although overshadowed by Bellini, Vittorio Carpaccio (*circa* 1465–1523/6) was the most Venetian of artists, with his vivid pictorial cycles and miniaturist precision.

Titian (*circa* 1487–1576) was the supreme artist. The church of the Frari contains two of his masterpieces, notably *The Assumption* (1516–18), a work whose revolutionary nature caused it to be rejected by the Friars; they relented, and the work made Titian's international reputation. Unlike his rivals, Titian could make his illusionistic altarpiece command attention from afar. Vibrant colours helped, with the counterpoint of a golden sky set against the glowing red of the Virgin's robes. Titian aligned the work exactly with the opening of the rood screen so that one's eye is drawn through the Gothic choir towards this magnificent altarpiece. In the same church, the Pesaro altarpiece depicts a theatrically illuminated yet off-centre Madonna in the presence of Saint Peter and of Titian's patrons, the Pesaro family. For the first time the portrait of a patron and his family was made part of a devotional painting, thus breaking the strict division between the sacred and secular worlds.

Tintoretto (1518–94) restricted his world to Venice. Despite being made official painter to the Doge in 1574, Tintoretto lived a precarious existence, often painting for the costs of the

poses. Tintoretto's parish church was Madonna dell'Orto, the most assured Gothic church in Venice. This is very much a shrine to the artist, who is buried there. The church contains a clutch of early works, with the *Presentation of the Virgin* showing Tintoretto's familiar theatricality and grandiosity.

Tiepolo (1696–1770) was the last great Venetian painter, graced with a sublime style and virtuosity reminiscent of the Old Masters. Tiepolo's credo was that "the mind of the painter should always aspire to the sublime, the heroic and perfection". According to art critic Adriano Mariuz, in practice this meant "a

materials alone; he died penniless. However his humble background gave him sympathy for the lives of the poor, a theme which, combined with religious fervour, distinguishes him from many contemporaries. The confraternity of the Scuola Grande di San Rocco represents Tintoretto's crowning glory. Magnificent Mannerist paintings adorn every surface; the works are larger than life, full of *chiaroscuro* effects and floating, plunging figures striking dramatic

LEFT: detail from the Bellini altarpiece (1505) in San Zaccaria, Venice.
ABOVE: the Rococo grandeur of Giovanni Battista Tiepelo (1696–1770).

sophisticated clientele who could appreciate the wit and sensuality of Tiepolo's interpretations of mythology". However, the greatest of Rococo painters also produced a riot of picturesque detail and enough charm to seduce the most casual observer. In Ca' Rezzonico Tiepolo proves himself a master of scenic illusion, creating mirages of light and air and orchestrating figures in large compositions.

Apart from the *trompe l'oeil* paintings here, Tiepolo's work can be admired in numerous Venetian churches. La Pietà, the waterfront church, is a feast for the senses, and Tiepolo's celebrated frescoes are best seen during a concert of Baroque music. ❏

THE MUSICAL TRADITION

*Italy has given the world opera, the musical scale, the piano,
the accordion and fabulous Stradivarius violins*

Without the Italian sensibility, the world of music would be deaf to the seductive strains of Vivaldi and the nobility and intensity of Verdi. Italy is rightly known as the home of music, with Milan's image inextricably bound up with La Scala. When opera houses burn down, as they still tend to do, people cry in public and the country grieves.

Fortunately, northern Italy still has more major opera houses than it deserves; opera is on home ground and rejoices in its natural mode of expression. One of the charms of such an instinctive approach is the superb staging, the art of the grand gesture, untempered by northern European reserve. Productions can be sweeping, sensual and lush, appealing to the heart, not the head. Yet, at its purest, the performers' skill at stirring elemental passions is matched by the cool perfectionism of the staging. In inimitable Italian style, the irreverence of opera-goers only serves to intensify the experience.

Vibrant tradition

However, northern Italy's contribution to Western music goes beyond plush Rococo interiors and impassioned outpourings of Verdi. Musical history has been shaped by a clutch of northern cities, from Milan and Venice to Mantua, Parma, Verona and Cremona, each with a separate, flourishing tradition.

As for composers, Monteverdi, Verdi, Vivaldi and Donizetti are northern names to conjure with. Dedicated opera-lovers are rewarded with Verdi's dramatic power and Donizetti's light touch and gift for melody. Musical form and development have a distinctive northern stamp; Donizetti dedicated himself to the art of *bel canto*, the traditional emphasis on fine tone and ornamentation. The language of music remains resolutely Italian.

Northern Italian music also embraces mem-

orable madrigals, solemn melodies and the purest Gregorian chant. The first violin sonatas of note were written by a Lombard, Biagio Marini of Brescia, in 1629: works of Baroque passion, energy and drama. Today the lush strings of the Venetian Albinoni perfectly chime with the public's taste for haunting Baroque music. As for musical instruments, Cremona has been the capital of violin-making since the 16th century (*see page 95*). Indeed, it is not too fanciful to see the curves of violins echoed in the spiral cornices of city palaces. Nor is it a coincidence that northern Italy is at the forefront of the trend towards a return to playing on authentic period instruments.

Venetian musicianship

"Venice was once the cradle of classical music, the birthplace of opera, the crucible of the concerto and the nerve-centre of a neo-classical revival." As critic Norman Lebrecht suggests, the city built the world's first opera house, cre-

---

LEFT: the genius of late Baroque music, Antonio Vivaldi (1678–1741).
RIGHT: Verdi is one of Italy's best-loved composers.

ated the first publicly-funded system of music education and inspired composers as great as Bach, Handel, Wagner and Britten. Although it took a Tuscan monk, Guido d'Arezzo, to devise the musical scale, a Venetian printer, Ottavino Petrucci, invented a method of printing music with moveable type. Other Venetian keynotes are struck by Albinoni (1671–1750), whose works are characterised by charm and urbanity, and by Antonio Vivaldi (1678–1741), who acted as a model for such composers as J.S. Bach. The popularity of *The Four Seasons* can blind one to Vivaldi's genius as a leading exponent of late Baroque music.

Operatic origins

Opera was Italy's crowning musical achievement, a rousing art form which may have emerged in 14th-century Florence but was perfected by Claudio Monteverdi (1567–1643) in Mantua and Venice. On becoming master of music at St Mark's in 1613, the Lombard composer spent two decades composing sacred services and sumptuous polyphonic music. The opening of San Cassiano in 1637, the first public opera house, provided Monteverdi with the impetus to restage his earlier works. He took the madrigal beyond its traditional form, forging the development of the dramatic madrigal

The northern lakes have inspired some of the grandest Italian opera. In 1813, Rossini composed *Tancredi* in Cernobbio, on the shores of Lake Como, an example followed in 1831 by Bellini, with the composition of *Norma*. Although Bellini was born in Sicily, he moved north, and his ravishing melodies helped make him the dominant composer in Milan. Equally entranced by Lake Como's subtle light, Verdi chose Cadenabbia to compose *La Traviata* in 1853. Further north, in the mountainous reaches of Alto Adige, Dobbiaco, near Bolzano, provided the peace sought by Gustav Mahler (1860–1911). The composer's quaint cottage has become an appealing restaurant.

that paved the way for Baroque opera. Until then opera had been confined to noble wedding celebrations and princely courts. In one sense, Monteverdi and Venice represent the true birth of opera; henceforth, opera was no longer a ducal distraction, the plaything of a courtly society, but a dynamic new art form favoured by a demotic public.

The emergence of opera was helped by the fashion for declamation, with strong emotions expressed as sighs and sobs rather than description. In Monteverdi's opera *Orfeo* the title role

ABOVE: Venice's La Fenice, before the fire of 1996.
RIGHT: an 1819 view of La Scala, Milan.

was taken by a *castrato*, a male soprano or contralto with an unbroken voice. *Castrati* were in great demand in the 17th and 18th centuries, because of their flexible and voluptuous voices.

Given that Rossini and Puccini were born just outside northern Italy, Monteverdi, Donizetti and Verdi represent the region's greatest operatic talents. Gaetano Donizetti (1797–1848) was born in Bergamo and trained in Bologna before becoming enamoured of Rossini and the Neapolitan style. His reputation, based on his light touch and

SEX APPEAL

Farinelli (1705–82) was the most famous *castrato*. His singing and stage presence caused women to faint from excitement.

feeling for melody and sentiment, was sealed by *Lucrezia Borgia* (1833), first performed at La Scala, and *Lucia de Lammermoor* (1835), his tragic masterpiece.

Giuseppe Verdi (1813–1901) was born in humble circumstances in Busseto, a village near Parma, and trained as a local church organist. Although he was denied entry to the prestigious Milan Conservatory, Verdi moved to Milan, where his first and last operas were premiered, and enjoyed a stormy relationship with La Scala. *Nabucco* and sub-

CREMONA: HOME OF STRADIVARIUS VIOLINS

Cremona is an exceptionally musical town. It is famous for the composition of medieval sacred music, and it was here that the composer Claudio Monteverdi) was born in 1567 (*see Lombardy, page 229*).

Cremona is also the home of the world's greatest cellos and violins: Antonio Stradivari (1643–1737) created instruments of incomparable workmanship, carved out of maple and spruce, with segments of pear, poplar and willow wood, which today rank among the highest-priced instruments in the world. The Stradivarius is still a byword for sublime sound and beauty of tone, an instrument so sensitive that it is considered to have a soul.

The city still basks in its musical reputation, with an internationally acclaimed school of violin-making and the Monteverdi Festival, staged in the city's neoclassical Teatro Concordia-Ponchielli, to which musical pilgrims come from all over the world.

Given their tangible sense of life, the Stradivarius violins on display in the Cremona civic museum are regularly taken out of their cases and played. Maxim Vengerov, regarded by many as the finest contemporary violin virtuoso, plays a Stradivarius (dating from 1723), which enables him to achieve an alchemy between maestro and instrument.

sequent operas were applauded as patriotic works and political gestures: the response of an oppressed people symbolised the Italians' suffering under Austrian domination. During the Risorgimento, walls were daubed with the acronym V(ittorio) E (manuele) R(e) D'I(talia), a reference to the first king of Italy, eventually crowned in 1861. However, Verdi's gifts marked him out as a genius rather than a mere patriot; he possessed intense dramatic power and a dark forcefulness, as well as a delight in humanity, subtle characterisation, and an ability to express contrasting emotions. By the time Verdi died in Milan, in the antiquated and

atmospheric Grand Hotel, he was regarded as Italy's best-loved composer, deserving of his enduring cult following.

Temples to tradition

"An opera house is like a sponge that absorbs the best of man's creativity," claims the film director Franco Zeffirelli, with classic Italian grandiloquence. Beyond the gilt and stucco interiors, the glittering opera houses (*teatri lirici*) are mostly neoclassical theatres rebuilt after numerous fires. Historically, the rivalry of noble courts gave birth to countless private opera houses, which gradually opened their doors to the public, the first in Venice in 1637. It is no coincidence that the greatest concentration of historic opera houses is found in Lombardy and Emilia, places linked to the great courts at Cremona, Parma and Mantua. The fashion spread, and by the 18th century there were 20 *teatri lirici* in Venice alone.

Today opera houses range from the proficient and praiseworthy to the lacklustre. Milan's La Scala (*see below*) is the premier opera house, even though all Italy's opera houses are prestigious symbols of regional pride. While there are major opera houses in Naples, Florence and Rome, La Fenice (the Phoenix) in Venice enjoys greater prestige, despite its tragic history. Venice's "Phoenix" has lived to rue its name after fires in 1836 and 1996. Diva Joan Sutherland mourned the loss of "the most beautiful opera house in the world"; singing in La Fenice, she said, felt like being inside a diamond. La Fenice burnt down a month before Woody Allen was due to play there. On hearing the news, the director's wry comment was: "It

---

LA SCALA

La Scala opera house in Milan, a symphony of red, cream and gold designed by Giuseppe Piermarini, opened in 1778 with a performance of an opera by Antonio Salieri, Mozart's great rival. All the great Italian composers have written for La Scala, in particular Rossini, Donizetti, Bellini, Puccini and Verdi. The opera house underwent a period of glory with performances of Verdi's patriotic works, and it experienced its early 20th-century heyday under Toscanini's direction.

Arturo Toscanini (1867–1957) was born in Parma but emigrated to the United States because of his opposition to Fascism. As musical director of La Scala, in the 1920s,

he had been hugely influential in shaping the repertoire and maintaining the prestige of the opera house. At the turn of the century he had also been responsible for bringing Wagner into the operatic repertoire. As a lover of Italian opera, the magnetic but autocratic Toscanini, with a gift for interpreting composers' intentions, won the admiration of Verdi and Puccini. In 1926 he conducted the premiere of *Turandot*, Puccini's last opera, to great acclaim. Despite Mussolini's attempts to promote Rome Opera over La Scala, the Milanese never lost their musical supremacy. After La Scala was damaged by bombing in 1943, Toscanini personally contributed to its rebuilding.

must be a music lover; they heard I was coming." The red-and-gold Rococo confection is being rebuilt as before, but until completion chic opera-goers must tolerate a tented affair. On the next rung down in terms of size, though not necessarily scope, are Parma, Genoa, Bergamo, Modena, Bologna and Turin. Parma's Teatro Farnese is a ravishing early 17th-century theatre modelled on Palladio's Teatro Olimpico in Vicenza. The all-wooden affair was built by the Farnese as an act of one-upmanship, to out-do the Milanese; it could seat

GLITTERING GLORY

"Singing in La Fenice is like singing inside a diamond."
– Dame Joan Sutherland

same level as the stage. Brescia's Teatro Grande, dating from the early 18th century, has also staged landmark performances of works by Verdi, Puccini and Rossini.

Mantua's musical tradition is as honourable as the enlightened Gonzaga court that fostered it: Monteverdi's *Orfeo* was first staged in 1607 in the Gonzagas' ducal apartments. Later, the city's Teatro Scientifico was finished in time to provide a stage for three of Mozart's newly-composed symphonies in 1770.

As for Verona, the city's Teatro Filarmonico

3,000 and was the largest theatre of its day. Parma's plush Teatro Regio was built at the behest of Empress Marie-Louise in 1828, and is considered the best place to hear a performance of anything by Verdi.

Bologna's Teatro Comunale, which opened in 1763, also has Verdi associations, having staged the premiere of *Don Carlos* in 1867. Given the demands of the Bolognese aristocracy, the auditorium was designed to double as a ballroom, with the raising of the floor to the

LEFT: a postcard celebrating Giuseppe Verdi (1813–1901) and his opera premieres.
ABOVE: the legendary diva, Maria Callas.

so impressed Mozart that he became musical director of the orchestra in 1771. Otherwise the city is best known for its operas in the open-air Arena (*see next page*).

Curtains for opera?

In recent years, opera houses have been buffeted by strikes, budgetary cuts and even arson attacks. In response to excessive bureaucracy and a funding crisis, the Italian government in 1997 announced the privatisation of all opera houses, starting with La Scala. As a result the opera houses became *enti*, state-run enterprises managed as self-financing institutions, although paradoxically still eligible for up to 40 percent

OPERA IN THE OPEN AIR

Italian opera and classical music are not restricted to Milan's La Scala. Northern Italy as a whole has some of the best music festivals in Europe, from the Rossini Festival performed in Pesaro to the Verona Opera Festival held in the Roman Arena, a glorious summer junket for Europe's opera-going elite. (The romantic Puccini Festival at the composer's lakeside home is held in Tuscany's Torre del Lago.)

Renowned international singers rise to the challenge of open-air opera: at times the unaccompanied voices struggle to make an impact, given the background babble – not to mention distant car horns and police sirens – that typifies any such Italian event. In the end, the sense of occasion, the spectacle and the elemental passions ensure that the occasion is a triumph. "Every time I step onto the stage and glance towards the stalls and tiers, my heart is squeezed in a vice-like grip. It's the immense embrace of a thousand lighted candles, of a thousand people that await my voice." Such was Pavarotti's emotional response to the impact of performing Verdi's *Requiem* in Verona.

The Arena di Verona Festival was devised in 1913 as a way of celebrating the centenary of Verdi's birth, and has continued ever since, save for interruptions during wartime. Travel companies often offer weekend breaks with tickets to the festival included. The festival's historic setting, in the ancient Roman Arena, and the latter's superb acoustics have drawn singers as great as Callas, Caballé and Domingo.

If filled to capacity, the Arena holds an audience of more than 16,000 people, as many as the combined capacity of La Scala, Covent Garden, Bayreuth and the Metropolitan Opera. Verona's favourite opera is Verdi's *Aida*, which makes the best use of the vast stage space. The spectacle of the triumphal march is something to behold, with over 400 spear-carriers, captives, soldiers, slaves, trumpeters, dancers and singers.

Any opera in Verona is a charming exercise in Italian class distinctions: the bars in the Arena serve only champagne and cola, with nothing in between. The *gradinata*, the cheap seats in the unnumbered stands, are populated by serious opera-loving locals who unwrap pungent picnics of salami and olives. As dusk falls in the steep tiers of the Arena, a brief hush descends and the audience lights candles in order to read the libretto. Just as the Arena is engulfed by tiny flickering flames, the privileged patrons commanding the best *poltrona* and *poltronissima* seats in front of the stage take their places, often accompanied by cat-calls from less fortunate members of the audience.

state funding. La Scala has traditionally been one of the most heavily subsidised opera houses in Europe. Compared with Covent Garden, La Scala stages fewer performances but receives double the subsidy. The cost of one Milanese production can equal an entire season's budget at a rival opera house. Italy's premier opera house has ostensibly been privatised, but with a sweetener of $57 million from the state; cultural supremos were fearful that their flagship would otherwise fall off its pedestal.

La Scala's justification for such largesse is that, at its best, it still stages lavish productions on an unparalleled scale. However, bol-

stered by sponsorship from banks and car companies, La Scala's future looks increasingly secure. The new Milanese foundation is looking forward to making further lucrative merchandising deals, raiding its prestigious musical museum to produce miniature busts of Verdi for the Japanese market.

Musical chairs

Although Italy has produced some fine young mezzos and sopranos, it has taken to importing tenors from the United States and other big voices from Eastern Europe. Italy suffers from a shortage of singers with big voices, who can sing loudly over heavy 19th-century orchestration. This is particularly true of the Verdi masterpieces, such as *Il Trovatore*, which makes casting problematic. According to critic Rupert Christiansen, the score requires "a strong yet exquisitely pure soprano of the type that the Italians label *spinto*; a rich and forceful *mezzo*; a tenor who can light fires; and a baritone who can be both villain and charmer". The charge is that most singers lack the stamina, physique and training to produce the amplitude, richness and fullness of sound

BLIND DATE

Bocelli is a great classical tenor whose blindness prevented him from following a conventional career. He was spotted singing in a piano bar by the rock star Zucchero, introduced to Pavarotti, and a musical marriage was born.

ian divas have graced the stages of the great *teatri lirici*, only Cecilia Bartoli stands out in the present-day. Even so, she is acclaimed for her Mozart roles rather than her interpretations of home-grown classics.

Yet any vocal disappointments are compensated for by the quality of conducting, an Italian forte since Toscanini. His first public performance was Verdi's *Aida*, which he conducted from memory after he had been asked to step in at short notice.

required of a live performance. Given the dearth of suitable home-grown talent, critics claim that the tradition of Italian dramatic sopranos and baritones is defunct.

Certainly, the gradual demise of the ensemble system means that it is no longer realistic to cast the great Verdi operas with Italian-speaking singers of the first rank. Apart from Pavarotti, one notable exception is Giuseppe Giacomini from Padua, a singer sought after because of the Verdian timbre of his voice. Although Ital-

Among today's *maestri*, Riccardo Muti is considered the world's most charismatic conductor of Verdi. He conducts at Milan's La Scala and runs the Ravenna Music Festival, close to his home. Muti's predecessor, Claudio Abbado, directs productions around the world, as well as in Ferrara. Conductors Daniele Gatti, Riccardo Chailly and Giuseppe Sinopoli have also found fame abroad, notably at Amsterdam's Concertgebouw, London's Covent Garden and the Dresden Opera House.

But to the outside world, Italy is forever linked with a clutch of tenors, from Caruso and Gigli to Pavarotti and the lyrical romantic Andrea Bocelli. ❑

LEFT: Alto Adige has its own distinct musical heritage.
ABOVE: Verona's Roman Arena provides a dramatic stage for many Italian operas.

RUSTIC AND CLASSIC CUISINE

"The cooking of Italy is really the cooking of its regions, regions that until 1861 were separate, independent, and usually hostile states." – Marcella Hazan

Culinarily speaking, Italy is more of a salad bowl than a melting pot. Northern taste-buds are tickled by distinctive regional styles, and dishes as diverse as the people themselves. Slav buffets, Balkan flavours and Hungarian goulash await visitors to Trieste. In Venice, filling Austrian pastries vie with Oriental spices. In Turin, culinary schizophrenia shows itself in peasant-style dishes covered with sophisticated French sauces. Emilia is the kingdom of pasta, while the Veneto and Piedmont favour risotto, leaving Lombardy torn between rice and polenta. With its sauerkraut and dumplings, the alpine Trentino-Alto Adige embodies the culinary clash between Italian and Austrian traditions. By contrast, seafaring Liguria relishes a summery, vegetable-based cuisine but makes less use of fish than one would expect of a coastal region.

Minestrone of tastes

"We have made Italy; and now we must make Italians," declared Massimo d'Azeglio, the Piedmontese statesman. But forging a common cuisine out of pasta and polenta has proved elusive. A national cuisine was first codified by Pellegrino Artusi in his influential *La Scienza in Cucina* (1891), still the most authoritative Italian cookery book. Artusi's aim was to "develop a common cuisine so that Italians could understand one another at table". However, the book promotes certain strands of refined northern cuisine at the expense of regionalism and rustic fare, elevating a pseudo-French concept of refinement over Italian regional authenticity. As British food critic Jonathan Meades points out: "There is only so much refinement Italian cooking can take before it becomes denatured." Not that culinary refinement is without an ancient lineage. The tradition of noble courts from late medieval and Renaissance times has enriched Italian regional cuisine.

PRECEDING PAGES: culinary adventures await you.
LEFT: fresh fruit for sale in Bolsano.
RIGHT: cutting the cheese.

Apart from pasta and pizza, little in Italy is national except such styles as *alla parmigiana*, cooking with cheese, bequeathed by Parma to the rest of the country. Yet the issue is not so much the struggle between national and regional styles, nor even between sublime cuisine and wholesome peasant fare. Instead, most

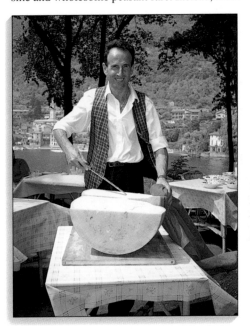

forward-thinking chefs are concerned with reinterpreting regional tradition: adapting the best of the past to contemporary trends and more health-conscious tastes. However, in the heat of the kitchen, lighter *cucina nuova* usually loses out to fare rich in red meat, butter and cheese and based on preparations and ingredients unchanged for centuries.

Geography on a plate

At the European level the Italians make pleas for protectionism, and their olive oil, *panettone* cake, Parma ham and Parmesan cheese are just a few of the products that have privileged status. Most Italians are against the globalisation of packaged food, but few realise that certain protected products are less local than they seem. Bresaola, dried salted beef, may be the pride of the alpine Valtellina area in Lombardy, but most of the beef is Argentinian; only the curing process is local. Even so, most northern Italians tend to eat more local food than their counterparts abroad. A typical meal might include pasta from Bologna; salad from Cremona; pizza yeast from Pavia; eggs from Vicenza; veal and milk from Lombardy; basil from Imperia in Liguria; flour from the Po Valley; Parmesan from Parma; sugar and peaches from Ferrara.

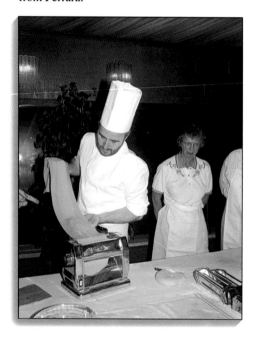

NOT FOR THE SQUEAMISH

Northern cuisine is not for the squeamish. All parts of pork go into the pot: ears, liver, bladder and guts. In Bergamo pitiful songbirds' beaks peer out of beds of *polenta*. Flavoured lard is enjoyed in Valle d'Aosta, as is sausage from castrated sheep in Valle Camonica in Lombardy. Horse is eaten in Emilia and Vicenza, while stewed donkey is devoured in Mantua, as is *torta di sangue*, a baked blood delicacy. (For this, the chicken's throat is slit, and the blood spills into a bowl of beaten egg yolks and sugar.) Also in gory Lombardy, *tinca* is a local fish either boiled alive or forced to swallow a tablespoon of white wine vinegar to cleanse its insides before cooking.

The best regional cuisine is both robust and refined: Emilia Romagna is the flagship of Italian gastronomy. Bologna, the capital, typifies the commitment and conviviality the world has come to associate with the finest Italian cooking. Pellegrino Artusi instructed his readers to "make a deep bow to Bolognese cooking, it deserves it". Bologna, a gastronomic paradise since the Middle Ages, remains Italy's undisputed culinary capital. The city is even known as "Bologna *la grassa*" – Bologna the fat. But "Bologna the rich" would be more appropriate given the city's feel for the good life, *il culto del benessere*. In this hearty, elaborate cuisine, the emphasis is on velvety sauces, pasta, meat, charcuterie and cheese. Foodies are enamoured of this opulent style, rich in pork fat, butter and oil, and equally high in cholesterol levels. *Fritto misto* is a case in point, delicious but dangerous: an array of breaded or deep-fried morsels, from sweetbreads to slivers of ham, chicken to courgettes, and brains to bananas, all bound in a *béchamel* sauce.

As for meat, Parma ham (*prosciutto di parma*) remains the Italian *antipasto* (first course) of choice, but the north abounds in distinctive cured meats. *Salama da sugo* from Ferrara is a succulent sausage made from minced pork, liver and tongue. Legend has it that the dish was created by Lucrezia Borgia to revive battle-weary troops; indeed, it is still served to soldiers home on leave. Neighbouring Modena produces ravioli stuffed with minced meats or *bollito misto*, mixed boiled meats, including beef, veal, tongue and pig's trotters. A *mortadella* from Bologna can have the circumference of a dinner plate and be studded with black peppercorns, with green pistachios protruding through the pale pink flesh. *Brodo*, a velvety meat broth, is matched by *stracotto*, a slowly simmered stew flavoured with cinnamon and nutmeg.

Ferrara is known for certain Jewish dishes such as smoked goose and marzipan desserts. Other regional sweets in Emilia Romagna include fritters, chestnut cakes, *tortelli* stuffed with chocolate, and myriad cholesterol-laden concoctions made with candied peel or brandy-soaked biscuits.

Venice and the Veneto

Like the winds across the lagoon, Venetian cuisine blows hot and cold. Much is filling, cold weather, comfort food: thick soup and creamy *risotto* suitable for sustaining marooned travellers as the mists close in. Yet the cuisine can also be sophisticated and light, from fish *risotto*, sprinkled with shrimps, to *carpaccio*, wafer-thin raw beef dressed with olive oil, rocket and Parmesan. For seafood lovers, the cuisine can be memorable, with soft-shelled crabs from Murano, plump red mullet, pasta heaped with lobster or black and pungent with cuttlefish ink (*seppie alla veneziana*). A trademark dish is cuttlefish

> **SLOW BUT SURE**
>
> The role of Italy's esteemed Slow Food Movement is "to be a bastion against the sadness of the hamburger and the pretensions of haute cuisine".

oriental influences; pine-nuts, raisins, almonds and pistachios play their part. Rice was introduced from Spain by the Arabs and remains the most versatile aspect of local cuisine. *Risi e bisi* (rice and peas) is a thick soup flavoured with ham, celery and onion. A Middle-Eastern inspired dish is *sarde in saär*, tart sardines marinated in the standard Venetian sauce, *saor*. Reflecting later conquests, the exoticism of Middle Eastern cuisine is tempered by French cuisine and stodgy Austrian fare.

risotto or *baccalà*– dried salt cod, prepared with milk and herbs or Parmesan and parsley.

As the hub of a cosmopolitan trading empire, Venice was bristling with foreign communities, each with its own culinary tradition. As a bazaar city, Venice raided the recipe books of the Arabs, Armenians, Greeks, Jews and Turks. Trading posts in the Levant gave the city access to *spezie* (spices), the secret of subtle cookery. Pimento, tumeric, ginger, cinnamon, cumin, cloves, nutmeg, saffron and vanilla show the

LEFT: making fresh pasta verde.
ABOVE: regional specialities on display in a Bolsano shop window.

If Venice, "the marketplace of the eastern and western lands", spells cosmopolitan cuisine, the Veneto remains more provincial, more rooted in the land. Treviso is the main supplier of *radicchio* (red endive) which, raw, grilled or fried, finds its way into *risotto*, pasta and salads.

As well as being a rice-growing region, the Veneto is Italy's chief area for poultry production, from chicken and goose to guineafowl and duck. Offal, spicy black pudding, horsemeat and kid (*capretto*) are also local delicacies, matched by wholemeal spaghetti (*bigoli*), subtle cheeses and honey. Pastries, cakes and desserts, flavoured with cinnamon and nutmeg remain a Venetian forte. The Venetians introduced cane sugar to Europe and have retained their sweet tooth, as has the Veneto at large. The chic resort of Cortina d'Ampezzo tempts après-skiers with deep-fried fritters, while Vicenza responds with *fugazza vicentina*, a popular Easter cake, and Verona brings Christmas cheer with *Pandoro di Verona*, a light, fluffy, mass-produced sponge cake.

The northeast

Austro-Hungarian and Balkan influences prevail in the least Italian of regions. In this rustic yet austere corner of the Balkans, Yugoslav-style raw beef is eaten with creamy Slav cheese, while a snack may consist of Hungarian pastries, stuffed with fruit and spices. Even so, the prominence of seafood, soups and risotto remains a legacy of Venetian rule, while the goulash, sausages, sauerkraut and strudel denote Austrian influence.

Trentino-Alto Adige is another distinctive border region, a mountainous area offering alpine food with an Italian twist. Wholesome peasant-style dishes prevail, from hearty pork and beef smoked sausages to *polenta* dishes and pulse-filled soups. Culinary keynotes are *minestrone* with beans and potatoes, alpine trout poached in white wine, and *ravioli* filled

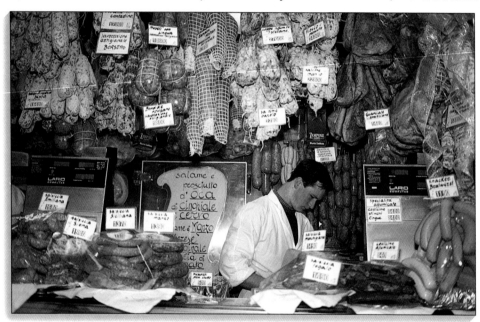

PASTA AND REAL BOLOGNESE SAUCE

Local lore has it that *tortellini* were inspired by Venus's belly button: when a Bolognese innkeeper espied the goddess in bed, he rushed to the kitchen to create his masterpiece. As if in homage to the goddess, the local *tortellini* association still claims that each sheet of pasta must be "as round as the moon and as soft as a caress". Each large Emilian town possesses a secret recipe for *tortellini* stuffed with minced meats, blended with herbs, broth and Parmesan. One shop even boasts *tortellini "buoni da ingannare i mariti"*, good enough to fool husbands.

Tagliatelle, another local pasta, was supposedly invented in 1487 to honour Lucrezia Borgia's golden hair, but a hairsplitting recent regulation determined that each strand should be precisely eight millimetres wide, one-12,276th part of the height of Bologna's main leaning tower. Since then, anything else is simply not *tagliatelle*. Equally well known is *cannelloni ripieni di tortellini,* a filling pasta dish stuffed with ham, mozzarella, cream and butter. *Cappelletti* are stuffed with brains and minced turkey breast. To go with the pasta is *ragu,* the authentic Bolognese sauce that bears little relation to bastardised versions served in restaurants abroad; the real thing contains 20 ingredients, from chicken liver, carrots and celery to ham, minced beef, mushrooms, nutmeg, parsley and red wine.

with chicken and roast and smoked meats. In practice, the cooking also embraces roast venison and rabbit, dumplings and sauerkraut. Trentino risotto can be made with wine, or with *finferli* mushrooms, second only to Tuscan *funghi porcini* (ceps) in quality. Variations include apple risotto or *risotto alle castagne o alle noci*, a rice dish with chestnuts or walnuts.

Austrian influence prevails in Alto Adige, and even in Trentino itself. Typical dishes include smoked meats, sauerkraut cooked in lard, roast venison with polenta, red cabbage goulash and other filling stews. Dumplings are preferred to pasta, and bread dumplings are confusingly known as *canederli* in Italian but *knodel* in German. The best-known dish is *strangolapreti* – gnocchi made with potatoes, bread or spinach and coated with butter or cheese. Desserts are Austrian-inspired pastries such as strawberry cake (*erdbeertorte*) or strudel stuffed with apples, nuts and raisins.

Lombardy

"Here, the foods of the rich, based on meat and dairy products, meet the staples of the poor – maize and pasta – overladen by the fast food of the modern world," states the cookery writer Claudia Roden. This is creamy cuisine designed for the palate of the northern industrialist, with saffron-tinted *risotto alla milanese* the signature dish. As in the Veneto, rice has been the natural choice of the urban upper classes since its introduction by Spanish rulers in 1535. This lavish Lombard cuisine favours combinations of rich, complex foods to display their sophistication. As such, it is a carnivore's delight, with beef, veal, pork and poultry dishes predominating. Yet it is also a poor *polenta* region: whether fried, baked or grilled, the white or yellow maize meal once formed the peasants' staple diet. Served in place of pasta or bread, white *polenta* accompanies fish, with filling yellow *polenta* usually served with the rest.

The region produces some of the best meat in the country, from veal and beef to pork and poultry: hence such stalwarts as *costoletta alla milanese*, veal fillet fried in breadcrumbs, and *osso buco*, shin of veal in white wine served with risotto. Less well-known outside Italy are *casseula*, a stew of mixed cuts of pork with

LEFT: salami and prosciutto for sale in Cipriani.
ABOVE: Venice is famous for its cakes and pastries.

vegetables, introduced from Spain by the Gonzagas, and *bollito*, boiled meats and offal cooked in a pot and served thinly sliced. The Lombards are also fond of sausages and cured meats (*salami*), such as mortadella, and bresaola, beef fillet, salted, dried, then smoked.

Good cheese

Gorgonzola, the greenish-blue veined cheese, originated in the foothills of the Alps near Milan. This cows' milk cheese has a piquant flavour and is ideally served runny or as a sauce for pasta, polenta or risotto. Grana Padano, originally made by the Cistercian monks of

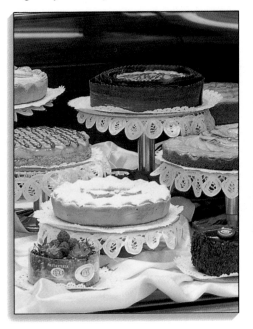

Chiaravalle in 1100, is similar to Parmesan. Moist chunks are eaten with fruit.

Taleggio, a strong cheese with a texture like Camembert, is used in risotto and terrines, or with *speck* or *wurst* salad. Bel Paese, the mild processed cheese, exists in its rustic incarnation, while creamy *mascarpone* is used in sauces.

Piedmont

The keynotes of Piedmontese cuisine are elegant French flourishes and filling country cuisine. The opulence of Piedmontese cuisine reflects the influence of France and the royal house of Savoy. Smooth truffle-scented risotto, rich cheeses and red meat represent the antithesis of *cucina nuova*. A classic dish is *vitel tonn*: sliced roast veal and tuna fish served cold in a mayonnaise, and garnished with capers and gherkins. Yet Piedmont also embraces robust peasant food. The creamy, buttery risotto is no accident: Vercelli and Novara are at the centre of European rice-growing. Beyond the rice plains Piedmont extends to barley fields, vineyards, game-rich woods and alpine cuisine.

Fontina, the best cows' milk cheese, comes from the alpine region of Valle d'Aosta. Fondues (*fonduta*) are made from this chewy semi-soft cheese, which can be mild or piquant.

Gnocchi alla bava are potato dumplings coated in Fontina cheese and white wine. This mountainous region is also noted for its salami, terrines and cured meats. By contrast, the woods around Alba are truffle-hunting country, providing such delicacies as *tagliolini* pasta coated in *salsa di tartufi bianchi*, white truffle sauce. The countryside was the inspiration for *bagna cauda*, a garlic and anchovy dip which accompanies raw peppers, artichokes, celery and potatoes. More substantial are meat dishes such as a *fritto misto* of brains, liver and sweetbreads fried in egg and breadcrumbs. Equally typical are *brusato al Barolo*, braised beef marinated in Barolo wine, or *bollito*, boiled meats.

Desserts include russet-skinned pears stewed in Barolo wine, baked peaches stuffed with amaretti macaroons from Saronno, or *zabaione*, a dessert made with Marsala and egg yolks. Turin is proud of its *gianduiotti*, hazelnut chocolates, a reminder of its 18th-century role as a founder of the European chocolate industry.

Healthy Liguria

Liguria is the most Mediterranean region, and it has the most vegetarian-friendly cuisine and the healthiest diet. There is little meat and dairy produce but an array of vegetables sandwiched into the narrow strip between the sea and the hills. The mild climate is ideal for tomatoes and artichokes, peaches, apricots and lemons.

Liguria's signature dish is pesto sauce, made from basil, olives, pine nuts or walnuts, Parmesan or sheep's cheese and garlic, ground and pounded into an aromatic pulp. It is usually served with *trenette verdi*, ribbon-shaped pasta or *trofie*, light gnocchi, and according to purists should only be made when the basil is in flower. Liguria also produces the only olive oil to rival the finest Tuscan varieties: a delicate sweetly scented, greeny-golden concoction. Other trademark dishes are *pansoti*, ravioli-like pasta stuffed with ricotta and herbs, often dressed in walnut sauce, and minestrone *alla genovese*, a vegetable soup laced with pesto.

For a coastal region, the fish is unexceptional, with favoured dishes including fish soup (*scippin*); stews (*buridda*) with anchovies and mixed fish, fried onions and pine-nuts; and *stoccafisso in umido*, salt cod cooked with tomatoes, potatoes, pine-nuts, garlic and sultanas.

Signature dishes

Italian cooking may be less coherent, less classic than French cuisine, yet the rich diversity of Italy's regional cuisine is greater than the sum of its parts. Even similar pasta dishes are distinguished by local preparations. Every region has its signature dishes, from *risotto alla milanese* (Milanese saffron risotto) to *fegato alla veneziana* (Venetian calf's liver), and *ragu alla bolognese* (Bolognese sauce). Above all, local dishes are a reflection of regional pride. As the old dictum runs: "*Dimmi come mangi e ti diro chi sei* (Tell me what you eat and I'll tell you who you are)." ❑

LEFT: some like it hot – chilli peppers.

Parmesan Cheese

Italy's most prestigious cheese has been praised since Etruscan and Roman times, with a Latin paean to Parmesan in Martial's verse. Correctly known as Parmigiano Reggiano, these hulking cartwheels of cheese originated in Emilia Romagna and were lauded in Petrarch's poetry and Boccaccio's Decameron. Parmesan's fame soon spread: Queen Elizabeth I shipped it to England in great quantities, and an elderly Molière even attributed the revival of his flagging dramatic powers to the chese. Today the cheese's praises are sung by a consortium which jealously protects its reputation. Despite the popularity of Parmesan on the world market, the majority of cheese is destined for Italy.

Parma and Reggio Emilia form the epicentre of the production zone, with a thousand small cheese-makers in the surrounding region. The straw-coloured cheese has been documented since the 13th century, and the production methods have remained unchanged ever since. Parmesan belongs to the Grana family of cheeses, including Gran Padano from Lombardy. However, Parmesan-makers insist that their "artisanal" cheeses are superior to industrially produced brands. Parmesan's cachet lies in its trusty artisanal methods and natural ageing process, as well as in the absence of preservatives or anti-fermenting agents. It takes 1.4 million tonnes of milk to yield 85,000 tonnes of Parmesan. The strictness of the specifications ensures the superb quality promised by the Parmigiano-Reggiano seal. Such superiority is reflected in the cost of this king of Italian cheeses.

Parmesan is made from a mixture of morning and evening milk from cows who graze on grass in spring and summer pastures. The cream is removed from the evening milk and turned into butter, with the resultant semi-skimmed milk mixed with full-fat morning milk. The concoction is then heated in huge copper cauldrons, shaped like inverted bells, with goat's kid rennet used as the curdling agent. After separation, the whey is fed to the local pigs while the curds are broken down, drained and pressed into round moulds. When firm, the cheese is floated in brine to absorb salt before being stamped with its name, date and provenance; Parmigiano Reggiano should be branded on the outer crust. The drums of cheese, weighing over 30 kilos (66 pounds) each, are then stacked on wooden slats in cellars that hold up to 200,000 cheeses at one time, and matured for between 18 months and three years. During the ageing process, the cheeses are constantly checked, turned and aired: more mature cheeses are drier and have a chalky look whereas younger cheeses are more moist. The golden Parmesan is stored in bank vaults, both to preserve its freshness and to protect it: in Emilia Romagna, cheese is as valuable as money.

Parmesan can be grated or eaten as a wedge, with the cheese "opened", rather than cut, using an almond-shaped knife. Since the 16th century, chunks of the best Parmesan have traditionally been served with grapes and pears. However, it

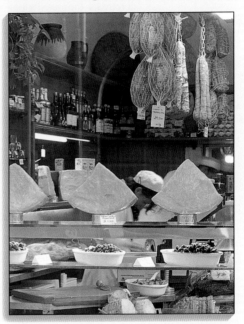

can also accompany an aperitif or a dessert of figs, apples, peaches or nuts. The popularity of Parmesan on pasta is due to its distinctive, lingering aroma and the fact that it melts without leaving a stringy residue. The best Parmesan crumbles in the mouth, while the edible crust can also be used in soups.

Parmesan enjoys a reputation as the most versatile and restorative of cheeses. Little wonder that Italian doctors have long promoted Parmesan's curative powers, particularly for those under six or over sixty. In order to hedge their bets, and perhaps to placate the powerful cheese lobby, doctors also prescribe Parmesan as an aid to digestion for greedy patients of all ages. ❏

RIGHT: wedges of Parmigiano Reggiano.

CAFÉ SOCIETY

Cafés – and coffee – are serious business in northern Italy, and the fine fin-de-siècle furnishings still make them atmospheric places to visit

The informal Italian *gelato* law stipulates that the further south one travels, the better the ice cream. Fortunately, the converse is that the further north one travels, the better the cafés. Turin, Trieste, Venice, Milan and Padua offer grandly historic cafés of great warmth and elegance. The northern climate favours formal, stylish retreats, intimate indoor cafés built against the vagaries of the weather. Yet the northern café culture owes much to Mitteleuropa, and the dowager ambience of the most monumental Italian cafés has much in common with cosmopolitan cafés in Vienna or Budapest, Paris or Prague.

Nobility and Art Nouveau

Caffè Cova is a Milanese institution on Via Montenapoleone. Founded in 1817, it was patronised by the 19th-century nobility. Students of Italian history can savour the genteel atmosphere where Mazzini and Garibaldi reputedly redrew the political map of Italy. Far grander is the Art Nouveau Giardino d'Inverno, in the Principe di Savoia, one of Milan's smartest hotels. Camparino, in Galleria Vittorio Emanuele, is also an Art Nouveau shrine, and a classic place for commuters to take *aperitivi* before they face the evening rush hour. Alternatively, Bar Giamaica, in the Brera district, is the place for erstwhile hippies who have mellowed into corporate suits. Although this 1960s bohemian rendezvous has been commandeered by models, designers and sundry creatives, it retains a raffish air.

Even the smaller provincial centres can conceal coffee houses of national repute. Trieste has a long and honourable tradition of coffee houses; the celebrated Caffè San Marco is a languorous study in elevated café style: frescoed Art Nouveau, gloomy mahogany fittings, polished brass and red velour drapes.

Venetian classics

Under the arcades of the Piazza San Marco is a cluster of distinguished coffee houses. Caffè Florian, considered the prince of coffee houses,

was founded in 1720 and is the oldest surviving café in Italy. Although heavily restored, it is a tribute to 18th-century splendour. As an erstwhile literary haunt, Florian's welcomed Byron, Dickens, Goethe, Mann, Proust and George Sand. It has long numbered musicans amongst, its patrons although Richard Wagner

kept away for fear of running into Giuseppe Verdi. Writers and artists still meet in Caffè Florian, though more for show than to listen to the melancholy airs of the cello and violin *virtuosi*.

On the basis that Harry's Bar is the best bar in the best city, the famed Bellini cocktail is cheap at any price. This is a legendary Venetian bar, resolutely unglitzy apart from a clientele of visiting celebrities and celebrity-watchers. The lure of classic cocktails and a good gossip have drawn prominent personalities, from Churchill and Chaplin to Bogart and Bacall,

ABOVE: the perfect cappuccino.
RIGHT: entertainment at Venice's Caffè Florian.

Fellini and Mastroianni, Sinatra and Madonna. Hemingway found inspiration in its "Montgomery", a Martini made with 15 measures of gin to one of vermouth, the same ratio of troops to enemy employed by the military strategist.

Savoy fare

Café culture reaches new heights in Turin's turn-of-the-century cafés, temples dedicated to pleasure and politics. Caffè Torino, once the favourite of the royal court, is still a high society haunt, noted for its elegance, cocktails and superb service. Caffè Specchi is one of a select band to line the bourgeois boulevards, a place to pass drowsy hours sitting and sipping cocktails or coffee. Caffè Mulassano, with faded gilt and panelled interior, is a rival turn-of-the-century temple to coffee, hot chocolate and cake-eating. By contrast, the glamorous bar in the Turin Palace strikes an exotic note, with a tented ceiling conjuring up an Oriental harem.

The intimate Al Bicerin is an early Ottocento café, originally a Sunday treat for prim dowagers attending Mass in the church opposite. The *bicerin*, the house speciality, is a heady mixture of hot chocolate, coffee and cream. Yet Al Bicerin is also a landmark in Piedmontese history, the preferred café of Count Camillo di

COFFEE THE WAY THE ITALIANS LIKE IT

The perfect *espresso* should have an aroma so intense that it bites. It should also have a *crema*, a head, whose consistency is determined by the fats and volatile oils in the coffee beans. To produce a good rounded taste, the beans should be a judicious blend of burnt arabica and robusta. *Caffè ristretto* is a double-strength *espresso* more akin to an electric shock than a cup of coffee. *Caffè latte*, an *espresso* mixed with steamed milk, can be drunk for breakfast, as can *cappuccino*, but never after a meal. *Caffè macchiato* is a single shot of *espresso* with a dash of foaming milk, while *caffè corretto* is fortified with a slug of spirits, whether *grappa*, cognac or whisky.

Cavour, the architect of Italian unification. Caffè-Pasticceria Baratti, set in a *fin-de-siècle* arcade, is a steamy spot for lovers of the *cioccolata calda*, a melting hot chocolate concoction. Caffè San Carlo, once frequented by Risorgimento patriots and intellectuals, claims to make the best coffee in Italy, rivalled only by Florian's in Venice.

Stefano Cavallero, its owner, sees the café as the lynchpin of Italy's social life, whether "neighbourhood cafés, football cafés, business cafés, bohemian cafés or intellectual cafés. Cafés are the first places where young people meet and the last places where old men say goodbye. Cafés keep Italians together." ❑

WINE ON THE MAP: TRAILS AND TASTINGS

Tracking down the greatest northern Italian wines is a delightful duty and a rewarding way of getting to know different regional landscapes

The region boasts many of Italy's best-known wines, from quaffable Valpolicella, fizzy Lambrusco and crisp Soave to Piedmont's powerful Barolo and Barbaresco, wines worthy of pilgrimages. The Veneto is a significant wine-producing region, encompassing the area from Venice to Lake Garda, and plays host to VinItaly in Verona, the country's largest wine fair. Amongst the biggest regional names are sparkling Prosecco and the red, cherry-like Bardolino, as well as fruity Valpolicella from around Lake Garda and dry Soave, produced east of Verona.

Although Lombardy cannot compete with the Veneto, its Franciacorta red, white and sparkling wines, produced around Lake Iseo, have been lauded since Roman times, and praised by Pliny himself. The Collio district of Friuli produces crisp, fine white wines, from Riesling Italico to Pinot Grigio, while Liguria is noted for red Dolcetto, and Emilia Romagna produces Italy's best sparkling red Lambrusco.

△ **BAROLO VINEYARDS**
At its best, Barolo, grown in southern Piedmont, is a powerful, individualistic long-lived red wine that lives up to its reputation.

THE KING OF WINES

However, Piedmont has a monopoly on the greatest wines. Barolo and Barbaresco are produced on the western shore of Lake Maggiore and benefit from a sub-alpine climate and southern exposure. These wines are justly famous, and have brought a quiet prosperity to the villages around Alba and Asti. They are made from the noble violet and raspberry scented Nebbiolo grape, the finest red grape in northern Italy, and matured in oak or chestnut casks. If Barolo is the king of wines, Barbaresco is the queen, lighter and more elegant. At the humbler end of the Piedmontese scale, the bubbly appeal of Asti Spumanti still enlivens a party.

◁ **BUBBLY**
Prosecco, which can be dry or sweet, works best as a dry sparkling aperitif.

▷ **TYROLEAN TASTES**
Eppan, in the Alto Aldige, sells wine with labels in both Italian and German.

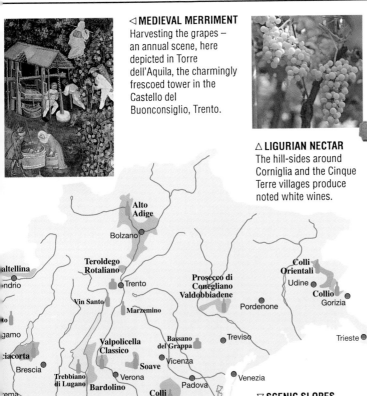

◁ MEDIEVAL MERRIMENT
Harvesting the grapes – an annual scene, here depicted in Torre dell'Aquila, the charmingly frescoed tower in the Castello del Buonconsiglio, Trento.

△ LIGURIAN NECTAR
The hill-sides around Corniglia and the Cinque Terre villages produce noted white wines.

WINE TOURS AND GRAPPA TASTINGS

Northern Italy is well-supplied with *enoteche*, centres of excellence for wine-tasting, sales and promotion. The best, such as Dozza and Barolo, are often sited in historic castles and make a convenient starting point for a leisurely trail around the region's best wine estates. In Emilia Romagna, Dozza boasts the medieval Sforza fortress of La Rocca, where, following a visit to the castle, you can sample Emilian wines such as Barbera and Lambrusco in the medieval cellars.

In the Veneto, the Strada del Prosecco is a celebration of Italy's most popular sparkling wine, with an accessible wine-tasting route centred on Conegliano and Valdobbiadene. In Lombardy, the Franciacorta area by Lake Iseo lends itself to wine-tastings and vineyard visits.

Trentino and the Veneto are the foremost producers of the famous firewater known as *grappa*, distilled from grapes.

For further information on wine tastings in the region, turn to Travel Tips at the end of the book.

▽ SCENIC SLOPES
Neat, vine-clad hillsides and prosperous estates represent harmonious northern wine country.

◁ HARVEST TOAST
Rossese di Dolceacqua, Napoleon's favourite wine, can be sampled in Liguria.

▷ KING OF WINES
Barolo, described as "earthy, truffly, smoky and mysterious."

VILLAS AND GARDENS

Lord Byron called Italy "the garden of the world", and the north, with its array of gorgeous Palladian villas and geometric gardens, does not disappoint

Bewitched by operatic gardens in the northern Italian lakes, Henry James described himself as "fairly wallowing in a *libretto*". Edith Wharton, who wrote the Edwardian travellers' bible to Italian gardens, praised such landscapes for their "breadth and simplicity", a composition of "marble, water and perennial verdure". From the Renaissance onwards, villas were embellished by sculptors, painters, cabinet-makers, plasterers and landscape gardeners. Whether models of Renaissance restraint, Classical Palladian design or Baroque theatricality, they possessed vistas framed by greenery, topiary and sculpture. Today the north still embraces some of the country's most enchanting villas and gardens.

The patrician ideal

From an architectural point of view, the Veneto possesses the greatest heritage, the blueprint for the patrician villa. Largely designed by Palladio (*see page 121*), these UNESCO-listed villas spread in an arc embracing Rovigo, Vicenza, Treviso and Venice. To the west, on the Ligurian Riviera, villas and gardens grace the outskirts of Genoa and hug the coast close to Portofino. Further north, lakeside Lombardy is noted for its patrician residences, from Baroque Isola Bella to exuberant Villa Carlotta on Lake Como, where landscaped gardens hug the hill in a shower of hibiscus, bougainvillea and citrus trees. Isola Bella was a barren rock before being landscaped by the Borromean princes in the 17th century. Their lasting testament is a series of lofty terraces encrusted with statuary and fountains, complemented by grottoes studded with shells, fossils and coloured coral.

While the patrician ideal was a country villa surrounded by formal gardens and a working farm estate, a number of northern gardens are showpieces in their own right. The botanical gardens in Padua, dating from 1533, are the oldest university gardens in Italy devoted to medicinal plants and scientific research. Also in the Veneto, the Giusti gardens in Verona are equally distinctive, embellished with grottoes and terraces, and used as an open-air theatre in Renaissance times. The Giardino Reale in Monza near Milan is an inspired Italianate ver-

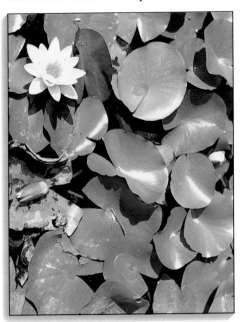

sion of English Romanticism: royal parkland studded with alpine glades, lakes and lawns.

Renaissance summer solace

During the Renaissance the villa was reinvented as a gracious retreat and framed by geometric landscaped gardens *all'italiana*. With airy loggias and panoramic belvederes, the Tuscan Renaissance villa broke the mould of enclosed medieval gardens. Steeply terraced gardens enjoyed vistas of parterres, stairways and pergolas, lemon groves, laurels and lilies, with olive groves and vineyards beyond. The Venetian nobility and merchant class soon followed suit, commissioning villas beside the

---

PRECEDING PAGES: Villa Hanbury botanical garden.
LEFT: the romantic gardens of Villa Carlotta, Como.
RIGHT: lilies at Villa Hanbury, Ventimiglia.

Brenta Canal and in the foothills of the Alps. Moving to the country also enabled polite society to escape the summer heat of the Venetian Lagoon and Po Valley.

A villa society

The early 16th century coincided with a fashion for country living and witnessed the emergences of villa society. The relationship between the rural economy and the ruling classes meant that the Venetians could invest any income earned from maritime trade and make profits from their new lands. In so doing, they could believe in the ennoblement of agri-

and greenery, and landscaped *all'italiana* to suit the tastes of the times. Mathematical order prevailed, with clipped cypresses, laurels and myrtles, topiary, scented herbs and sculpture. Dwarf fruit trees were popular, with lemons, quinces and pomegranates generally grown.

In Renaissance times the villas became the hubs of prosperous agricultural estates, and a harmonious part of the landscape. The leading architects of the day were summoned to design the villas, from Michele Sanmicheli and Jacopo Sansovino to Palladio. By the same token, the greatest artists, from Veronese to Tiepolo, were invited to decorate the interiors.

culture whilst also achieving their less noble goal: the glorification of the dynasty. The merchant class was as industrious on *terra firma* as it was in the lagoon city. The land was drained and farmed. In summer, the villa became a society haunt for noble Venetian patrons, first as a focus for humanist gatherings and finally as a setting for festivities.

From the 1520s a stream of city-dwellers built country retreats, villas adorned with waterside gardens. Villas were often designed so that they would be reflected in the Brenta River or Canal, and formal pools were integral to the overall composition of the grounds.

An architectural garden was traced with paths

Palladian trail

Palladio treated his creations as Roman stages encased in theatres of greenery. He favoured superb natural settings, airy porticoes, and loggias crowned by triangular pediments. The blend of architectural coherence and compositional elegance pleases the eye as simplicity personified. However, the Classical design and decorative detail mask the virtuosity of the design, cast as it is in mathematical ratios.

Villa Rotonda, technically known as Villa Capra, is a Palladian masterpiece famed for its photogenic setting, shallow dome and four identical façades. Set in the hills outside Vicenza, this summer retreat was designed as an architectural set-piece, a stage for admiring the undulating view flowing from the majestic columns and staircase. Villa Foscari, known as La Malcontenta, vies with La Rotonda as Palladio's most admired creation. The villa, raised on an elevated pedestal to protect it from floods, displays a temple-like façade reflected in the Brenta River.

Villa Emo, east of Vicenza, is another Palladian gem, and, like Villa Saraceno to the south, accepts paying guests. Villa Barbaro in Maser, in the foothills of the Dolomites, is one of the Veneto's grandest villas, designed by Palladio and frescoed by Veronese.

The northern lakes, particularly Como and Maggiore, are home to some of the region's most splendid villas and gardens. Lake Como has long had the most exclusive lakeside villas, many of which are owned by celebrities. Villa Carlotta was the work of Princess Carlotta of The Netherlands, who landscaped the formal gardens and park in the 1860s. The dazzling azaleas and rhododendrons provide a colourful contrast to the villa's cool Neoclassical interior. By contrast, the Baroque splendours of Isola Bella on Lake Maggiore often blind visitors to the charms of the neighbouring Isola Madre and its luxuriant botanical gardens.

Dignity and harmonious proportions have served as a model for later villas in the Veneto. Villa Arvedi, set in Cuzzano, near Verona, dates from 1650 and has a complex Classical garden, with allegorical statues, geometrical hedges, a grotto, amaze and an orangery. By contrast, Villa Pisani in Strà is an 18th-century affair, decorated by Tiepolo. The garden owes much to French classicism, with the villa and the outbuildings set some distance apart, and a maze, rustic portals, and a belvedere with a spiral staircase leading to a raised loggia.

LEFT: Villa Cordelina, Montecchio Maggiore.
ABOVE: the terraces of Villa Serbeloni, Bellagio.

Geometry and perspective

Italianate gardens conjure up a picture of graceful geometry. Attention is paid to the proportions between the height of a wall and the width of a path, or to the alternation of sunny parterres and shady woodland. The grandest gardens may indulge in sweeps of landscape, with waterworks and pergolas in the foreground, possibly culminating in the *pièce de résistance*, a *scaletta d'acqua:* a water staircase with a grotto, fountains and classsical statuary. Though less dependent on artifice and dramatic effects than Roman and Tuscan models, the Renaissance gardens in the Veneto play the same games with geometry and perspective.

Given that Renaissance man saw himself at the centre of the universe, the wish to impose his will on the countryside was ever-present.

Villa Cicogna Mozzoni, in the hills north of Varese, was a hunting lodge until it was remodelled in 1559 as a classic Lombard Renaissance villa. The *trompe-l'oeil* Mannerist frescoes and loggia painted with plants and peacocks complement the framed vistas of parterres and forested slopes. The Renaissance garden is a tiered affair, inspired by Medici gardens in Florence and Papal gardens in Rome; a double staircase framed by cypresses and dotted with statuary connects the villa and grounds. The

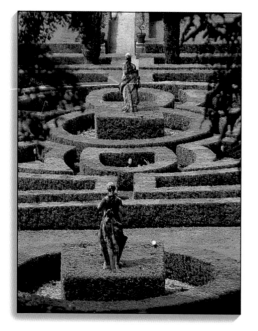

effect is seamless, a procession of loggias, box hedges, classical pools, fountains and a grotto.

French influence

The formality of French Classical gardens was difficult to transplant to the more rugged Italian terrain but succeeded in parts of the flatter Veneto, even if on a far smaller scale than the Classical châteaux garden around Paris. By comparison, Isola Bella is a deeply Italian Baroque extravaganza in the lake district, a fanciful terraced pleasure garden bursting with vegetation from all over the world.

Villa Trissino Marzotto, near Vicenza, has medieval gardens remodelled in Rococo style

in the 18th century. In the grounds, striking features include the wrought-iron gates and curtain of cypresses leading up to the belvedere; wooded areas give way to sweeping lawns and terraced gardens with statuary and arches.

Anglo-Saxon attitudes

As fashions changed, some Classical gardens were transformed into *giardini inglesi*, English Romantic parkland and woods. The Italian tendency to remodel nature to man's own design gave way to the English approach, whereby man saw himself as aiding nature in creating a naturalistic effect.

Villa Pallavicino, set in Stresa, on Lake Maggiore, is a 19th-century villa whose gardens combine Romantic and Classical elements. Enlarged by the Duca di Villambrosa, who had a passion for tree-planting, the park abounds in horse chestnuts, copper and purple beech, maple and magnolia, majestic sequoia and oak. The parkland is complemented by Italianate gardens dotted with secret arbours, rose bowers, statues and fountains, as well as greenhouses filled with exotic and ornamental plants.

The lush gardens at Sigurtà, on Lake Garda, are an Italianate approximation of English parkland, full of flowering plants and majestic trees interspersed with terraces, lakes and a ruined castle. In the Edwardian heyday of genteel tourism, the northern lakes delighted visitors with seemingly careless vistas of azaleas, rhododendrons and camellias. At the same time the Italian Riviera, the Riviera dei Fiori, lived up to its floral name, with a profusion of camellias, magnolias and palms along the seafront.

A privileged minority still strives to recreate the classic villa garden of the aristocracy, an ornamental affair of statuary, topiary, fountains and stone paths. But to most Italians a garden means crops, vines, olives and an orchard, or at least an untidy vegetable patch.

Chic city-dwellers may have recently taken to spending a fortune on minuscule, status-symbol balcony gardens, but even those with more space tend to focus on creating a lovely terrace and ignoring the rest. Even here, tomatoes, a lemon tree or basil plants often take pride of place over pots of geraniums; in Italian minds, there is no contest between the rival claims of food and flowers. ❑

LEFT: Verona's Giusti gardens.

Palladian Style

Palladio's treatise *The Four Books of Architecture* was hugely influential in popularising Classical architecture. If the term "Palladian" has entered the language, it is a compliment both to the Italian's superb buildings and to his legacy as a scholar. The Renaissance genius Andrea di Pietro della Gondola was dubbed Palladio by Count Tressino, his patron and mentor, one of the enlightened Venetian landowners who had the foresight to commission Palladio's villas.

Palladio was born in Padua in the Veneto in 1508, and worked as a mason on Mannerist monuments in Vicenza, but he only fully formulated his Classical philosophy after visiting Rome in the 1540s. As the leading architect of his day, he pioneered a radical classicism that was too bold for Venetian tastes. Consequently he received few public commissions, and none for city palaces, which made him dependent on the patronage of the religious orders and the largesse of the Venetian landed gentry.

Authentic Palladian villas are found in the Po Valley between Venice and Vicenza, with some of the most celebrated situated along a stretch of the Brenta Canal. The architect also designed a bridge at Bassano del Grappa, in the foothills of the Alps, before dedicating the end of his career to transforming the Venetian skyline with his bold buildings. Be it church, bridge or villa, Palladianism is noted for its Classical restraint, a chaste and restrained style at odds with theatrical Baroque. Yet the villas, in particular, often pose architectural puzzles, from a square house built around a dome to a circular house constructed with square walls.

Palladio's designs for villas were a marriage between ancient Rome and the modern world, with the elevated tastes of the leisured classes allied to a sober and humane classicism stripped of excess. In the Roman hills, Palladio was impressed by the Tivoli villas, from the curved staff wings to the elevated monumental façades and stylised projecting pediments. He then proceeded to reinterpret the greatest Roman architecture for the Venetian bourgeoisie. Inspired by the Pantheon in Rome, certain villas are designed on the lines of a votive temple. An unwavering sense of proportion and perspective is reflected in the façades, the pedimented

porticoes and the bold, airy interiors. The subtle, spare designs are enhanced by broad domes, graceful columns and Corinthian capitals.

Taken as a whole, Palladio's work on Venetian churches and the villas of the Veneto make him one of the outstanding architects of all time. Tempered by Palladianism, even Venetian Baroque was a relatively sober form. The rest of northern Italy witnessed a return to Palladian values in the 18th century, with dignified villas built for the nobility, and grandiose city palaces designed for wealthy *arrivistes*.

Palladian villas in the Veneto influenced architectural styles all over the Western world, especially in the United States, England and Ireland.

The use of the Graeco-Roman temple front as a portico was probably the most imitated feature. Villa Rotonda provided the model for London's Chiswick House and countless English stately homes, as well as inspiring imitators in Ireland and America. London's National Gallery, the Capitol in Washington DC and the Metropolitan Museum in New York are testaments to the pervasiveness of Palladianism. Thomas Jefferson, the American President and author of the Declaration of Independence, transplanted Palladian style to Virginia, where he cultivated a transatlantic Italian renaissance. Nonetheless, in terms of Classical design and decorative detail, the villas in the Veneto represent the purest form of Palladianism. ❏

RIGHT: Villa Foscari, Veneto, designed by Andrea Palladio and built c.1560.

WALKING AND WILDLIFE

Green tourism is a growth area in northern Italy, with spring and autumn the best seasons for hill-walking

Walkers drawn to the penitential aspect of mountain-climbing can satisfy their bodies and souls in the uncharted wildernesses of northern Italy. They will encounter jagged mountain peaks looming menacingly, stony mule tracks, torrential rain, and scrambles up strata of unyielding rock. Unattainable summits spur the walker to greater endeavours in the metaphysical sense. Yet, in a flash, vistas open up to reveal a clear blue sky over snow-capped peaks, serene woodland or a sighting of a chamois or an ibex. The descent may take in panoramic views from natural balconies, thundering waterfalls and copses of oak and chestnut. Beyond awaits a more ordered landscape, with alpine meadows punctuated perhaps by olive groves and vineyards. Material rewards take the form of filling polenta, venison and red wine in a cosy alpine refuge.

Mountains to coastal paths

Le Corbusier, the great French architect, described the Dolomites as the most beautiful natural sculpture in the world. British and German pioneers of alpine tourism "discovered" them in the 19th century, since when their landscape of peaks and perpetual glaciers has become a popular destination for foreign hikers. Yet so have the Ligurian coastal paths climbing through vineyards and terraced olive groves; the mists and marshland of the Po Delta; the coppiced woodland of the Emilian Apennines; and the balmy micro-climates of the great northern lakes.

Apart from gentle hill-walking and strenuous hiking, the north offers the full range of associated sports, from mountaineering and orienteering to rock and glacier-climbing. Winter adds alpine and cross-country skiing to the menu, as well as dog-sledding and long-distance excursions on snow shoes.

A number of walking itineraries are rich in

LEFT: the Stelvio Pass.
RIGHT: hiking amid the hills and mountains of Trentino.

military sites. Trentino, for instance, offers the Path of Peace, a World War I line of fortifications and communication trenches carved out the mountains separating Italy and Austria (*see page 126*). Further south, in the Apennines, on the border between Emilia Romagna and Tuscany, walkers can explore the war sites along

the Gothic Line. During World War II the Germans built substantial fortifications in these rugged valleys.

Taking the high road

The Alps are criss-crossed with long-distance paths linking chestnut groves with rugged alpine panoramas. The *strade bianche* are the dusty white roads of rural Italy, while the *alte vie* are high long-distance paths, with the most spectacular being the *alte vie delle Dolomiti*, the high Dolomite trails. The most arduous routes are the so-called *"vie ferrate"*, iron ladders, named after the spaghetti lines of iron cables that are implanted into the steeper rock gradients. Real ladders are used to scale sheer cliff walls in a sport that is still considered walking rather than mountain-climbing and is popular with the Italians and Germans in the Trentino Dolomites. Ice picks and a head for heights are a prerequisite for such alpine trails.

The north provides a taste of the region's best parks and nature reserves. Gran Paradiso, Italy's foremost national park, is a magnificent wilderness, with its waterfalls, meadows, glaciers and rare alpine flora. On a par with its northern neighbour is the sprawling Parco dello Stelvio, Italy's largest national park, which straddles Lombardy, Trentino and the Alto Adige. The profusion of lakes has led to the area being dubbed "the Finland of Italy". Most major parks have visitor centres where one can usually hire a bicycle, find detailed walking itineraries or book a local guide. National parks are patrolled, and keepers impose on-the-spot fines for such infractions as disturbing animals or picking flowers, mushrooms or berries.

Piedmont and the Gran Paradiso

The ruggedness of the terrain makes the region more suitable for long-distance walking, mountaineering and skiing than for gentle strolls. While the cultivated land is among the most

THE ITALIAN ALPINE CLUB

The CAI, the Italian Alpine Club, with recognised centres and schools in the main resorts, provides qualified mountain guides and instructors in every imaginable sport. The *rifugi*, invaluable mountain refuges providing hearty meals and even simple rooms, also tend to be run by the CAI. Turin and Trento have museums showing its members' achievements, including their participation in Antarctic expeditions.

Upmarket independent tour operators offer hiking holidays, with accommodation varying from converted palaces, castles and convents to the simplest farms and *agriturismo (see page 126)*.

profitable in the country, particularly the prized vineyards, almost half the region is mountainous. The alpine landscape was modelled by glaciers during the last Ice Age. Today the Dolomites abound in spruce, Scots pine, mountain pine, silver fir, larch, ash, silver birch and rowan. The wilder areas allow sightings of the golden eagle, chamois and marmots. Long-distance walks link the area around Cuneo to the Valle di Susa and Gran Paradiso. However, committed hikers tend to head straight for the Gran Paradiso. Swathes of woodland and precipitous peaks provide a background for fast-flowing streams, botanical gardens and carpets of alpine flora. The sure-footed ibex is the symbol of the park and, along with the chamois, is best seen in May or June on the lower valley slopes, or in late summer on the higher slopes. Since the last lynx was killed here in 1914, visitors must be content with sightings of chamois, marmots and mountain hares, or golden eagles, black woodpeckers and snow finches. The Val di Cogne area provides easy access to the park and is not far from the alpine garden in Valnontey, with its dramatic views of glaciers. Paths are well-marked, including *alta via 4*, a

BEAR FACTS

The Adamello Brenta national park is the preserve of roebuck, chamois and foxes as well as being the last northern Italian refuge of the rapidly disappearing brown bear.

and roe deer, eagles, owls and chaffinches – a reasonable tally for a region devoted to hunting.

Trentino

The region proclaims itself a walkers' paradise. Mountains crown the landscape; over half the region is covered by woods and alpine pastures, with high-altitude hiking popular in all seasons. In terms of guides, facilities, organisation and the sheer variety of outdoor pursuits, Trentino is unparalleled in Italy. Hikers are rewarded with tumbling

long-distance trail that crosses the park.

Oasi Zegna, set in the alpine foothills near Biella and Trivero, was founded in the 1930s by Ermenegildo Zegna, a far-sighted industrialist. Although the product of paternalism, the park has served its purpose as a pastoral retreat for the company's textile workers. The nature reserve, which embraces alpine pastureland and fir woods, is dotted with wildlife trails. The wolf may have died out in the area, but badgers, marmots and stoats survive, as do chamois

streams, dramatic mountain gorges, and crags looming overhead. Brenta, an archetypal Dolomite group, intimidates with its towering pinnacles of limestone and rock surfaces that have an orange sheen when they catch the light. Equally appealing in the summer months are Trentino's 300 lakes. Particularly delightful are the walks around the lesser lakes, with Lake Tenno, Lake Cavedine and Lake Molveno encircled by footpaths. In summer, Lake Tovel can be tinged red by red algae.

Trentino offers numerous archeological and geological trails as well as organised excursions in search of alpine flora, usually beginning in the local botanical gardens. Fans of military

LEFT: monarch of the South Tyrol.
ABOVE: marmots of the Oasi Zegna nature reserve.
RIGHT: the endangered brown bear.

history can follow the Path of Peace (*see page 123*). The path, which covers the Adamello, Ortles, Cevedale and Marmolada glaciers, would take a month to complete so is best restricted to certain stages.

The largest alpine park

The impressive Parco dello Stelvio, known as Stilfs in German, is the largest national park in the Alps, encompassing 40 lakes and the alpine massif of Ortles-Cevedale. As an indication of the ruggedness of the terrain, a tenth of the area is covered by glaciers. The Passo di Stelvio, Europe's second highest mountain pass, con- nects with Bolzano and the Alto Adige and is a hiking centre in summer, doubling as a ski resort in winter.

There are visitors' centres in Cogolo and the Val di Rabbi, in addition to access from Bormio. Marked trails and numerous alpine refuges permit observation of chamois, mar- mots, ibex and golden eagles.

Valle di Peio, part of the park, is a noted trekking centre, with summer routes equally suited to winter excursions on snow shoes. Walkers travelling in small groups may be rewarded by occasional sightings of deer, ibex, marmots or eagles.

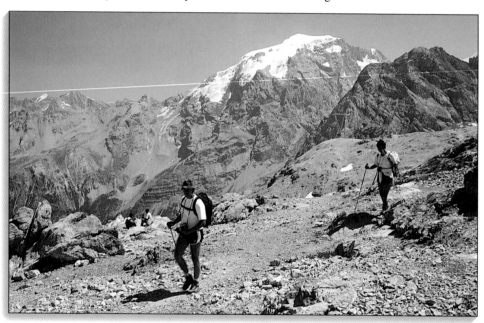

RURAL TOURISM

Agriturismo originally referred to spartan rooms in working farms. Now the term can be used to describe any rural accommodation, from simple renovated cottages to restored medieval farms or luxurious converted convents. *Agriturismo* flourishes in much of the north, including Liguria, Emilia Romagna and Trentino–Alto Adige.

The larger or more luxurious rural enterprises may organise hiking or horse-riding excursions. Well-organised regional tourist offices provide lists and accurate descriptions of the *agriturismo* facilities. Successful rural ventures make profits from selling specialist honeys, truffle pâtés, bottled artichokes, olives and jams. A *degustazione*, or tasting of the estate wines and farm produce, is the best part of rural life.

Agritur is a rural initiative popular in the Trentino region. Although it tends not to provide accommodation, it is usually a specialised farm with a simple restaurant. Legally, it can only sell its own products, such as honey, cheese, yoghurt and salami. In Trentino, *Agritur* also offers the opportunity to meet bee-keepers and cattle-farmers at work. Standards of *Agritur* establishments vary enormously: the inn could be a simple place in which to hang up one's walking boots for a while, or represent a gastronomic experience serious enough to draw committed skiers from the slopes.

The chic winter ski resort of Madonna di Campiglio lies at the head of Val Rendenna, a typical pastoral valley. From Cles, near Tuenno, a wooded path leads to Mostizzolo, which opens out into the mountain pass of Campo Carlo Magno. From there, there is a descent to Madonna di Campiglio, a place for well-deserved après-ski posing in one of the trendy local inns. In summer this is also an ideal base for exploring the Brenta and Adamello ranges as well as for following the "five lakes" itinerary.

NEOLITHIC ART

Europe's finest rock carvings can be found at Val Camonica north of Boario Terme. Created by Neolithic hunters and farmers these sheer rock faces were used as a canvas for scenes of everyday life as well for drawings to appease the gods.

For serious hikers, the cable car from Madonna di Campiglio connects with Groste, where a beguiling path leads to Rifugio del Tucket, a mountain refuge. From here, there is access to one of the most popular *vie ferrate*, the "iron paths" along the stunning Sentiero Orsi in the Brenta group. Progress along these paths is aided by a mountain guide provided with ladders or by rungs fixed to the rock.

Mountaineers and climbers are well served by this craggy region. Mountaineering across glaciers of varying difficulty is available in the Valle di Fasse, Valle di Fiemme or Lagorai. Experienced rock-climbers can attempt the vertical ascents around Lake Garda and the Colodri near Arco. The mild lakeside micro-climate makes climbing possible in winter. Sheer cliffs also await expert and novice climbers near Cavalese, in the Valle di Fiemme, as well as in the Val di Sole, Predazzo and Moena.

Alto-Adige

Better known as the South Tyrol, this is Germanic borderlands with a Tyrolean feel, a landscape dotted with hamlets and onion-domed churches. Beyond the quaint villages await dramatic glaciers and scenes of intrepid paragliders floating amidst the snow-capped peaks. Gentler trails wind through domesticated rolling farmland, a patchwork of well-tended fields, orchards and vineyards. These hikes trace the charming meadows around Bad Ratsches and Compatsch, with an opportunity for stops in rustic inns and Germanic spas.

LEFT: the Parco dello Stelvio is the largest national park in the alps.
RIGHT: winter hiking in Madonna di Campiglio.

Tougher challenges are posed by the Schnals (Senales) glacier or the Seiser Alm range in the Dolomites. The Sciliar national park, accessible from Bolzano, has steep rock faces and peaks.

The Lakes

Compared with the serious hiking on offer in the Dolomites, this region favours a gentle pace. Tucked into the foothills of the Alps, the silvery-blue lakes offer alpine walks in pearly mists or more Mediterranean strolls

closer to the shore. Framed by majestic mountains, the lakes abound in balmy micro-climates favourable to citrus fruits and palm trees. Lake Maggiore is well served by paths and cycle tracks, on both the Lombard and Piedmontese banks. From Laveno, a 5km (3-mile) climb leads to the rocky sanctuary of Santa Caterina del Sasso. Around unspoilt Lake Iseo, Provaglio represents the start of a nature itinerary that takes in the peatbogs at the foot of Monte Provaglio and the reed-beds which provide refuge for water fowl. Monte Isola, the traffic-free fishermen's island in the centre of the lake, is best explored by bicycle.

From the centre of Como a gentle stroll leads

to Villa Olmo, a gracious villa on the lake. A cable car also connects the town of Como with Brunate, the starting point for scenic hiking in the hills. With its confluence of dramatic peaks and a serene lake shore, the quaint resort of Bellagio is a good base. An invigorating afternoon's stroll can be made from the lakeside Villa Melzi to Monte San Primo by way of streams and mills. At Tremezzo one can join the lakeside route known as Tremezzina, linking several villas and gardens.

Lake Garda, despite being the most developed lake, offers good walking routes, whether from the Brescia, Verona or Trento shores.

blessed with a steamy micro-climate producing palms, banana trees and tropical plants.

Lombardy's great art cities, including Bergamo, Mantua and Cremona, offer unusual walks in their vicinities. West of Mantua lies the Mincio reserve, a network of canals and reed beds which is the preserve of marsh turtles, river crab and otters. In Cremona a riverside route leading from Via del Sale traces the floodbeds and wends past poplars and birches to Porto Polesine. North of Boario Terme lies Val di Camonica, Europe's finest park of rock carvings, an "open-air museum" created by Neolithic hunters and farmers. Reached via

From the lakeside resort of Malcesine, a cable car connects with a number of mountain paths and convenient *rifugi* for lunch. The adventurous can choose to make the return journey by mountain bike. The castle resort of Sirmione is an ideal base for exploring the Grottoes of Catullus, while the picturesque villages of Tremosine and Tignale, perched on rocky crags, open onto a series of inviting footpaths.

On the Veneto shore, an appealing walk leads from the wine-producing village of Bardolino to Garda itself. Closer to Desenzano is a Mediterranean landscape of vineyards and olive groves. The lush atmosphere is even more pronounced around Gardone Riviera, a resort

Capo di Ponte, these sheer rock faces bear scenes of everyday life as well as magical, propitiatory drawings to appease the gods.

The Veneto and Emilia Romagna

This is varied terrain, from the watery Po Plain, a bird-watching paradise, to the Emilian Apennines, rugged hill-walking country. While the Veneto can offer both mountains and hills, the marshland and waterscapes are arguably more distinctive. However, given the relative flatness of most of the terrain, the Veneto is perfect cycling country. The regional tourist office provides clear guides outlining the best cycling itineraries, whether linked to Palladian villas, lakeside retreats and the coastal route, or giving more energetic rides through the verdant Euganean hills or the vineyard-clad slopes of Soave. The river Sile, which connects Castelfranco Veneto and Treviso with Venice, includes inviting stretches of marshland. Although sections of the nature reserve can be explored on foot, more enterprising visitors will take to canoes or *burchi*, typical flat-bottomed boats built to traverse the reed-beds. The rural route to Treviso passes mills, dams, brickworks, villas and large country estates.

The Po Delta lies in a maze of waterways between Ferrara and Ravenna. This precious nature reserve, shared between the Veneto and Emilia Romagna, and just beyond the bustling Adriatic beach resorts, is a timeless landscape characterised by shallow lagoons and dunes, mudflats, low dykes and salt pans. For those who value solitude there are opportunities to walk or cycle along the high banks of the *valli*, the fishing lagoons curled into the delta branches of the meandering river Po. The only signs of life are wealthy weekenders using the *casoni*, the shuttered fishing huts, as a base for catching eels, sea bass and flounder. The eels for which this region is famous are caught in reed-walled traps as they try to answer the call of the Sargasso Sea. The misty marshland is the preserve of herons, egrets and mallards, as well as Camargue-style white ponies.

The Emilian Apennines, within easy access of Bologna, provide rugged hill-walking country. Covering the mountains on the Tuscan border, the terrain spans sharp ridges, coppiced woodland and mysterious leafy hollows dotted with dilapidated sanctuaries. Less arduous walks traverse valleys littered with long-abandoned hamlets. In the hills are traces of the loamy platforms used by the *carbonari* who worked the soot-encrusted charcoal-burners. Walkers seeking historical trails would do well to trace the war sites along the Gothic Line (*see page 123*).

Liguria

The rocky Ligurian coast, riddled with coves and creeks, makes for beguiling walking country, complete with spellbinding sea views. The lush landscape, sandwiched between the Alps and the Apennines, provides a backdrop of juniper, myrtle and lentisks and the scent of thyme, rosemary and lavender. The rocky hinterland provides sightings of marmots, white hares and lizards, as well as walks to mountain sanctuaries.

The Impero Valley, close to Imperia, has walks through olive groves, chestnut and oak woods. Monte di Portofino is a protected area which embraces the chic resort of Portofino. Walks through the wooded countryside afford spectacular views over the idyllic gulf and a jagged coastline rich in Mediterranean flora.

One of the loveliest walks is to the renowned abbey of San Fruttuoso.

The Cinque Terre coastal villages have the most rewarding walking trail in the region. Idle ramblers can choose to follow a short stretch of the so-called "lovers' path" that hugs the dramatic coast. Serious hikers will tackle longer stretches of the rocky coastline, travelling between the five quaint fishing villages. The arduousness of the steep slopes and sheer drops into the sea is compensated for by the sight of terraced vineyards and olive groves clinging to the hillsides. After such exhilarating sights, the relaxing boat trip to Portovenere proves a sore temptation for tired feet. ❑

LEFT: apricot trees in blossom.
RIGHT: cherry trees abound in the fertile country of Emilia Romagna.

PLACES

*A detailed guide to the entire region, with principal sites
clearly cross-referenced by number to the maps*

Despite its surface gloss and bourgeois air, northern Italy is far from being either a cohesive entity or yet another pocket of modern cosmopolitan Europe. The region's charm resides instead in its local character and customs. Sophisticated Milan may embody most visitors' preconceptions of the entrepreneurial north, but Trieste and Bolzano offer the unmistakable whiff of Mitteleuropa with their alpine scenery, chalets and cowbells, sauerkraut and strudel.

Since most northern regions retain their local character, this book presents places within their official demarcations. The only exceptions are the Lakes, which span several official regions but are more naturally treated as a whole, and Emilia Romagna, which, given its diversity, is accorded an additional chapter dedicated to the Adriatic Coast.

As a general rule the rural north is best explored by car while, conversely, the historic cities reveal their secrets more readily to pedestrians. However, each region abounds in convenient touring bases and unusual thematic itineraries. In the Veneto, travellers can follow the Palladian villa trail or simply succumb to the romance of Romeo and Juliet in Verona. Just west, in Trentino-Alto Adige, the spectacular Great Dolomites Road links the two regions, crossing dramatic mountain scenery en route to prestigious ski resorts and scenic Tyrolean castle trails. Friuli-Venezia Giulia represents the exotic gateway to the Balkans and the Austro-Hungarian legacy evoked by Trieste. The genteel Lakes district encapsulates the best of the north, with its beguiling resorts and palatial villas. Even prosaic Lombardy has historic Bergamo and musical Cremona, not to mention Milan, the country's business, fashion and design capital.

As for the Ligurian Riviera, visitors can choose between chic Portofino and the gentrified fishing village of Camogli, while the Adriatic coast dismisses such pretensions with its brashly appealing resorts. The coherent time capsules of Bologna and Ferrara make ideal springboards for exploring the art cities of Emilia Romagna while, further north, cool Piedmont responds with the vivid contrast between Turin, Italy's suave car capital, and the mountain wildernesses and rolling vineyards of the hinterland. Asti is synonymous with sparkling Spumante, while neighbouring Barolo and Bardolino represent the region's finest red wines. Indeed, any geographical tour of northern Italy would also be a gastronomic feast, embracing wine and truffles from Piedmont, *polenta* dishes from Trentino, Milanese risotto, Venetian seafood, *tortellini* from Bologna and succulent Parma ham and Parmesan cheese from Parma. Although visitors are advised to march on their stomachs, the north is a feast for all senses. ❑

PRECEDING PAGES: summer in the Dolomites; the monastery of San Giorgio, Venice, at dusk; façade of the Duomo, Milan.
LEFT: Galleria Vittorio Emanuele, Milan.

VENICE

"A commercial people who lived solely for gain – how could they create a city of fantasy, lovely as a dream or a fairy tale?" – Mary McCarthy

Venice is the city we have all been to, if only in our imaginations. Yet its essence remains as elusive as the slippery lagoon-dwellers themselves. Venice is a state of mind, a canvas for projecting one's poetic fantasies: there are monumental Venice and mournful Venice, domestic Venice and eclectic Venice, seductive Venice and secret Venice. In a city awash with ghosts, melancholy and nostalgia await around most dark canal corners, from Hemingway's bar to Wagner's bed, or the Jewish ghetto to the cemetery islands.

Monumental Venice dazzles with its Baroque stage sets, Palladian churches and Gothic palaces; eclectic Venice beguiles with Byzantine mosaics and carnival capers; seductive Venice can go serenading in the grandest cafés or catch one unawares in a wisteria-clad garden. Henry James gives us domestic Venice: "a narrow canal in the heart of the city, a patch of green water and a surface of pink wall, a great shabby façade of Gothic windows and balconies".

Yet even this fails to do justice to the watery chimera of the city, with its mercurial climate, shimmering light and mood of impermanence. The physical uniqueness of Venice can only be felt, not described.

A living museum

In a city that provokes possessive passion, tourism is almost as ancient as Venice itself. "His gondolier, being in league with various lace-makers and glass-blowers, did his best to persuade his fare to pause." Even in Thomas Mann's Venice, the fleecing of tourists was part of the Venetian experience.

Although traditionally cosmopolitan and tolerant, Venetians will admit to an impatience with mass tourism; nor do they wish to live in a museum but in a living city. To them, Venice is not a frozen expression of beauty but an everyday affair of neighbourhood cafés and fish markets, gondolas and garbage barges. A Venetian elite may still meet to strains of Vivaldi at the fireside of a freshly gilded salon. However, most Venetians prefer a prosaic stroll and a meal out: understandable when a stroll encompasses more magic and drama than are available on the formal stage. Proust best captures the poetic and prosaic nature of a place in which "the simplest social coming and going assumes at the same time the form and charm of a visit to a museum and a trip to the sea".

San Marco

Venice is traditionally divided into six *sestieri* (districts), a practice followed here, with the addition of the Grand Canal, which winds its way through the heart of the city. An astonishing 50 per cent of visitors fail to stray further than St Mark's Square. Yet, unlike

LEFT: fishing nets in the lagoon.
BELOW: a gondolier.

The Lion of St Mark.

BELOW: Basilica di San Marco.

many official city squares, **Piazza San Marco ❶** belongs to the citizens as well as to visitors; Venetians drink at the grand cafés, even if they often save money by standing up, and some may attend Mass at the Basilica or even dance at the open-air Carnival. However, for most of the day, St Mark's belongs to the pigeons, crowds and souvenir-sellers; only in early evening does it revert to a semblance of solitude. Piazza San Marco has acted as the heart of the Republic ever since the earliest settlement shifted from Torcello to central Venice. Yet Venetian notions of glory caused it to be remodelled in Renaissance times, with such success that it was later famously dubbed "the finest drawing room in Europe" by Napoleon. Like many visitors to Venice, he then proceeded to repaint it in his own image, even rearranging the furniture and literally moving the walls. However, given the city's talent for fusing influences into a beguiling Venetian whole, the square has retained its essential character.

In spite of high prices, contemporary visitors to Venice should not spurn San Marco's opulent cafés. With their stagey string quartets and pretentious airs, they are part of the performance art that is Venice. Each café has its charms: **Caffè Quadri** basks in the morning sun and an 18th-century ambience, while **Caffè Florian**, its more celebrated rival, lies in the shade until noon; Lavena simply serves the best coffee without the *beau monde* atmosphere. Even out of season, these historic haunts captivate. Here one can sip hot chocolate in a café adorned with elegant stucco-work, red damask walls, Murano chandeliers and gilded mirrors.

Basilica di San Marco (St Mark's Basilica) ❷ (open Mon–Sat; Sun 1.30–5pm) is the centrepiece of the square. San Marco, modelled on Byzantine churches in Constantinople, transposes the essence of an eastern basilica to the

SAVING VENICE

Floods have become a way of life in Venice, and the city faces a soggy future. As global warming continues and sea levels rise, Venice has been subjected to increasing flooding. Its position at the head of the lagoon also makes the city vulnerable to storm surges. Until recently the most posited solution to the problem was the installation of flood gates which would span the three entrances to the lagoon and be closed whenever high waters threatened.

But the scheme faltered on environmental grounds. In 1999 the government decided that it risked undermining the lagoon's fragile ecosystem: by being shut off from the sea too many times a year, the lagoon would be turned into a quagmire. Instead, experts favoured raising the ground level of the city and cleaning waters polluted by industrial waste and maritime traffic. However, supporters of the dam have not given up. As the head of a European Union research body declared: "Do you prevent the lagoon from turning into a lake or do you save Venice and its historic heritage? Personally, I would save Venice."

However, the mayor of Venice believes that the international community does not, subconsciously, wish to save Venice: "From Byron to Mann to Woody Allen, they have all hankered after Atlantis."

Map
on pages
140–141

West. Indeed, to critic Mary McCarthy it was "an Oriental pavilion, half pleasure house, half war tent, belonging to some great satrap". Charles Dickens was spellbound: "Opium couldn't build such a place… dim with the smoke of incense; costly in treasure of precious stones and metals; glittering through iron bars; holy with the bodies of deceased saints." The Basilica was consecrated in 832, intended as a mausoleum for St Mark's relics and as the Doge's ceremonial chapel. In 976 the church burnt down after a riot but was rebuilt between 1063 and 1094, probably supervised by a Greek architect. Since Venice still recognised the cultural supremacy of Byzantium, the Basilica echoed eastern models. At the same time Doge Selvo (1071–84) asked merchants to return with rare marbles and semi-precious stones to adorn the Basilica.

The Greek cross plan is inscribed in a square, and crowned by a cluster of five cupolas, one over each arm of the cross and its centre. These are linked to one another by loggias and arcades. The bewildering contrast is between the Oriental domes and rounded Byzantine arches and the Gothic ornamentation of the central roofline. Most of the garish mosaics on the façade are 17th-century copies, with the only intact 13th-century one depicting the arrival of St Mark's relics in the Basilica (set above the doorway on the far left). The exterior brickwork of the central apse is reminiscent of Santa Fosca in Torcello. The Baptistry doors are framed by the **Pilasters of Acre**, two ancient Syrian pillars plundered from Acre in the Holy Land after a victory over the Genoese in 1258. These sculpted 6th-century marble columns stand beside a porphyry stump known as the *pietra del bando*, where the laws of the Republic were proclaimed. In the corner are the **Tetrarchs** or Moors, a 4th-century Egyptian work representing Diocletian and his fellow rulers who governed the Roman Empire.

Carved detail, St Mark's central door.

BELOW: view from the Campanile.

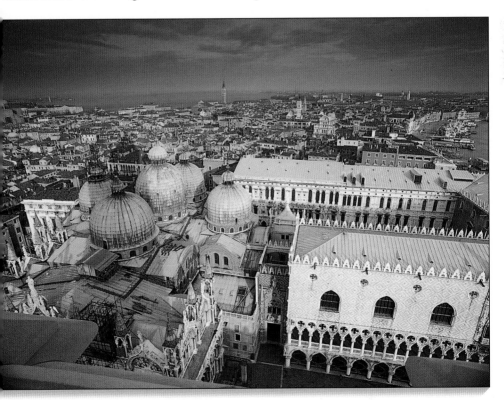

After the conquest of Constantinople in 1204, Venice celebrated with lavish cycles of mosaics and the display of looted treasures. The classical **horses** were Byzantine booty and once stood on top of a triumphal arch in Rome before gracing the hippodrome in Constantinople and adorning the façade of San Marco; because they symbolised the Venetian Republic's untrammelled independence, Napoleon had them harnessed to a chariot in Paris for 18 years. Now returned, the original horses are on display in the **Museo Marciano** inside, with copies on the façade.

Other plundered treasures include the **Madonna Nicopeia**, a sacred 10th century icon adorning the Altar of the Virgin. Officially, St Mark's remains are encased in a sarcophagus under the altar, but sceptics believe that they were destroyed in the fire of 976. Behind the altar, often swamped by crowds, is the **Pala d'Oro**, a superb Byzantine altarpiece studded with gems. The **Treasury** incorporates a 9th-century corner tower from the first Doge's Palace and displays Byzantine gold, silver and glassware.

The interior is studded with **mosaics**, one of the chief glories of San Marco. They date from 1071, and were first created by craftsmen from Constantinople; while the majority are from the 11th century to the 14th, more continued to be added until the 18th century. The result is a an illustrated Bible using 4,000 square metres (43,000 sq. ft) of mosaic. Even the windows of this extravaganza were walled up to make more space for mosaics. As a rule of thumb, the lower walls depict saints, with the middle section featuring the Apostles, and the domes dedicated to Christ Pantocrator, the Ruler. The Basilica pavement is an Oriental carpet interweaving floral, animal and geometric motifs. The mosaics of marble, porphyry and glass depict allegorical and naturalistic scenes.

BELOW:
the distinctive stonework of the Palazzo Ducale.

A striking feature of the square is the **Campanile ❸** (open daily), a replica of the original tower that collapsed in 1902. From the top there is a superb view across the city and lagoon to the Dolomites, even if the canals themselves are not visible. In the past, foreigners were only permitted to climb the tower at high tide to prevent them from espying secret navigational channels. The belltower was at the centre of controversy in 1997 when it was briefly captured by a Separatist group before being rescued by Venetian commandos.

The piazza's other tower is the Renaissance **Torre dell'Orologio ❹** (1496), which boasts a gilt and blue enamel clockface featuring the signs of the zodiac and the phases of the moon. Naturally, it also tells the time, with two bronze Moors striking the bell on the hour.

Behind the Clocktower, keen shoppers can plunge into the **Mercerie ❺**, the shadowy maze of alleys running between the Rialto and San Marco. Named after the haberdashers' shops that once lined the route, this engaging bazaar specialises in marbled paper, Murano glass and carnival masks.

Map on pages 140–141

The clockface on the Torre dell'Orologio.

The Doge's Palace

Palazzo Ducale (the Doge's Palace) ❻ (open daily) was the seat of the Venetian government from the 9th century until the fall of the Republic in 1797. Yet while rival mainland cities were building grim fortresses, the Venetians indulged in a light and airy structure, confident of the natural protection afforded by the lagoon. Apart from being the Doge's official residence it acted as the nerve centre of the Republic, containing offices and armouries, council chambers and chancellery, courtrooms and dungeons. The Palace was a symbol of political stability and independence as well as a testament to Venetian supremacy and a

BELOW: the Palazzo Ducale is a magnificent showcase of Venetian art and craftmanship.

* *The secret itinerary*
(itinerari segreti)
offered at the Doge's
Palace explores the
"shadow palace",
with its secret
passageways, state
inquisitors' room,
torture chamber and
prisons.

glorious showcase of Venetian art, sculpture and craftsmanship. Yet there was also a shadow palace, a secretive machine with state inquisitors, spies and torturers in residence.

Architecturally the palace is a Venetian hybrid, a harmonious fusion of Moorish, Gothic and Renaissance. Although often considered the symbol of Gothic Venice, the palace's distinctive façades were inspired by the Veneto-Byzantine succession of porticoes and loggias. However, the Gothic inversion of spaces and solids reached perfection in the floriated style of the southern corner, with a mass of masonry seemingly floating on air. The palace has two of the finest Gothic façades in existence, visions of rosy Verona marble supported by delicate Istrian stone arcades.

The **interior** is magnificent, but visitors are usually channelled along specific routes. Many of the carved capitals on the portico were replaced by 19th-century copies, but the restored originals can now be seen in the **Museo dell'-Opera** beside the entrance hall, set in the former prisons. The rooms reveal the inner workings of the Serene Republic, from the voting procedures to the courts of law. The Scala d'Oro, designed by Sansovino in 1555, was a ceremonial staircase intended to overawe ambassadors.

Museo Correr ❼ (open daily), the museum of Venetian civilisation, is housed in the Procuratie Nuove, with the entrance in the Napoleonic Wing. The Neoclassical rooms make a fitting setting for Canova's sculptures. The first section is a romp through Venetian history, from Doges' caps to the fall of the Republic. Those without a taste for coins and battle memorabilia can proceed to the charming gallery, which focuses on 13th–16th-century Venetian art. Nearby, the Marciana Library, **Libreria Sansoviniana ❽** (open daily by appointment only, tel: 041-5208788), is a cool classical building set in an extended loggia. Designed by Sansovino in 1537, this long, low building houses the precious collection of manuscripts bequeathed by Petrarch in the 14th century. The superb salon of the original library is covered with paintings by Veronese and Tintoretto. Just west, on Calle Vallaresso, is **Harry's Bar ❾**, the world-famous watering hole where the Bellini cocktail was invented.

By boat, the island of **San Giorgio Maggiore ❿** lies just a few minutes away. Seen from afar, the majestic Benedictine monastery appears suspended in the inner lagoon. Today the monks remain the sole island residents, enhancing the mood of spiritual seclusion. **San Giorgio** (open daily, 10am–noon, 2.30–5pm) is the finest monastic church in the lagoon. Here Palladio showed his mastery of the Classical idiom, using the basic geometric volumes of cube, pyramid and sphere. Based on Alberti's precepts, this is a Christian church founded on Classical principles and mathematical proportions. The façade is composed of two overlapping temple fronts, with a central portico. A lift whisks visitors to the top of the **belltower**, modelled on St Mark's, for fabulous views.

From the ashes

A few minutes from San Marco is **La Fenice ⓫**, the ravaged site of the legendary opera house. Although

BELOW: Bocca di Leone, Palazzo Ducale.

DE NONTIE SECRET
NTRO CHI OCCVLTE
GRATIE ET OFFICII
Ō COLLVDERĀ PER
NASCONDER LA VER
RENDITA D ESSI

destroyed by fire in 1996, "the Phoenix" was expected to rise from the ashes by the year 2000. In typical Italian fashion, a dispute between rival building firms has taken on a political dimension and frozen the project. Still, this remains an appealing district, with atmospheric restaurants tucked around the encircling canals.

Palazzo Contarini del Bovolo (open daily, 10am–6pm), concealed in a maze of alleys off Campo Manin, is a late Gothic palace celebrated for its arcaded staircase. *Bovolo*, meaning snail shell in Venetian dialect, describes the delightful spiral staircase which is linked to loggias of brick and smooth white stone. Nearby is **Campo Santo Stefano** ⓭, a long, theatrical space lined with palaces and cafés. The Augustinian monastic church of **Santo Stefano** has a Gothic main portal and an entrancing ship's keel ceiling; a canal flows under the church, which gondolas can pass along if the tide is low.

Castello

If St Mark's Square is "the drawing-room of Europe", in Napoleon's celebrated phrase, then **Riva degli Schiavoni** is its sumptuous bedroom. The waterfront is awash with cultural links, reminders of famous past residents, from Wagner and Tchaikovsky to Dickens. But sailors, shipwrights and merchants also came here, from Dalmatia, Eastern Europe, Greece and Egypt, attracted by the prospect of work at the Arsenal shipyards and quaysides. The cosmopolitan legacy lingers on in sizeable Greek and Slav communities as well as a small Armenian quarter. The sights are scattered, with much space occupied by the Arsenal, whose looming walls and towers are visible from afar.

Ponte dei Sospiri ⓮, the most famous bridge in Venice, crosses the canal to the "new" prisons. Built between 1595 and 1600, the Bridge of Sighs provided

Map on pages 140–141

The famous Ponte dei Sospiri (the Bridge of Sighs).

BELOW: San Giorgio Maggiore.

Part of the city's impeccable front.

BELOW: gondolas on the Canale Grande.

a link between the Doge's Palace and the courtrooms and cells, allowing interrogators to slip back and forth. This covered stone bridge acquired its legendary name after the lamentation of prisoners as they confronted their inquisitors.

The bridge marks the beginning of **Riva degli Schiavoni** ⓫, the best-known stretch of Venetian waterfront. Now bustling with tourists and souvenir sellers, this quayside once thronged with slave-dealers and merchants. (Its name refers to either slaves or Slavs, who were often synonymous in Venetian minds.) The quayside was widened and paved in 1782 and has been a popular Venetian promenade ever since. Over the bridge stands a horseback monument to **Vittorio Emanuele** (Victor Emmanuel), the first king of a united Italy.

San Zaccaria ⓰, set on the Campo of the same name, is a Renaissance masterpiece graced by Coducci's curvilinear facade and a Gothic belltower. The church was founded in the 9th century and acted as a Venetian pantheon, with eight early Doges buried in the crypt. The original Byzantine basilica forms the crypt below San Tarasio chapel, an atmospheric spot usually lying under water. The chapel itself is decorated with Gothic frescoes and several lovely 15th-century altarpieces. In the north aisle of the main Gothic church is a glowing altarpiece by Bellini.

A stroll along bustling Riva degli Schiavoni leads past waterfront cafes to **La Pietà** ⓱, Vivaldi's (1678–1741) musical base in Venice. The church was superbly remodelled by Massari in the 18th century and transformed into the city's leading concert hall. The cool oval interior was designed with acoustics in mind, aided by curving lines, low vaulted ceilings and the filigree-like choir galleries. The church is a feast for the senses, with Tiepolo's celebrated frescoes best seen during a concert of baroque music.

Tucked into Calle dei Furlani, **San Giorgio degli Schiavoni** ⓲ (open Tues–Sun, 9.30am–12.30pm, 3.30–6.30pm) is the loveliest confraternity seat in Venice. Dating back to the Middle Ages, these *scuole* were charitable lay associations close to the heart of Venetian life. This one was intended to protect the interests of Slavs from Dalmatia (Schiavonia), the first Venetian colony. On its completion in 1501 the confraternity commissioned Carpaccio to create a painting cycle in honour of the Dalmatian patron saints. The *scuola* boasts the only Venetian pictorial cycle to have survived in its original site. This cycle is characterised by dramatic storytelling. In particular, the St George paintings are bold chivalric scenes, depicting a veritable knight in shining armour and a dying dragon in a place of desolation, with the ground littered with skulls, vipers and vultures.

Further east along Riva degli Schiavoni is the vast expanse of the **Arsenale** ⓳. The best way to see it begins with a walk or boat ride to **Campo della Tana**, the landing stage for the 52 or 23 boats that run through the naval complex. Founded in 1104, the Arsenal was the symbol of Venetian maritime might. This secretive military and naval complex became the largest medieval shipyard in Europe and a powerhouse of industrial planning. It was also an armaments site. The earliest part is the **Darsena Vecchio**, sandwiched between St Mark's Basin and the lagoon.

The complex remained in continuous use until 1917, when the dockyards were dismantled lest they fall into enemy hands. Since then the Italian navy has been ensconced, with the dockyards used as a storage and repair site.

On the waterfront stands the **Museo Navale** ⑳ (open Mon, Wed, Fri–Sun 8.45am–1.30pm, Tues and Thur 2.30–5pm). Apart from naval maps, nautical instruments and weaponry, the intriguing collection displays models of Egyptian and Phoenician craft and Greek triremes. The Venetian focus is naturally on gondolas and galleys, but includes a replica of the last Bucintoro, the legendary state barge. Nearby, the **Giardini Pubblici** are the permanent location of the **Biennale** ㉑, a glamorous summer forum for contemporary art. The Biennale has been held in these Napoleonic gardens in odd-numbered years since 1895. Described as Disneyland for adults, the event is garish, sprawling and pretentious but also chic and challenging. The gardens are home to about 40 permanent pavilions.

San Francesco della Vigna ㉒ (open daily 8am–noon, 3.30–7pm) is set in an isolated, somewhat shabby area. Goethe even required a compass to reach this remote spot. However, this Franciscan church represents an architectural milestone: both Sansovino's first creation in Venice and the first flowering of the High Renaissance in Venice. The façade and crowning pediment were designed by Palladio, and the tall belltower is a familiar city landmark.

SS Giovanni e Paolo ㉓, known as **San Zanipolo**, is set on the square of the same name. Guarding the great Gothic church is the finest equestrian statue in northern Italy. This restless horse and rider commemorate Bartolomeo Colleoni (1400–76), a celebrated *condottiere*. The church is dedicated to Saints John and Paul, and its sheer scale invites comparisons with the Frari, its fellow giant.

Map on pages 140–141

The waterfront is the location of Venice's finest hotels, like the Danieli. Even Proust was enchanted by his room here: "When I went to Venice I found that my dream had become my address." The hotel's terrace is still a superb place to toast the end of a war or the beginning of a romance.

BELOW: Venice's historic Hotel Danieli.

San Zanipolo, too, is an austere church, founded in the late 13th century but only consecrated in 1430. Its Gothic pinnacles can be seen from both banks of the Grand Canal, with the roofline displaying statues of the Dominican saints. The church is the Pantheon of Venice, honouring illustrious leaders from admirals and noblemen to the odd artist. Above all, this was the last resting place of the Doges, with magnificent monuments to 25 of them, including the sculpted Renaissance tomb of Doge Giovanni Mocenigo.

Campo Santa Maria Formosa ❷ is a lovely asymmetrical space dotted with flower, fruit and junk stalls. Set in the heart of Castello, it is the archetypal Venetian square. The *campo* rests on its laurels, sure of each Venetian element: the shadowy alleys running into a sunlit space; a striking Renaissance church; palaces from three different periods; a covered well-head surrounded by pigeons; everyday cafés filled with stallholders; even a gondola station *(stazio)*. The Renaissance parish church of **Santa Maria Formosa** is an endearing sight, with its bulging apse and Baroque belltower.

Grand Canal (Canale Grande)

The Grand Canal was considered the register of the Venetian nobility, with the palaces symbolising patricians' status and success. Once a waterway for merchant vessels, the canal now welcomes simpler craft, from gondolas to garbage barges. The palaces remain as a testament to the city's imperial past, but the sea is a great leveller, with low tide revealing the slimy underpinnings of the noblest *palazzo*. The palaces represent a subtle fusion of styles: a Gothic design may be graced with round Renaissance arches and pilasters, while a sweep of Oriental tracery echoes the Byzantine tradition.

Known affectionately as the *Canalazzo*, the Grand Canal makes an appealing evening diversion. After most tourists have returned to the mainland is the ideal time for a leisurely look. Pick up a No 1 *vaporetto* and slip into one of the coveted seats on the prow. The palaces present a seductive face: the illuminated windows, revealing gleaming Murano glass chandeliers, red silk-clad walls and the odd summer party spilling onto the balconies are an invitation to dream.

Day or night, **Punta della Dogana** ❷ is the start of a popular Venetian walk around the point. **Dogana di Mare**, the sea customs post, occupies the triangular tip where ships and cargoes were inspected before being allowed to drop anchor in front of the Doge's Palace. Still used as a customs house, this is the only Republican civic building to have maintained its original function. Guarding the entrance to the Grand Canal is the Baroque basilica of **La Salute** ❷ (open daily 8.30–noon, 3–6pm). Officially dedicated to the Madonna, the church was begun in 1631 as a thanksgiving for delivery from the Plague. Longhena, the architect, wished it to be "strange, worthy and beautiful" and succeeded magnificently. La Salute marks the end of Venetian Mannerism and heralds an era of bold Baroque statements. Devised before Rome's Bernini and Borromini masterpieces, it became one of the few Italian churches to challenge the supremacy of Roman Baroque. The clinical interior

… "like some great lady on the threshold of her salon … with her domes and scrolls, her scalloped buttresses and statues forming a pompous crown, and her wide steps disposed on the ground like the train of a robe."

– HENRY JAMES
(Description of La Salute)

BELOW: the magnificent interior of the palace of Ca' Rezzonico.

boasts a spectacular central plan, with its revolutionary octagonal space surmounted by a huge dome.

Another waterside landmark is the gently listing **Ca' Dario** ㉗, one of the most delightful palaces on the canal. Henry James adored the façade for its intricate pattern of roundels and plaques of precious marble and porphyry. Known as a *cielo-terra*, a self-contained structure, it is only accessible by water or through a door in the walled garden. However, five centuries of scandals, suicides and suspicious deaths have left Venetians wary of this unfortunate palace. Next door, **Palazzo Venier (Guggenheim)** ㉘ is a white, truncated structure also known as "*Nonfinito*" (unfinished). Legend has it that the owners of Ca' Grande opposite forbade further building as it would block their view.

The building now houses the **Guggenheim Foundation** (open Wed–Mon, 11am–6pm), named after the American modern art collector Peggy Guggenheim (1898–1979). On show is work by such names as Chagall, Dali, Klee, Braque, Giacometti, Kandinsky, Bacon and Sutherland. Most major movements are represented, from Picasso's Cubist period to Severini's Futurism, from Mondrian's Abstract works to Surrealist masterpieces by de Chirico, Delvaux and Magritte. The gardens are filled with sculptures, including works by Henry Moore and Marino Marini.

Virtually opposite is the **Palazzo Pisani Gritti** ㉙, a legendary Venetian hotel. The Gritti terrace offers a grandstand view of the Grand Canal, lying diagonally opposite the church of La Salute. This is one of the most sumptuous hotels in Venice, linked to writers as diverse as Hemingway and Graham Greene.

The **Accademia** ㉚ is a popular meeting-place for Venetians. The distinctive wooden bridge, built in 1932 and restored in the 1980s, replaced a cast-iron

Map on pages 140–141

To ponder on the ghosts of Venice, choose from the sophisticated stage sets at the glitziest hotels: the Gritti Palace, overlooking the Grand Canal, was one of Hemingway's haunts; or the Art Deco Hotel des Bains, where Visconti shot Death in Venice.

BELOW: the famous Grand Canal (Canale Grande).

An example of Venetian Gothic – Villa Barbaro, where Henry James stayed.

BELOW: the quayside near the Ponte di Rialto is home to numerous cafés and restaurants.

bridge dating from the time of the Austrian occupation. Beside it is the Accademia boat stop, with the world's greatest collection of Venetian paintings in the **Galleria dell'Accademia** ➌ (open Mon–Sat; 9am–7pm, Sun 9am–2pm). Not surprisingly, this is the city's most popular gallery. The collection is housed in La Carità, a complex of church, convent, cloisters and charitable confraternity. Since the gallery is lit by natural light, it is best to choose a bright day. The early rooms display Byzantine and Gothic works noted for their symmetry and static decorative style on a gold background. The gallery's masterpieces include Renaissance and Mannerist works by Carpaccio, Bellini, Giorgione, Titian, Tintoretto and Veronese, and 17th and 18th-century works by Tiepolo, Guardi and Canaletto.

Ca' Rezzonico ➋ lies on the left bank, by the boat stop of the same name. Designed according to Longhena's plans, this ponderous palace was where the poet Robert Browning (1812–89) died. Inside, the **Museum of 18th-Century Life** (open Sat–Thur, 10am–5pm) is an opulent showcase for Tiepolo's *trompe l'oeil* ceilings and Guardi's 18th-century genre paintings. The interior is magnificent boldly restored, daringly frescoed and richly embellished with glittering chandeliers and period pieces.

Ponte di Rialto ➌, which traditionally divides the city into two, was the only bridge across the Grand Canal until 1854. The single-span bridge, created in 1588–91 by Antonio da Ponte, is lined with shops selling shoes, silk scarves and jewellery. The quaysides where iron, coal and barrels of wine used to be unloaded are now overrun by restaurants and souvenir stalls. From the bridge one can admire the majestic sweep of palaces and merchants warehouses swinging away to the great bend in the canal.

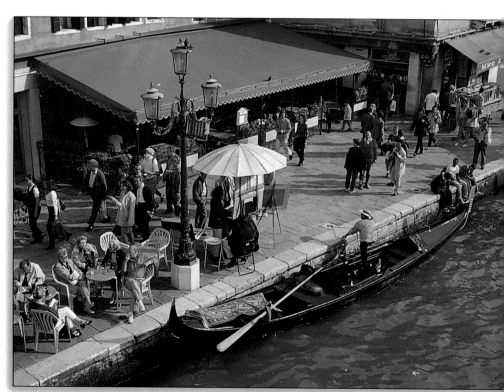

Beyond is the **Ca' d'Oro** ❸❹ (open daily, 9am–2pm), one of the loveliest Gothic palaces, set beside the landing stage of the same name. The Veneto-Byzantine influence is clear in the design, from the Oriental pinnacles to the ethereal tracery. On the sumptuous façade the friezes of foliage and mythological beasts were originally picked out in gold, giving to its popular name "the golden house". Inside, the artistic highlights include a delightful *Annunciation* by Carpaccio, Titian's *Venus*, and Andrea Mantegna's poignant *St Sebastian*.

 Palazzo Vendramin-Calergi ❸❺, set on the same bank of the canal, was inhabited by aristocrats, Doges and even Wagner before becoming the city casino. Although built before 1500 by Coducci, the palace was inspired by Classical principles and built in a familiar three-part design. The casino has coffered ceilings, chandeliers and marble fireplaces, as well as jasper columns looted from Ephesus in Turkey. Opposite is the **Fondaco dei Turchi** ❸❻, a former trading base for Turkish merchants. It was built in 1227 for the noble Pesaro family but in 1621 was leased to the Ottomans, who created bedrooms, shops and servants-quarters. In keeping with Muslim custom, doors and windows were sealed off, and the building contained a mosque and Turkish baths.

Dorsoduro

Dorsoduro is the most charming quarter for idle wandering, with wisteria-clad walls, secret gardens and distinctive domestic architecture. Its name simply means "hard back" since the district occupies the largest area of firm land in Venice. This is the chicest *sestiere*, with the grandest section defined by the Punta della Dogana, the Gesuati and the Accademia.

 The **Zattere** ❸❼ stretches all the way round Dorsoduro's southern shore, with

Map on pages 140–141

TIP

To chance your luck in the casino in Palazzo Vendramin-Calergi, get off at the San Marcuola stop.

BELOW: the Ca d'Oro.

Carnival masks – the perfect souvenir of the theatricality of Venice.

BELOW: the Palladian splendour of the church of Il Redentore, on the island of Giudecca.

its quaysides flanked by cafés and churches, boathouses and warehouses. This promenade was created in 1516 and named after the cargoes of wood that were unloaded here (*zattere* are floating rafts). Its southern spur makes the most beguiling Venetian promenade, bracing in winter and refreshing in summer.

Further along the Zattere stands the grandiose church of the **Gesuati** ❸ (open daily, 8am–noon, 3–7pm), a supreme example of 18th-century Venetian architecture. The façade, with its lofty Corinthian columns and Palladian motifs, was designed by Massari, an early Rococo architect. The theatrical interior boasts illusionistic Tiepolo frescoes (1739), visible in their original setting.

The **Zattere boarding stage** lies on this stretch of quays, with ferries to San Marco and the Giudecca. Set on the island of Giudecca, **Il Redentore** ❸ (open daily 8am–noon, 3–7pm) is a Venetian landmark. The Church of the Redeemer was built in thanksgiving for the end of the 1576 Plague. Architectural purists feel that this Palladian masterpiece, inspired by the Pantheon in Rome, surpasses San Giorgio. Certainly, the façade is more subtle, resting on a rusticated pediment, with a sweeping flight of steps. From here, the eye is led to the lantern surmounted by the figure of Christ the Redeemer.

From the Zattere it is a charming stroll to **San Trovaso** ❹ (open daily, 8–11am and 3–5pm), set on the canal of the same name. Originally medieval, the church was remodelled at the end of the 16th century in Palladian style. Opposite the church is Cantine del Vino, an engaging canalside wine bar. The **Squero di San Trovaso**, a picturesque gondola repair yard, is best viewed from further down the canal.

Following the Zattere westwards leads to **San Sebastiano** ❹ (open Mon–Sat, 3.30–5.30pm), an early 16th-century church which is a Classical canvas for Veronese's opulent masterpieces, painted between 1555 and 1565. The church is praised as a perfect marriage of the arts, with architecture, painting and sculpture in complete accord. Veronese's *trompe l'oeil* interior is an architectural flight of fancy created by frescoed loggias, columns and statues.

San Nicolò dei Mendicoli ❹ (open daily, Mon–Sat 10am–noon, 4–6pm) is the most remote waterside church in Dorsoduro. Set in a dilapidated district, this former fishermen's and artisans' church is surprisingly sumptuous. It is one of the oldest in Venice, founded in the 7th century but remodelled between the 12th and 14th centuries. The interior is one of the best-loved, with a single nave ending in a Romanesque apse and embellished with Renaissance panelling and gilded statues.

I Carmini ❹ (open Mon–Sat, 9am–12.30pm, 3.30–6pm) is the headquarters of the Carmelite Scuola Grande. Longhena's uninspired façade conceals a frescoed 18th-century interior. The Carmelites prospered during the Counter-Reformation, with the cult of Mary acting as a counterweight to Protestantism, and could afford to summon the services of the greatest Rococo painter. Tiepolo repaid their confidence with a series of sensuous masterpieces, a floating world of pale skies and illusionistic effects. Just beyond lies **Campo Santa Maria Margherita** ❹, the liveliest square in the district. One side of the square is bordered by palaces with overhanging roofs, a style rare in Venice both because of the fear of fire and through a desire to let light into dark alleys.

Map on pages 140–141

San Polo and Santa Croce

Centred on the bustling Rialto market, these adjoining districts *(sestieri)* are curved into the left bank of the Grand Canal. The hub of the left bank is the Rialto, "the marketplace of the morning and evening lands". Goethe's poetic description is fleshed out by writer Jan Morris, who loved the Rialto's "smell of mud, incense, fish, age, filth and velvet". The labyrinthine Rialto also contains several of the grandest churches and paintings in Venice. It is also the ideal place to indulge in a Venetian bar crawl, a *giro di ombre (see panel below)*.

The **Rialto** is often described as "Venice's kitchen, office and back parlour". For Venetians it is not restricted to the graceful bridge but embraces the district curved around the middle bend of the Grand Canal. Its name (derived from *rivo alto*, high bank) refers to the first settlement of central Venice, which became and became the capital from 814. It was the powerhouse of the Venetian empire, a crossroads between East and West, home to a mix of races and a babble of tongues. In this exotic marketplace, cargoes of spices and silks from the Levant were sold along with Slav slaves. Here northern Italian grain dealers and Flemish wool merchants rubbed shoulders with Jewish money lenders, Arab spice traders and German metal traders, as well as with Florentine and Lombard cloth merchants.

Threading the labyrinthine alleys of the Rialto is an intoxicating experience. It remains a hive of commercial activity, with everything on sale between here and the Mercerie. The markets extend along the bank to the **Pescheria ⓯**, the

At the Pescheria (fish market).

BELOW: you'll find numerous *osteria* and *bàcari* in Venice, serving delicious snacks.

BÀCARI: TRADITIONAL BARS

Venice abounds in historic cafés and glitzy hotel bars, sophisticated stage sets for posing. However, beyond Harry's Bar and Florian's a humbler, cosier world awaits. Venetian wine bars, known as *bàcari*, are the places to indulge in the bitter cough mixture that passes for *amaro*, the classic Italian aperitif. More Venetian is a *spriz*, made with white wine, *amaro* and soda water. Nor is a beer out of the question, whether a *birin*, a tiny glass, or the slightly bigger *birèta*.

A *giro di ombra*, as they say in dialect, is a serious "wine crawl", with each tasting accompanied by a Venetian version of *tapas*. Delicacies include *crostini* covered with cheese, salmon or *baccalà* (dried salted cod). More substantial nibbles are *sorprèssa*, a dark-red creamy, black pudding; home-cured salami; and *sarde in saòr*, sardines in a marinade of onions and pine nuts.

Typical *bàcari* are clustered in the Rialto market district. If early, try the rumbustious Do Mori (9am–1pm, 5–8pm) on Calle de Do Mori, just off Ruga Vecchia di San Giovanni. At the end of the alley is Do Spade (9am–2pm, 5–11pm, Sottoportego delle Do Spade), marginally more genteel. Easier to find is the rustic Antico Dolo (10am–3pm, 6.30–10pm, Ruga Vecchia di San Giovanni 778).

The celebrated cookery writer Elizabeth David was entranced by "the light of a Venetian dawn so limpid and so still that it makes every separate vegetable and fruit and fish luminous with a life of its own".

BELOW: the Erberia fruit and vegetable market.

fish market, set in an arcaded Neo-Gothic hall by the quayside. Brightly-painted boats from the lagoon supply the main markets with fish and fresh vegetables. The adjoining **Campo delle Beccarie**, once a public abattoir, contains market overspill and a lively bar. The **Erberia** is the canalside fruit and vegetable market. Foodies find sensuous pleasure in the profusion of succulent salads, asparagus, baby artichokes, bunches of red peppers and peachy *borlotti* beans.

The greatest Gothic church on the left bank is the **Frari ④**, officially known as **Santa Maria Gloriosa dei Frari** (open Mon–Fri 9am–noon, 2.30–6pm; Sat, Sun 3-6pm). This Franciscan complex was founded in the 13th century but rebuilt over the next 200 years. The adjoining monastic cloisters house the state archives and a thousand years of Venetian history. In keeping with Franciscan strictures, the bare brick is unadorned: poverty was the guiding principle of the mendicant orders. The barn-like interior is a stark framework for the artwork, a pantheon of Venetian glories. The choir chapels are lined with tombs of the Doges, including the monument to Doge Francesco Foscari, deposed in 1457. The nave is dominated by a Gothic choir screen and lovely choir stalls, the only such ensemble to survive in Venice. The high altar is the focal point of the Frari, a space illuminated by Titian's *Assumption*. The revolutionary nature of the painting led to its initial rejection by the friars; they relented, and the work made Titian's reputation. Henry James adored Bellini's altarpiece, a radiant *Madonna*: "It is as solemn as it is gorgeous as it is simple as it is deep."

Scuola Grande di San Rocco ④ (open daily 9am-5.30pm), dwarfed by the Frari, is Tintoretto's crowning glory. Mannerist paintings adorn every surface, the works full of *chiaroscuro* effects and plunging figures striking dramatic poses. The confraternity's mission was the relief of the sick, a noble aim that became conflated with the prestige of the *scuola*. The painter's bold Biblical scenes, executed between 1564 and 1587, provoke strong responses. Henry James found the air "thick with genius" yet palpably human: "It is not immortality that we breathe at San Rocco but conscious, reluctant mortality." In the evening, this splendid stage acts as a backdrop for baroque recitals.

Campo San Pantalon ④, a canalside square lined with crumbling palaces, is home to the astonishing church of **San Pantalon**. It follows common Venetian practice by which interiors are often finer than exteriors. The unfinished façade gives no indication of the splendours within. The Baroque ceiling paintings by Fumiani (1650–1710) depict the martyrdom and glory of St Pantalon in a *tour de force* of perspective which projects the nave high into the sky. The ascent into heaven is peopled by boldly foreshortened figures clambering, floating or flying. On completion of the ceiling, the artist supposedly stood back to admire his work before slipping off the scaffolding to his death.

For a burst of everyday Venetian life, head towards **Campo San Polo ④**. After San Marco it is the largest square, an amphitheatre once dedicated to bull-baiting, tournaments and processions. Today it makes do with carnival balls, film screenings, impromptu football matches, student gatherings and romantic assignations, an appropriate end for a square linked to the devilish exploits of Giovanni Casanova.

Cannaregio

Cannaregio is the most northerly district, designed for those who have tired of monumental San Marco. The name comes from *canne*, meaning reeds, indicating Cannaregio's marshy origins. As the district closest to the railway station and the mainland, Cannaregio is the most densely populated. Yet it is also an ancient quarter, the last bastion of working-class Venetians, often scorned by the snobbish in favour of the more stylish Dorsoduro. Walks in the melancholic backwaters at the edge of the city trace a landscape of peeling façades and humble workshops, broad canals and wind-buffeted quays.

Santa Maria dei Miracoli ⑤⓪ (open daily,10am–5.30pm) rises sheer from the water, marooned like a marble siren awaiting the call of the sea or the embrace of a foolish sailor. No wonder the church is a favourite with Venetian brides. Perfect proportions and seductive charm make this a Renaissance miracle in miniature. Its dazzling display of pastel marble presents a vision of pale pinks and silvery greys, of pilasters adorned with interlaced flowers, mythical creatures and cavorting mermaids. Visitors are dazzled by the cumulative effect of this bridal church, with its inlaid marble, bas-reliefs and statues.

The Gesuiti ⑤① (open daily 8am–noon, 5–7pm*)* is often confused with the Gesuati, the other major Jesuit foundation, in Dorsoduro district. The Jesuits were never popular in Venice, a city which put patriotism before the Papacy and declared: "Venetians first and Christians second." After their banishment was revoked, the Jesuits returned to Venice and in 1715 started to rebuild on the site of a medieval church. The Gesuiti is still run by the Order and is the seat of the American Jesuit University. Set into a line of severe houses, the baroque, angel-bedecked façade reveals an exuberant interior, graced by Titian's *Martyrdom of St Lawrence* and Tintoretto's *Assumption.*

Fondamente Nuove ⑤②, the windswept "new quays" bordering the northern lagoon, was actually created in the 1580s. Before that, this now desolate stretch was a desirable residential district, with summer palaces and gardens lapped by the lagoon waters. Fondamente Nuove is the main boarding stage for the islands, with services to San Marco in the other direction. Although the quays seem inhospitable, especially in winter, the stirring lagoon views, encompassing the cemetery island of San Michele, count for much. These quaysides are the best departure point for visits to the outlying islands of **Torcello, Murano and Burano**. Torcello, the most remote, was the first settlement, and contains magnificent Byzantine mosaics in the basilica. Burano is a lively, painted fishing village, while Murano has been the centre of the Venetian glass industry since medieval times.

Madonna dell'Orto ⑤③, set on a harmonious square of herringbone design, is a shrine to Tintoretto (*see* "Venetian Artists"). Tintoretto apart, the church is a treasury of Venetian painting from the 15th century to the 17th. The quirky *campanile* is topped by an onion-shaped cupola, the first belltower to greet visitors as they speed across the lagoon from the airport. Often bathed in a warm light, the church is a masterpiece of Venetian Gothic. The austere, brick-faced interior also makes a good starting point for exploring

Map on pages 140–141

"From alley to alley we had got deep into Cannaregio, into a Venice quite different from the pretty city of water colours."

– THÉOPHILE GAUTIER

BELOW: your gondola awaits…

Map
on pages
140–141

A bronze relief in the Ghetto Nuovo recalls the deportations and deaths of 200 Venetian Jews in World War II.

BELOW: an artisan opens up shop.
RIGHT: a canalside walkway in Cannaregio.

Tintoretto's temperamental genius; the painter lived nearby and this, his parish church, is decorated with works he created *in situ*. His humble background gave him sympathy for the lives of the poor, a theme which, combined with religious fervour, distinguishes him from many of his contemporaries. A memorial bust of the artist watches over his grave in a side chapel.

Before crossing the bridge over Fondamenta Madonna dell'Orto to **Campo dei Mori** ㉞, stand on the quayside and glance across at the Gothic Palazzo Mastelli opposite. To the right of the filigree balcony is a relief of a laden camel, lending the palace an eastern flavour. The owners were Levantine merchants whose origins are alluded to in the worn reliefs of turbaned Moors on the Campo dei Mori façade. On Rio della Sensa, beyond the *campo,* is **Tintoretto's house,** marked by a plaque and a bas-relief of the painter. This relatively humble abode was where the artist lived from 1574 until his death in 1594.

These faintly mournful waterways are flanked by Flemish-looking houses and neglected palaces, a contrast to the tall tenements of the **Ghetto** ㉟ *(see box opposite)* further west. In the 1890s the de Goncourt brothers were moved to describes these melancholy, slightly menacing canals as "a district in decay, like an antique sculpture eaten away by rain and sun".

Despite its name, **Campo del Ghetto Nuovo** is the heart of the world's oldest ghetto, a fortified island created in 1516. Three of Venice's five remaining synagogues are unobtrusively set around the square, as is the **Museo Ebraico,** a museum of Jewish history (Sat–Thur tours 10.30am–4.30pm except Friday). Beyond the spacious square and bridge lies the **Ghetto Vecchio,** an overspill ghetto created in 1541, with two more synagogues. Visitors may follow in Woody Allen's steps by lingering by the Jewish bakery or kosher restaurant.❑

The Jewish Ghetto

Jews were first mentioned in Venetian records in the 10th century, as passengers banned from travelling on Venetian ships. As an ambitious trading city, Venice feared competition from Levantine merchants. Persecution soon drove waves of refugees to Venice, but Venetian policy was ambivalent, wavering between toleration and persecution.

While Jewish doctors, traders and textile merchants were tolerated, pawnbrokers and money lenders were resented. Although hefty levies on money lending meant that Venice profited, Jews were treated as second-class citizens, forbidden to settle in Venice. As Shylock says in Shakespeare's The Merchant of Venice: "I will buy with you, sell with you, talk with you, walk with you... but I will not eat with you, drink with you, nor pray with you."

From the 14th century onwards there were attempts to restrict Jews to the mainland, resulting in the decree of 1423 forbidding them to own property. Jews were forced to wear distinguishing badges, yellow skull caps or red hats. When Mestre was destroyed in 1509, the Jews sought refuge in Venice until rampant prejudice led to the creation of the ghetto. In 1516 the expanding Jewish community was given its own closed living quarters, the ghetto, both as a reward for contributing funds for the defence of the city and as a means of future control. Since this new home was within sight of the former foundry or ghetto, the term came to mean a closed Jewish quarter.

The ghetto was damp and dark, and the living space was cramped because the local community multiplied in spite of persecution. In time the houses grew as high as the foundations permitted, an exception to normal Venetian building practice. The population density was three times greater than that the most crowded Christian suburbs. After the Ghetto Nuovo (1516) two newer settlements, the Ghetto Vecchio (1541) and the Ghetto Nuovissimo (1633), provided temporary relief from overcrowding.

RIGHT: buildings as tall as those found in the ghetto are unusual elsewhere in Venice.

The decline of Venice ultimately affected the Jews; in 1655 there were almost 5000 people in the ghetto, with numbers falling to 1500 a century later. The Jewish tax burden often led to bankruptcy or emigration. This long farewell ended in 1797 with the Napoleonic invasion; at last the ghetto gates were flung open: even Jews were entitled to liberty, equality and fraternity. This brief dream was soon dispelled by the restoration of Austrian rule. But times had indeed changed, and Jews were among the most passionate upholders of the revolutionary aims of 1848. Jews only became full citizens in 1866, when Venice became part of the Kingdom of Italy.

Today the local Jewish community numbers 600, with few choosing to live in the former ghetto. Nonetheless, the ghetto remains at the heart of Jewish life, with fine synagogues and a cultural centre; a nursery and an old people's home; even workshops selling liturgical objects and a kosher bakery offering unleavened bread. The Jews may live elsewhere but they break bread here.　❏

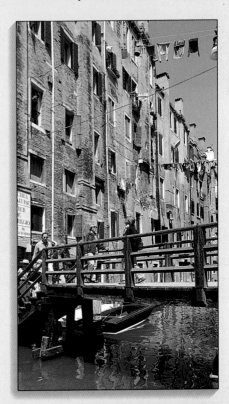

LIFE AS A MASQUERADE

Carnival in Venice is supreme self-indulgence,
a giddy round of masked balls and private parties
suggesting mystery and promising romance

Carnival in Venice is a 10-day pre-Lenten extravaganza, culminating in the burning of the effigy of Carnival in Piazza San Marco on Shrove Tuesday. As an expression of a topsy-turvy world, carnival is a time for rebellion without the risk of ridicule. The essence of the "feast of fools" lies in the unfolding Venetian vistas: masked processions heading towards Piazza San Marco past shimmering palaces, with surreal masqueraders tumbling out of every alley. As the revellers flock to Florian's café in Piazza San Marco, the air is sickly-sweet with the scent of fritters and the sound of lush Baroque music. Carnival capers include costumed balls, firework displays and historical parades, all staged by the carnival societies.

SPIRIT OF RESISTANCE

Carnival is often dismissed as commercialised and chaotic but Venetian traditionalists view it differently. The leader of a venerable carnival company sees the event as saving his city: "Life in Venice is inconvenient and costly. With the carnival, we give a positive picture and show the pleasure of living here. Carnival is a form of resistance. By resisting the temptation to leave, we are saving the spirit of the city for future generations."

△ SELECT CARDS
A select group of Venetians still appears as *tarocchi*, fortune-telling tarot cards. These famous cards supposedly reached Europe from the East, through Venice. The star of the pack is the Queen of Swords, her costume rich in silver cabalistic signs.

▽ WINDOW DRESSING
Masks originally allowed the nobility to mingle incognito with the common people in *casini* (private clubs), but are now an excuse for all-purpose revelry. This shop window displays fantasy masks, which are creative rather than authentic, and appeal to individual tastes.

▽ THE GREAT LEVELLER
A mask makes everyone equal. Masqueraders are addressed as *"sior maschera"* (masked gentleman) regardless of age, rank or even gender. One way of preserving some individuality is face-painting.

MASTERS OF DISGUISE

Mask-makers had their own guild in medieval times, when a *mascheraio* (mask-maker) helped a secretive society run smoothly. Modern masqueraders must choose between masks in leather *(cuoio)*, china *(ceramica)* or papier-mâché *(cartapesta)*. Papier-mâché and leather masks are the most authentic.

Antique masks are rare since neither material readily stands the test of time or the Venetian climate. Authentic mask-makers both reinterpret traditional designs and create new ones. In the case of papier-mâché masks, the pattern is made from a fired clay design, which generates a plaster-of-Paris mould. Layers of papier-mâché paste are used to line the mould and thus create the mask. When dry, the paste gives the mask a shiny surface akin to porcelain. Polish and a white base coat are applied before the eye holes are cut and decorative detail is added. This painting process can be simple or highly artistic.

Of the alternatives to papier-mâché, leather masks are hard to fashion; ceramic designs, ideal as hand-held masks or as wall decorations, are often adorned with fine fabrics. Places to browse include Laboratorio Artigiano Maschere (Barbaria delle Tole), founded by a family of puppet-makers, and the bohemian workshop of Ca' del Sol (Fondamenta dell'Osmarin).

△ THE NOBLE LOOK

Costumes can be historical, traditional or simply surreal. The classic Venetian disguise of the 17th and 18th centuries was known as the *maschera nobile*, the patrician mask. The carnival companies wear noble Renaissance and Rococo costumes *(left)* as a matter of course.

▽ VOLTO FACE

The patrician *maschera nobile* and witty *commedia dell'arte* masks are among a number of authentic disguises. While this cumbersome ruff is pure fantasy, the white mask looks to the past for inspiration: it is a modern variant on the slightly sinister *volto*, the traditional Venetian mask.

THE VENETO

Sandwiched between the seemingly dreary plain, the dramatic Dolomites and the exotic lakeside, the Veneto is very far from uniform

Maps:
Area 168
City 170

At first sight the *terra firma* towns pale into insignificance before Venice, the shimmering capital. As a centre of European art and architecture, Venice colours the local culture: graceful Venetian-style loggias adorn modest hilltop towns; the soft, sensuous Venetian atmosphere shines through the paintings of Giorgione and Titian. In the Veneto's civilised cities and landscaped countryside, trade with the famed Republic has left a legacy of impressive merchant palaces and Palladian villas. The presence of paintings and sculpted images of the Lion of St Mark also testifies to the Venetian influence. However, certain *terra firma* towns have resisted the cultural imperialism of Venice; Verona, Vicenza and Padua have had sharply separate identities since Roman times. Yet even the smaller centres possess clear personalities, whether castellated cities or hill spas, Adriatic resorts or chic ski stations.

The landscape is often dismissed as dull, marshy or nondescript, but the Veneto is a fertile plain bounded by the Adriatic coast and the Po to the south, and by Lake Garda to the west. Around Vicenza and Padua the plains and gently rolling hills are prime villa country, revealing world-famous Palladian villas. In economic terms, the Veneto is Lombardy's keenest competitor, and often outdoes its dominant neighbour, with a concentration of efficient companies in sectors as diverse as furniture and high-tech, clothes and wine. Only Venice (*see pages 143–60*) is an exception to the economic boom: with business costs 10 percent higher than on the mainland, the city simply relies on tourism.

PRECEDING PAGES: the rolling, wooded hills of Bassano. **LEFT:** café society in the Piazza Bra. **BELOW:** Romeo's beloved Juliet, immortalised in bronze.

Romantic Verona

As the largest city after Venice, **Verona ❶** is a place of great provincial charm. It also exudes the sophistication that comes of being a significant centre, long before the Venetian empire presumed to swallow it up. Verona has a rich Roman and Etruscan past but was dominated by feudal families until the Venetian Republic took control (1402–1797). From 1797 to 1859 it was ruled by Austria, and it was only 20 km (12 miles) from the frontier of the old Austro-Hungarian Empire until the end of World War I.

Verona could name-drop on a grand scale: as the birthplace of Catullus, the Latin lyric poet, and of Veronese, the great Venetian painter. As the setting for Shakespeare's *Romeo and Juliet*, the city is still a magnet for lovers. Yet contemporary Verona is a prosperous city at ease with itself, an aesthetically pleasing swathe of pale pink stone curling along the banks of the River Adige, its streets paved with precious marble and lined with discreet restaurants and chic designer shops.

Piazza Bra ❹ stands at the centre of civic life, presenting an elegant, languid space lined with cheerful

Veneto and Friuli-Venezia Giulia

0 — 20 km
0 — 20 miles

cafés. The square is completely dominated by the **Arena** ❸ (open Tues–Sun, 9am–12.30pm, 2.30–6pm; admission charge), the greatest of the city's Roman monuments. The elliptical amphitheatre, dating from the 1st century AD, is the third largest in existence. Built of pale pink Veronese limestone, it provides the backdrop for Italy's most theatrical open-air operatic festival. **Piazza delle Erbe** ❹ is a sociable, domestic square, revealing the cosy heart of the city. Occupying the site of the Roman forum, it is dotted with cheerful market stalls and flanked by impressive palaces. The adjoining **Piazza dei Signori** ❺, the main public square during the Renaissance, has an impressive array of civic buildings.

Casa di Giulietta ❻, just off Piazza delle Erbe, complete with the requisite marble balcony and romantic courtyard, is the supposed home of Juliet, Shakespeare's tragic heroine – a fictional shrine, even if the Montagues and Capulets did actually exist. **Sant'Anastasia** ❼, the city's largest Gothic church, with a a charming fresco by Pisanello, is set just north in the medieval quarter. Around the bend in the river waits the red-and-white striped **Duomo** ❽ (Cathedral), which is mainly Romanesque in the lower sections and Gothic towards the top. Nearby stands Ponte Pietra, a Roman bridge detonated by the retreating Nazis in 1945 but rebuilt using the original materials. Further along the river looms **Castelvecchio** ❾, a 14th-century fortress that controls the main city bridge. An innovative and imaginative civic art gallery (tel: 045-594734) is carved into the castle walls. The collection is rich in medieval, Renaissance and Mannerist works, from Pisanello to Bellini and Tintoretto.

San Zeno Maggiore ❿ (open daily, 7am–noon, 3.30–6.30pm) lies to the west; an impressive church dedicated to Verona's patron saint, it is popular for weddings. Founded in the 5th century, it is essentially Romanesque; the lofty interior is adorned with an altarpiece by Mantegna. The Romanesque and Gothic cloisters are part of the former Benedictine abbey.

The **Tomba di Giulietta** ⓫ (tel: 167-853040, freephone), set by the river, south

The ruling Scaligeri dynasty who ruled Verona from 1277 to 1387 were patrons of learning and benefactors to painters and poets, including Dante Aligheri (above).

of the Arena, is a slightly spurious Juliet shrine. The so-called tomb lies in a crypt below the cloisters of **San Francesco al Corso** a former monastery which is now a museum devoted to Shakespeare and 16th-century Verona. Just north, also beside the river, stands **San Fermo Maggiore **, a complex of two super-imposed Benedictine churches dating from the 8th and 11th centuries. Highlights are the frescoed interior and the wonderful ship's keel ceiling. From here, a short stroll across the bridge leads north to the Renaissance **Giardino Giusti ** (open daily 9am–dusk), grand formal gardens with shady arbours and waterfalls.

Further north still is the **Teatro Romano ** (open daily, Tues–Sun, 8am–1.30pm; admission charge), occupying a pleasing position on the hill. Like the Arena, the Roman theatre is used for the summer festival of dance and opera. Steps beside the theatre lead up to **Castel San Pietro **, a characterless fortress constructed by the Austrians on the site of a ruined Visconti castle. Just beyond the theatre is the Romanesque church of **Santo Stefano **, the city cathedral until late medieval times. On the far side of Ponte Garibaldi, around the bend in the river, is the Renaissance church of **San Giorgio in Braida **, studded with precious paintings by Veronese and Tintoretto. The riverside *piazza* beside the church presents a fittingly romantic farewell to Verona.

It is no coincidence that Verona plays host to VinItaly, the country's major wine fair: the city is the hub of a thriving wine-producing region. **Sant'Ambrogio di Valpolicella **, just west of Verona, is wine country noted for the eponymous fruity red wine. **Soave **, which lies in the Verona hinterland, is best known for its dry white wine. The fortified town is enclosed by Gothic defensive walls, hemmed in by towers and crowned by a castle known as **Rocca Scaligeri** (tel: 045-7860036), named after its 14th-century founders.

The Palladian trail

Vicenza ❹, which lies equidistant between Venice and Verona, is set against a backdrop of mountains. Palladio (1508–80), the leading 16th-century architect, was responsible for at least a dozen of its city palaces, not to mention countless villas in the surrounding countryside. The impressive array of Palladian buildings belies the fact that the city was heavily bombed during World War II. Contemporary Vicenza is sleek and smug, content with its cool classical image; the city centre, partly bounded by medieval walls, feels a world away from the city's current source of wealth, a "silicon valley" electronics industry.

The historic heart is best explored on one of the free guided tours provided by the tourist office (tel: 0444-544122), a pleasant stroll which takes in the city bridges, from Ponte Foro, with its remaining Roman arches, to Ponte Pusterla, with a quaint mill race. The Roman theatre which inspired Palladio was dismantled in his lifetime, the marble recycled in city palaces. Palladio's main works include Palazzo Chierati, the Teatro Olimpico and, on a hill just outside town, the famous Villa Rotonda.

On Piazza dei Signori, the city centre, stands his imposing **Basilica**, his first public project: a classical remodelling of a Gothic courthouse. A daily market takes place in the shadow of the basilica, with canny shoppers more interested in cheese and salami than in the copper-clad roof and double order of loggias. On the same square, Palladio's stately **Loggia del Capitaniato** (1571), now the town hall, was the residence of the Venetian military commander. Just south is the **Cattedrale,** a gloomy Gothic affair incorporating elements from earlier basilicas, with a door designed by Palladio.

Teatro Olimpico (open Tues–Sat, 9.30am–12.30pm, 2.30–5pm; Sun 10am–

Map on pages 168–169

Vicenza's 1st-century Roman Criptoportico remains, as does a stretch of Roman road on Corso Fogazzaro, with crafts workshops clustered in the adjoining porticoes.

BELOW: built in 1580, the Teatro Olimpico is claimed to be the world's oldest surviving indoor theatre.

Padua's golden age between the 12th and 14th centuries left an impressive cultural legacy, including many works by great artists, such as the Guattamelata *by* Donatello.

BELOW: the magisterial elegance of La Rotonda.

noon; admission charge), Palladio's theatrical last work, was begun in the year of his death and finished by his gifted successor, Scamozzi. Intended as a stage set for classical tragedies, it lays claim to being the world's oldest surviving indoor theatre. Essentially a covered amphitheatre, this masterpiece of wood, brick, stucco-work and statuary represents a coherent piece of classical reconstruction.

At the end of Corso Palladio, on the site of the former docks, stands **Palazzo Chiericati** (open Tues–Sat, 9am–noon, 2.15–5pm; admision charge), dating from 1551 and housing the civic museum and art gallery. The highlights of the collection are Venetian paintings by Tintoretto and Veronese and Flemish works by Memling and Van Dyck. **Palazzo Barbaran da Porto** (open Tues–Sun, 10am–6pm; admission charge), set on Contra Porti just off Corso Palladio, is exceptional in being the sole building in Vicenza entirely designed and supervised by Palladio. Its chief features are an impressive loggia, a grand entrance, and sumptuous decoration by Veneto artists. In 1999 it opened as a centre for Palladian studies and aims to be the world's main display case for his work.

La Rotonda (daily visits to grounds; Wed only for the interior, 9.30am–noon, 3–6pm; admision charge; tel 044-321793) nestles in the hills south of Vicenza. This exquisite villa, graced by solemn flights of steps and a ravishing dome, is an ostentatious monument to the owner's vanity.

Centre of learning

Padua ❺ (Padova in Italian) ranks with Florence and Bologna as one of the main Italian centres of learning. The 12th–14th centuries represent a vigorous period in the city's history, typified by the building of basilicas and the expansion of the university. Although Venice held sway after 1405, Padua experienced a Renaissance flowering with Mantegna and Donatello, and benefited from grand Venetian schemes, including new public buildings and ramparts. The locals are proud of their city as the last resting place of St Anthony of Padua, honoured with a seven-domed basilica that closely resembles a mosque. Outsiders are more likely to refer to its ugly industrial suburbs and notorious drugs problem, but these present no risk to visitors and the city offers art treasures aplenty.

Most visitors instinctively head to the **Cappella degli Scrovegni** (open Tues–Sun; admission charge), which contains the most complete cycle of frescoes ever attributed to Giotto (1267–1327), who created it at the height of his powers (1303–5). Dedicated to the Virgin, the Life of Christ and the Last Judgment, the cycle displays great narrative force and naturalism, with vivid, humanised figures. The artistic impact is enhanced by softly burnished colours, framed by a celestial blue sky.

The neighbouring **Eremitani Musei Civici** (open Tues–Sun 9am–7pm; admission charge), housed in the cloisters of a reclusive Augustinian order, is a cluster of different collections, including archaeological, Roman and Venetian sections. Among the artistic highlights are Renaissance bronzes, a Giotto Crucifixion, and Venetian paintings by Bellini, Titian, Tintoretto and Tiepolo. Nearby, facing the remains of the Roman amphitheatre, stands the church of the **Eremitani** (open daily, 8.15am–noon, 4–6pm). Inside the Ovetari chapel are fragments of frescoes by Mantegna (produced from 1454–57), the survivors of an Allied bombing raid in 1943, one of the worst artistic tragedies of the war.

From the Eremitani it is a short stroll to Piazza Cavour, town's heart, and a historic coffee house. **Caffè Pedrocchi**, facing the university, is designed like a Classical temple, and lined with Empire mirrors and velvet banquettes. The café has been a salon for students, academics and intellectuals since 1831. It was in these Egyptian Revival surroundings that Stendhal debated political utopias, and political plots were hatched during the Risorgimento. Today the café also functions as an arts complex and exhibition centre.

Palazzo del Bo, the seat of the university, lies a stone's throw from Caffè Pedrocchi, on Via VIII Febbraio. The building is named "the ox" after an old inn sign that once hung nearby. Founded in 1221, the university is second only to Bologna in seniority and can name Galileo among its professors; the great Tuscan mathematician and astronomer taught physics here from 1592 to 1610. Among the sights visited on the guided tour is the anatomy theatre, founded in 1594 as part of the university's school of medicine.

Further south, just within the city walls, lies the lush **Orto Botanico** (open daily, 9am–1pm, 3–6pm), the oldest university botanical gardens in Europe, founded in 1545. Around the corner from the university, separating the bustling **Piazza delle Erbe** and Piazza della Frutta, looms the monumental **Palazzo della Ragione** (open Tues–Sat; admission charge). These arcaded medieval halls housed the city council and law courts in the early 13th century. The upper floor displays a keel-shaped roof and frescoes with astrological themes.

Map on pages 168–169

TIP

"Padova Arte", a combined ticket, provides access to all major city monuments and museums.

BELOW: Giotto's *Adoration of the Magi*, Scrovegni Chapel, Padua.

The **Basilica di Sant'Antonio** (open daily, 6.30am–7pm), is a splendid place of pilgrimage erected in honour of St Anthony, a 13th-century Portuguese missionary shipwrecked in Italy. The basilica is a poor man's St Mark's, echoing the Venetian model but also incorporating Lombard and Tuscan styles. The assimilation of Eastern and Western traditions can be felt in the fusion between the Byzantine domes and minarets and the Romanesque-Gothic structure. Inside are works by Donatello and Titian.

Elsewhere in the city, Paduan churches are often memorable. On Piazza Duomo stands the plain 16th-century Cathedral flanked by the more impressive Romanesque baptistry. The recently restored **Battistero del Duomo** (open daily, 9.30am–1.30pm, 3–7pm) is adorned with 14th-century frescoes. By contrast, **Santa Sofia** (open daily, 9am–noon, 4–6.30pm), the city's oldest church, is a remodelled 6th-century brick basilica graced by a lovely Veneto-Byzantine apse.

Rovigo, south of Padua, marks the Veneto gateway to the Po Delta. Rovigo itself is an uninspiring town that borders a singularly flat, wild and wet landscape, notorious for its muggy summers and freezing winters, and its sense of watery desolation. Known as the *bonifica*, this eerie reclaimed land is not to everyone's taste, but beach-lovers can find consolation in the cluster of bustling coastal resorts in the Veneto *(see The Adriatic, page 341).*

The Po Delta

The **Po Delta** has the misfortune to straddle two administrative regions, the Veneto and Emilia Romagna. The Emilian authorities are more environmentally aware than their counterparts in the Veneto, who have been slower to grasp the fundamental conservation-equals-tourism equation. But, prompted by government and environmentalists, the lethargic regions are finally tackling the pollution of the Po, which causes a yellowish haze to pervade the atmosphere.

Although much of the Venetian plain is flat and featureless, the rolling **Colli Euganei** ❻ (Euganean Hills) make a refreshing change from cultural pursuits. Southwest of Padua, this region is noted for its spas and mud treatments. The healing properties of these hot springs have been recognised since Roman times. The sweetest spa is **Arquà Petrarca**, a medieval village where Petrarch spent his last years (1369–74); he is buried in a tomb in his former home.

The slow journey along the **Canale Brenta** ❼ provides a placid showcase for the Veneto's rural treasures. A *burchiello*, a long Venetian boat, leaves Venice every Tuesday, Thursday and Saturday and crawls along the canal to Padua, en route passing about 70 Renaissance villas as well as the Villa Pisani at Stra, infamous as the setting of Mussolini's first meeting with Hitler in 1934. (The alternative road route connects Padua and Stra.)

The trip takes in visits to the 18th-century **Villa Pisani** (tel: 0429-81368), which rivals a palace in ambition and scale, and the distinctive **La Malcontenta** (open Tues and Sat, 9am–noon; admission charge), also known as Villa Foscari. This showy villa (1558–60) has a vaulted *piano nobile* modelled on the interiors of the ancient Roman baths.

While **Venice ❽** (*see pages 143–160*) is universally acclaimed, the industrial own of **Mestre ❾** on the mainland is best known as the badly polluting hinterland. Still, the mundane yet mysterious aspects of Mestre are colourfully captured in Donna Leon's detective fiction. Further east, **Caorle ❿** was a traditional fishing port until transformed into a bustling Adriatic seaside resort. With its Romanesque belltower and pedestrianised historic centre, Caorle also makes a pleasant place for browsing. Just inland, **Portogruaro ⓫** is a Venetian-style town with significant Roman remains and an archaeological museum (tel:)421-72674), a testament to the once thriving Roman city of Concordia.

Map on pages 168–169

Proud and prosperous

Treviso ⓬, situated between Portogruaro and Venice, is a prosperous provincial town and a beacon of economic excellence. Treviso's origins are Roman, but the city flourished during the Middle Ages, when it minted its own coinage. After annexation by Venice in 1389 it assumed strategic importance as the guardian of the Republic's northwestern frontier. The city walls date from the period of Venetian domination. A single bombing raid in 1944 destroyed almost half the city, but much has been restored. What remains is a beguiling townscape of balconied houses and porticoed streets criss-crossed by picturesque canals.

    Calmaggiore, the grandest commercial street, is lined with frescoed Gothic façades and porticoes. It connects the **Duomo** (Cathedral) with Palazzo dei Trecento, the rebuilt town hall; both were casualties of the 1944 bombardment. The Cathedral; is notable for its Romanesque crypt and a frescoed chapel containing Titian's *Annunciation* (1570). Set in the lee of the 16th-century town walls, the Dominican church of **San Nicolo** outshines the Cathedral; amid

Treviso is proud of its cuisine, based on traditional local produce. Radicchio is used in salads, soups and risottos; and local asparagus, famed for its fragrance and succulent flavour, is usually served with hard-boiled eggs and oil.

BELOW: negotiating the Brenta canal.

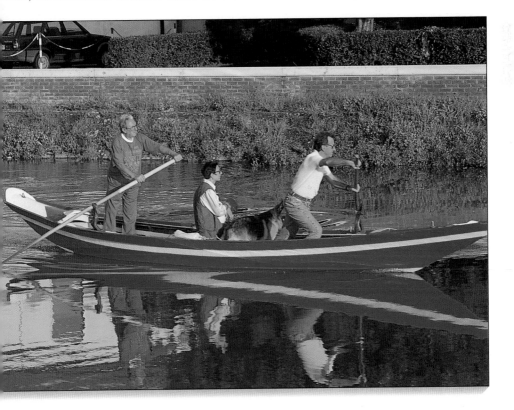

The Good Ski Guide *describes Cortina's spider's web runs as "flattened and widened in typical Italian style so that the beautiful people do not become too tired to enjoy the extensive après-ski afterwards".*

impressive Sienese frescoes are works by Tommaso di Modena (1325–79). **Buranelli** is the most pleasing quarter, characterised by ancient palaces overhanging the water and by a low stone bridge. Further west, on Borgo Cavour, is the **Museo Civico** (tel: 0422-51337), which houses an archaeological collection and a picture gallery displaying works by Titian, Bellini and Tiepolo.

Between Treviso and Casale is the watery region of **Il Sile** dotted with old mills, farmhouses and villas. The walled town of **Castelfranco-Veneto** , which once defended Treviso's western borders, lies between Treviso and Bassano del Grappa. Attractions include porticoed palaces and a Palladian cathedral with an altarpiece by Giorgione (1478–1511). The town makes a good springboard for a Palladian villa tour, with the magnificent **Villa Emo** within easy reach, at Fanzolo di Vedelago (weekends and Tue, 2–6pm; admission charge).

Marostica is a delightful medieval town, tucked inside 14th-century walls. It is celebrated for its delicious cherries and its bizarre chess festival: every alternate May (in even years) the porticoed main square is transformed into a giant chessboard with costumed citizens acting as chess pieces. This is supposedly a re-enactment of a 15th-century end game which resulted in the feudal lord giving his daughter away in marriage to the victor.

Favourite firewater

Bassano del Grappa sits astride the River Brenta in the lee of Monte Grappa. This lovely castellated town is noted for its ceramics and for the famous firewater known as *grappa*. The Veneto is a leading maker of the spirit, which is produced from the lees left over from wine production. Weekend strollers are drawn to the arcaded squares and quaint alleyways lined with frescoed houses. Despite war damage, much of the medieval fabric has remained, notably the **Ponte Coperto**, the covered timber bridge designed by Palladio. Piazza Garibaldi, the heart of the town, is dominated by a 13th-century tower and overlooked by the Gothic church of San Francesco. Housed in the adjoining monastery, the **Museo Civico** (open Mon–Sat, 9am–12.30pm, 3.30–6.30pm; admission charge) contains works by Longhi and Tiepolo.

BELOW: Bassano del Grappa.

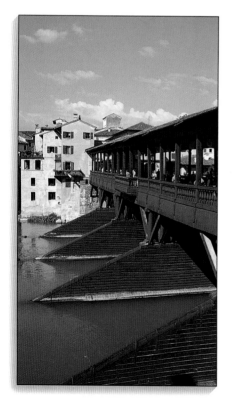

Monte Grappa, 32 km (20 miles) north, is a scenic route through forests and pastures culminating in vistas stretching towards Venice and Trieste. The mountain is popular with skiers in winter and hang-gliding enthusiasts in spring. Such is the loveliness of the terrain that it is easy to forget that the summit witnessed some of the deadliest battles on the Austro-Italian front during World War I.

Just east is **Asolo** , a picturesque walled town set amid the lumpy foothills of the Dolomites and dominated by the high-walled Rocca, the hilltop fortress. Its winding alleys are flanked by frescoed Renaissance palaces and Gothic arcades. The town has long been beloved of writers and aesthetes, from Henry James and Robert Browning – who dedicated a book of verse to Asolo – to the travel writer Freya Stark, who lived in a local villa. From the fortress and similar vantage points there are views of snow-capped Monte Grappa, the lower slopes covered by cypresses

Map
on pages
168–169

and vineyards, olive groves and pomegranate orchards. No wonder the poet Giosue Carducci described Asolo as "the city of a hundred horizons".

Villas and vineyards

The Veneto abounds in 16th–18th century villas designed as rural retreats. Around the smaller towns and villages of the Veneto are idyllic rural estates, not the hubs of working farms but showy suburban villas, giving the impression that nobles were above such lowly matters as agricultural revenues. Even Palladio was only there to cater to the nobility's rustic pretensions.

In Maser, close to Asolo, in an arcadian setting, stands **Villa Barbaro** (open Tues, Sat and Sun pm; admission charge). The interior is a *trompe l'oeil* frescoed affair by Veronese. Just outside Vicenza is **Villa Valmarana ai Nani** (tel: 0444-543976), a grandiose 18th-century villa noted for its Tiepolo frescoes. Visitors keen to sample villa life can stay at the recently restored Palladian **Villa Saraceno** (tel: 0444-891371) at Agugliaro.

Valdobbiadene ⓱ is unremarkable in itself, but its vineyard-studded hills produce some of the Veneto's best wines, from sparkling Prosecco to light Chardonnay and Verduzzo, full-bodied red Cabernet Sauvignon and Refosco. Nearby, in Crocetta del Montello, the harmonious 17th-century Palladian **Villa Sandi** is attributed to Andrea Pagnossin, an architect from Treviso.

Conegliano ⓲ enjoys an appealing setting amid orchards, vineyards and gentle hills. The name is synonymous with Prosecco, a sparkling white wine best drunk fruity, light and young. The town is the birthplace of Cima da Conegliano (1459–1518), a colourist influenced by Bellini, who favoured idealised, luminous landscapes. His beguiling *Madonna and Saints* adorns the high altar of the 14th-century Cathedral in the heart of the town. The adjoining Scuola dei Battuti is a frescoed palace decorated in Venetian and Lombard style. The castle stands sentinel over the countryside and contains the Museo Civico, with a collection of regional paintings.

Belluno ⓳ stands on a rocky spur at the meeting of the Piave and Ardo rivers, encircled by lofty peaks, with the Dolomites to the north and the Belluno pre-Alps to the south. The **Piazza del Duomo** contains a 16th-century Cathedral and baptistry with a baroque belltower; on the other side of the square is the Palazzo dei Rettori, graced by a porticoed facade, a loggia and mullioned windows. The **Piazza delle Erbe**, set on the site of the Roman forum, is lined with Renaissance palaces. Belluno's cuisine betrays alpine and Venetian influences, with mountain *gnocchi* and game flavoured with spicy Venetian sauces.

Cortina d'Ampezzo ⓴, the self-proclaimed capital of the Dolomites, vies with Zermatt and Kitzbühel as the loveliest alpine resort. Although only two hours from Venice, it feels like a Latin enclave in the South Tyrol. Ringed by spectacular peaks and spires, with pink towers and cliffs soaring out of forests and snow-fields, Cortina offers 140 km (88 miles) of *pistes,* extended to over 1,120 km (700 miles) on the linked "Dolomiti Superski" area. As a ritzy resort in the world's largest ski area, Cortina is a delightful playground of parading fashion victims. ❏

The road from Conegliano to Valdobbiadene is known as the "Prosecco trail".

BELOW: the terraced hillsides of the Veneto.

FRIULI-VENEZIA GIULIA

Map
on pages
168–169

This is where the Venetian and Austrian empires met between lagoons and limestone mountains. Its attractions number churches, castles and the delightful backwater port of Trieste

he name of Friuli-Venezia Giulia implicitly suggests a botched job, and the region is all too frequently portrayed as a briefly favoured child of the Austrian Empire which made Trieste its principal port and Grado a health resort, a half-breed Slavic region in cahoots with Yugoslav communists, or a fascist enclave that produced the only concentration camp in Italy in World War II. But as you travel around its extremities – and even venture into neighbouring Austria and Slovenia – it is quite clear that all of this is not only still homogeneously Roman territory but also, more recently and more lastingly, is still in the thrall of the Venetian Lion of St Mark, a figure that appears on gateways and public buildings everywhere.

That is not to say it doesn't have its interesting corners, regional dialect differences and special charms. It also has its special problems: the region suffered badly in an earthquake in 1976, when several towns were severely damaged, particularly in the northeast. Other fatal earthquakes occurred in 1222 and 1516.

The central plain

The last Doge of Venice had his country residence at the palatial Villa Manin in **Passariano** ㉑, some 25km (15miles) east of the manufacturing town of **Pordenone** ㉒, built to resemble St Peter's in Rome. Its spacious rooms house exhibitions, and there is a large formal garden. In this building the Venetian Republic was assigned to Austria by Napoleon in the Treaty of Campoformio.

The villa lies in the heart of the flatlands, sea-level terrain which stretches out around the River Tagliamento. As well as fish and game, the area is famous for its smoked meats; the "Strada dei Castelli e del Prosciutto", a route of castles and meats, runs near the river, reaching a high spot at the town of **San Daniele del Friuli** ㉓, set on a hillock. This is a good stopover, where a plate of meat with some bread and a carafe of wine can be wholly sustaining. Here, too, is a small church with what are considered to be the best Renaissance paintings in Friuli-Venezia Giulia; lines of chairs are drawn up for visitors to be seated and make up their own minds.

Udine ㉔, 48km (30 miles) east of Pordenone, is one of the great finds in Friuli-Venezia Giulia. Animated and full of *osterias* where the local white wines are drunk in generous balloon glasses, it has a mix of architecture that blends into an exciting, historical whole – a true satellite of the great Venetian Republic. Visitors will immediately fall upon the lovely Renaissance Piazza Libertà where the arcaded, pink-and-white-striped **Loggia del Lionello** is a pristine relic of a glorious past. It is named after its benefac-

PRECEDING PAGES: the Villa Manin, Passariano.
LEFT: Piazza dell'Unità, Trieste.
BELOW: Trieste's waterfront.

The Lion of St Mark
above a doorway at
Gorizia Castle.

BELOW: Cividade
del Friuli, Gorizia.

tor, a goldsmith named Nocolò Lionello. The building opposite, the Loggia di San Giovanni, is by Bernadino da Morcote, and the columns with the Lion of St Mark and the statue of justice are from 1614. Beneath an arch in the corner of the square, a cobbled hill, flanked by a Venetian Gothic portico built in 1487 under the Venetian governor, Tommasso Lippomano, leads to the **castle** he inhabited. Destroyed first in the 1511 earthquake, and damaged in that of 1976, it is now a museum and art gallery (open daily; closed 12.30–3pm and Mon pm and on festival days). Beside this great civic building is the church of **San t'Odorico**, a graceful Romanesque relic with a certain grace. Within walking distance of the Piazza Livertà is the **Archbishop's Palace** where Giambattista Tiepolo created a triumphant ceiling, with The Fall of the Rebellious Angels.

Earthquake towns

East of Udine the land rises in the Cast mountains and the borderlands of Slovenia. **Gorizia** is dominated by a castle, and an onion-domed church gives it a distinctly Slav flavour. **Cividale del Friuli** is a delightful stopover above a deep river gorge. Among the town's treasures is the Tempietto Lombardo, a remarkable 8th-century Lombardic relic with fine 14th-century frescoes.

The country road from Cividale to **Gemona del Friuli** in the Carnia mountains is a rural ride, among vineyards, although the houses are suburban. The earthquake that struck in 1976 wreaked its worst at Gemona where 1,000 died. It is an old town rebuilt, with vestiges of that fateful day, but it still has the antique shop for which it has long been famous. **Venzone** , 18km (11 miles) further north, also suffered severely in the earthquake, particularly the church, now rebuilt and containing an excellent wood sculpture of villagers trying to hold up the falling roof.

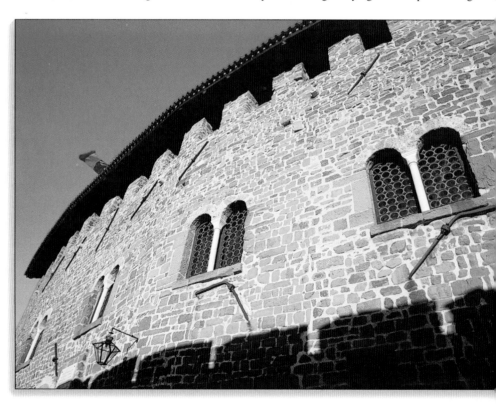

Above Venzone the high roads of the Carnia mountains go west to Cortina, north to Austria and east to Slovenia. **Forni di Sopra** ㉙ on the western route is a clutch of villages and a base for mountain hiking and riding, as is **Arta Terme** ㉚ on the northern road, where walkers enjoy the flower-filled meadows. The last main town before the Slovenian and Austrian borders in the east is **Tarvisio** ㉛, a mountain resort with an Austrian flavour.

Map
on pages
168–169

The coast

The Venetian lagoon continues round into Friuli-Venezia Giulia, flat and full of marshes, sand spits, duck shoots, bird sanctuaries and fishermen's thatched *casoni*. Much of the lagoon is not accessible, but the two principal resorts, Lignano and Grado, both cul-de-sacs off the main road to Trieste, are well-established holiday spots. **Lignano Sabbiardoro** ㉜ has 8km (3 miles) of beach, eight marinas and an aquatic park. **Grado** ㉝, at the end of a causeway, has an old-town heart, but this is hardly relevant. A spa resort built up by the Habsburgs, this is where people come to rent umbrellas in serried ranks on beaches, eat seafood and have fun with family and friends.

Just inland from Grado is the jewel of Friuli-Venezia Giulia, **Aquileia** ㉞. A major Roman port with a waterfront, which was abandoned to the marshy wastes after attacks by the Huns in the 5th century, it is not much more than a village now. Its major attraction is the basilica, which has a stunning Roman mosaic floor (open daily; summer 8.30am–7pm; winter 8.30am–12.30pm and 2.30–5.30pm; free admission). Measuring 37 by 20 metres (120 by 65 ft), it was laid down in 314, but the current building was consecrated in 1031 under Patriarch Poppo, who had the mosaics covered; they did not see daylight again until

BELOW: fishing boats moored at Grado's harbour.

Mosaic in the 13th-century apse of Duomo San Giusto, Trieste.

BELOW: the waterfront, Trieste.

1909. They depict Biblical tales, scenes from the life of Jonah and mythological moments. There are also fine frescoes in the crypt.

East of Aquileia there is little access to the coast until **Monfalcone** ③ and the last strip of Italy that squeezes between the Carso hills and the Gulf of Trieste. This coast is mainly a concreted promenade where sun-worshippers bask and slip into the sea.

Halfway down is **Miramare** ③, the castle of the Archduke Ferdinand Josef Maximilian of Habsburg-Lorraine who became Emperor of Mexico and there met his fate (open daily summer 9am–6pm; winter 9am–4pm; admission fee). With his wife Charlotte, daughter of Leopold I of Belgium, he built his dream palace on a promontory between 1856 and 1860, designing his rooms like the interiors of ships. Fully furnished, it is the best relic of the Austro-Hungarian Empire in Italy and itself plays a part in that story, which in summer is re-enacted in a *luce e suoni* (*son et lumière*). The Italianate gardens go down to the sea, which is a conservation area, and a building in the garden explains the work of the marine biologists here.

Trieste ③ is both an intriguing modern port town and a delightful backwater. Caught under the hills, it seems almost relieved that it is unable to expand, though it attracts scientists, particularly physicists, mathematicians and biotechnological engineers. Its modern prosperity dates from 1719 when it was made a free port and an important outlet for the Austro-Hungarian empire, and Empress Maria Theresa oversaw its rebuilding. It was the headquarters of the Italian high command in World War I, and after a turbulent World War II it did not come under Italian administration until 1954. The great traveller Richard Burton, the German poet Rainer Maria Rilke and the Viennese psychoanalyst

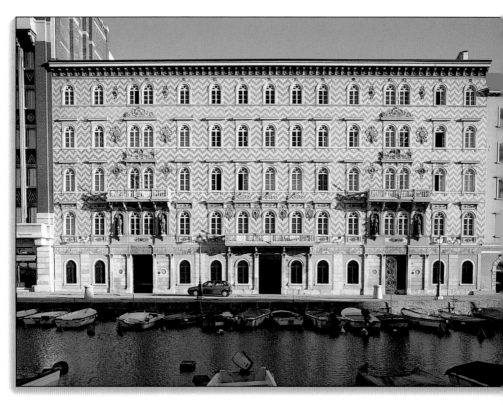

Sigmund Freud were among its famous visitors. James Joyce taught and drank and leched around the town, and it is easy to see a similarity between Trieste and Dublin:, both uncosmopolitan cities where nobody is passing through; visitors come here deliberately.

Trieste's generous waterfront, unblighted by late-20th-century tarting up, is centred on the 19th-century **Piazza dell'Unità d'Italia,** surrounded by the serried portals of the Town Hall (1877), Palazzo del Governo, Lloyd Triestino building, Hotel Duche d'Aosta and the Baroque Palazzo Piterri (1790). A further showpiece by the sea is the canal and former harbour that runs up to the Neoclassical church of S. Antonio Taumaturgo, designed by Pietro Nobile in 1849.

First stop after these must be the castle and cathedral looking down on the town. The cathedral of **San Giusto** is a simple Romanesque basilica once joined to another, giving it no fewer than four naves, with a lovely mosaic floor. Many religions worship in the town, including Serbian Orthodox at the neo-Byzantine San Spiridione, Greek Orthodox at San Nicolò and Jews at the 1912 Tempio Israelito, one of the largest synagogues in Europe. There is no shortage of museums in Trieste, and pleasant surprises include the Pasquale Revoltella collection where there are some excellent, large genre paintings such as Lionelli Balestieri's *Beethoven*, acquired at the 1901 Venice Biennale (open 10am–1pm and 3–8pm; closed Wed–Mon pm on public holidays).

There is not much left of Italy south of Trieste. The last resort is **Muggia** ㊳, a developed fishing village where the Lion of St Mark still roars above archways. Beyond is the border, painless these days, and Slovenia, where the concrete sea wall is replaced by grass. ❑

Map on pages 168–169

TIP

Trieste has some wonderfully atmospheric cafés, such as Caffè San Marco, where you can breakfast on *cornetto* or *briosce*, feast on Viennese pastries for tea, or while away the early evening with an *aperitivo*.

BELOW: the understated elegance of San Giusto cathedral.

TRENTINO-ALTO ADIGE

Map on page 190

As a region with a dual identity, Trentino-Alto Adige keeps one foot in Italy and the rest of the body in the South Tyrol, with its spirit adrift somewhere in the mountains

Trentino-Alto Adige and cultural ambiguity go together like snow and mountains. Its mind and passport may be in Italy, but its history is Austrian, its heart is in the South Tyrol, and its stomach is in *Mitteleuropa*. Austro-Hungarian culinary influences are clear, from dumplings and apple *strudel* to the typical winter dish of *polenta e crauti*, with *sauerkraut*. In 1946 the area was granted a greater degree of autonomy by the sanctioning of a special statute for the creation of the Trentino-Alto Adige region, containing the two autonomous provinces of Trentino and Alto Adige.

The region's linguistic identity is torn between Italian and German. Compared with the Tyrolean Alto Adige, where many speak German as a first language, Trentino generally feels Italian in language and culture, although a Ladin-speaking minority lives in the valleys. Ladin is a Romance language, once spoken over much of Central Europe but now restricted to the South Tyrol, parts of Switzerland and Friuli. Trentino's other linguistic minority is the German-speaking group in the Valle dei Mocheni, an attractive rural area inhabited by people of German origin, descendants of those who came to work in the mines in the 16th century. In Alto Adige (South Tyrol) most signs appear in both Italian and German. As soon becomes apparent, Trentino-Alto Adige does not typify Italy pure and undiluted, yet the shared alpine identity often cancels out cultural differences.

PRECEDING PAGES: Runkelstein, Bolsano (Bozen). **LEFT:** harvesting among the hills. **BELOW:** it is hard to miss the region's German cultural heritage.

Alpine culture

Ever since Roman times, the Brenner Pass and the Adige Valley have been the easiest crossing points over the Alps. The Adige Valley was also the main route from Innsbruck and western Austria, via the Brenner Pass, to the cities of Venice and the Po Valley. Both Trentino and Alto Adige lie in the heart of the Alps and share traditions of conservatism, hospitality, environmental concern, quiet prosperity and a passion for the mountains. The shared man-made landscape embraces alpine villages and onion-domed churches, frescoed façades and fortified castles, remote refuges and welcoming *weinstuben* (inns).

The scenery ranges from the domesticated to the wild, from sunny lakeside vineyards to the stark peaks and spires of the haunting Brenta range. Much of the region is wooded or mountainous, covered in spruce, fir, larch, pine, beech and silver birch. Yet the valley floors are carpeted with apple orchards, mainly of the golden delicious and Canadian *la reinette* varieties. The Valle di Non, set between Lombardy and the South Tyrol, is traditionally the wealthiest alpine valley, as is shown by the verdant pastures and spring blossom. The lakes, with their slopes often covered in olives or vines, enjoy the most temperate climate in

*A sign you are in
mushroom country.*

Trentino. The local parks are home to roe deer, chamois, mouflons, marmots, eagles, black grouse and the bearded vulture. The brown bear is the emblem of the Adamello Brenta park, but there are probably fewer than 10 left. Strict environmental laws ensure that nature is protected: lake water is constantly monitored, and even mushroom-picking is regulated.

Given that over half the terrain is covered in woods and mountains, the appeal of the great outdoors is obvious. Sports enthusiasts can indulge in hang-gliding in the Dolomites, as well as hiking, mountaineering and rock-climbing. For those who don't want to brave the rocky ascents, hiking is a beguiling option. In winter there are ski resorts to suit every taste, with snowboarding, dog-sledding or scenic excursions on snow shoes as alternatives. In summer the lakes offer sailing and windsurfing, while the River Noce in the Val di Sole is the place for rafting and kayaking. Although some organised cruises ply the lakes, private motor boats are banned; even on wide Lake Garda, they must hug the Brescia shore on the Lombardy side of the lake.

Capital of Trentino

Trento **❶**, the capital of the autonomous province of Trentino, lies at the foot of Monte Bondone. This prosperous yet provincial city exudes a curious air of alpine homeliness and quiet sophistication. Trento was part of the Holy Roman Empire from the 10th century; it owes its fame to the Council of Trent, summoned in 1545 to face the crisis in Catholicism, notably the threat posed by the popularity of Lutheranism and Calvinism. The Pope and Emperor Charles V quibbled about the location, but Trento, set at the intersection between the Italian and Teutonic worlds, seemed an ideal choice: an Italian-speaking town within the German-speaking empire, situated on the easiest alpine crossing.

Map on page 190

Trento was ever a model of Roman Catholicism, as is revealed by the local dish, strangolapreti *("priest stranglers"), distinctive gnocchi which evoke the popular indignation against the avarice of some clerics.*

The partly-pedestrianised town centre is lined with impressive mansions. Via Manzi, Via Belenzani and the area around the Duomo, in particular, have richly frescoed Renaissance palaces. The Cantone is one of several quaint city corners which open onto attractive loggias and balconies. The profusion of pastry shops and homely *weinstube* (inns) paint a convincing picture of *Mitteleuropa*, but Trento nails its Italian colours to the mast: in the Piazza Dante gardens stands a monument to the great Florentine poet Dante Alighieri (1265–1321), erected in 1896 as an act of national pride, in defiance of the Austrian rulers.

Piazza Duomo, the bustling heart of the town, is home to summery café terraces and boisterous Tyrolean bands. The Baroque fountain of Neptune with trident recalls the city's Roman name, Tridentum. During the June *Mangiarbene* food festival the square is strewn with tables laden with salami, meat stew, *polenta, canederli* (dumplings) and apple strudel. The Romanesque **Duomo** (Cathedral) is surprisingly harmonious, considering it was built over an extended period and incorporates the remains of a 6th-century basilica. The highlights are the Romanesque apse, the gaudy Baroque altar and a rose window representing a wheel of fortune. Behind looms the crenellated **Castelletto**, the first fortified seat of the prince-bishops. Adjoining the Cathedral is the fiercely battlemented **Palazzo Pretorio** (open Mon–Sat, 9.30am–noon, 2.30–6pm) which houses the Diocesan museum and displays paintings of sessions of the Council of Trent.

BELOW: the Piazza Duomo, at the heart of Trento.

The **Castello del Buonconsiglio** (open daily, 9am–noon, 2–5.30pm) is one of Italy's most underrated castles. This was the seat of the prince-bishops of Trento until the secularisation of the bishopric in 1802. The bastion contains an exquisitely frescoed Gothic tower, late-medieval and Renaissance wings and sumptuous Baroque apartments. The castle served as an Austrian military court during World War I, and played a symbolic role in the myth-making of Italian irridentism. In the "martyrs' moat", below the medieval town walls, the Austrians executed three patriots for high treason in 1916.

Castelvecchio (1239–1486), the oldest part of the castle, is centred on an arcaded courtyard. A loggia in Venetian Renaissance style leads to the Bishops' Room, frescoed with images of princely clerics. The **Magno Palazzo** (1528–36) is a Renaissance affair, with the frescoed walls and elegant loggias acting as a counterpoint to the medieval town walls and towers. However, the showpiece is the Gothic **Torre dell'Aquila**,

The arcaded courtyard at Castello del Buonconsiglio.

containing a cycle of the months (1390–1419). The frescoes contrast the peasants' labours with the noble high life: pig-slaughtering, harvesting and tree-felling give way to patrician fox-hunting, frolicking lovers and snowball fights.

Just outside the town lie the slopes of **Monte Bondone ②**, the place for leisurely walks. Once the preserve of charcoal-burners, the kilns are now as abandoned as the ruined watchtowers. Set beside a mountain refuge is the **Giardino Botanico** (open daily 9am–noon, 2.30–5.30pm). Among the common alpine flowers in these botanical gardens are foxgloves and edelweiss, gentians, orchids and lilies. From here stretch panoramic views of the Brenta range.

Castel Toblino ③ (tel: 0461-864036), west of Trento, is one of the most romantic castles in the region, a lakeside fortress which has been sensitively converted into a restaurant. Toblino is set on a small island, which becomes a peninsula when the water is low in the aquamarine Lago di Toblino. The 12th-century castle, built over Roman remains, was remodelled in Renaissance times, and the fierce military aspect has been softened by the porticoes and loggias gracing the inner courtyard. The turreted **Maso Toresella**, set on the shores of the enchanting lake, is the loveliest-looking wine estate in Trentino. Founded by the Renaissance prince-bishops of Trento, it has a perfect microclimate for grape-growing.

Lakes and fortresses

Between Castel Toblino and the massive Lake Garda lies **Lago di Cavedine ④**, a lake created by an enormous post-glacial landslide. Now used to generate hydro-electric power as well as pleasure, the peaceful lake is subject to strict environmental controls, as in all Trentino territory. Further south, **Riva del Garda ⑤** is an engaging resort on Lake Garda, the largest inland lake in Italy.

TRENTINO CASTLES

As a border region, Trentino has always been a bulwark against outside enemies. The strongholds encompassed feudal tower houses, lofty medieval bastions clinging to the rocks, and Venetian Renaissance courts. The mountain ridges are also dotted with Austro-Hungarian forts, often turned into military outposts during World War I. Recently the region has restored its finest castles, with some converted into hotels, restaurants, conference centres or the seats of wine estates. In summer they become the cultural focus for folklore and fireworks, exhibitions and classical concerts. During Trentino's Vinum Bonum – a summer wine and music festival – wine-tastings take place in lovely settings, including such historic haunts as Castel Toblino Castel Pergine and the Castello di Rovereto (*see page 194*)

The Adige Valley has long been an important trading route and eased the path of invading armies. Thus the Adige has the greatest concentration of castles, but the region as a whole bristles with bastions. In the prosperous Valle di Non there are patrician castles, tower houses and fortified manors, but many are privately owned and not open to the public. The design of the castles reflects changing tastes, with Gothic frescoes giving way to Renaissance loggias or lavish Baroque stucco-work.

The town, set on the fjord-like tip of the lake, is dominated by a rocky escarpment. On the lake stands the truncated **Rocca di Riva**, a moated medieval fortress linked to the town by a drawbridge. The castle belonged to a succession of feudal lords and prince-bishops before serving as an Austrian barracks. From here it is a short stroll to the picturesque maze of the old town, a pleasant place for shopping and idling.

Despite the sea-like expanse of **Lago di Garda** ❻, only the northern tip of the shore is in Trentino, with the rest shared by the Veneto and Lombardy. Garda is subject to the *ora*, a bracing breeze that blows over the lake every afternoon, helping to make neighbouring **Torbole** the best place for windsurfing. Just north of Riva stands **Castello di Arco** (tel: 0464-583511), a castle perched on a jagged peak. The ruined watchtower and imposing bastions survey the Valle di Sarca, once the route to the Po Valley for armies from the north. The ruins, dotted with cypresses, overlook olive groves and Lake Garda beyond. When water levels are low, **Lago di Ledro** ❼, which lies just west of Garda, reveals the soggy stumps of a prehistoric village off the south-western shore.

East of the two lakes is an impressive castle, visible from the main north–south motorway. Scenically set on grassy slopes framed by jagged peaks, **Castel d'Avio** ❽ (open Tues–Sun, 10am–1pm, 2–5pm) is a striking feudal bastion. The strategic location, overlooking Val Lagarina, enabled it to protect trading routes between the Mediterranean and northern Europe. Also known as Sabbionara d'Avio, the castle is reached by a steep path from the car park. The overwhelming impression is of terraces, towers and three sets of solid walls. The interior contains a baronial court extended by the Venetians, with Gothic frescoes depicting the battlefields of love and war.

Map
on page
190

A breeze on Lake Garda.

BELOW:
the Varone gardens,
Riva del Garda.

The vineyards of Trentino.

Second city

Rovereto , Trentino's second city, reveals an engaging medieval and Renaissance heart, despite unprepossessing modern quarters. Although it marked the northern outpost of the Venetian empire in the 15th century, Rovereto remains imbued with Italian irridentist spirit. The citizens also consider themselves more cultured and entrepeneurial than their bureaucratic counterparts in Trento, and are proud of Mozart's visits in the 1770s and of their long-standing musical tradition. The city was shelled by the Italians in World War I, and the scars remain. In the Miravalle quarter the Maria Dolens bell rings daily at sunset in memory of the fallen in all wars. A long-distance **Path of Peace** also traces the line of the battlefields, leading to the Adamello and Marmolada glaciers.

In the town centre the River Leno is lined with silk-workers' tall houses. Silk-making was introduced in the 16th century and helped make Rovereto the region's chief industrial centre 200 years later. World War I caused great damage, but the historic centre still has a faded charm, with frescoed façades, loggias and portals adorned with family crests. The winding **Via della Terra** is the backbone of the picturesque medieval quarter, linking the church of San Marco with the Gothic civic tower and the **Castello** (open daily, 9am–6.30pm), which came into being as a moated military fortress guarding the Adige Valley crossing. The crenellated bastion was remodelled by the Venetians but still follows the rugged contours of the rock. Since the 18th century the castle has served as a poorhouse, a Napoleonic garrison and an Austrian barracks before becoming a war museum and a school of hotel management.

Until the 18th century much of the surrounding countryside was given over to mulberry orchards and the silk-worm breeding that supplied the local industry. Today, however, the slopes are covered in vineyards. In the Lavini di Marco area south of the town a bizarre **Dinosaur Trail** can be picked out, but is best followed on a guided tour. Two hundred million years ago dinosaurs left their tracks in sandy causeways, which became fossilised in hard grey limestone.

BELOW: the "Bell of Peace" at Rovereto.

Wines and spas

Isera , an otherwise undistinguished area, is home to vineyards producing the dry, full-bodied ruby-red Marzemino wine. Production, extending between the mountains of Baldo and Bondone, is centred on the slopes of the Lagarina Valley overlooking Rovereto. De Tarczal (tel: 0464-409134) is one of the finest producers of the noble varietal wine most which was favoured by the Imperial court. During the Vinum Bonum summer wine and music festival, concerts and tastings take place in numerous settings, from the de Tarczal villa to rustic cellars and historic castles. The local **Casa del Vino** (tel: 0461-822820) is a wine centre that promotes prestigious local brands, harvest festivals and wine and food fairs. North of Rovereto, near the village of Besenello, looms **Castel Beseno** (open Tues–Sun, 9am–noon, 2–5.30pm; admission charge), the largest castle in Trentino, incorporating massive bastions and gun emplacements.

Valsugana, about 20 km (16 miles) from Trento, covers Lake Caldonazzo and a cluster of spa towns centred on Levico Terme. The hills are dotted with ruined Austro-Hungarian forts. The long-distance **Path of Peace** runs along the 1914–18 front line, connecting the Tonale Pass, Rovereto and Marmolada. The valley makes a relaxing centre for alpine and cross-country skiing, trekking, riding, water cures or simply sheer indulgence.

Map on page 190

Lavarone ⑫ is a small resort set on the hillside above a tiny lake of the same name. The crest of the hill is dotted with Austrian forts, trenches and war cemeteries, while the lakeside path is named after Sigmund Freud, who spent a few psychoanalytical summers there. Separated from Lake Lavarone by a mountain ridge is **Lago di Caldonazzo** ⑬, which offers swimming, sailing, windsurfing, canoeing, water-skiing and fishing. Part of the appeal lies in the purity of the water. Moreover, this is the only lake where water-skiing is permitted.

TIP

Substantial local dishes worth sampling in the Valsugana region include polenta with mushrooms or game, salmon trout, sausages and cured meats.

At 1,500 metres (4,900 ft) above sea level, in the oldest part of the town, **Levico Terme** ⑭ claims to be the highest spa resort in Europe. The waters descend from a great height through galleries dug in the Middle Ages to facilitate the extraction of minerals. The 19th-century spa has a dignified air and is dotted with Art Nouveau villas, mostly hotels set in spacious grounds. Italians still set store by the healing properties of the water, which has a high iron and arsenic content. Patients seeking distractions from diseases can shop for local handicrafts, from copper and brassware to hand-carved wooden toys and furniture. At **Panarotta 2002**, a ski resort north of Levico, the use of snow cannons for artificial snow ensures skiing until April.

Just north is the **Valle dei Mocheni**, a curious cultural enclave inhabited by descendants of 16th-century German miners, who uphold many of their forebears' traditions as well as their language. Attractive wooden farmhouses are

BELOW: Tyrolean gentlemen of the Alto Adige enjoy a game of cards.

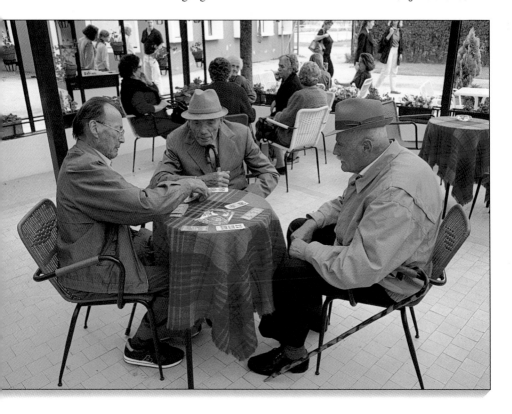

visible in such villages as Palu del Fersina, as are stretches of abandoned mines. Towering over Lake Caldonazzo is **Castel Pergine** ⓯ (tel: 0461-531158), an impressive Gothic castle, remodelled in the Renaissance. It is now a renowned (but reputedly haunted) hotel and restaurant.

Cembra ⓰, a wine-producing town between Trento and Cavalese, has the steepest terraces in Trentino. Cembra is also the gateway to the rugged **Valle di Cembra**, noted for its alpine climate, steep gorges and flower-bedecked hamlets. Part of the valley has been scarred by porphyry quarrying, which provides paving stones and building slabs for cities all over Europe. The **Sentiero Rosa** is a relaxing 7-km (4-mile) trail linking villages on the north-western side of the valley; en route are views of vineyards, porphyry quarries and alpine terraces. In **Segonzano**, just east of Cembra, there is the strange spectacle of curious natural pyramids, carved over thousands of years by the wind and the rain.

Madonna di Campiglio ⓱, the most stylish ski resort in Trentino, is second only to Cortina d'Ampezzo as a haunt of the sleekly pampered winter sports set. The *settimana bianca*, the annual skiing trip, is seen as a northern Italian right rather than a privilege. The winding main street is the scene of a nightly parade, a *passeggiata* encompassing window-shopping for skiwear and shades followed by *vin brulé* (mulled wine) in cosy rustic inns. Madonna is situated at the head of Valle Rendena, nestling between the Adamello and Brenta groups, and is part of a cluster of well-groomed slopes that connect with the vast Dolomiti Super-Ski area. For non-skiers there is *après-ski* a-plenty, plus spectacular hang-gliding over the slopes.

Set in west Trentino, the **Parco Nazionale Adamello-Brenta** ⓲ is the last refuge of the brown bear, but red deer, roe deer, foxes and marmots are more in

In Pinzolo, close to the Madonna di Campiglio resort, the church of San Vigilio displays macabre frescoes of a Dance of Death (1539).

BELOW: the alpine meadows of Seiser Alm.

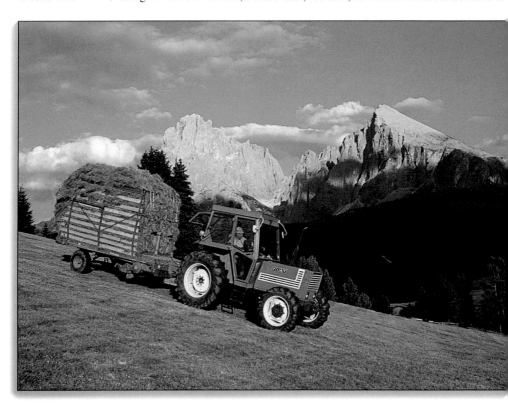

evidence. (The elusive brown bear is best seen in the Spormaggiore or San Romedio sanctuaries in the upper Valle di Non.) For most visitors, the austere landscape is the greatest draw, embracing majestic glaciers, such as Mandron, and alpine lakes, streams, waterfalls, deep fir woods and dolomitic rocks. The visitor centre is on Lake Tovel, but Lake Molveno further south is also appealing. This was the base for the ascents of the Brenta group made by the 19th-century British and German mountaineers who pioneered alpinism in Trentino.

Map on page 190

Cavalese ⓳ is the chief resort for the **Valle di Fiemme**, a valley carpeted with spring flowers. The grandest building in the town is the sumptuously frescoed Palazzo della Magnifica Comunità, the seat of the ruling medieval council. Fresher in the world's mind is the controversial crash of 1998, in which American pilots based in Italy, flying too low, hurtled into the ski slopes, cutting the cable car lines and killing 20 skiers.

The Valle di Fassa was the fiefdom of the prince-bishop of Bressanone (Brixen) until 1802. As such, it had to pay tithes of 68 sheep and pigs.

San Martino di Castrozza ⓴ basks in archetypal Dolomites landscape, lying at the foot of the pinnacle-crowned mountains. Rising to almost 3,200 metres (10,500 ft), the Pale di San Martino is the main mountain group in the southern Dolomites. Chair-lifts give access to stunning views over glaciers and craggy peaks soaring over meadows and woodland. San Martino is also the springboard for visits to the **Lagorai** mountains, a popular place for horse-riding and hiking. In summer the *Suone delle Dolomite* Festival combines a passion for mountains and music in open-air concerts conducted in alpine meadows.

Valle di Fassa

Canazei ㉑ is the main resort for the Ladin-speaking Valle di Fassa. The Ladin Campitello carnival is both a cheerful interlude and an affirmation of local culture. The resort has expanded to absorb surrounding hamlets, but the valley's tradition of hospitality survives, as do the typical alpine chalets with painted façades still visible in the upper part of the town. Spectacular views of the Dolomites lie in wait at Belvedere and Sass Pordoi, reached by cable-car. For skiers, the popular **Sellaronda** skiing area is centred on the Sella Pass, with a free ski shuttle connecting the hamlets and hotels with the slopes. Canazei is also the best base for challenging climbs of the **Marmolada** range, the highest Dolomite peaks.

BELOW: the valleys and rocky crags of Valle di Fassa.

The **Valle di Fassa**, which takes in the western slopes of the Marmolada range, includes the towns of Moena, Soraga and Campitello. **Moena** is noted for its Gothic church, welcoming inns and wood-carving. **Soraga** remains a rural community, as does **Campitello**, which marks the start of strolls along mule-tracks lined with votive crosses. The most magical landscape awaits beyond Predazzo, in the Lagorai and the jagged Catinaccio, where sunsets and refracted rays create a soft effect known as *enrosadira*, bathing the crags in a rosy glow.

Alto Adige (Südtirol)

Known as the South Tyrol in English, this landlocked province dissociates itself from the rest of Italy, at least in cultural terms. The Tyrolean nature of the architecture in the Alto Adige is matched by the alpine blond people, who are more lugubrious than Latin. The Tyrolean influence is present too in the soft alpine meadows, the geranium-bedecked chalets and strudel-scented bakeries.

Capital of the Alto Adige

Bolzano (Bozen) ㉒ is the German-speaking capital of the Alto Adige (Südtirol). It lies on the Brenner transalpine route, linking the Latin south with the Germanic north. The bilingual signs, gabled mountain chalets, brass bands and neat window boxes all seem distinctly un-Italian. The Tyrolean mood is a reflection of the cultural and artistic influences that prevailed from the 16th century until 1919. Culturally, Bolzano still feels like an Austrian city, and the triumphal arch, built by Mussolini, raises thorny issues of race, identity and language. The finest houses lie in the area from **Piazza Werther** to Via dei Portici, an arcaded street lined with 17th-century patrician mansions, and home to a colourful market, spilling out from Piazza Grano. The **Duomo** is a pink sandstone affair roofed with multi-coloured tiles, scrupulously restored after World War II bomb damage. Dating from the 6th century, the Cathedral incorporates Romanesque and Gothic elements. A pair of medieval churches, the Chiesa dei Dominicani and the Chiesa dei Francescani, decorated with School of Giotto frescoes, are also noteworthy; both have attractive cloisters.

The **Museo Archeologico dell'Alto Adige** (open Tues–Sun) is set on Via Museo, a street of pastry shops. This is the final resting place of the mummified Oetzi the Iceman, a Bronze Age man found in the meltwaters of a glacier in 1991. Austrian nationalists lost the battle to keep him on home soil, and he was reluctantly returned from Innsbruck to Italy. Since 1998 he has

Map on page 190

been on display in a capsule of solid ice, protected behind bullet-proof glass. He is dressed in a superior leather loincloth, fur leggings, cape and cap, and waterproof grass boots, and has a food satchel and copper axe. Despite mysterious burn marks, and a small hole in his skull, the cause of death is unknown, but exposure is considered likely.

In summer, Bolzano's climate is stifling, but cable cars swiftly transport citizens to the alpine meadows. For motorists, the majestic **Dolomite Road** stretches from Bolzano to Cortina d'Ampezzo, following the central depression of the massif. The route came into existence in the Renaissance, but this masterpiece of engineering was built in 1895 and served a military purpose during the 1914–18 campaigns.

Water therapy

Merano (**Meran**) ㉓, set at the head of the Val Venosta Valley, is a sedate spa town, popular with genteel visitors from all over Europe who enjoy the *Belle Epoque* tea-rooms, gentle strolls and grim water cures. On Corso Libertà is the Kurhaus, the former pump-rooms, now converted into a concert hall. The Duomo di San Nicolo is a Gothic cathedral with a crenellated gable. The **Castello Principesco** (tel: 0473-237834), with its gabled façade, is the ancestral home of the Counts of Tyrol and the palatial residence of the Habsburg Archduke Sigismund. The interior displays many of the original antiques.

A stroll through the medieval centre of town can take in Via Portici (Laubengasse), an arcaded promenade lined with painted houses. Merano's flower-decked promenades have boutiques and cafés as well as terraces and waterfalls. One of the most appealing strolls is **Passeggiata Lungo Passiro**, a "winter walk" linking the north bank of the river with the so-called Roman bridge. The "summer walk" meanders through a park planted with palms and pine trees. From the town, a cable-car sweeps winter sports enthusiasts up to **Merano 2000**, a ski resort set on a conifer-clad plateau.

Parco Nazionale dello Stelvio (**Stilfs**) ㉔ is the largest park in the Alps, extending into Trentino and Lombardy (*see page 237*). The best access to this land of snow-clad peaks and perpetual glaciers is via the visitor centres at Cogolo di Peio and the **Valle di Rabbi**. From there, park rangers accompany visitors on hiking trips through larch and spruce forests with the sharp scent of resin in the air. A rural region characterised by mountain streams and alpine meadows, scattered hamlets and solid home cooking, Valle di Rabbi provides a good base for exploring the park. It is here that chamois decend to their summer pastures from the glaciated peaks. The landscape is dotted with *masi*, farm buildings consisting of a cowshed on the ground floor and a barn or hay-loft above.

Malles Venosta (**Mals im Vischgau**) ㉕, the largest town in the west of Val Venosta, is a popular resort. The frescoed Carolingian San Benedetto church has a graceful Romanesque belltower, while the spires of the Gothic San Michele echo the jagged mountain peaks. The surrounding **Val di Senales** (**Schnals Valley**) ㉖ is a scenic ski centre. Just north

The spa town of Merano also delights in a notorious "grape cure", which involves a copious diet of grapes for the duration of the regime.

BELOW: cooling off in Pragerwildsee.

Map on page 190

Seiser Alm is oddly named, as "alm" means alp but confusingly refers to a wide plateau here.

BELOW: cycling the Pordoi Pass.

of Malles, close to Burgusio (Burgeis) is the Benedictine **Abbazia di Monte Maria** (tel: 0473-831306), an impressive but much remodelled abbey whose fine crypt is decorated with 12th-century frescoes. At Sluderno (Schluderns), 4 km (2½ miles) south-east of Malles, looms medieval **Castel Coira (Churburg)** (tel: 0473-615241), housing a collection of weaponry and armour.

Vipiteno (Sterzing) ㉗ is unquestionably a Tyrolean town, linking Bressanone with the Brenner Pass. As the centre of a previously prosperous mining district, Vipiteno was the possession of the Fuggers, the legendary banking dynasty, who redesigned the centre in lofty Renaissance style. Via Città Nuova is flanked by grand palaces, including the late-Gothic town hall, the Palazzo Comunale. The arcaded main street is lined by Renaissance Tyrolean houses, graced with oriel windows and wrought-iron signs. The **Museo Multscher** (tel: 0472-766464), set on Via della Commenda, displays Renaissance sculptures. The mineral-encrusted valleys outside town include the appealing **Val di Racines**, noted for its waterfalls.

Bressanone (Brixen) ㉘, south of Brunico and Vipiteno, is also typically Tyrolean. The medieval heart is centred on the Cathedral and the **Palazzo Vescovile** which retains a pleasing galleried courtyard. The grand interior contains the Diocesan museum (tel: 0472-830505), with Romanesque sculptures and wood carvings, Renaissance altarpieces and a collection of cribs *(presepi)*. The remodelled Romanesque **Duomo** displays a Neoclassical west front but retains its Romanesque cloisters, adorned with Renaissance frescoes.

To the southwest of the town is **Castello di Velturno** (tel: 0472-855525), the summer palace of the rulers of Bressanone. Just north of the town stands the **Abbazia di Novacella** (tel: 0472-836189), a fortified monastery with fine frescoed cloisters, a Bavarian Baroque church and a Rococo library.

Ortisei (Sankt Ulrich) ㉙ is an attractive resort serving the Valle di Gardena and Alpi di Susi area, both delightful areas for alpine hiking. The valley is a centre of Ladin culture, and the library traces the origins of the language, whose grammar was not written down until 1864. South of town is the compelling **Alpi di Siusi (Seiser Alm)**, an alpine area with quaint farmhouses and onion-domed churches.

From Ortisei, a cable car connects with Seiser Alm, a truncated peak encircled by the spiky spires of **Sassolungo (Langkofel)**. This table mountain is dotted with old chalets and carpeted with fragrant alpine orchids in spring. Sassolungo itself enjoys a view of the Sella, a seemingly castellated mass topped by towers. The **Passo di Sella**, the pass linking Canazei and Valle di Fassa with Ortisei and Valle di Gardena, provides one of the most panoramic views in the whole region.

East of Vipiteno is **Brunico (Bruneck) ㉚**, a quaint town surveyed by an impressive Gothic castle. Brunico's appealing narrow alleys lead to a medieval gate and the church of Saint Ursula, which displays fine altar reliefs. To reach the popular winter sports area, visitors can take the Riscone cable-car to Plan de Corones, either to ski or simply to enjoy a superb view over the Dolomites. ❏

Italy with a German soul

Alto Adige, Südtirol, Trentino-Alto Adige, South Tyrol: this region goes by a succession of highly charged names. Most ethnic Germans felt wronged at the hands of the Italian Fascists after World War I. Until then the region had been part of Austria, and 97 percent German-speaking. Indeed, German-speaking irridentists have never accepted the Italian annexation of the South Tyrol, which was part of the deal the Italians struck with the Allies in return for joining the war against Austria-Hungary in 1915. By claiming all the territory up to the Brenner Pass, the Italians put the desire for clearly defensible borders above the demands of linguistic and ethnic distinctions. The South Tyrol was duly split.

In the 1920s Mussolini transformed the population, bringing in Italians from the Veneto and the south as well as erasing German place-names and suppressing German culture and language. In 1939 Mussolini held a plebiscite to offer German-speakers the option of moving to post-*Anschluss* Germany. Over 200,000 chose Nazi Germany over Fascist Italy, proof that Il Duce's Italianisation policy had failed. In 1946 an international agreement stipulated that Austria renounced any territorial claim on condition that the rights of the German-speaking minority were respected.

In 1948 the Italian state engineered the creation of a new province to ensure an Italian-speaking majority in the enlarged entity. The provinces of Trento and Bolzano were duly merged to form Trentino-Alto Adige, with its own regional parliament and administration based in Trento. However, aggrieved German extremists perpetrated terrorist attacks from the late 1950s onwards, making a new political accommodation a priority.

With the aid of the United Nations, a *pacchetto*, or package of concessions, was finally agreed between Italy and Austria, and adopted in 1969. The measures allowed for greater local autonomy, with Bolzano able to protect the rights of all language groups.

Today German-speakers outnumber Italian speakers by two to one in Alto Adige, with the latter mainly settled in the towns, and the former in the country. Since 1996 there has been a political drive to 'Germanise' place-names across the region, which has provoked an Italian backlash. Italian-speakers claim that their racial forebears had inhabited the region since Roman times. Equally aggrieved was the minority population of 20,000 Ladins who speak Ladin, a language close to Latin, and claim to have been settled in the region for 2,000 years. Ladin-speakers, who live mainly in the valleys, are noted for their entrepreneurial flair.

In recent years South Tyroleans have been granted increased autonomy by Rome, and showered with mammoth subsidies. This has served to dim the secessionist ambitions of the materialistic *Südtiroler* (South Tyroleans). As the richest and best-protected minority in Europe, they have simply no reason to envy their poorer Austrian neighbours living in the North Tyrol. ❑

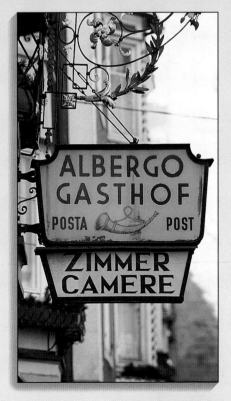

RIGHT: a sure sign of Trentino-Alto Adige's bilingual heritage.

MILAN

*The fashion industry has put the city on the international map
as a sophisticated place. But it's a one-dimensional image:
the reality is much more complex*

Map
on page
206

As the country's fashion capital, Milan is not slow to flaunt its credentials: even the airport is emblazoned with the Armani logo in sky-high lettering. In the chic Montenapoleone shopping district, Bar San Babila sells designer sandwiches named after Moschino, Versace and other dead fashion legends. At its sartorial best, Milan is a well-tailored, cosmopolitan city that puts on a show with panache. During fashion week, the *modelari*, the louche men who chase models, are encased in leather trousers and regulation shades.

By night, La Scala's marbled and mirrored lobby is awash with Milanese opera-lovers in deep-pile furs and Bulgari jewels. At a Dolce & Gabbana party, foreign stars gather by fountains overflowing with rose petals and pick from silver platters piled with pomegranates. Yet this picture of the city at its most hedonistic is only a party snapshot. Behind the scenes lies the cool practicality of a prosaic capital: serious, sober and locked into its quintessential northernness.

Undisputed capital

Once an inconsequential city on the Lombard plain, Milan rose to fame as the Roman stronghold of Mediolanum. After developing as an early Christian centre connected with Saint Ambrose, it consolidated its power as an independent medieval commune. The Visconti (1277–1447) were enlightened despots whose empire-building caused them to be regarded as the city-state's natural rulers. Under Gian Galeazzo Visconti (1385–1402) the mercantile city prospered and the northern empire expanded. The pragmatic Sforza dynasty then turned Milan into a vibrant Renaissance centre until Spanish rule (1535–1713) spelt cultural stagnation. Nonetheless, during the Counter-Reformation the Spanish viceroys instilled a Catholic paternalism which still marks contemporary Milanese society. During the Enlightenment, Austrian rule replaced Spanish decadence with economic progress and helped engender the industrious spirit that characterises the city today.

Italian unification led to the integration of the northern industrial cities into a cohesive national economy and gave a further boost to Milan. Since 1900 the city has led industrial design, a position consolidated by the impact of Bauhaus rationalism in the 1920s and the advent of mass production in architecture in the 1930s. After enduring Fascism and Allied bombing, Milans was confirmed in its pre-eminence by the economic miracle of the 1950s when the burgeoning design industry came into its own. Today Milan still dominates the fashion and industrial design calendar, from international trade fairs to the spring and summer couture and ready-to-wear collections.

Milan remains the undisputed business capital, a

PRECEDING PAGES: the umbrellas of Milan; the Duomo cathedral in a downpour.
LEFT: the Duomo's Gothic spires.
BELOW: fashion central.

ophisticated modern metropolis dedicated to money-making and the plea-
ure principle. As the engine of economic growth it is also a symbol of the
ountry's north-south divide, contrasting favourably with the cemetery of
ublic works that is the south. This dour but ponderously handsome city will-
ngly sells its soul for profit, while poverty-stricken Palermo would sacrifice
vealth for prestige and power. As Luigi Barzini states in *The Italians*: "South-
rners tend to make money in order to rule, northerners to rule in order to
nake money." Fortunately, the northern city has recovered from *Tangentopoli*,
he "Bribesville" corruption scandals of the early 1990s. According to Roberto
Peretta, an expert in Milanese affairs: "*Tutto come prima ma non proprio*"
"All is as it was – but not exactly".)

Map on page 206

A local expression, "lungo come la fabbrica del Duomo" (as long as the building of the cathedral)", can refer to anything that seems unending.

The civic centre

Piazza del Duomo ❶ has been the historical heart of the city since the Middle
Ages when the archbishop, the city's political ruler, maintained a palace beside
he cathedral. Despite its sense of solidity, the square only attained its present
orm after Italian unification, when medieval buildings were demolished to
emphasise grandeur. The square is dominated by the Duomo, the city's landmark
athedral, but is lined by severe palaces, notably the two monumental blocks
ouilt under Fascism. However, any architectural severity is softened by the
presence of busy commuters, buskers and bag-sellers. The *piazza* is always
oustling, particularly when open-air concerts enliven summer evenings.

    The Duomo ❷ (open daily, 6.45am–6.30pm) remains Italy's most famous
unfinished masterpiece, which patrons continue to endow with statuary and
stones. The work was begun under Gian Galeazzo Visconti in 1386 but continued until Napoleonic times, seamlessly blending
Gothic, Baroque, Neoclassical and neo-Gothic styles.

    The building is considered Europe's biggest Gothic
cathedral, but its authenticity is slightly compromised
by the Baroque main doors and the main façade,
which was added during the Counter-Reformation.
Nonetheless, it is the clearest model of Gothic architecture in Italy, with French-style flying buttresses
and soaring pinnacles contrasting with the excessive
width preferred by the native Lombard builders. The
finest view is from the Piazzetta Reale, which reveals
the full sweep of its Gothic Flamboyant glory, with
arched buttresses and gables embellished with delicate spires and gargoyles. On the highest pinnacle
stands the sacred *Madonnina*, the city protector,
resplendent in glittering gold. From the roof of the
Duomo, accessible by lift, there is a memorable view
of the *Madonnina* soaring over the Gothic spires.

    In a small square to the right of the Duomo is the
royal palace, **Palazzo Reale ❸** (open Tue–Sun,
9.30am–7.30pm). The 18th-century building, the
home of the Spanish and Austrian governors, was
built on the site of the Viscontis' 14th-century fortress.
It suffered in the 1943 bombardments, and the damage
is still visible in the loveliest room, the partly demolished Sala delle Cariatidi.

    One section of the palace has recently been turned
into the **Museo d'Arte Contemporanea** (open

BELOW: the
Duomo is a temple
of astonishing
craftmanship,
as seen in this
intricate cast-
bronze door.

BELOW: feeding the pigeons in the Piazza del Duomo.

Tue–Sun, 9.30am–5.30pm), which houses a notable collection of Italian modern art. The Futurists, such as Carlo Carrà and Gino Severini, are well represented, as are de Psisis, de Chirico and Giorgio Morandi. The permanent collection is complemented by regular temporary exhibitions, from contemporary art to photographic retrospectives. One wing houses the **Museo del Duomo** (open Tue–Sun, 9.30am–12.30pm and 3–6pm), a collection of stained glass, Gothic tapestries and paintings.

Galleria Vittorio Emanuele ❹, the magnificent arcaded gallery leading off the square, is known as "*il salotto di Milano*", Milan's front parlour. Since its creation in 1864 the gallery has served as a meeting-place for Milanese of all ages and backgrounds. The gallery, originally created to honour the Austro-Hungarian emperor, was instead dedicated to Victor Emmanuel, the Italian king. The designer, Giuseppe Mengoni, intended the passage to link the Cathedral with La Scala and the prestigious Via Manzoni. The gallery, surmounted by a magnificent iron-and-glass cupola, and lined by cafés and bookshops, has lost none of its lustre.

The gallery opens onto the austere Piazza della Scala, home to **Teatro alla Scala ❺**, Italy's premier opera house. The Neoclassical façade was built by Giuseppe Piermarini in 1776, but the main auditorium, which seats 2,800, was faithfully reconstructed after bomb damage. Opera is a national passion, and is celebrated by the Milanese with typical Italian fervour. In this melodious city the perfect pitch of the singers is matched by the sumptuousness of La Scala's red plush, and by the choice of neighbouring bars that play on a musical theme. Caffè Verdi, around the corner, is decorated with posters of the Three Tenors, Callas and Nureyev, while the neighbouring Grand Hotel et Milan contains the

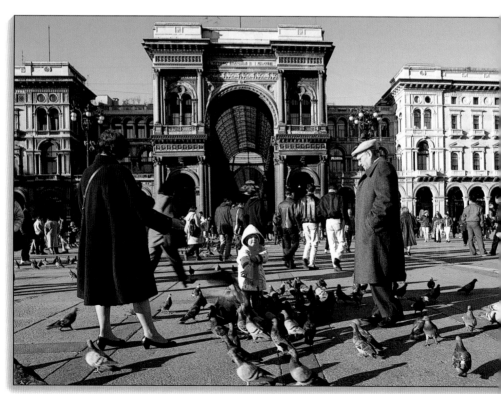

Map on page 206

famous suite where Verdi died. In honour of the *Maestro*, who lay on his deathbed, the citizens covered the street outside his room with straw to muffle any noise from passing carriages.

La Scala's season traditionally opens on 7 December, dedicated to St. Ambrose, the city's patron saint. This is the high point of the Milanese social calendar, signalling a season running until July, with opera interspersed with orchestral concerts. The student unrest of the 1960s forced this world of privilege to face public hostility. After the audience was pelted with rotten eggs at the opening performance of the 1968 season, La Scala adopted a more enlightened policy: aggrieved students, teachers and factory workers were given discounted tickets. Since then, in common with other opera houses, La Scala has been guilty of wanton extravagance, from wayward staging and costly costumes to a failure to revive successful productions. The newly-privatised opera house closes for restoration until the centenary of Verdi's birth in January 2001. Until then the company relocates to the city outskirts, much to the consternation of its fur-coated clientele.

Opera-goers who wish to show their appreciation should shout "bravo" for tenors, "brava" for sopranos, and "bravi" for all.

The famed **Museo Teatrale alla Scala** (open Mon–Sat; 9am–noon, 2–5pm) displays a rich collection of musical instruments, operatic costumes and masks, as well as busts of the great operatic composers and conductors. Milanese audiences are hard taskmasters, with applause led by the official clapping societies. If the opera falls short of perfection, the *loggionisti*, those sitting in the gods, are ready to rain down abuse on fallen divas, with booing and hissing commonplace.

Casa del Manzoni ⑥ (open am–noon, 2–4pm; closed Sat, Mon), set on Via Morone, is a shrine to Alessandro Manzoni, one of the country's best-known novelists. The house was where the writer lived from 1822 until his death in

BELOW: contemporary *trompe l'oeil* murals.

Museo Poldi-Pezzoli, a testament to 19th-century patrician tastes.

BELOW: the Galleria Vittorio Emanuele has been a favourite Milanese meeting place since 1864.

1873. It is now a small museum and, for all but literary sleuths, represents a rather arid centre of Manzoni studies.

On Via Manzoni is the **Museo Poldi-Pezzoli** ➐ (open Tues–Sun, 9.30am–12.30pm and 2.30–6pm; closed Sun pm). This museum was founded by a Milanese nobleman who bequeathed his home to the city on his death in 1879. The interior is a testament to 19th-century patrician tastes, with sundials and ceramics, clocks, carpets and jewellery. Poldi-Pezzoli, the founder, particularly loved Venetian art, especially by Bellini, Tiepolo and Mantegna, and appreciated work by schools in central Italy, represented by Pollaiolo, Perugino and Botticelli. The highlights of the collection are the Renaissance paintings by Botticelli, Bellini, Piero della Francesca and Mantegna.

From Via Manzoni, Via Santa Margherita leads to **Palazzo Clerici** ➑ (ring the bell). Set on Via Clerici, this impressive 18th-century palace is noted for a famous fresco by, the Rococo artist Tiepolo. Further south, just off Piazza Duomo, is the tiny **Piazza Mercanti**, the sole surviving corner of medieval Milan. Surrounding the square are former guildhalls and civic biuldings that have been converted into banks and offices. The finest building is the **Palazzo della Ragione** ➒, also known as the Broletto Nuovo. As the seat of the independent commune of Milan, this medieval gem served as the council chambers and city law courts until 1779.

Il Quadrilatero

From Piazza Mercanti it is a short stroll or metro ride to the chic fashion district, centred on Via Monte Napoleone. The fashion showrooms are located between the elegant Brera district and Piazza San Babila in the *"quadrilatero"*, a quad-

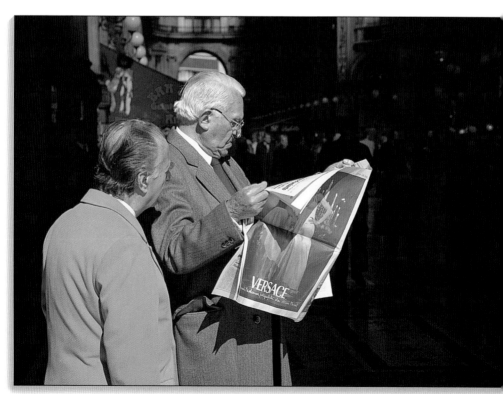

rangle often dubbed the "golden triangle". **Via Monte Napoleone** , known to cognoscenti as 'MonteNapo', offers Italy's greatest concentration of design and jewellery houses. Milan's fashion industry thrives on a ready supply of home-grown talent and a contemporary feel, essentially a creative twist on classic lines. These deep design roots lie in medieval craftsmanship, traditional skills which are prized in textiles, jewellery and leather goods, as well as in *haute couture* (*see Alta Moda, page 219*). Yet so confident are the Milanese of their impeccable refinement that they can even do gross bad taste with aplomb, as Versace, Moschino and Dolce & Gabbana have often demonstrated.

Via Monte Napoleone is lined with 18th- and 19th-century patrician palaces, most of which have been converted into chic boutiques. A stroll down the street takes in La Perla seductive underwear, Beltrami shoes and Cartier jewellery by way of Versace glitz, Gucci chic and Alberta Ferretti's Philosophy. Caffè Cova, a Milanese institution founded in 1817, is an obligatory stop on the fashion circuit. These tea-rooms were favoured by Mazzini, Garibaldi and 19th-century nobility but today welcome the *Milanese bene*, well-off citizens eager to exchange shopping tips over a Fernet Branca in this chic *pasticceria*.

Famous names abound in this chic area.

On Via Santo Spirito is the quirky Renaissance museum of **Palazzo Bagetti-Valsecchi** (open Tues–Sun, 1pm–5pm). Much like the Museo Poldi-Pezzoli, this is an eclectic collection set in a nobleman's residence. Created by the Bagetti-Valsecchi brothers as an elegy for Renaissance era, the palace is also a tribute to Victorian eclecticism. Authentic 16th-century furniture, ceramics and weaponry are mixed with reproductions of Renaissance art. Even so, the overall result is more than a pleasing pastiche.

Piazza San Babila is a popular meeting-place for Milanese youth. Nearby

BELOW: friends meet and greet on the Via Manzoni.

TIP

For weary shoppers, the glamorous bar of the Four Seasons Hotel, set in a delightful former monastery on Via Gesu, provides a cosseted escape from rampant consumerism.

BELOW: the Pinacoteca di Brera houses one of Italy's finest art collections, with works by Mantegna, Raphael and Piero della Francesca.

stands **Basilica di San Babila** ⑫, a 5th-century church sensitively remodelled in 1905 in an attempt to restore it to its 12th-century splendour. The adjoining streets of Via Sant'Andrea and Via della Spiga also worship at the altar of high fashion. Sleek addicts of designer wear scour Via Sant'Andrea in search of Prada, Trussardi, Moschino, Fendi and Kenzo labels, while Via della Spiga is home to Krizia, Ferré and Blumarine, leaving Via Pietro Verri to the Ermenegildo Zegna menswear designers and Corso Venezia to fashion and diffusion lines, from Ferré to D&G.

From here Via Palestro leads through a chic residential district to **Villa Reale** ⑬, set in romantic grounds dotted with follies. The Neoclassical villa, built for a Milanese count in 1790, accommodated Napoleon and Josephine as well as Napoleon III. Today the villa houses the **Galleria d'Arte Moderna** (open Tues–Mon 9.30am–5.30pm), a collection of modern Italian paintings. On the other side of Via Palestro are the **Giardini Pubblici** ⑭, the city's finest parkland. Created in the 1780s, the landscaped grounds incorporated the monastic kitchen gardens that bordered Corso Venezia. In the 18th century Corso Venezia was at the heart of Milanese intellectual life, and it still abounds in grand palaces that were once literary salons. Today the pony trails and pavilions make the park a popular spot for Milanese families. Off Corso Venezia, just inside the park, is Planetario Ulrico Hoepli (tel: 02-29531181), the city planetarium.

The Brera quarter

This chic district adjoins the "golden triangle" and the castle quarter. The Brera was once a bohemian rendezvous for artists and rebels, but 1960s flower power has long since given way to *fin-de-siècle* materialism. This is *Milano bene*, an elegant district where well-to-do Milanese browse in designer boutiques and art galleries before flitting to fashionable cafés. Fortunately relics of the old Brera remain, not least in the discreet palaces graced by secret courtyards and old portals. A handful of quaint cafes and theatres is testament to the intellectual flavour of old Brera.

A stroll from La Scala along Via Verdi leads to the Brera quarter, which is also served by Lanza metro station. The best of the Brera lies in the small pedestrianised area sandwiched between Via Pontaccio and Via Brera, lined by 18th- and 19th-century palaces. Bar Giamaica on Via Brera is the place for erstwhile hippies who have mellowed into corporate executives. This 1960s haunt now welcomes top models and designers. **Via Fiori Chiari** ⑮ is the heart of a bustling little area packed with fashionable bars, restaurants and designer boutiques. This characteristic street is an obligatory stop on the evening summer *passeggiata*, with passers-by waylaid by African street-vendors selling fake Vuitton or Prada bags. On the third Saturday of the month an atmospheric antiques market spills over onto Via Fiori Chiari.

Pinacoteca di Brera ⑯ (open Tues–Sat, 9am–10pm; Sun 9am–12.45pm and 2.30–8pm), founded by the Habsburgs in the late 18th century, represents one of the country's greatest art collections. The museum, set on Via Brera, was dramatically enlarged in Napoleonic times, enriched by paintings confiscated from churches in French-occupied Italian regions. Napoleon sought to create a collection worthy of a new capital, albeit one subject to Paris. Since his fall did not result in the return of the art works, the Brera remains a treasure trove of northern European art. The somewhat austere palace has been modernised, with the remodelling of certain rooms and the creation of a pleasant café and bookshop. The collection is particularly strong in Venetian and Lombard works dating from the 15th century to the 18th, with Renaissance artists particularly favoured. Italian masterpieces include works by Mantegna, Raphael, Piero della Francesca and Caravaggio, as well as modern works by Boccioni, Carrà and Morandi. The Venetians are represented by Veronese, Tintoretto, Titian and Carpaccio, with Bellini's *Madonna and Child* one of the finest works. Amongst foreign old masters, paintings by Rubens, Rembrandt and Van Dyck can be singled out.

Via Pontaccio and Corso Garibaldi lead to **San Simpliciano** ⓱ (open daily, 7am–noon, 3–7pm). Set on Piazza San Simpliciano, this is one of the city's most ancient churches, dating from the 5th century. Behind the church are fine 15th-century cloisters. From here, it is a short stroll back to Via Tivoli, which leads to the castle quarter.

Madonna in Prayer, attributed to Pietro Solari, in the Picture Gallery of the Castello Sforzesco.

The castle quarter

The castle quarter adjoins the banking district and is signalled by Foro Bonaparte, a grandiose semicircle created by the French Napoleonic forces. Dominating the district is **Castello Sforzesco** ⓲ (open Tues–Sun, 9.30am–5.30pm), the imposing Sforza Castle rebuilt by the princely family in 1450. The castle was largely dismantled by the Napoleonic forces, who downgraded it to a barracks.

BELOW: the "English gardens" of Castello Sforzesco.

Fresco of St Ambrose in the Basilica di Sant'Ambrogio.

The shell was rebuilt in 1893 to incorporate mock medieval and Renaissance flourishes such as the Filarete tower which dominates the facade. Charming Renaissance interiors include Leonardo da Vinci's Sala delle Asse, a room decorated with its pattern of intertwined foliage. The castle museums house a display of Lombard sculpture, ceramics, furniture, tapestries, arms and musical instruments. The picture gallery features works by Bellini, Titian, Correggio, Tintoretto, Canaletto and Van Dyck. The highlight is Michelangelo's last work, the unfinished *Pietà Rondanini*.

The castle is surrounded by so-called English gardens, which connect with the sprawling **Parco Sempione ⑲**. The park, which was created in 1893 on the castle's old parade grounds, terminates in a Neoclassical arch, l'Arco della Pace. On the edge of Parco Sempione is the **Acquario ⑳** (open Tues–Sun 9.30am–5.30pm). The aquarium is housed in an appealing Art Nouveau building and displays the main marine habitats as well as a specialist library.

Porta Romana and the university quarter

This is a mixed neighbourhood, with student cafés and historic sights part of a pleasant residential patchwork. The quarter comes alive in early December for the city's medieval fair, Oh Bej, Oh Bej, set in Piazza Sant'Ambrogio. Stalls then sell speciality sweets, pork snacks, children's toys and artisanal furniture.

Ca' Grande (Università Statale) ㉑, set on Via Festa del Perdono, is the most imposing university building. The "big house", as it is known in Milanese dialect, is an attractive 15th-century brick building that housed the city's main hospital for five centuries. Now home to the humanities faculty, the Ca' Grande is at the heart of Milanese student life. Closer to Sant'Ambrogio is the Università Cattolica, the Catholic rival to the state university. On Piazza Velasca, just around the corner, looms **Torre Velasca**, a bizarre tower built in 1958 to echo the city's predilection for massive medieval towers.

Beyond, on Piazza Sant'Ambrogio, is the **Basilica di Sant'Ambrogio ㉒**. The Basilica is seen as a prototype for a Romanesque Lombard church, with its harmonious proportions and geometrical cross-vaulting. For many Milanese this solemn church is closer to their hearts than the lofty Duomo. A mood of subdued spirituality prevails in a place dedicated to the city's beloved patron saint. Work began under Saint Ambrose in 386, but the church was only completed in the 12th century. The legacy of Saint Ambrose lives on in the liturgy of the Milanese church as well as in Ambrosian chant. Traces of the early Christian church remain: portions of walls and columns; marble and mosaic decorations; a medieval high altar encrusted with jewels; and a ciborium supported by columns of red porphyry. From here it is a short walk to Corso Magenta and Leonardo da Vinci's masterpiece.

BELOW: the Corso Venezia was once the centre of Milanese intellectual life; it still features the occasional debate.

Leonardo's *Last Supper*

The **Cenacolo Vinciano ㉓**, housing Leonardo da Vinci's *Last Supper*, lights up the refectory of Santa Maria delle Grazie (since its restoration in 1999 the popularity of the painting means that it is best to book your visit as soon as you arrive in Milan; freephone: 199 199 100; viewing is limited to 15 minutes only). Leonardo's famous fresco, painted between 1495 and 1497 on a wall in the Dominican monastery, has been damaged by humidity, bomb damage and over-enthusiastic restoration, not to mention as a direct result of Leonardo's experimental methods. Nevertheless, it remains a symbol of Western art.

In deciding not to paint on wet plaster, Leonardo rejected received wisdom: dry plaster would allow him more time to retouch the work. However, excessive humidity combined with the faulty mixture used for binding the paint caused the fresco to deteriorate even during the artist's lifetime.

The masterpiece was finally unveiled in 1999 after a 22-year restoration, with later accretions being stripped off to reveal the artist's original intentions. As a result the restorers have revealed wonderfully vivid details, such as flowers and bread, with the familiar murky brown sludge giving way to a startling luminosity.

The controversial restoration has divided critics, but Signora Brambilla, the chief restorer, is clear about her guiding principles: "I'm an artisan, not an artist, still less a scientist; aesthetic sensitivity is the most important thing for restoring any work of art." Although the public tends to approve of the brilliancy of the colours, the results of the restoration have dissatisfied many art critics, who feel that posterity has been given a pale ghost, a virtual Leonardo.

Facing the refectory is the lovely Renaissance church of **Santa Maria delle Grazie** (open daily, 8am–noon, 3–7pm), with cloisters attributed to Bramante. Also on Corso Magenta is the **Palazzo delle Stelline ㉔**, an impressive cluster of palaces converted into a major exhibition centre and congress complex. On

Map on page 206

When the prior accused Leonardo da Vinci of dawdling over the fresco, the master tartly replied that he was having difficulty imagining the face of anyone as evil as Judas, but that the prior's portrait could be used if the Church were really in such a hurry.

BELOW: flawed genius: da Vinci's masterpiece, *The Last Supper.*

RENAISSANCE MAN

Leonardo da Vinci lived in Milan and France as well as in his native Florence. In Milan he was suppported between 1482 and 1515 by the Sforza, his powerful patrons, and he has left numerous masterpieces in his adoptive city. Yet despite the sublime beauty of his work and a supreme mastery of painting technique, Leonardo was chiefly interested in solving intellectual and philosophical problems of composition. As the quintessential Renaissance man he was ready to apply his mind to a wide range of fields, from the arts to applied sciences, from poetic portraiture to war machines, from anatomy to botany.

In addition to his paintings, Leonardo bequeathed the city new techniques in irrigation, canal-building and hydraulic engineering. As well as being a philosopher, a visionary, an architect, a medical draughtsman, a musician and a cartographer, he was the first artist to be universally acknowledged not as a skilled artisan but as an inspired genius whose mind encompassed the sum of human knowledge. However, whether this brilliance is visible in the restored *Last Supper* is open to debate, nor has Leonardo's flawed experimental technique confirmed optimists' expectations of a "reborn masterpiece".

the same sedate boulevard is the palace from which the whole *Tangentopoli* political corruption scandal exploded in the 1990s. Milan has yet to live it down.

The canal quarter: the Ticinese and Navigli

Strictly speaking, this is the Ticinese and the Navigli, two overlapping districts with shared characteristics. The Ticinese is the most atmospheric of Milan's *quartieri popolari*, the old working-class districts, and is named after the river Ticino, a tributary of the Po. The sprawling Ticinese runs into the youthful and faintly bohemian Navigli quarter, equivalent to the Parisian left bank. The Navigli were the navigable canals that used to flow across the city; now largely covered over, the canals survive in this quirky district, reached by Porta Genova metro station. They have recently been re-opened to pleasure boats, bringing new life to an area already populated by painters, artisans, students and self-conscious intellectuals.

The **Pinacoteca Ambrosiana** ㉕ (open Tues–Sun, 10am–5.30pm), set on Piazza Pio XI, is a picture gallery founded by Cardinal Federico Borromeo in 1609. His more serious aim, represented by the illustrious library in the same building, was to defend Catholic orthodoxy against the challenge of Protestantism, and for this purpose, he created a research institute complete with a superb collection of illuminated manuscripts and ancient Bibles. The manuscripts in particular were intended to establish the only "true" version of the Bible, a response both to Luther's radical German translation and to the freer interpretation of sacred texts favoured by Protestantism.

The collection contains Cardinal Borromeo's favourite work, Caravaggio's *Basket of Fruit*, and also reflects the founder's preference for Flemish and

Map on page 206

Venetian art. However, later bequests have broadened the Pinacoteca's appeal by including medieval Lombard sculpture, German old masters and Tuscan Renaissance masterpieces. Foremost amongst the Venetian treasures is Titian's *Adoration of the Magi* and Rococo works by Tiepolo. Renaissance paintings include a luminous Botticelli Madonna, Raphael's cartoon for *The School of Athens*, and enigmatic masterpieces by Bramantino which delight in games of perspective. The collection also boasts *The Musician*, a masterpiece attributed to Leonardo da Vinci. Certainly, it fulfils Leonardo's dictum that: "There are only two subjects worthy of the painter: man and the concept of his mind."

On the ground floor is the **Biblioteca Ambrosiana** (open Tues–Sun, 10am–5.30pm), one of Europe's oldest public libraries, founded by Cardinal Borromeo in 1607. The library houses a collection of illuminated manuscripts, Hebrew parchments, Oriental and European Bibles, letters and antiquarian books. In addition to drawings by old masters, the collection contains a 5th-century copy of the *Iliad* as well as the *Codex Atlanticus*, complete with over a thousand pages of scientific and technical drawings by Leonardo da Vinci. Other treasures include Petrarch's annotated copy of Virgil's poems, letters from Boccaccio and Machiavelli, and Piero della Francesca's treatise on painting.

A stone tablet still preserved in the library warns potential thieves that the penalty for stealing a volume is no mere fine but instant excommunication.

Via Torino leads to the **Basilica di San Satiro 26**, a landmark church created with exquisite artifice. Although founded in the 9th century, San Satiro was completely remodelled in Renaissance style in 1478. Bramante's skilful use of a Classical idiom disguises the lack of space and, by integrating gilded stucco and *trompe l'oeil* effects, creates the impression of a chancel. While the 9th-century baptistry was incorporated into the remodelled church as the Cappella della Pietà, and graced with a Renaissance exterior, the Romanesque brick bell-tower is a testament to the earlier church.

San Lorenzo Maggiore 27, on Corso di Porta Ticinese, is often cited as the first centrally planned building in the Western world. Founded in the 4th century, this is a powerful evocation of an early Christian basilica. The 16th-century reconstruction remained faithful to the early Christian plan. The vast dome creates an awe-inspiring interior, with chapels radiating in a sunburst pattern. The most affecting section is the Sant'Aquilino chapel, the 4th-century mausoleum decorated with original mosaics. Outside stand the **Colonne di San Lorenzo**, a cluster of Roman columns forming a portico in front of the church. Opinion is divided as to whether the Roman remains formed part of a temple or of public baths.

Nearby are the Portoni di Porta Ticinese, the medieval walls which were restructured in the 19th century. Corso di Porta Ticinese connects with Piazza XXIV Maggio, running south to the canal quarter. The Corso is lined with specialist shops, often devoted to crafts or cuisine. **Sant'Eustorgio 28** lies on Piazza XXIV Maggio, at the end of the Corso. The church dates back to the 5th century but was rebuilt from the 11th century onwards. The Dominican foundation conceals a chapel in Tuscan Renaissance style. Also on the square stands **Porta Ticinese 29**, a Neoclassical arch built on the former Spanish walls.

Just beyond is the **Darsena 30**, or canal basin, rep-

BELOW: statue of Constantine, San Lorenzo Maggiore.

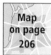
Map on page 206

The designer of the Pirelli Tower, Giò Ponti, proves the versatility of Italian industrial designers; apart from conceiving a Milanese landmark, he created the espresso machine, founded the magazine Domus and established the Milan Triennale.

BELOW: snacking on the Piazza del Duomo

resenting the hub of the Navigli. **Alzaia Naviglio Grande ㉛**, which hugs the northern bank of the main canal, changes its mood according to the time of day; a sleepy afternoon spent browsing in antique and craft shops gives way to an exuberant summer scene. Vicolo Lavandai, just off the Darsena end of the canal, is one of the most charming corners, with rustic cottages and a quaint wash-house. Beside it a mill is converted into the El Brellin restaurant, which combines traditional dishes and an old-fashioned Milanese atmosphere.

The station quarter

As a slice of monumental Milan, the station quarter offers some of the city's grandest hotel, as well as a section of seedier Milan. Travellers leaving from the airport bus terminal or taking the train to other cities will have no choice but to pass through the district. However, the area has a certain appeal for fans of innovative modern architecture.

The **Stazione Centrale ㉜** is overwhelming in its conception and sheer size. With its marble terraces and mosaic floors, this Fascistic, triumphalist affair is still the most splendid station in Europe. Facing it, **Hotel Gallia**, one of the city's most traditional luxurious hotels, offers a taste of the highlife in its sedate bar and restaurant, and on the adjoining Piazza d'Aosta soars the **Grattacielo Pirelli ㉝**, Milan's brutalist Pirelli Tower, designed by Giò Ponti in 1956.

The neighbouring **Piazza della Repubblica ㉞** is a soulless square that is, paradoxically, home to several of the city's finest hotels and hotel bars. Giardino d'Inverno, set in the smart Hotel Principe di Savoia, has an Art Nouveau design, known as *lo stile liberty*, complemented by a classical fountain and statues in Carrara marble. As an escape from the hordes it cannot be bettered. ❑

Alta Moda

Commercially, the Milan-based fashion industry is far more successful than its Parisian counterpart, with the Italian *alta moda (haute couture)* collections considered more wearable. Milan's reputation for style is enhanced by the presence of well-known *couturiers* who contribute to the city's prestigious design courses, from Romeo Gigli to Luciano Soprani.

The fashion world fields designers with the aspirations of Renaissance princelings the kitsch eroticism of Versace clashes with Armani's fluid lines, Romeo Gigli's romantic fantasies and Dolce & Gabbana's sense of fun. Certain designers cleave to tradition with quiet confidence. Cerutti continues to produce status-symbol suits for the rich and powerful-while Missoni, the grandparents of designer knitwear, have spent 50 years perfecting their blend of bright colours and eccentric hippy attitudes. If Armani reigns supreme as the king of classicism, Milan-based designers such as Dolce & Gabbana and Versace remain in the vanguard of youth culture, using techno fabrics to liberate youngsters from the straitjacket of classic Italian good taste. In the late 1990s, however, such sartorial pre-eminence was challenged by Prada, Gucci and Moschino. These reinvigorated logos were seen as provocative and playful yet glamorous.

Armani, the master of minimalism, specialises in sophisticated styling and softly tailored suits. His trademark deconstructed suits are object lessons in rigour and refinement, the quintessence of Italian classicism. Versace, the first superstar designer, was his sartorial polar opposite: vulgar, glamorous and sexually explicit. Armani's rivalry with Versace's 'rock and royalty' label was a running theme until the death of the 'emperor of excess' in 1997. Despite the loss of the creative design genius, the firm thrives under his sister, Donatella. Dolce & Gabbana, whose credo is to 'blur the lines of femininity and masculinity', are equally enslaved by sexual chutzpah. As for Moschino, although the

founder died in 1994 the house still produces glitzy sunglasses and scarves as well as wittily self-referential T-shirts.

The 1990s witnessed the battle for the high ground between Gucci and Prada, former luggage firms that became the most coveted labels of the decade. Gucci, as famous for its feuds as for its frocks, no longer belongs to the Florentine family founders. Guccio Gucci is one of the few remaining dynastic members since the murder of Maurizio Gucci in 1995, a contract killing ordered by his former wife. Gucci designs are marked by a contemporary androgyny.

By contrast with the cool chic of Gucci girl, Prada woman depends on a creative alchemy in which kooky ideas become functional clothes. As founder Miuccia Prada admits: "I am not exactly a designer but I know how to pull design elements together."

Certainly the quilted bag made from nylon, inspired by military bivouacs, has become a design classic. However, given the Italian beauty aesthetic, it isn't surprising that *stropicciato*, the grunge look, never caught on. ❏

RIGHT: Valentino's designs are among the most elegant in Italian fashion.

WHY "MADE IN ITALY" MEANS SO MUCH

Furniture, clothes, cars, typewriters, even kitchen appliances – the influence of Italian design has permeated the way we live and work today

Italian designers bask in their reputation for refinement, innate good taste and an eye for colour and line. "Quite simply, we are the best," boasts architect and cultural commentator Luigi Caccia. "We have more imagination, more culture, and are better mediators between the past and the future. That is why our design is more attractive and more in tune with the times than in other countries." Italian design is nothing if not inclusive. The traditional distinction between architect and industrial designer is blurred, with practitioners dabbling in fields as diverse as factory building and furniture design, office lighting and graphics. In the words of Ettore Sottsass, one of the most influential designers "Design should be a discussion of life, society, politics, food and the design itself."

△ FERRARI FORMULA
The Ferrari Spider is in a long line of fabulous cars from the most admired Italian manufacturer. Enzo Ferrari (1898–1988), the firm's founder, was also a noted racing-car designer.

MODERNISM TO POP ART

Since the turn of the century Milan has led industrial design, reaching its apogee in the 1970s and 1980s. The Italians produced seminal designs for cars and lamps in the 1930s, matched by radios and motorbikes in the 1940s. Milan also pioneered innovative design in the 1950s, with the mass production of household appliances from cookers and washing machines to kitchen utensils. Italian modernism supplanted the post-war European taste for the safe, hand-crafted homeliness of Scandinavian design. Stylish kettles and coffee percolators became cult objects in the 1960s, followed by quirky Pop Art furniture and the fashion designer chic of subsequent decades, from cool Armani to pared-down Prada. The inimitable character of *la linea italiana*, Italian style, still sets the standard for international design values.

▽ WINDOW SHOPPING
A highly structured Prada suit adorns Milan's fashion district. Prada is the fashion company that best captures the *Zeitgeist* of the 1990s. Its designs made it the most copied (faked) label on the city streets.

▷ WASHED OUT
Zanussi's rigorous designs, streamlined look and user-friendly features have long made it a European market leader in the field of washing machines, refrigerators and other "white goods".

CLASSIC CAR STYLE

△ PLASTIC FANTASTIC
A Post-Modern bookcase in laminated plastic, a bold design for the Memphis studio by Sottsass (1981). Memphis was the design event of the 1980s, a playful and much-imitated school inspired by Bob Dylan's song *Memphis Blues*.

◁ TALKING POINT
Italian design often takes ideas to their extreme, as in these eye-catching New Tone sculptural sofas by Atrium. This is subversive, unconventional, avant-garde living.

Ever since the 1930s, Italian car design has been characterised by stylistic restraint, versatility and timeless elegance. At one end of the scale, the Italians still produce some of the greatest status symbols in the world. In the 1950s the beautiful Alfa Romeo convertibles spelt playboy raffishness; Ferrari's Spider, the ultimate in glamour, was produced from 1966 to 1992 – the only sports car to boast a longer production run than Germany's Porsche 911.

Yet the Italians have also had great success with Fiat's bland but eminently practical models. Topolino ("the little mouse") was launched to great acclaim in 1939, and continued into the 1950s. Giovanni Agnelli studied American mass-production techniques, and from the 1950s the family dynasty had a captive market, with customers eager for the inexpensive Fiat 500.

The car industry is based in the North, with Fiat in Turin, Alfa Romeo in Milan and Ferrari in Modena. The huge Fiat Lingotto plant was set up near Turin in the 1920s, and today the city's fortunes are still inextricably linked to Fiat. The Italians also design for foreign manufacturers, including Mercedes and Rolls-Royce.

DESIGN CLASSIC
The Piaggio Vespa ("wasp"), first produced in 1946, became the symbol of freedom for the post-war generation. The Vespa Lifestyle bag (*above*), part of a trend for brand recognition and product diversification, is an austere minimalist offering from the Piaggio stable.

LOMBARDY

Map on page 226

"Beneath is spread like a green sea
The waveless plain of Lombardy, Bounded by the vaporous air
Islanded by cities fair" – Percy Bysshe Shelley

L ombardy, the Milanese hinterland, is the richest and most populous region in Italy, producing a quarter of its GNP and a third of all Italian exports. With an average income double that of the south, it has had a reputation for entrepreneurial flair since the Middle Ages, when the Como silk industry and the Milanese banks made the region a byword for reliability. Lombardy's prosperity was founded by its powerful independent cities, representing the antithesis of feudalism. The success story continues in modern times, with Brescia, Lombardy's second city, acting as New Jersey to Milan's Manhattan. If Brescia is synonymous with light industry and middle-class commuter-belt land, then Varese and its hinterland compete with helicopters, silks, confectionery and specialised foodstuffs.

Although economically progressive, Lombardy is socially more conservative, a product of its chequered past and deep local roots. The resourceful Lombards are descended from waves of Teutonic tribes, with Pavia becoming the capital under the Goths. During the Middle Ages the cities rose to prominence as independent communes, but later came to be run by paternalistic aristocracies. Bergamo, Brescia, Como, Pavia, Mantua and Cremona were powers in their own right. Under the Gonzagas, Mantua boasted a Renaissance court illustrious enough to engage Mantegna (died 1506) as a court painter. The region also prospered under the Visconti and Sforza dynasties, with the arms and textile industries favoured. Both are thriving, with arms manufacturing still based in Brescia, and textiles produced throughout the region. Venetian rule, which lasted until the 18th century, brought stability and a sophisticated veneer of superb palaces and villas.

Separatist sentiments

Lombardy regained a sense of leadership during the Risorgimento, the movement for Italian unity. In 1860, when Garibaldi set sail for Sicily, half of his volunteers were from Lombardy. This progressive region also led the way in industrialisation after World War II. Since then, however, feelings of resentment have set in, compounded by the Lombards' strong sense of identity. The desire to keep control of their regional riches has led to a rise in separatist sentiments. The Lombard resurgence of civic pride, in particular, followed in the wake of the corruption scandals of the early 1990s.

Lombardy embraces diverse territory, from the Alps to the plains, from watery rice paddies around Mantua to the lush Mediterranean climate of Lake Garda, rich in olive groves and oleanders. However, to most Italian minds it is synonymous with the misty, oppressive climate of the Po Valley which afflicts the area

PRECEDING PAGES:
poplars near
Mantua.
LEFT: alpine cattle
in Lombard
mountain pastures.
BELOW: Renaissance
fountain, Brescia.

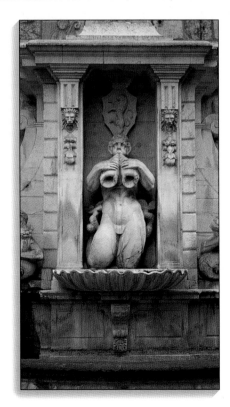

To nostalgic separatists the 12th century represents the flowering of Lombardy, with its rich civic culture, burgeoning guilds and Gothic churches.

around **Milan** , among other places. The city *(see pages 205–218)* is th starting point for rural excursions. South of the city lies the Bassa Milanese, curious region dotted with historic abbeys, border castles, extensive parks an large farms. The abbeys are the legacy of Benedictine monks who settled th marshy area during the Middle Ages. By contrast, the ruined fortresses reflec Milan's determination to defend its borders against threats from its rival, Pavia

A stone's throw from Milan

Monza ❷, just 10 km (6 miles) from Milan, makes a pleasant trip, particu larly for motoring fans. The Neoclassical Villa Reale adjoins the spacious **Parc di Monza**, one of the largest enclosed parks in Europe. Once part of the Habs burg and Savoy hunting estates, this was created in its present form in 1805 b Eugènè de Beauharnais, Napoleon's Viceroy. The spacious grounds are ampl enough to conceal a golf course and a cluster of working farms, plus the Auto dromo di Monza, the Formula One racing track situated in the grounds.

Abbiategrasso ❸, once an important port, is now a mere market town on the banks of the Naviglio Grande, which connects Milan with its rural hinterland. The Castello, a Gothic fortress, was partly destroyed by Spanish troops in the 17th century but retains a ruined tower and mullioned windows. Outside the town is Abbazia di Morimondo (open Fri–Wed, 8.30am–noon, 2.30–5.30pm), the remains of a Cistercian abbey. The complex, one of the earliest examples of Gothic in Italy, was created by Burgundian Benedictines, who were the first to drain and cultivate the once insalubrious marshes. The brickwork church, which dates from 1182, contains notable frescoes and 16th-century choir stalls. Adjoining Abbiategrasso is the **Parco del Ticino** ❹, which stretches from Turbigo to Pavi, following the course of the River Ticino, meandering through woods, water meadows, cultivated fields and rolling hills. The park offers a variety of activities, from hiking, cycling and riding to canoing and rafting.

Facade detail, Certosa di Pavia.

Vigevano ❺, just south of Abbiategrasso, boasts the huge Castello Sforzesco, occupied by two of Milan's major ruling dynasties, the Visconti and the Sforza. The 15th-century castle and the Piazza Ducale, a monumental Renaissance square, provide the setting for the historical Palio, a colourful competition which is staged in late spring and autumn. The surrounding countryside is noted for its rustic specialities, from salami risottos to omelettes made with wild herbs.

Chiaravalle ❻ (open Tues–Sun, 9am–noon, 2.30–6pm), set in a hamlet of the same name just south of Milan, is one of the loveliest abbeys in Italy. This Gothic masterpiece was founded by Saint Bernard in 1135 and was Italy's most important Cistercian abbey. Chiaravalle, which still enjoys a rural setting, conforms to rigid Cistercian principles but reflects the Lombard preference for brick. The church, decorated with 16th-century frescoes, is flanked by Gothic cloisters and a distinctive belltower.

BELOW: the garden cloisters of Certosa di Pavia.

Further south, before Pavia, stands the remarkable **Certosa di Pavia** ❼ (opens Tues–Sun, 9–11.30am and 2.30–6pm). The Carthusian monastery was founded in 1396 on the edge of the extensive park surrounding the Visconti castle in Pavia. Although created as a pantheon for the illustrious Visconti dynasty, the Charterhouse is better known as a decorative masterpiece in Lombard Renaissance style. However, since the Certosa took two centuries to build, the resulting complex also embraces Gothic and Baroque elements. The stunning Lombard façade (1473–9) is studded with marble sculptures and sumptuous lacey windows. The late Gothic interior is dotted with ornate vaulted chapels displaying Lombard sculptures, paintings and frescoes, including Renaissance funerary monuments to the d'Este dynasty. The cloisters form an atmospheric backdrop to the complex, with the Chiostro Piccolo, the small cloisters, distinguished by their decorative terracotta friezes.

By contrast, the Chiostro Grande houses the relatively luxurious monastic cells, which are still in use. In 1784 the monastery passed into Cistercian hands before being entrusted to the barefoot Carmelites. Although now state property, the Certosa is still run by the Cistercians whose vows of silence are relaxed enough to permit visitors to be shown around.

Just south is the historic city of **Pavia** ❽, set on

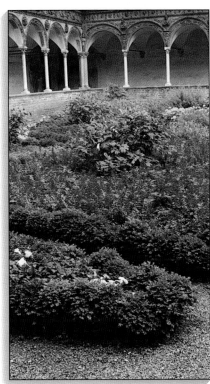

BELOW: the Ponte Coperto, Pavia.

the banks of the River Ticino. Although founded in Roman times, Pavia rose to prominence as the capital of the Goths from the 6th century to the 11th and witnessed such historic events as the coronation of Charlemagne in 774. The city later prospered as a medieval trading centre, with links with Amalfi and Venice. It was also resplendent during the Renaissance, when its court became the focal point for festivities throughout Lombardy. While Pavia has preserved a number of Romanesque and Renaissance buildings, the city's mood owes more to the Austrian domination, from the citizens' air of self-composure to the stucco-faced buildings, decorated in ochre, russet and cream colours.

Castello Visconteo (open daily, 9am–1.30pm), in the north of the city, was built by Gian Galeazzo Visconti in 1360. Although designed as a pleasure palace rather than as a castle, it is flanked by two corner turrets, the remains of mock-defensive fortifications. Inside, the archeological museum displays Roman, Etr-uscan and Egyptian exhibits, as well as statuary, mosaics and frescoes salvaged from demolished Romanesque and Renaissance churches. The east wing of the castle contains the Pinacoteca, a picture gallery focusing on Lombard painting from the Middle Ages to the Renaissance.

San Michele, on Via Paolo Diacono, is a Romanesque church built in mellow sandstone over a 7th-century Lombard basilica. The solemn, austere interior, reminiscent of Sant'Ambrogio in Milan, was where Federico (Frederick) Bar-barossa was crowned Holy Roman Emperor in 1155. The neighbouring **Strada Nuova**, the elegant main street, is built over a Roman road that linked the north and south of the city. Lined with smart cafés and boutiques, Strada Nuova crosses the river over a grand covered bridge that was reconstructed after bomb damage in World War II. The street's dignified air is underlined by the presence

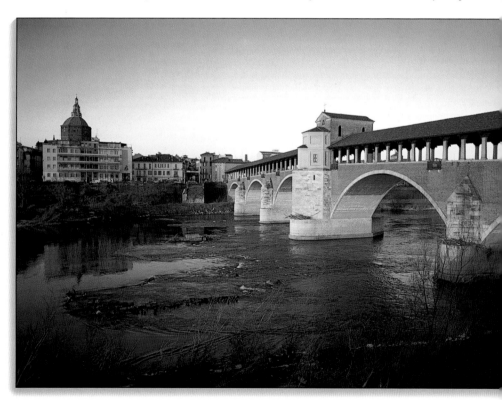

of an ancient university, famed for its faculties of law and medicine. Founded by the Visconti in 1361, the university owes more to Renaissance designs, despite later remodelling in Neoclassical style. A series of inner courtyards leads to the historic anatomical theatre and the Museo per la Storia (open Mon 3.30–5pm, Fri 9.30am–noon), the science-based university museum.

Lodi **❾** has always been overshadowed by Milan, Mantua and Pavia. However, the signing of the Peace of Lodi in 1454 signalled a period of peace and prosperity for the city, and marked the end of a long struggle between Francesco Sforza and the Venetians for control over the Duchy of Milan. Although indisputably a minor town, Lodi has some impressive Renaisance architecture. L'Incoronata, in particular, is a richly decorated church graced with a Renaissance portico and a gilded, stuccoed interior designed in the style of Bramante.

City of Monteverdi

Cremona **❿**, languishing on the plains of the Po, relishes its reputation as the cradle of fiddle-making and the birthplace of Monteverdi. The violins came into being in 1556, when Andrea Amati developed the modern violin industry. Since then their spirit and form have been likened to an essay in Baroque architecture: the subtle, curvaceous forms of the instruments, cut from the finest woods in Lombardy or the Dolomites, are reflected in the cornices and pediments of the city palaces. The great Stradivari was part of a long musical tradition that continues to shape city culture; other than at music festivals and violin museums, Cremona boasts more violin masters and workshops (*botteghe liutarie*) than any other European city.

Cremona was a pawn of the Visconti and Sforza dynasties before falling into

Map on page 226

Portrait of Claudio Monteverdi by Domenico Feti.

BELOW: one of the many violin workshops in Cremona, home of Stradivari.

TIP

Cremona makes for interesting shopping. Musicians can browse in the hundred violin workshops, while foodies can track down Cremona's wonderful nougat (*torrone*), cheese and salami shops.

Venetian, Spanish and Austrian hands. However, its greatest square belongs firmly to the medieval period. **Piazza del Comune** is a beguiling piazza with a cluster of imposing monuments. The sombre Lombard Romanesque Cathedral is decorated with loggias and faced with polychrome marble; inside are Flemish tapestries and a 16th-century Lombard fresco cycle. The adjoining **Torazzo,** the lofty crenellated belltower, is the symbol of the city, linked to the Cathedral by a Renaissance loggia, and the octagonal Romanesque baptistry has a portico supported by a pair of weathered lions. Opposite the cathedral stands the **Loggia dei Militi**, the headquarters of the captains of the citizens' militia, built in 13th-century Lombard style. Completing the square is the **Palazzo del Comune**, the grandiose town hall, which dates from the 13th century. On display inside are some of the greatest violins ever made, of which the undoubted star is the Cremonese 1715, a Stradivarius complete with its original mysterious varnish.

The **Museo Stradivariano** (open Tues–Sat, 9am–noon, 3–6pm) is set among the baroque palaces on Via Palestro. The collection contains casts and models which attempt to explain Stradivari's genius. Nearby, on Via Dati, is the Museo Civico (times as above), a grand palace housing an archeological section and an art gallery presenting an overview of art from Cremona and the rest of Lombardy from Renaissance times onwards.

Glorious ghost town

BELOW: Cremona's Romanesque cathedral.

Sabbioneta ⓫, set between Cremona and Mantua, is a rational expression of the Renaissance ideal, an orderly urban space provided with winter and summer palaces, a theatre, a hospital and a humanist a library, schools and a synaogue, a printing office and a mint. In 1444 it was an undistinguished village, but by he end of the century it had been transformed into a glittering Renaissance court. As one of the first consciously designed Renaissance cities it drew on humanist architectural treatises and the precepts of Vitruvius. The city is also a tribute to the fertile mind of Vespasian Gonzaga, an extravagant and impetuous prince of a patron. (In a moment of rashness, he accidentally killed his son by kicking him in the genitals.) At his best, Gonzaga sought to create a humanist utopia bounded by star-shaped Renaissance walls. Sabbioneta fell into decline with Gonzaga's death in 1591 and became something of a glorious ghost town.

Piazza Ducale, the main square, has a pink-and-white-marble parish church and an elegant Ducal palace, graced with a tower and loggia. The interior abounds in frescoed chambers and gilded ceilings. Behind the palace is the church of the Incoronata, with the austere façade contrasting with the ornate interior. Designed as Vespasian Gonzaga's tomb, the octagonal church delights in chiaroscuro effects and games of perspective.

At the end of the neighbouring Piazza Castello stands Palazzo del Giardino, a noble pleasure palace. The frescoed interior sports designs inspired by classical mythology. The other highlight is the Teatro Olimpico, a theatre modelled on Palladio's original in Vicenza. The monuments in this rural backwater can only be seen on a guided tour (tel: 0375-52039).

The Po Valley

Cremona and Mantua are set in the Po Valley, an area with great resonance for northern Italians. The Pianura Padana, the interminable northern plain, is broken only by screens of scrubby poplars and mulberry trees. Summers are stultifying and winters freezing, hence the popularity of the beach scene. Urban

Map on page 226

Reading matter on a city newsstand.

BELOW: rice, the main crop of Lombardy.

sophisticates may baulk at the brackish fishing lakes, the silted-up river mouths, the canyons of poplars, the lone belltowers, the watery bleakness and unpeopled pall of it all. Close to Mantua is a watery rice-growing area, reminiscent of the Lomellina rice paddies near Vigevano and Pavia. Lombardy, which has always employed advanced agricultural methods, introduced rice cultivation during the Renaissance, thus providing work for the peasants while satisfying the pampered palates of the urban rich.

TIP

Mantua's marshy location, bordered by lakes on three sides, produces a muggy climate, but this makes for atmospheric boat trips on Lago Superiore, the western lake. The Parco del Minclo, close to the city, is a wetlands zone with opportunities for bird-watching, boating and cycling.

BELOW: the sun sets over Mantua.

Melancholy Mantua

Mantua (**Mantova**) ⓓ is a stern, inward-looking, ponderously noble city. Surrounded by swampy lakes, this melancholy, masculine place was once a busy port. As an isolated city-state, protected by its waters, it was ruled by the extravagant Gonzaga dukes, and survived as a showy but canny buffer state between Milan and Venice. From 1328 until 1630 the Gonzaga led one of the liveliest and richest princely courts, attracting artists of the calibre of Pisanello, Italy's Gothic master, and Mantegna, the leading Renaissance artist in northern Italy. The last great Gonzaga, Vincenzo I, was the patron of Rubens and of Monteverdi, who composed *Orfeo* for the court of Mantua.

Foreigners tend to associate Mantua with Mantegna's magnificent cycle of frescoes. In Italian eyes, however, modern Mantua is known for its staunchly separatist politics. It has a strong sense of identity and became a member of the Lombard League in 1167. As a sign of the recent revival of regionalism, in 1992 it became the first city to be ruled by a Northern League mayor, and is known as a powerbase for separatists.

Mantua is blessed with a trio of impressive squares: the bustling marketplace of **Piazza dell'Erbe**; the medieval civic centre of **Piazza del Broletto**; and the cobbled Piazza Sordello, containing the seat of the ruling dynasty and the site of the Duomo. The cathedral's curious 18th-century façade gives way to a Renaissance interior, frescoed by Giulio Romano (circa 1492–1546). Just east of the Broletto, set on Via Accademia, is the **Teatro Scientifico**, an 18th-century gem of a theatre. **Piazza dell'Erbe** is dwarfed by the domed Renaissance **Basilica di Sant'Andrea** designed by Alberti, the great architect and theorist, and based on Vitruvius's idea of a Roman temple. Fittingly, Mantegna, who died in Mantua in 1506, is buried inside the city's greatest church. From here one can wander through austere red-brick arches and admire the dignified façades of a seductive city which is rarely soft and mellow.

Palazzo Ducale (open Tues–Sat, 9am–1pm, 2.30–5pm; Sun, and Mon 9am–1pm), the palatial playground of the Gonzaga dukes, monopolises the north-eastern section of the town. The Renaissance palace incorporates a basilica, political prisons and offices as well as Castello San Giorgio, the Gothic fortress that served as the family apartments. The 500 rooms, frescoed by artists as great as Pisanello or Mantegna, provide a snapshot of courtly life. Apart from the intimacy of Isabella d'Este's private chambers, the so-called dwarfs' apartments present a clear recognition that dwarfs were fashionable accessories in royal courts. Elsewhere, Arthurian legends or coffered ceilings illustrated with the signs of the zodiac bring to life the lavish world of the Gonzaga court.

The centrepiece of the palace is the **Camera degli Sposi**, a chamber decorated with Mantegna's frescoes of Ludovico II, his family, court and retinue. Painted between 1465 and 1474, these are frank portraits, painted without fear or favour, depicting hunting scenes, with pure-bred horses and sturdy mastiffs. The circular ceiling painting features a sumptuous garland with a glossy peacock and cherubs blessed with gosssamer wings. The *trompe l'oeil* ceiling is also an early attempt (1474) at perspective painting.

At the far end of town stands the **Palazzo del Te** (open Tues–Sun, 9am–6pm), an elegant country palace doubling as palatial horse stables and a boudoir for Gonzaga mistresses. The villa, constructed in harmonious classical style, has a frescoed interior (1525–35) which is largely the work of Giulio Romano, a gifted pupil of Raphael.

Map on page 226

Military minded

As a solid Lombard workhorse, **Brescia** ⑬ is not immediately appealing a: lumbering economic force with little natural grace. However, a recent re-evaluation of its artistic heritage, prompted by the superb restoration of the Santa Giulia complex, has tempted the city to take tourism more seriously. As Brixia, Brescia was a Gaulish and later a Roman city which still retains vestiges of its glorious past. Medieval Brescia was a member of the powerful Lombard League but by 1421 the Brescians, tired of regional rivalries and internal strife, had invited the Venetians to rule the city. Venetian domination signalled a period of prosperity and rebuilding, characterised by the remodelling of the cityscape.

A meeting of like minds in Brescia.

BELOW: the Palazzo Ducale in Mantua, home of the Gonzaga dukes.

Ruins of the Roman Temple, Brescia.

BELOW: the Piazza Vecchia, Bergamo.

Neighbouring iron-ore deposits also provided the basis for a firearms manufacturing industry so profitable that the Venetians imposed severe emigration restrictions on producers. Indeed, Brescia's reputation as Italy's chief armaments producer stems from this period.

The sinister and soulless **Piazza Vittoriale** is a ponderous tribute to Fascism, a symbolic hole where the heart of the city should be. The square only comes alive during the *Mille Miglia,* Italy's celebated vintage car rally. Fortunately the adjoining **Piazza della Loggia** is as vibrant and harmonious as Piazza Vittoriale is vainglorious and heartless. It is dominated by the clocktower and **Palazzo del Comune**, the Renaissance town hall. A note of grace is added by the square's Renaissance loggias, including one on **Monte di Pieta**, now the tourist office, with its façade studded with recycled Roman inscriptions.

Behind the clocktower looms the dome of the **Duomo Nuovo**, the curious 17th-century "new" cathedral, set on **Piazza Paolo VI**. On the east of the square squats the Romanesque **Duomo Vecchio** (open daily, 9am–noon, 3–7pm),has the site of the Roman baths. Known as the Rotonda, this softly-lit basilica has a cylindrical dome supported by eight pillars. The impressive crypt incorporates medieval and Roman columns as well as mosaics from the Roman baths.

Santa Giulia Museo della Citta' (open Tues–Sun, l0am–9pm), set on Via dei Musei at the foot of the castle, is an innovative new museum complex that showcases Brescia's past in relevant monuments from the Bronze Age to the present day. It incorporates an 8th-century nunnery, the Renaissance church and cloisters of Santa Giulia, the Romanesque oratory of Santa Maria in Solario, and the Lombard Basilica of San Salvatore. This church alone is a major monument, with its Byzantine influences and Lombard nave flanked by Roman

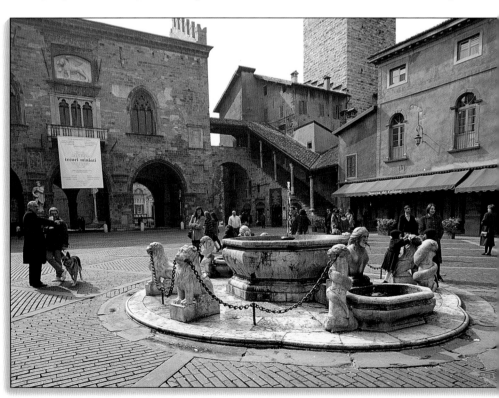

columns. The Longobard and Carolingian section is set in San Salvatore and displays frescoes, gold jewellery and 8th-century terracottas. The Venetian section, rich in statuary and frescoes, depicts the city from the late Gothic and Renaissance periods, while the Roman section is notable for mosaics, bronzes and sarcophagi unearthed while excavations were taking place in San Salvatore.

The route from Santa Giulia to Via Piamarta passes the ruins of the city's remaining Roman gate. The Cydneo (Chydnean) hill that looms up behind Via dei Musei was the core of Roman Brixia. Via dei Musci, formerly the Decamanus Maximus, leads to the ruins of the forum in **Piazza del Foro.** Above stand the Corinthian colonnades and pediment of the Capitoleum, the Capitoline temple built by Vespasian in AD 73 and probably dedicated to Jupiter, Juno and Minerva. Next to the temple is the insignificant-looking **Teatro Romano,** which once held 15,000 spectators. The medieval Castello, set atop the Cydneo hill, possesses a Gothic tower built over Roman remains. The most interesting castle museum is the remodelled **Luigi Marzoli** (open Tues–Sun, l0am–5pm), a tribute to Brescia's military might and the focus for leafy walks that connect the castle grounds with the lower city.

Pasticceria in Bergamo.

Great escapes and Donizetti

Franciacorta ⓮, sandwiched between Brescia and Lake Iseo, is an appealing wine-growing region. **Lago d'Iseo** ⓯ itself *(see Lakes)* is one of the least visited yet more engaging lakes.

The combination of cobbled streets, cypress-clad hills and mountain air makes **Bergamo** ⓰ a refreshing diversion. Memories of the stifling Lombard plains are banished by Bergamo's delightful skyline and softly-hued stonework. Although a significant settlement in Roman times, the city owes more to the late-medieval and Renaissance periods.

Medieval Bergamo experienced independence before falling under the sway of the Venetians from 1428 to 1797. Today Bergamo is essentially two cities: the well-preserved *citta alta,* or historic upper city, and the spacious but uninspiring *citta bassa,* or lower city. The city on the plain possesses one extraordinary art gallery, but otherwise the sights are concentrated in the lofty *citta alta.*

The fortified upper city, framed by Monte Vigilio, is easily reached by cable car. Bergamo is bound by a circle of defensive walls, built by the Venetians in 1560 after the city had outgrown its medieval ramparts. At its heart is the **Rocca**, the former fortress built to protect the Venetian empire against the Milanese state. The Rocca spans the site of Roman ruins and now encompasses landscaped gardens. A leisurely stroll along the 5km (3 miles) of city **walls** makes a fitting prelude or postscript to a summer visit.

With its winding streets and mountainous climate, the wintry upper city is particularly appealing under a snowfall. At the heart of the town lies **Piazza Vecchia**, a harmonious Gothic ensemble. Flanking the porticoed square are the lofty civic tower and the Palazzo della Ragione, the much-remodelled medieval council chambers, complemented by a graceful fountain, and the Palladian-style Palazzo Nuovo, housing

BELOW: the richly sculpted stonework of Cappella Colleoni.

the city library. The adjacent Piazza del Duomo is the religious centre, home to the Gothic Cathedral and the more memorable **Santa Maria Maggiore**, an austere Romanesque basilica. Attached to the south wall is the **Cappella Colleoni**, built in the 1470s as a funerary monument for Bartolomeo Colleoni, a legendary *condottiere.* The richly sculpted chapel, on the site of the original sacristy, is one of the earliest set-pieces of Renaissance architecture in Lombardy.

In the lower town, the **Accademia Carrara** (open daily, 9.30am–noon, 2.30–5,30pm) cushions the blow of coming down to earth. The collection, one of the grandest arrays of Lombard and Venetian art, contains paintings by such masters as Tintoretto, Bellini, Veronese, Tiepolo, Pisanello and Mantegna.

On the pedestrianised Sentierone is the **Teatro Donizetti**, dedicated to Bergamo's celebrated native son (1797–1848). Opera-lovers are rewarded with Gaetano Donizetti's light touch, gift for melody and art of *bel canto*, the traditional emphasis on fine tone and ornamentation. (The composer's birthplace is in the upper city, in the picturesque street of Borgo Canale, with a Donizetti museum in Via Arena nearby.)

Cookery writer Claudia Roden is one of many to single out the local cuisine: "Bergamo, once part of the Serenissima, is more Venetian; Mantua has refined aristocratic traditions and is more like Emilia, to the south. But they do have things in common: they use enormous quantities of butter, lard and cream and all their cuisines are based on risotto, polenta and *minestre*."

Prehistoric carvings

Val di Camonica 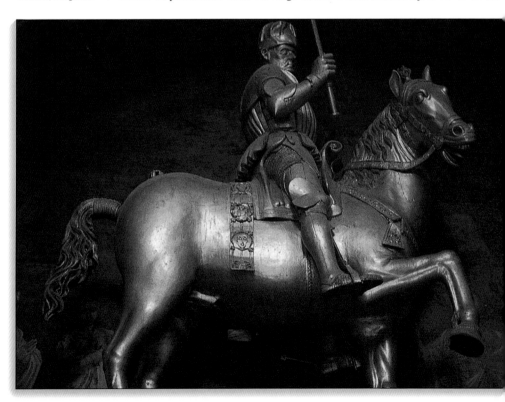, also known as Valcamonica, has the greatest concentration of prehistoric rock-carvings in the world. Situated just north of the spa town of Boario Terme, this rural valley has been inhabited since the Neolithic era. The carvings span a period of thousands of years, from Neolithic times (before 2200 BC) until the Roman era. For generations the Camuni tribes of hunters and farmers made their mark by recording their symbols of everyday life and propitiatory rites, warfare and weaponry. Altogether there are approximately 200,000 carvings on this glacier-seared sandstone, of which about 30,000 represent figures. All the images are presented in varying degrees of sophistication, from Stone Age scratchings to Bronze Age narratives. A wide selection of mystifying images is visible on Naquane rock, including solar discs, roses and labyrinths.

Capo di Ponte ⓲ (tel: 0364-42212) marks the main entrance to the Unesco-recognised **Parco Nazionale delle Incisioni Rupestri**, the largest open-air display of rock-carvings in Europe.

Springboard for the Dolomites

As a popular winter and summer resort, **Bormio** ⓳ provides a convenient base for exploring the glacier-encrusted Dolomite mountains. It is also a gateway to the Stelvio National Park (*see Walking, page 126*), the largest park in the Alps. **Parco Nazionale dello Stelvio** ⓴ straddles Lombardy, Trentino and the Swiss border, encompassing alpine meadows, myriad lakes and dramatic peaks. Although hunting is illegal on the Lombardy side, the wildlife over the Trentino border have been slow to sneak over.

Access to the park is from numerous sites in Lombardy as well as from Trentino (*see page 199*). These exhilarating snow-capped mountains could not make a more dramatic contrast with the muggy Lombard plains. ❑

Map on page 226

The park claims to possess the oldest representation of a rose, an image duplicated throughout the valley and now adopted as Lombardy's official regional symbol.

BELOW:
Capo di Ponte.

Valle d'Aosta and Piedmont

VALLE D'AOSTA

Map on pages 240–241

The "Valley of Castles", centred on the Roman town of Aosta and surrounded by the highest peaks in Europe, is a great region for driving, hiking and taking cable-car rides

Torino

The Valle d'Aosta is the highroad in and out of Italy. Bordering France on the western side is Mont Blanc (Monte Bianco, 4,810 metres/15,780ft), and bordering Switzerland in the north are the Matterhorn (Monte Cervino, ,478 metres/14,692ft) and Monte Rosa (4,634 metres/15,203ft), the three highst mountains in Europe. On the south side is the highest mountain entirely within Italy, Gran Paradiso (4,061 metres/13,323ft), which gives its name to he spectacular surrounding National Park. The region takes its name not from he river that created the valley – the thundering Dora Baltea, which feeds to River Po – but from its main town, Aosta, named after Emperor Augustus who et up one of his chain of mini-Romes in the centre of the valley.

Accessible only along the river's course, the "Valley of Castles" is clearly of trategic importance, and its mountain passes, *fenêtres*, have been used by the great armies of European history, from Hannibal to Napoleon. The most important of these glacially eroded saddles are the Great St Bernard pass, north of Aosta, leading to Switzerland, and Little St Bernard, south of Mont Blanc, leading to France. The 5.6-km (3½-mile) road tunnel through Great St Bernard was opened in 1964, the 12-km (7½-mile) Mont Blanc tunnel the following year.

This is the supreme alpine region of Italy, home to marmots, ibex, ermines and eagles, laid out with orchards, vineyards and meadows, bright with flowers and singing with trout-filled torrents. Wildlife is conserved in one national and one regional park, and in nine nature reserves. Glaciers glisten and snow is visible all year, though rainfall here is the lowest in Italy. Dairy farming is important; local "red-dappled" and "black-dappled" cattle move up and down the pastureland clunking their bells. Minerals have been exploited since the 15th century, and there is still some iron and steel production.

Mountain men

Woodcarvers, herdsmen and adroit mountaineers, the people are conservative and pious – St Anselm, an archbishop of Canterbury, was born in Aosta in 1033. The French language, imposed by the Savoy Duke Emanuel Filiberto in 1561, is in evidence, and a Franco-Provençal culture dominates, with a minority Walser, German-Swiss, tradition in the upper valleys in the northeast.

In 1943 there was a move towards annexation with France after 20 years of Fascism under which local languages had been suppressed, workers were mandatorily imported from poorer areas, and an "Italianisation" of the region had been attempted. In 1944 several well-respected local nationalists were murdered by the Fascists. Three years after the end of the war the region was granted a degree of autonomy.

PRECEDING PAGES: Valle d'Aosta; where the towns meet the mountains. **LEFT:** meadow in bloom, Val d'Ayas. **BELOW:** a mountainman of Valle' d'Aosta.

The Lower Valley

Pont-St-Martin ❶, overlooked by 12th-century Castello du Pont, was the main iron and steel town in the Valle d'Aosta until the end of the 19th century. The *pont* crosses the River Lyss, the first of half a dozen tributaries on the northern side of the valley, and the 34-km (21-mile) road traces it up the **Val di Gresonne** to the foot of Monte Rosa. The 100-sq-km (39-sq.-mile) Lys glacier on the Italian slope is a clue to the naming of the mountain after the word *roise*, local dialect for glacier. The 16th-century church of St James the Elder at **Issime ❷** has a splendid external fresco of the Last Judgment executed by the d'Enrico brothers.

Further up, the Lys is fed by a number of spectacular waterfalls. **Gressoney-St-Jean ❸** was apparently founded by shepherds from the Swiss Valais, and *titsch*, an ancient German dialect, is still spoken here. Nearby is **Savoy Castle** (open Fri–Wed, 1 April–30 September, 9am–7pm; 1 October–1 March 9am–noon, 3–6pm, closed Thurs) and botanical gardens, summer residence of Queen Margherita, widow of King Umberto I, who had it built in 1894. The simple, Nordic-looking buildings of the Walsers are scattered through the upper valley, which draws to a halt at **Gressoney-la-Trinité**, a major winter resort.

Beyond Pont-St-Martin the main road passes the sturdy, cold fortress at **Bard**, to which Cavour was confined in 1831 for his liberal ideas. One of the most interesting castles in the valley is 10km (6 miles) further on at **Issogne ❹** (open daily, 9am-7pm, tours every 30 minutes; entrance fee). More château than fortress, the three-storey building overlooking a courtyard with a pomegranate fountain was begun in 1480 by the local noble Challant family. Restored in the last century, it contains period furniture and objects, and some delightful frescoes on the lunettes of the entrance portico which show every-

BELOW AND RIGHT:
friendly locals.

Map
on pages
240–241

day street life at the end of the 15th century. The next village on the same side of the river is **Champdepraz** ❺, the entry point to the **Mont Avic Regional Park**, a curious landscape of lakes and peat bogs which support a rich flora and 1,000 species of butterfly.

Opposite Issogne is **Verrès**, where Ibleto de Challant built a castle in the 14th century, and from here a road winds up the **Val d'Ayas**, which follows the River Evançon 27 km (17 miles) to **Champoluc** ❻, another resort beneath Monte Rosa. En route are the 50-metre (165-ft) waterfall at **Isollaz**, a 10th-century castle at **Graines**, wooden houses at **Brusson** and a sparkling blue reservoir by the **Colle de Joux**.

Back in the valley, the main road climbs around **Montjovet** and then opens on to the broad valley around **St Vincent** ❼, a spa town and leisure centre, to **Châtillon** where a third valley, the **Valtournenche**, runs north. The town the valley is named after lies 18km (11 miles) away, and the great sliver of the Matterhorn beckons at each twist and turn.

In the small town square at **Valtournenche** ❽ tablets have been struck on the walls to commemorate the guides and climbers who have risked their lives in the mountains. **Breuil-Cervinia**, the great ski resort of the 1930s, is at the end of the road 9km (6 miles) further on.

Of all the Challant family's castles, the finest is beyond Chatillin at **Fénis** ❾ (open daily, 9am–7pm; tours every 30 minutes). Every inch a proper castle, with towers, keeps, crenellations and a double curtain wall, it was built by Aimone de Challant in 1340. There are good frescoes in the courtyard, attributed to the school of Giacomo Jaquerio (1375–1453), and the building is used as the Museum of Valle d'Aosta Furnishings.

In chilly Valle d'Aosta, the locals have a penchant for fortified caffè valdostano nella grolla, *laced with wine, grappa and sugar. The* grolla, *or drinking vessel, is supposedly descended from the Grail, the chivalric cup of yore.*

BELOW: the castle at Issogne has some fine frescoes.

Aosta, the Roman hub

Beyond Fénis the valley opens generously to encompass **Aosta ❿**, the region's capital (population 36,000). Built in 25BC as a military camp, Augusta Praetoria was dissected by the roads to the passes of Little St Bernard and Great St Bernard. However you enter Aosta, the best way to understand it is as a traveller would have done in the time of Augustus, arriving at the lower end of the town over the Roman bridge, and crossing the River Buthier to the Roman **Arch of Augustus**, now squatting on a traffic island. From here the Roman road is a pedestrian precinct, Via Sant'Anselmo, where clogs, cuckoo clocks and mountain hooch are displayed for the passing tourist.

To the right is an intriguing series of ancient church buildings built outside the city walls around the **Collegiate di Sant'Orso**, perhaps the most important in the whole valley. It has a highly original 15th-century façade, opposite a free-standing Romanesque belltower (1131). High under the church roof, between the middle nave and the loft, are some fine 15th-century frescoes. The handsome 16th-century wooden choir stalls were carved by Jeninus Braye. The crypt dates from the 11th century, as does the cloister, which has richly carved and animated capitals.

Via Sant'Anselmo leads to **Porta Praetoria**, even now a massively impressive stone entrance into the city. Made of "pudding stone slabs", the two arched walls are 4.5 metres (14ft 9in) and 3.45 metres (11ft 4in) thick, and some three metres of them are hidden beneath the rising level of the ground. The entrance pierces the centre of the eastern wall, and most of the Roman city walls, a perfect rectangle 572 metres by 724 metres (1,875ft by 2,375ft), remain intact. Inside the Porta Praetoria and to the right are the remains of the **Roman theatre and amphitheatre**.

BELOW: Aosta's Arch of Augustus.

The shopping lane then opens up into the main square, Plaza Emilio Chanoux, named after one of the leading Aosta nationalists murdered by the Nazis. This is a fine square for a coffee and a look at life. The tourist office and town hall are situated here, the latter built in 1839 after French troops had destroyed the Franciscan convent on the site. A lane in the far right corner leads up to the **Cathedral**, which has an intriguing façade with a polychromatic tableau above the main portal. The **Museo de Tesoro**, housed in the ambulatory, has some of the finest treasures of Christian art in the valley (open 1 April–30 September: daily, 10am–noon, 3–6.30pm; 1 October–31 March, ask for permission from the custodian, tel: 0165/40413; entrance fee). The nearby **Archaelogical Museum** has plans of the Roman city and finds from the valley.

The upper valley

The Buthier torrent heads towards the Great St Bernard Pass to the north of the city. It soon divides, the right fork going east up the **Valpelline** valley and where, there are old wood-balconied houses. During the French Revolution the Bishop of Paris holed up here in **Bionaz**. The valley ends at a vast dam which flooded the upper reaches in 1965. To the left, the road heads to **Colle del Gran San Bernardo ⓫**, where a hospice was founded in 1050 by St Bernard of Montjoux, patron saint of mountaineers, and, later, dogs named after him were trained to find people lost in snowstorms. The present building dates from 1825.

On the main road above Aosta is the castle of **Sarre ⓬**, Victor Emmanuel II's hunting lodge, decorated with horns from a thousand mountain goats. The king had set up a Royal Hunting Reserve in 1856 on the facing slopes of Gran Paradiso. In 1929 Victor Emmanuel III donated 5,200 acres (21 sq. km) of the park

Map on page 240–241

Bernard of Montjoux, born in 996, was a canon in Aosta Cathedral with responsibilities over the mountain passes. He did much to minister to the peoples of these remote areas, and built rest houses at the top of the passes (Great and Little St Bernard). In 1932 Pope Pius XI made him patron saint of mountaineers.

BELOW: Fénis castle.

Mountain flora.

Map on page 240–241

to the state; this became the **Parco Nazionale del Gran Paradiso**, which stretches over the mountain into Piedmont. On the Aosta side it lies between the **Valle Rhêmes** and the **Valle de Cognes**, the best entry point to the park. The drive up the **Cogne Valley** beside the river is delightful. **Cogne ⑬** is a modest town and a good springboard for the hills. Just above it, at **Valnontey**, 1,700 metres (5,580ft) up, is the **Paradisia Alpine Botanical Gardens** (open 2nd weekend in June–2nd weekend in September, 9.30am–12.30pm, 2.30–6.30pm; period of maximum bloom end of June to mid-July), which has more than 1,000 flower species found in mountain regions all over the world .

The flora and fauna of the mountains is otherwise laid out in the **Natural Science Museum** at the fairytale castle at **Saint Pierre ⑭** just beyond Sarre. There are description of lichen and displays of the colourful local minerals.

The valley is now closing in as it heads towards Mont Blanc, and tempting glimpses of this majestic white lady come around each bend. The last major town in the valley is **Courmayeur ⑮** where, along the pedestrianised Via Roma, shops brim with produce and outdoor music plays in summer. The **Museo Alpino Duca degli Abruzzi** (9am–6.30pm; closed Mon) has a collection of snow-wear and memorabilia from mountain climbs and Antarctic expeditions. From here there are many excursions to make, by ski in winter and on foot in summer.

The Mont Blanc Tunnel lies ahead, or you can scale the mountain by cable car across the Aiguille du Midi to Chamonix in France. To the south, the S26 road winds past the Pré Saint-Didier gorge to **Thuile** and the **Colle del Piccole San Bernardo (Little St Bernard Pass) ⑯**, where a stone circle is known as Hannibal's Circle after the Carthaginian and his invading band of elephants.   ❑

Skiing

Less expensive than their French, Swiss and Austrian counterparts, Italy's ski resorts are full of good food and relaxed Italian fun. Snow lasts roughly from Christmas to Easter, pistes come in all shapes and sizes, and sports include snowboarding, snowmobiling, snow-shoeing, snow-rafting, skijoring, dog-sledding, sleigh rides, parapenting, ice-climbing, and polo played on frozen lakes. Après-ski is fully catered for, and restaurants can always be looked forward to; Italians do not consider a long lunch a waste of skiing time.

Skiing in Italy began at the turn of the century in the Susa valley, Piedmont, when Adolfo Kin in Sauze d'Oulx and the Smith brothers in Bardonecchia imported wooden skis to help them get about in the snow. Today these two towns are part of the **Milky Way** (Via Lattea), 400km (250 miles) of piste that make up one of Europe's great ski circuits, taking in Montgenèvre in France. The circuit's centre is **Sestriere** in Piedmont, where the Alpine Skiing World Championships were held in 1997.

Further north is **Courmayeur**, beneath Mont Blanc at the head of the Valle d'Aosta. This is an old town with a good social life and abundant restaurants, which are appreciated by Italians, particularly visitors from Milan. Linked to Chamonix in France, it lies on the sunny side of the slope, which in no way diminishes its snowfall. **La Thuille**, an old mining town nearby, is a good choice for escaping crowds, for both beginners and intermediates.

Cervinia (the Matterhorn) in the Valle d'Aosta is the most reliable resort for snow. Built up by Mussolini, it is rather lacking in soul. The village of **Valtournenche** just down the valley is a more attractive proposition. Cervinia is linked with Zermatt in Switzerland, and ski passes are valid in both resorts. More ethnic, and quieter, are the Walser settlements in the nearby **Monte Rosa** area: **Alagna**, **Champoluc** and **Gressoney-la-Trinité**.

One of the most typically Italian resorts is **Bormio**, a Roman spa town with a pedestri-anised centre of cobbled streets, chic shops and low-key nightlife. Snow stays late, and the town is linked to the more lively **Santa Catarina** and in reach of St Moritz in Swizerland. **Livigno** in the Spol Valley is linked to both St Moritz and Davos in Switzerland and is one of the cheapest resorts. Both Lombardy resorts are around five hours from Bergamo or Milan.

The Dolomites in northeastern Italy offer the best-value skiing in Europe. Skiers in Verona head for **Madonna di Campiglio**, which has good woodland cross-country trails, while skiiers in Bergamo also head for **Passo Tonale**, and for **Pontedilegno**, which is inexpensive and has easy slopes for beginners. The top Dolomite resort is **Cortina d'Ampezzo**, two hours from Venice. This is the smartest place to ski in the country. It is not overpriced, and anyone can watch the rich climb aboard helicopters in search of new snow thrills.

Where skiers go walkers can go, too, and ski lifts and cable cars operate in many places throughout the summer. ❑

TURIN

Map
on page
254

*With a royal palace, more than 30 museums, smart shops,
elegant cafés and a replica of the famous Holy Shroud,
there's plenty to see and do in Piedmont's capital*

Italy's fourth largest city (population 1.2 million) is a harmonious and noble collection of 18th- and 19th-century streets built where three rivers join the Po. From 1574 this was the seat of the House of Savoy, a duchy that once not only included Piedmont and the Valle d'Aosta but also extended into Switzerland and took in all the Savoie in France as well as the island of Sardinia.

It was here that the Turin-born aristocrat Count Camillo di Cavour colluded with Victor Emmanuel (Vittorio Emanuele) of Savoy against the empires of France and Austria to bring about an independent and unified Italy (though Nice and Savoie were lost in the process) and, in 1861, provide Italy with its first capital. In every piazza and at every junction huge, moustached Emanueles and Umbertos rise on plinths and warhorses, leaving no doubt about the satisfaction the House of Savoy felt in providing blue blood for an Italian monarchy.

For all their heroism, the aristocracy were wimps in the wet, insisting that colonnades line the main streets so they would never be bothered by rain. The result is that the heart of the city has a grand Baroque and Neoclassical air, with seamless arcades shading discreet cafés and smart shops suggesting nothing of the industrial city of Fiat and factory workers, of Antonio Gramsci and red-brigade targets, of the tough working city that Turin really is.

PRECEDING PAGES:
the Caffe Torino,
off Turin's Piazza
San Marco.
LEFT: the dome of
the chapel of San
Lorenzo.
BELOW: Turin
grandeur.

Orientation

At first this seems like a one-street town. From the gates of the royal palace there is a clear view straight down the Via Roma and its handsome, colonnaded *piazzas* to the glass-and-iron greenhouse of the grand railway station 1.2km (¾ mile) away. This is the first street to stretch your legs in. Two lesser streets lead off from the castle in front of the royal palace: the colonnaded Via Po heads down to the attractive Piazza Vittorio Veneto and the River Po, and in the opposite direction the pedestrianised Via Garibaldi makes for the older part of town.

The cathedral and old town

There was a bishopric in Turin from around the 5th century, but the present Cathedral was not completed until 1498. The **Duomo di San Giovanni ⓐ** is a small but elegant Renaissance design by a Tuscan architect, Meo del Caprina da Povere. Beside it is a 60-metre (200-ft) brick campanile built 30 years earlier, topped by an 18th-century bell house by Filippo Juvara. At the back of the Cathedral is an outstanding Baroque octagonal cupola built by Guarino Guarini in 1694, illuminating the black **Capella del Sindone**, the chapel of the Holy Shroud (*see page 259*), entered from inside the church and also accessible through the royal palace behind. In 1997 the cupola was seri-

Turin

ously damaged by fire. Guarini was a monk from Modena, and Juvara, who was working in the mid-18th century, some 50 years later, was from Messina in Sicily. Both contributed enormously to the city's architecture, evolving a distinctive local Baroque style.

Map on page 254

From the cathedral steps the remains of the Roman city are evident on the right in some fragments of the wall, theatre and **Porta Palatina ❸**, the main gate to the Po Valley. Walk through it to reach the **Piazza della Repubblica ❹**, the site of a market every morning and all day Saturday. There is also a flea market, the Balôn, on Saturdays, which becomes the Gran Balôn antiques market on the second Sunday of the month.

Beyond the market, by one of the Roman city's five corner towers, are the Piazza Consolata and Guarini's round **Church of the Consolata ❺**. Around this ancient square are an old herbalist's shop and Al Bicerin, a café famously frequented by the composer Puccini and still serving its renowned hot drink, the *bicerin*, made of coffee, chocolate and cream.

There are a number of old shops and manor houses in this former heart of the city. Jean-Jacques Rousseau lived at 11 Via dei Cappelli (now a wine shop) and was converted to Catholicism at a neighbouring hospice in 1728. The **Palazzo Città ❻** is the former grass market, just off the old Roman Via Dora Grossa, now Via Garibaldi, a pedestrianised throughfare that is one of the most characterful streets in the city.

On the Porta Palatina, gateway to the Po Valley.

Royal Turin

Via Garibaldi arrives at the centre of the town at **Piazza Castello ❼**, where the only medieval monument in the city is found; it is known as the Palazzo Madama since two royal widows, Marie-Christine d'Orléans and Giovanna Battista of Savoy, made it their home. The Senate of the Kingdom of Savoy met in its Salone degle Svizzeri between 1846 and 1861, and for the next three years it housed the Senate of the Kingdom of Italy. The Swiss connection is confirmed by the statue of the Standard Bearer of the Swiss Army by Vincenzo Vela on the south side of the building, presented to the city in 1857 by the municipality of Milan. The Castello now contains the **Museo Civico di Arte Antica** (open Tues–Sat, 2–7pm; Sun, public holidays, 9am–7pm).

BELOW: window shopping in Turin.

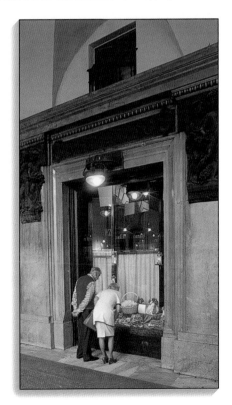

The royal buildings which lie to the north of the castle will not have gone unnoticed. Their near wing contains, on the ground floor, the **Biblioteca Reale** and, on the first floor, with Oriental as well as Risorgomento and Napoleonic weapons, the **Armeria Reale** (royal armoury, Wednesday, Friday, Saturday 9am-2pm; Tuesday, Thursday 1.30–7pm, closed Monday and public holidays).

Beyond, through the Piazza Reale, is the **Palazzo Reale ❽**, which it is essential to visit (regular guided tours, Tues–Sun, 9am–1pm and 2–6pm). The Royal Palace was built in 1660 by the architect Amadeo di Castellamonte and was used by the Savoy dukes until 1865. Dripping gold and velvet, chinoiserie and chandeliers, the first-floor apartments around a plain courtyard are furnished with pomp and pretension. The

In Turin, café life is in the blood. The citizens have a passion for pastries and desserts, many of which were first created for the royal court of Savoy. For more information on Turin's cafés, see page 111 in the chapter entitled "Café Society".

palace grounds are modest but pleasant for a stroll. On the far side of the Castello, beside the 18th-century façade of the **Teatro Regio**, the Via Po leads down to the river, passing, on the left, Via Montebello where the extraordinary **Mole Antonelliana** ❶ points its 167-metre (548-ft) spire at the sky as an emblem of the city. Named after its architect, Alessandro Antonelli (1798-1888), it was originally a synagogue and is now being prepared as a cinema museum. The shops among Via Po's arcades includes the aristocratic **Caffè Florio**, an ice-cream specialist, where Cavour drank and dreamed in its plush red 19th-century décor. The street ends in the wide **Piazza Vittorio Veneto** ❶, an elegant square looking across the Ponte Vittorio Emanuele to the 19th-century Gran Madre de Dio on the opposite bank.

The Risorgimento relived

On the south side of the Castello, near the grand Caffè Mulassano, the Via Accademia della Scienza leads down to **Piazza Carignano** ❶, Turin's political centre in the 19th century when it seethed with optimism and grand plans for an emergent independent state.

On one side of the square are Il Cambio, where Cavour dined, which is still a prestigious restaurant serving traditional local dishes, and the Teatro Carrignano; on the other side is **Palazzo Carignano**, designed by Guarini, where Italy's first king, Victor Emmanuel II, was born in 1820. It now houses the **Museo Nazionale del Risorgimento** (open Tues–Sat, 9am–7pm; Sun, 9am–12.30pm, entrance charge), and though 27 rooms may be more than one wishes to see concerning the movement, the experience should not be missed, particularly the fledgling Italian parliament chamber, built like a small plush theatre.

BELOW: one of a pair of statues representing the Po and Dora rivers.

Guarini designed the **Pallazzo dell'Accademia delle Scienze** ⓚ on the south side of the square for the Jesuits; it now houses the **Museo Egizio** (open Tues–Sat, 8.30am–10pm; Sun and public holidays, 8.30am–8pm). Turin may not be the place in which visitors would expect to learn more than they already knew about Egyptian civilisation, but this is one of the world's largest collections. It has some fine paintings, and the commentary is also available in English. On the top floor of the building is the **Galleria Sabauda** (same opening times), an extensive art collection of Italian and Dutch paintings based on the original collection of the dukes of Savoy.

Opposite the museum is **San Filippo Neri**, the city's largest church and a product of both Guarini and Juvarra. On the far side of the Palazzo Carignano is **Piazza Carlo Alberto**, dominated by Marocchetti's equestrian statue of Carlo Alberto, Victor Emmanuel's father, who was also born in the palace. On the corner of Via Carlo Alberto is a plaque commemorating "Frederico" Nietzsche's stay in the city in 1888.

Walk back up to Via Roma and **Piazza San Carlo** ⓛ, the heart of this elegant thoroughfare, designed by Castellamonte, where a pianist might be playing at the Caffè Torino. Another equestrian statue by Marocchetti, that of Emanuele Filiberto (1831–38), is in the centre of this grand space of former noble homes and exclusive establishments, including, at No. 183, the still existing Circolo de Whist founded by the card-carrying Count Camillo di Cavour.

Map on page 254

Elegant façade, Piazza San Carlo.

BELOW: Turin's Il Cambio is typical of the city's many upmarket restaurants.

Via Roma and the railway station

Beyond the piazza, Via Roma becomes a street again where statues of two figures, refreshingly naked and unhorsed, represent Turin's two major rivers, the Po and the Dora. Ahead lies the final elegant square, **Piazza Carlo Felice** ⓜ, with bandstand and ponds, sitting in front of the **Porta Nuova railway station** and the slightly seedier end of the town. The Corso Vittorio Emanuele runs in front of it, leading on the right hand to the **Galleria Civica d'Arte Moderna e Contemporanea** ⓝ, which has mainly 18th- and 19th-century Italian and foreign art, with continual temporary exhibitions (open Tues–Fri,10am–5pm; Sat, Sun, 10am–7pm).

To the left the road leads to the **Parco del Valentino** ⓞ down by the Po. This is a popular park, with cafés, restaurants and a "medieval village" built for the 1884 Italian General Exhibition as a replica of 15th-century buildings from Piedmont and Aosta. The park attracts families, lovers and evening and weekend strollers, and boats stop here for ferry trips up and down the Po. Italy's first airline operated half a mile upriver at the turn of the century, when seaplanes made a daily run to Pavia, Venice and Trieste.

Further afield

A number of sites outside the centre of Turin are accessible by public transport, taxi or car; check opening times locally before venturing out. South of the Parco del Valentino, at Corso Unità d'Italia 40, is the **Museo Nazionale dell'Automobile** ⓟ (open Tues–Sun, 10am–6.30pm), one of the most important

Map
on page
254

motoring museums in Europe, as one might expect from the home of Fabbrica Italiana di Automobili Torino – FIAT. It has more than 150 models, posters, paraphernalia and a good bookshop.

Superga is a hill opposite **Piazza Veneto** on the other side of the Po. Filippo Juvara took 40 metres (130ft) off its top to create a flat space for his masterpiece, a Baroque basilica built to fulfil a vow made by Vittorio Amedeo II before the Battle of Turin in 1706, in which besieging French and Spanish forces were routed, and it subsequently became the resting place of the Savoy kings. A plaque also commemorates a tragedy which particularly touched the people of Turin: the death of the entire Turin soccer team, who were returning from Lisbon in May 1949 when their plane crashed behind the basilica.

Upriver from Parco del Valentino, accessible by ferry, is **Moncalieri**, a Capuchin monastery, housing in one wing the **Museo Nazionale della Montagna**, founded in 1874 by the Italian Alpine Club (open Tues–Fri, 8.30am–7.15pm; Sat–Mon 9am–12.30pm, 2.45–7.15pm). The Alps are visible, on a clear day, from the belvedere.

Three royal residences are also within reach. To the north is the **Castello di Venaria Reale**, a vast echoing Baroque summer residence of the Savoys (open Tues, Thur, Sat, Sun, 9–11.30am, 2.30–6.30pm). To the west of the city is another summer palace, **Castello di Rivoli**, by Juvara, which has a permanent modern art collection (open Mon–Fri, 10am–5pm; Sat, Sun, 10am–7pm). But the most impressive is **Palazzini di Caccia di Stupinigi**, a grand hunting lodge and grounds to the south of the city (open Tues–Sun, 10am–7pm). Built by Juvara for Vittorio Amedeo II, the lodge was a favourite of Napoleon when "visiting" Italy. ❑

BELOW: an original Fiat 500 (Cinquecento), one of Turin's most famous exports.

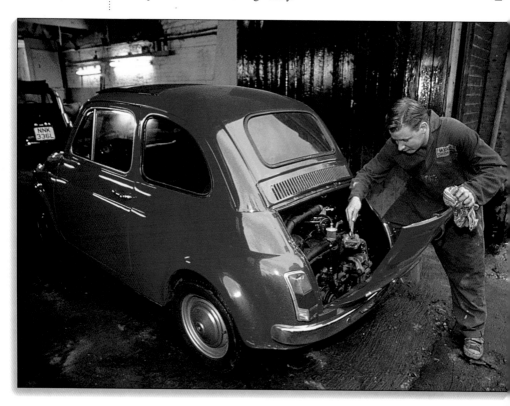

The Turin Shroud

The most venerated piece of cloth in Christendom is 4.34 metres (14ft 3in) long and 1.09 metres (3ft 7in) wide. This length of linen was wrapped lengthways around a corpse, from heed to toe, leaving a faint image of both the back and the front of a naked body, a long-haired, bearded figure which has its hands clasped over its groin. Joseph of Arimathea is said to have wrapped it round the body of Christ after He was taken down from the Cross.

The shroud was bequeathed to the Holy See on the death of Umberto II of Savoy in 1983. It had belonged to the House of Savoy since 1448 when it was given to Anne of Lusignan, the wife of the Duke of Savoy, by Marguerite de Charney. The de Charney family had kept it since 1353 when Geoffrey de Charney, Lord of Lirey, gave this "True Burial Cloth of Christ" to his collegiate church in northern France. The Savoy household kept it in Chambéry in southern France, where it was slightly damaged in a fire, until 1578 when it was brought to Turin.

The cloth was one of many miraculous sitings reported from Jerusalem by pilgrims as long ago as the 6th century. It later apparently turned up at the church of Our Lady of Blachernes in Constantinople. The city was sacked by French Crusaders in 1202, and the shroud was not reported in the Near East after that date, making the connection with Geoffrey de Charney plausible.

In 1898 the shroud was photographed by a Turin photographer, Secondo Pia, who realised that the image was a negative, and that the negative he made of the shroud appeared as a positive image. This made the picture of the figure much clearer. It apparently confirmed a crown of thorns, wounds to the right foot, the left side, the left wrist, the back of the head and the forehead. It also seemed to show bruises, presumably caused by the weight of the cross, and lines on the back from the scourging. Darker marks along each edge were attributed to the fire at Chambéry, water marks to the extinguishing of the fire, and two small patches to the handiwork of the Chambéry nuns who repaired the fire damage.

The shroud is kept in a silver chest in a special chapel of black marble in Turin Cathedral and seldom goes on display, but a full-size copy is shown in the church for visitors to examine.

A scientific study carried out in 1978 revealed the three-dimensional impressions made by the body and confirmed the bloodstains. However, in 1989 carbon-dating tests by scientists from Oxford, Zürich and Tucson, Arizona, proved that the shroud was made between 1260 and 1390 – roughly the time it disappeared from Constantinople and appeared in France.

But the mystery is far from solved, and the Institute of Sindonology in Turin is dedicated to continual study of the cloth. In 1998 the Institute's Pier-Luigi Baima Bollone said that it showed "signs of fatigue, the pain of 19 hours of torture, shock, dehydration and mechanical asphyxiation from being crucified". He concluded that the victim had died with a cry of pain and a heart attack. ❑

RIGHT: the Turin Shroud – the face of Christ?

PIEDMONT

Risotto, truffles and some of Italy's finest wines are rich rewards for the traveller among the mountains and plains of Piedmont

Map
on pages
240–241

A s its name suggests, Piedmont, Piemonte in Italian, lies at the foot of the mountains, a great encircling wall of rock and ice where two dozen valleys beckon winter skiers and summer hikers. Some 40 percent of the land is hilly or mountainous, forming a crescent around the regional capital, Turin. To the northeast the Apennines border Switzerland and descend to the edge of the popular lake district (*see pages 271–286*). In the northwest is the Gran Paradiso National Park, shared with the Valle d'Aosta; to the west are the French Alps of Haute Savoie; to the south, rising through some of the best winelands in Italy, are the Maritime Alps that lead to Liguria.

The remaining 60 percent is flat and fertile, spreading east around the wide valley of the Po which produces cereals and most of Italy's rice.

Mountains in the West

The southern slopes of the Gran Paradiso National Park, less accessible than those of the north, are wilder and less populous. Main access to the park is up the **Valle di Locana** ⓱ to the Orco Valley, where the road climbs to the 2,612-metre (8,570-ft) peak of Colle del Nivolet and a pass over the mountains which leads to the Val Savarenche in Aosta.

The main road west of Turin goes through the Susa valley to France. After some 32 km (20 miles) it passes **Sacra de San Michele** ⓲, a hugely impressive monastic bastion sitting on top of the 962-metre (3,156-ft) Monte Pirchiriano. **Susa** ⓳ is an attractive small mountain town and a good centre for the exploration of the surrounding Alps. Shops brim with pastries, gifts and multicoloured alcoholic delights. Remains of Roman Segusio include an amphitheatre, an aqueduct and the 3rd-century Porta Savoia, which owes its present wide arch to an enlargement in 1750 to accommodate the wedding procession of Vittorio Amedeo. The Arco di Augusto (8 BC) was put up by Cottius, a local Gallic chieftain who threw in his lot with the Romans. There is a small museum in the castle at the top of the town.

From Susa the old road goes over the **Col du Mont Cenis** pass into France, but the motorway and main road head for the **Fréjus** tunnel. Susa is as much a summer as a winter resort: the main winter resort is **Sestriere** ⓴, to the south in the Valle del Chisone (*see Skiing, page 249*), reached through **Pinerolo** ㉑, an attractive town with an interesting history, an old centre and a fine 15th-century cathedral. There are a large number of forts in the area, notably the extraordinary complex at **Finistrelle**.

Two other attractive mountain valleys are the upper **Po Valley**, which begins beneath Monteviso

PRECEDING PAGES:
Barolo country.
LEFT:
cycling through the streets of Barolo.
BELOW:
some of Italy's finest wine comes from this region.

dove sta di casa il
BAROLO
DOLCETTO
BARBERA D'ALBA
NEBBIOLO

Cantina
Terre del Barolo
COOP TRA PRODUTTORI Castiglione Falletto·Alba

*Barolo vineyards.
Piedmont has 20
denominated wines.*

(3,841 metres/12,602ft), where Italy's longest river starts its journey to the Adriatic sea, and **Valle Varaita**. Both are approached through **Saluzzo ㉒**, which makes a pleasant stopover. **Cuneo ㉓** 32km (20 miles) south of Saluzzo leads to the southern valleys, including the Stura and Vermengagna, verdant places with abundant flora.

Alba, Asti and the winelands

Southeast of Turin the flat landscape begins to roll into a sea of hills topped by castles and hamlets, most of which have only a few hundred inhabitants. First come the Roere and then the Langhe hills, running into the chalk Monferrato district in the east and rising to 900 metres (2,950ft) as they approach the High Langhe and Liguria to the south. These are the winelands of Barbaresco and Barolo, often called the Burgundy of Italy, not least because of the wines' very high prices. The government has set up nine Enoteca Regionale, regional wine-tasting centres, in castles and other historic buildings, and these are backed up by numerous wine shops and high-quality restaurants.

This is a gourmet corner of the country, and tables are filled with white truffles, mushrooms and hazelnuts; it is also marketed as "the hills of salami, cheese and bread". Many of the villages have cellars and places to taste wine as well as small rural and wine-related museums.

Barolo ㉔ is the king of the wines, and it comes from a village of the same name set in a triangle of vineyard between Alba, Dogliani and Cherasco. A modest village which can seem almost deserted, it has a castle with a museum of the former residence of the Falletti family, and of wine (open Feb–Dec: Mon–Wed, Fri–Sun, 10am–12.30pm 3–6.30pm). The last Falletti marquesa

BELOW: the
14th-century
facade of Asti's
cathedral.

is credited with vinifying the wine to make it last longer, thus creating the famous Barolo brew. Wines from the whole region are available in the Enoteca in the bowels of the castle; they include less expensive Nebbiolo, as well as the noble Barolo.

On the edge of the region is **Grinzane Cavour**, which also has a good selection of wines in its 13th-century castle (open Feb–Dec Mon, Wed–Sun; closed lunchtime). This was the family home of Count Camillo di Cavour, whose rooms can be visited, and there is also an interesting ethnographic museum. The Order of the Knights of the Truffles and the Wines of Alba meets here. The Enoteca at **Barbaresco**, just east of Alba, is in the middle of the village, in the deconsecrated 19th-century church of San Donato.

Alba ㉕ is a quiet and genial country town which comes alive when it's ready to eat. There is a good local market on Saturdays. This is the truffle capital of Italy, and the national truffle fair is held here every October. **Asti** ㉖ is a livelier town which is at it most boisterous during the *palio*, a bare-back horse race that thunders around the Campo de Palio on the third Sunday in September, when a wine festival also takes place. The banners of the riders are kept in the Collegiato di San Secondo in the square, where a Sunday antiques market takes place.

Only a handful of the 122 40-metre (130-ft) towers which loomed over the powerful 13th-century town remain, and the highlight of the modern town is the airy 14th-century Cathedral, one of the finest Gothic works in Piedmont. It has an attractive portico of brick and tufa, in front of which outdoor concerts take place in summer. The Enoteca for Moscato d'Asti and Asti Spumante is the castle at **Mango** ㉗ some 30 km (20 miles) due south of Asti.

Map
on pages
240–241

Second to wine comes rice.

BELOW: stonework on Asti's magnificent Gothic cathedral.

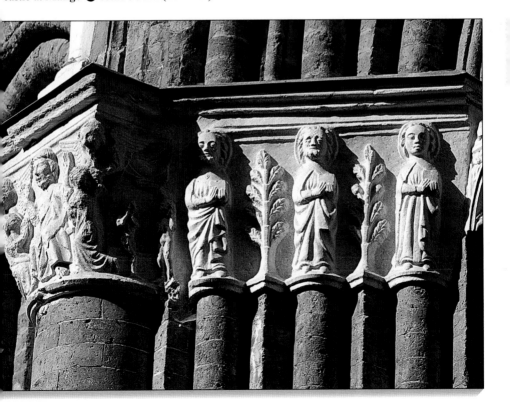

Map on pages 240–241

Flat lands of the Po Valley

From Asti the Po Valley travels some 40km (25 miles) to **Alessandria** ㉘, once a heavily fortified and now a busy modern town. Towns are broad and generous in these flat lands of maize and rice fields, among them **Casale Monferrato** ㉙, a fortified town beside the Po where there is a particularly fine synagogue and Museo d'Arte e Storia Antigua Ebraica (open Sun, 10am–noon, 3–5pm, otherwise apply to the director's office, 44 Vicolo Olpes, tel 1042 71807). **Vercelli** ㉚ is the rice capital of the area and is a pleasant town, though mosquitoes are active in the heat. Its most notable building is the Basilica of St Andrew, completed in 1227 and one of the first Cistercian Gothic buildings in Italy. The **Lago di Viverone** ㉛, 32 km (20 miles) west on the S228, is good place to drop in for a swim.

Ivrea ㉜, 16 km (10 miles) further on, lies on the Dorea Balteia emptying out of the Valle d'Aosta. The home of Olivetti, it has a lively shopping street leading up to a vast, rotting castle. The textile town of **Biella** ㉝ is a 30-km (18-mile) country drive north, and 8km (5 miles) above it is **Oropa**, where an intriguing collection of churches has created a place of Marian pilgrimage.

The northern mountains

Biella lies in the lower hills that rise north to the Swiss border. Val Sesia and Valle Anzasca lead up to Monte Rosa, the former passing through the quaint village of **Varallo** ㉞ where cobbled streets and manor houses show signs of a prosperous past. **Domodossola** ㉟ is the main centre for the Val d'Ossola, Piedmont's most northerly valley, tucked up among the Swiss Alps. This small medieval town is the starting point for a railway that takes an hour-long scenic route east across the border to Locarno at the head of Lake Maggiore. ❑

BELOW: Muscat grapes are the oldest variety in the region.
RIGHT: roadside harvest.

WINE

Italy's greatest red wines – Barolo and Barbaresco – come from around Alba. Rich, ruby red, aged for two years in oak or chestnut and made from the Nebbiolo grape, these are the Burgundies of Italian wine. But there are other wines, too, ranging from young whites and slightly sparkling reds to the more characteristic reds, such as the Nebbiolo d'Alba. In all, there are 20 denominated wines in Piedmont, including Asti Spumanti.

Most wines with the word Alba in their title suggest full reds that age well, whether they are made from the Barabera, Dolcetta or Nebbiolo grape. Other Dolcettas are drunk young. Lighter and younger are the Roero wines, which have the local Arneis grape added; a Roero Arneis is a light white which can be an aperitif. Asti Spumanti is a sparkling dessert wine. Made from grape-must, it goes well with Panettone Christmas cake. Moscato d'Asti is a slightly fizzy wine that is drunk young. Both are made from Muscat grapes, the oldest variety in Piedmont, which are also used in distilling one of the best kinds of *grappa*.

There are Enoteca Regionale (government-backed wineries) where you can taste and buy at Acqui Terme, Barbaresco, Barolo, Anale, Canelli, Crianze Cavour, Mango, Roppolo and Vignale Monferrato.

THE LAKES

Map on page 272

"What can one say about Lake Maggiore, about the Borromean Isles, about Lake Como, unless it be that one pities those that are not madly in love with them" – Alexandre Dumas

The lakes, set against snowcapped peaks or vine-clad slopes, evoke dreamy images of passing steamers, with the waterside cloaked in mysterious winter mists or summer heat hazes. Since their 19th-century heyday the lakes have drifted in and out of fashion, symbolising mournful sanatoria, inspiring poets or simply soothing the spirit. The lakes entranced Byron and Shelley, Stendhal and Ibsen, Freud and Nietzsche, Goethe, Rilke and Thomas Mann. On Garda alone each classic resort has its literary lion: Kafka is associated with Desenzano, James Joyce with Sirmione, D. H. Lawrence with Gargnano.

Lake Garda, the largest, seemingly as wide as a sea, was the first lake to be "discovered" by Grand Tourists, and it remains the most commercial, the one favoured by Italians, the one with the greatest range of hotels and water sports. By contrast, Lake Lugano naturally exudes a Swiss atmosphere, while majestic Lake Maggiore is blessed with delightful islands, and Lake Iseo feels aloof, faintly sad and haunted. To connoisseurs, Lake Como, cradled by mountains, is perhaps the loveliest, both the most distinctive and the most refined.

Yet all the lakes have their share of sophisticated resorts, pastel-coloured fishing villages and sumptuous villas. On the major lakes, Baroque or Classical villas are surrounded by verdant gardens, while gracious Art Nouveau hotels enjoy azalea-framed views. The vineyards and olive-clad hills are reminiscent of languid Mediterranean landscapes. The mild climate favours this lush vegetation, with azaleas, rhododendrons and camellias set in the lee of majestic mountains. The palette of shades encompasses sludgy greens, browns and greys as well as Mediterranean pinks, reds, ochres and lemon yellows. The lakes are best savoured from a waterfront terrace, from the shelter of camellia-scented gardens, or the deck of a leisurely steamer. Hydrofoils are faster, but open-decked steamers are more in keeping with the mood of the lakes, slowing one down and stilling the mind.

PRECEDING PAGES: the lakeside town of Varenna.
LEFT: Bellagio, Lake Como.
BELOW: the lake at Villa Melzi, Bellagio.

Lago di Garda (Lake Garda)

Despite the presence of secluded villas in the shadow of the Alps, Garda is less status-seeking than Como and Maggiore. As the most southerly of the great lakes, it is also blessed with the warmest climate and least "Swissified" atmosphere. The Dolomites to the north shelter Garda from the cold north winds, helping to create delightfully mild conditions. The distinctly Mediterranean micro-climate is emphasised by the profusion of olive groves and citrus plantations, palm trees and vineyards, lofty cypresses and vivid flowerings of magnolias, oleanders and bougainvilleas. The southern end of the lake is more tropical and languorous, broadening out over the Lombard plains;

closer to the Dolomites the air can carry a hint of a chill and the scent of juniper Although water-skiing and motor boats are banned in the northerly Trentino end of the lake, there are fewer restrictions in the south, which makes it both busier and more at risk from pollution.

Riva del Garda **, one of the liveliest resorts on the lake, has a charming town centre with a castle and compact medieval quarter. However, despite a pleasant beach, upmarket boutiques and turn-of-the-century hotels, the effect is tarnished by the summer crowds and the undistinguished sprawl along the shore. Water-skiing and motor boats are banned in this stretch of the lake, as they are at neighbouring **Torbole ②. Yet Torbole remains a burgeoning water sports centre, popular with young Austrians, Germans and Scandivians who are eager to race their windsurfers when the *ora*, the fierce local wind, whips up the right afternoon breeze.

Malcesine ③, set on the slopes of Monte Baldo to the south, is a family resort which combines the charms of a Mediterranean resort with the complexity of a medieval town. A crenellated castle soars over the red-tiled rooftops, the quaint café-lined port and a labyrinth of steep, cobbled streets overhung by balconies. From the Venetian **Palazzo dei Capitani** the 16th-century rulers controlled the port and acted as customs officials. From the town, a cable car leads up to Monte Baldo and superb views over the Dolomites.

Halfway down the shore stands the former bastion of **Torri del Benaco ④**. This former Lombard stronghold lies on the Riviera degli Olivi, named after its olive groves. A crenellated feudal castle dominates the little port and overlooks the frescoed church of Santissima Trinità. Just around the headland and the resort of Garda is **Bardolino ⑤**, the highpoint of the wine-growing hills (*see*

The Venetian authorities in Malcesine arrested Goethe (1749–1832) as a spy when they saw him sketching the castle. The event is now commemorated by a bust of the poet in an upper courtyard.

page 266). The family resort itself has a cobbled, pedestrianised centre and is popular with Austrians and Germans. It possesses the curious Carolingian church of San Zeno and the Romanesque church of San Severo, as well as a ruined castle. However, wine-lovers will focus on tastings in the celebrated *cantine* or visits to the vine-clad slopes. Beyond, in the wide, southern section of the lake, lies **Lazise** ➏, ringed by medieval walls and dominated by a fine castle. Close to the small port is the Romanesque church of San Nicolo, graced with School of Giotto frescoes. The 16th-century Dogana Veneta is a reminder that Lazise was a key customs post and an important Venetian military base.

    Peschiera del Garda ➐, at the southeastern end of the lake, occupies a strategic site near the mouth of the River Mincio that drains the lake. **Gardaland**, just northwest of town, is Italy's most popular theme park (open Mar–Sept, daily). From Peschiera it is a short drive (10 km/6 miles) to **Sigurta** ➑, near Valeggio, where the well-tended villa gardens (open daily) are among the finest in the region. An exotic array of banana and palm trees gives way to lily ponds and an avenue of irises; dramatically-sited cypresses frame a colourful display of Chinese and Japanese plantings.

Map on page 272

Bardolino, a favourite resort.

Scenic Sirmione

As the quaintest resort on the Lombardy bank, **Sirmione** ➒ sits snugly on a narrow peninsula jutting into the lake. The centrepiece of this scenic walled town is the moated fortress known as the **Rocca Scaligera**, with the drawbridge on its landward side the only means of reaching Sirmione. Nearby stands the porticoed church of **Santa Maria Maggiore**, carved out of a feudal tower. Although slightly claustrophobic and self-consciously cute, Sirmione's cobbled pedes-

BELOW: the imposing fortress of Rocca Scaligera.

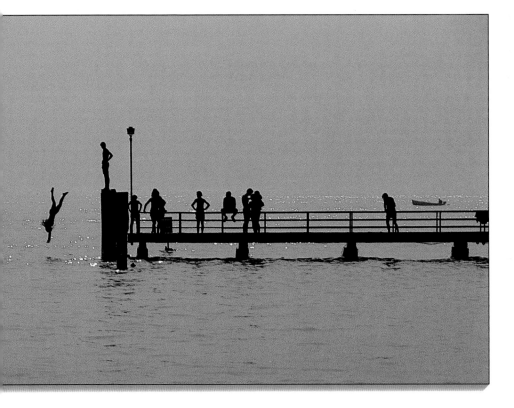

trianised quarter is pleasant, with its chic boutiques, cafés and cake shops. Most of the hotels are strung along the uninspired strip that leads into Sirmione, but the lakeside promenades and archaeological trails are rewarding enough.

Long before Salò became identified with unsavoury politics, Lady Mary Wortley Montagu, a privileged visitor in 1750, praised the local setting as "an amphitheatre covered with woods of orange, lemon and pomegranate trees".

Via Catullo leads along the rocky promontory through olive groves to the church of San Pietro in Mavino, which dates from the 8th century. At the end of the peninsula lies the Roman archaeological site known as **Grotte di Catullo**, linked to the poet Catullus (87 BC–AD 54), who died in Sirmione. The remains of ancient baths and vaulted disrobing chambers are reminders that the local thermal springs have been active since Roman times. Sirmione's spas now channel the sulphurous springs into a range of dubious water cures.

Desenzano del Garda ⑩, often considered the gateway to the lake, is by no means the most relaxing resort. The traffic-choked centre gives way to a picturesque port before sprawling along the waterfront. Apart from the porticoed Piazza Malvezzi, the sites include a Roman villa and the Duomo, which dates from the 16th century and displays a Last Supper attributed to Tiepolo. On Via Gramsci lie the remains of a 4th-century Roman villa.

The wide stretch of water at the southern end of the lake, between Desenzano and **Salò ⑪**, resembles an inland sea. Although a charming lakeside resort, Salò is synonymous with one of the most shameful periods of Italian history, the notorious wartime Republic of Salò (*see below*). In 1943–45 Salò was a playground for the idling Italian aristocracy and war malingerers, with decadent German officers and Italian officials leading self-indulgent lifestyles while the Jewish round-ups were going on. Salò boasts a late-Gothic Cathedral in Venetian style, but its sites are less compelling than the weight of history.

BELOW: Fascist leader Benito Mussolini – *Il Duce* – addressing his people in 1929.

Gardone Riviera ⑫ became a favoured halt in the days of the Grand Tour.

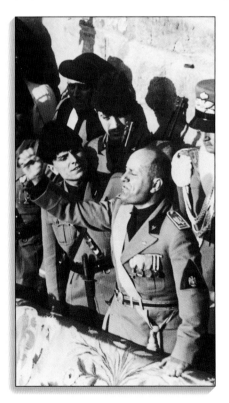

PLAYGROUND AND PUPPET STATE

In 1943, Mussolini, who had fallen from grace and been imprisoned by the king and the Fascist Grand Council, was rescued from a mountain-top prison by the Nazis. Il Duce was swiftly installed as the ruler of a puppet republic operating from a sleepy resort on Lake Garda. The Republic of Salò represented Mussolini's last stand, a government with little power but all the trappings. Here he occasionally paraded for the benefit of German newsreels, discussed casualties over lunch with his neighbour, the German ambassador, and met his favourite mistress, Claretta Petacci, at 5 o'clock. In 1945 he was shot by partisans near Lake Como, with Claretta by his side; both were strung up by their heels with piano wire.

Gardone Riviera's honey-coloured Villa Fiordaliso was where Mussolini installed his mistress. Most features remain, down to the door handles embellished with swastikas. The villa is now an elegant hotel, and the Claretta Petacci suite is perfect for romantic encounters. Mussolini's wife, Rachele, was ensconced in Gargnano, 10 km (6 miles) away, in Villa Feltrinelli, which also became a hotel. Donna Rachele was more interested in her pet hens than in her sumptuous villa, which included 16 bedrooms, a billiard room and a private bunker.

Nestling amongst lush gardens, with its air of fusty grandeur, Gardone remains the most elegant and exclusive resort on Lake Garda. Steamers still dock by the cobbled quayside, while the lakeside promenade offers views over the whole southern section of the lake. Via Roma leads to the splendid **Giardino Botanico Hruska** (tel: 0336-410877). Alpine plants and Mediterranean vegetation grow happily on this rocky spur, lying in the shadow of the Dolomite peaks. A delightful trail winds past artificial streams, exotic blooms, papyrus-filled pools and Buddhist shrines. The hotel **Villa Fiordaliso** (Via Zanardelli, tel: 0365-20158), a secluded pink-and-white lakeside villa, was where Mussolini dallied with Claretta Petacci, his favourite mistress (*see previous page*). The chandelier-hung Grand Hotel also has a history: it was patronised by writers, from Vladimir Nabokov to Somerset Maugham, while Winston Churchill used it as his base during painting holidays.

Above the resort is **Il Vittoriale** ⓑ (open Tues–Sun, 8.30am–8pm), an extraordinary shrine to Gabriele D'Annunzio, one of Italy's most flamboyant pre-war figures (*see page 287*). The villa, framed by cypresses and oleanders, is set on gentle slopes overlooking the lake. The grounds are cluttered with bizarre monumental structures, from the brutalist open-air theatre to the lofty mausoleum containing D'Annunzio's body and the hangar on the hillside displaying the plane he used to fly over Vienna. The overall effect is of ugly monumentalism almost disfiguring the enchanting lakeside setting.

Bogliaco ⓮, just south of the better-known Gargnano, makes an inviting lunch stop. This erstwhile fishing village has a 15th-century parish church and the Villa Bettoni, encircled by Baroque gardens. Further north, named after the luxuriant lemon groves that represented the town's claim to fame before tourism

Map on page 272

Vibrant bloom in the Hruska Botanical Gardens.

BELOW: taking a breather at Torbole, by the shores of Lake Garda.

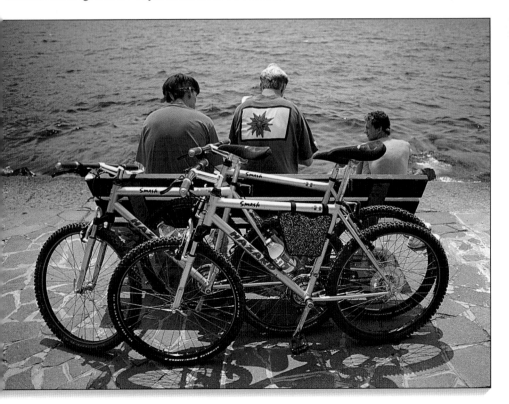

took over, **Limone sul Garda** completes the circuit back to Riva del Garda. Set amid the surviving lemon groves and cedars, Limone's ochre-coloured houses and cobbled streets are hung with bougainvillea.

Lago d'Iseo (Lake Iseo)

Lago d'Iseo measure 5 km (3 miles) at its broadest point, but most of the space is occupied by Monte Isola, the largest lake island in Europe. This resolutely untouristy lake depends on fishing and boat-making, and on the fabrication of nets of all descriptions. Its charms reside in the peaceful hamlets fringed by mountains and the cosy local inns, and its position, sheltered by two sets of mountain ridges, reinforces the residents' independent natures. The atmosphere is compounded by fogs and fitful thunder storms that descend without warning.

Iseo , set on the southern part of the lake, is a pleasant resort and a lively provincial town, its lack of sights compensated for by a refreshingly unpretentious, friendly atmosphere. The bustling shops in the medieval quarter display a slice of provincial life, with huge Parmesans, salamis and mounds of fresh pasta eagerly devoured by local eyes. The liveliest part of the market occupies the recently-restored Jewish ghetto. Not far from Iseo is the large peat bog and nature site known as Torbiere, noted for its water-lilies and marsh reeds.

Monte Isola , the island at the centre of the lake, resembles a mountain more than an island. The fishing villages, which can be explored on foot or by bicycle, are characterised by red-tiled roofs, cobbled streets and an inward-looking air. With its sudden mists, steep banks and timeless fishing traditions, the island can feel aloof and slightly menacing, a mood dispelled by an invigorating walk up through the chestnut groves. The summit of the island, from

BELOW: a ferry on Lake Iseo.

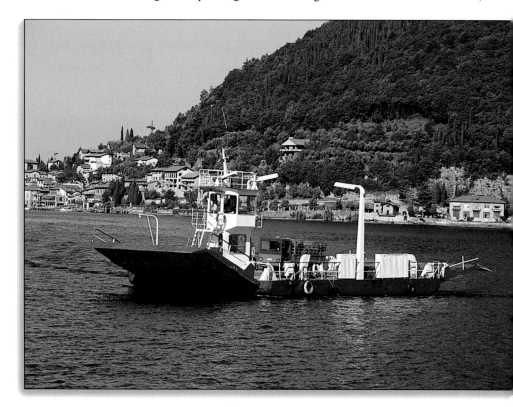

where there are panoramic views across to Bergamo and the Alps, is crowned by the frescoed church of Madonna della Ceriola.

On the eastern shore of the lake, **Cislano** ⓲, near the village of Marone, provides a curious natural spectacle of so-called erosion pyramids, bizarre rock formations similar to those found in the Dolomites. **Lovere** ⓳, the major lakeside town in the north, is a pleasant resort with terraces tumbling down to the shore, but the narrow northern end of the lake is about 250 metres (820 ft) deep, which acts as a psychological deterrent to swimmers. The dramatic northern end is framed by high ridges and sheer cliffs that rise up from the shoreline.

Sarnico ⓴, at the southern end of the lake, served by the steamer which also chugs over to Iseo, marks the end of the circuit around the shore. This fishing village abounds in cluttered fortifications and breezy boatyards. Further inland lie the extensive vineyards of **Franciacorta** ㉑, a region which produces champagne-method sparkling wine, and superior reds and whites. Franciacorta is also dedicated to the cult of Foodism, with the quality of wine estates often matched by the standards of the local cuisine. Its gentle hills are home to one of the finest gourmet restaurants in Italy, set in the hamlet of Erbusco. **L'Albereta** (tel: 030-7760562), an elegant villa-hotel and restaurant, is run by Gualtiero Marchesi, the country's best-known chef.

Lago di Como (Lake Como)

Lake Como, in mood if not in reality, is most closely associated with the days of grand dukes and dowager empresses, of *fin-de-siècle* balls before the chill winds of democracy swept away the doomed, cobweb-encrusted aristocrats. The sight of sluggish steamers and snow-capped peaks, shady arcades and entic-

Map
on page
272

TIP

You won't be disappointed by Erbusco's L'Albereta where Marchesi, an exponent of reinterpreted nouvelle cuisine, shows that superb seasonal produce and creative flair can go hand in hand with sensibly-sized portions.

BELOW: a stroll by the water's edge, Lake Como.

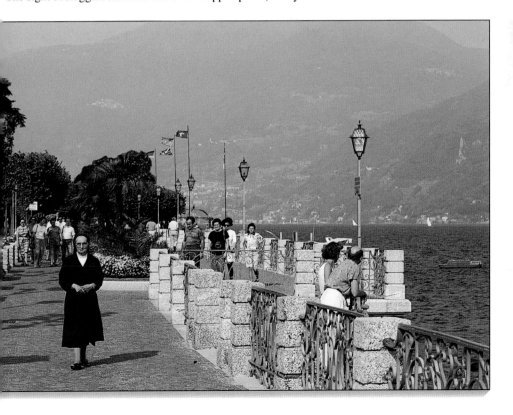

ing waterfront cafés, still provokes visitors to Victorian-style promenading. This celebrity-studded lake has entranced writers of the status of Flaubert and Stendhal, and been appreciated by stars from Greta Garbo to Gianni Versace. Consequently, the hotels tend to be as historic as the so-called sights.

With its pewter-coloured water and darkening mass of mountains, the deep, fjord-like Como has a less balmy climate than Garda, but it still has its sparkling days of serene blue waters, plus lakeside villages with steeply cobbled streets and cascades of geraniums, pastel villas and prettified hotel terraces, creaky jetties and cedar-framed views of the waterfront.

The town of **Como** ② also retains a tangible charm and a gentle atmosphere which makes it an engaging base for a lake-hopping holiday. It was a prosperous centre in the Middle Ages, and many of the city monuments owe much to the craftsmanship of the Maestri Comacini, the medieval master builders and sculptors who perfected the Lombard style. The silk and textile industries, which still flourish, also contributed to Como's prosperity and gracious living.

Just inland from the lake, the heart of the harmonious medieval quarter centres on the **Duomo** Ⓐ. This splendid solemn Cathedral represents the transition from Gothic to Renaissance. The highlights are the Gothic rose window and richly sculpted façade, with the central portal framed by Renaissance statues to Pliny the Elder and Younger. Adjoining the façade is the **Broletto** Ⓑ, the former town hall, an elegantly arcaded Gothic affair with triple-arched windows. A complete contrast to this is provided by the Fascist **Casa del Popolo** Ⓒ (1936), a surprisingly harmonious piece of Fascist architecture which is a masterpiece of the only style that Italy pioneered in the 20th century.

The **Tempio Voltiano** Ⓓ (open Tues–Sun, 10am–noon, 3–6pm; admission

When Gianni Versace was murdered in 1998, his family chose to scatter his ashes in the grounds of his beloved Montrasio villa near Como.

BELOW: standing at ease; a wine press awaits the next season's harvest.

WINE LAKES

The fertility of the lake district emerged in the wake of the glaciation that formed the lake basins, and retreated at the end of the Ice Age. One extremely fortuitous effect of the mild climate and myriad microclimates is the number of fine vineyards in the region. The range of wines produced is greater than in most other Italian regions; types run from a simple, sparkling Asti Spumante to the dry complexity of Bardolino.

Asti Spumante is produced in pressure tanks, using a special technique for processing the must of muscat grapes. The full-bodied red wines of Barolo and Barbaresco come from the western shore of Lake Maggiore. Both are produced from Nebbiolo grapes, and aged in oak or chestnut casks – Barolo for at least three years, Barbaresco for two. Dry Soave, fruity Valpolicella and dry Bardolino come from around Lake Garda. There are also white wines from the plains of Lombardy, including Moscato and Riesling. These are complemented by red Valtellina wines from the mountains, or by the superior range of Franciacorta wines from Lake Iseo. As if this were not enough, the region is a noted producer of distilled alpine drinks, made with forest fruits or herbs, not to mention the powerful fire-water known as *grappa*.

charge) set in the public gardens, is named after Alessandro Volta (1745–1827), the self-taught physicist who invented both the battery and the units of electricity now known as volts. Volta's deeply enquiring mind was also rewarded with the discovery that methane was an organic gas, proved by a series of experiments with methane in the marshes around Lake Maggiore. In his honour the Italian 10,000-lire note reproduces a picture of the scientist and the Classical-style temple that contains a museum of his work.

Maps:
Area 281
Town 279

In 1999 the bicentenary of the invention of the battery was marked by the opening of a series of walking tours.

Porta Vittoria ❺, south of the Duomo, at the end of Via Giove, is a 12th-century gate topped by five tiers of arches. Just southwest, on Via Vittorio Emanuele, on the site of a pagan temple, stands **San Fedele ❻**. The present much-remodelled church dates from the 7th century but it is essentially a masterpiece of Lombard Romanesque architecture. The **Pinacoteca ❼** (open Mon–Sat, 9.30am–noon, 2–5pm; entrance charge), in Palazzo Volpi on Via Diaz, contains the city art gallery, with paintings dating from the 14th century to the 18th. The **Musei Civici ❽** (open daily, 9am–noon, 2–5.30pm), which flank **Piazza Medaglie d'Oro Comasche**, contain an archeological collection plus a museum dedicated to the Risorgimento.

Just east is the **Museo della Seta ❾** (open Tues–Fri, 9am–noon, 3–6pm), a silk museum devoted to the town's traditional industry which has flourished since the 16th century. Although silkworms are no longer bred on the lake, Chinese thread is woven and dyed here to the specifications of the top Milanese fashion houses. Mantero and Ratti supply such designers as Chanel, Dior, Yves Saint Laurent and Versace.

TIP

Fine silk can be bought at local factory outlets or at the Centro della Seta (on Via Volta and Via Bellinzona).

BELOW: the Gothic rose window at Como's cathedral.

Sant'Abbondio

Languishing in the industrial suburbs is the **Basilica di Sant'Abbondio** N, a frescoed Romanesque complex built by the Maestri Comacini and well restored in the 19th century. **Villa Olmo** N (open Mon–Sat, 9am–noon, 2–6pm), 3km (2 miles) north of Como, is an imposing Neoclassical affair, built in 1782 and set in formal gardens and wooded parkland. However, since most visitors will eventually succumb to lake-hopping, the waterside **Piazza Cavour** is the obvious place to go. Flanked by café terraces and ice-cream parlours, the utterly touristy square lies a stone's throw from the main steamer and catamaran jetties. Visitors in search of peace and quiet can take the cable car from the waterfront by the main beach to Brunate, a village perched above a hill overlooking the city, which marks the start of several appealing trails.

Neighbouring **Cernobbio** N was the stylish resort favoured by the exiled Queen Caroline of England. In 1815 the then Princess of Wales bought the Villa d'Este as a bolthole, but debt eventually forced her to sell it. Then, as now, the magnificent Renaissance estate was framed by cypresses and formal gardens and dotted with Italianate grottoes and topiary. The **Villa d'Este** (open in summer only; tel: 031-3481) has been one of Europe's leading hotels since 1873.

Island retreat

Isola Comacina N is a charming patch of greenery in the middle of Lake Como, best known as the setting for a spectacular folk festival and firework display on 24 June. Facing the island is the gorgeous **Villa Balbianello** (open Tues–Sun, 10am–noon, 3.30–6.30pm). The villa, which is now state property, is set on a rocky spur near Lenno and can only be reached by boat from Isola

Elton John and Michael Schumacher are among the people who come as guests of the Villa d'Este today.

BELOW: the baroque splendour of Villa Carlotta.

Comacina. In 1786 Cardinal Durini bought Balbianello as a retreat and transformed it into the most romantic villa on the lake. It was restored in the 1970s by explorer and supermarket heir Count Guido Monzini, who filled it with exotic artefacts. A short lakeside stroll leads to the pale pink **Villa Carlotta** (open daily 9am–6pm), a Baroque residence which overlooks splendid formal terraced gardens. A wilder section of the grounds features a giant sequoia and a glade of lush ferns, with rhododenrons and a rockery. Elsewhere the tropical vegetation focuses on shrubs, succulents and trees from Australian and the Orient. The interior of the villa is somewhat disappointing, although the statuary includes Canova's erotic *Eros and Psyche*.

   Menaggio ㉖, the next port of call, is a health resort with a young and sprightly atmosphere. There's a cluster of ochre and red houses by the harbour, plus an onion-domed church and a hillside studded with villas and gardens. **Colico** ㉗, further north on the eastern shore, nestling below the conical Monte Legnone, is the gateway to the nature reserve of **Piano di Spana**. **Varenna** ㉘, also set on the eastern shore, is a delightful steamer stop, with a beguiling old quarter stacked up on the lower slopes. The lush resort is surrounded by terraced gardens, cypresses and pine groves. The gardens of **Villa Monastero** (open daily, 10am–noon, 2–6pm) are the finest on the eastern shore. This former Cistercian abbey was converted into a palatial residence in the 16th century and complemented by landscaped Classical grounds.

Poetry and promenades

Bellagio ㉙ rises up on a promontory that separates the two southern arms of Lake Como. This gentrified, rather old-fashioned resort commands a gorgeous

Map on pages 280–281

TIP

Isola Comacina is well known for the Locanda dell'Isola Comacina (tel: 0344-55083), an inn with good rustic food.

position on the cusp of the lake. While neighbouring Menaggio has traditionally been popular with Germans, Bellagio has always appealed to the British and French. Stendhal (1783–1842) spent many summers here, whiling away his time attending the opera, fighting duels or falling for a woman "not conspicuously chaste", whom he had to pursue for 10 years before she succumbed.

From the bustling café-lined waterfront, Salita Mella leads up to the sheltered centre of Bellagio and the pleasing main shopping street at the top. The main square is graced by a Romanesque church with an intriguing baptismal font. From here it is an enjoyable stroll past pink and ochre houses and discreet villas to the Neoclassical **Villa Melzi** (open daily, 9am-6pm). The exotic gardens are dotted with gazebos and banks of camellias, with formal terraces complemented by classical statues.

On the crest of the hill stands a hotel that is part of the history of Bellagio. **Villa Serbelloni** (tel: 031-950216) is the quintessential grand lakeside hotel, once patronised by Russian princes and German counts. In 1901, Prince Gagarin requested 14 rooms for his entourage. Now a palatial hotel and conference centre run by the Rockefeller Foundation, the Serbelloni still opens its gardens to non-residents. For diners on the romantic lakeside terrace there are views of the mountains softening in the twilight, with lights coming on on the distant shore.

South of Bellagio, on the Lecco arm of the lake, **Oliveto Lario** ㉚, set amid olive groves as the name suggests, presents a rural farewell to the lake.

Lago di Lugano (Lake Lugano)

Compared with Lake Maggiore and Lake Como, **Lugano** is wilder and more wooded yet distinctly less majestic. The waterfront is often inaccessible, with

Such is the spell of Bellagio and the Villa Serbelloni that in 1998 Las Vegas unveiled a replica of the resort in the guise of a casino and hotel complex.

BELOW: Baveno, Lake Maggiore.

its shoreline too steep for a road, let alone a straggling hamlet. Two-thirds of the lake comes within the Swiss canton of Ticino, which contains much of the best scenery. **Ponte Tresa ③** is a steamer landing and curious border village with both a Swiss and an Italian side. The Italians claim that the polluted waters of Lake Lugano drain into Lake Maggiore at this point, but the Swiss reject this as a racial slur. **Morcote ③**, known as "the pearl of the lake", is a charming village en route to Campione d'Italia, and makes an inviting lunch stop.

Beyond is **Campione d'Italia ③**, an Italian enclave in Switzerland, which is wedged halfway between Lugano and the border at Chiasso. Italian law may prevail, but the cars have Swiss number-plates, the postal service is Swiss, and the principality's budget is calculated in Swiss francs. Campione has a chequered past, but it looks cheerfully modern. For neighbouring Italians the glitzy casino is the main attraction, with wins spent in local designer boutiques. The greatest surviving historical monuments are the Oratorio di San Pietro (1326) and the Gothic and Baroque Madonna dei Ghirli, both the work of the Maestri Campionesi, who rivalled the Maestri Comacini from Como as the most skilled medieval master builders. These travelling Lombard craftsmen helped create some of Italy's greatest Romanesque cathedrals, including Cremona, Modena and Verona.

From Campione there are views across the lake to **Lugano ③**, set in Ticino, and one of the leading Swiss cities. The Swiss took control of Lugano in 1512 and have held it ever since. Highlights of the old quarter include the Renaissance-frescoed church of Santa Maria degli Angeli and the Duomo, graced with a Lombard-Venetian façade. For most visitors, however, this smart resort is an opportunity to sample lakeside promenades and Swiss cuisine.

Porlezza ③, at the northernmost end of the lake, is an appealing town where Italian flair prevails over Swiss sobriety. At Santa Margherita, further south, a cable car conects with the scenic Belvedere, known as "the balcony over Italy". Even more panoramic views unfurl from **Lanzo d'Intelvi ③**, the ski resort above. The alpine village, tucked into thick pine and larch woods, enjoys views over Lake Lugano and the Alps. The resort is part of the scenic Via d'Intelvi, a series of rural valleys centred on village churches decorated by the Maestri Comacini, the master builders. As a vital link between Lake Como and Lake Lugano, this route was heavily fortified in medieval times and also saw action during the Risorgimento battles of independence. **Fedele d'Intelvi ③**, nestling among alpine valleys and conifer forests, has the best Romanesque church in the region.

Concluding the lakeside circuit is **Ponte Ceresio ③**, a port set on a sheltered bay south of Campione.

Lago Maggiore (Lake Maggiore)

Although the northern part of the lake is centred on Locarsa, **Stresa ③**, with its faded *belle époque* charm, was once one of the grandest 19th-century resorts. The elegant waterfront is still flanked by lovely Art Nouveau hotels and well served by steamers which spirit visitors away to the Borromean islands. The Grand Hotel des Borromees, featured in Hemingway's

Map on pages 280–281

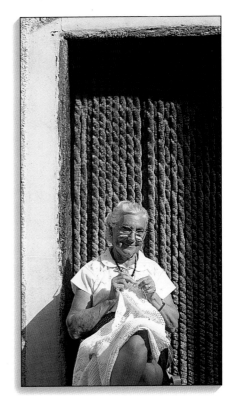

BELOW: lacemaking is one of the traditional crafts of the region..

A Farewell to Arms, is a relic of past glories. Just behind the waterfront, Piazza Cadorna is a pleasant café-lined square and shopping quarter. At Stresa Lido a cable car leads up to Monte Mottarone, with views of glacier-crested peaks, the Monte Rosa ski slopes and the valleys around Domodossola, as well as a panorama of the Lombardy plain.

The Borromean dynasty originally intended Isola Bella as a pleasure palace, Isola Pescatori a rural retreat, and Isola Madre as an enchanted garden.

Just outside Stresa, off the Arona road, stands **Villa Pallavicini** ⓴ (park open daily, 9am–6pm), encircled by romantic "English" gardens. Gentle parkland and streams are complemented by more formal terraces, ornamental gardens and pergolas. The grounds are also home to a small zoo of llamas, antelopes, deer and kangaroos.

The **Isole Borromee** ㊶, which have belonged to the Borromean family since Renaissance times, present three enchantingly different faces: the Baroque fantasy of Isola Bella; the fishing village of Isola Pescatori (also known as Isola Superiore); and the verdant villa-park of Isola Madre. The Milanese Borromean family still owns the fishing rights over the entire lake. Steamers from Arona, Stresa, Verbania and Laveno criss-cross the lake, making frequent stops at the islands.

Isola Bella (palace open daily, 9am–noon; gardens, open daily 9am–5.30pm) is the centrepiece of these picturesque islands. This sumptuous palace and its lush pleasure gardens were a labour of love begun by the Cardinal of Milan, Count Carlo III Borromeo, in 1632, in honour of his consort, Isabella. The Baroque palace was largely completed by the couple's sons in the 1670s. The terraced gardens represent a Baroque masterpiece, graced with statuary, fountains and dramatic perspectives. The garden is a riot of colour in summer, with butterflies darting in and out of shady arbours, and is crowned by a shell-shaped

BELOW: outside Locarno's Madonna del Sasso church.
RIGHT: the gardens of Villa Palavicino.

amphitheatre, the setting for concerts and spectacles. A cobbled courtyard opens onto high-ceilinged rooms decorated with stucco-work and frescoes, often emblazoned with a unicorn, the Borromean crest. The palace's lavish interior also displays a Tiepolo ceiling, Murano glass chandeliers, Flemish tapestries and Florentine marquetry. The highlights are the magnificent Empire-style ballroom, the cantilevered spiral staircase and the domed great hall.

Isola Pescatori once sheltered the lake's main fishing community. Today the village's secret passageways and tiny courtyards, accompanied by the sweet sound of birdsong, provide unexpected views of the lake or lead to the frescoed medieval parish church. **Verbano** (tel: 0323-30408) is a rustic inn overlooking the lake, and a sought-after destination for lunch. From the rocky beach beyond there are views of Isola Bella framed by fishing nets and snoozing cats.

Isola Madre, set closer to Pallanza than to Stresa, is the largest and most languorous of the islands, with a 16th-century villa surrounded by lush gardens (opening times same as Isola Bella). The gardens, landscaped into five terraces, are the highlight of any visit, although the overall effect is curiously naturalistic. Planted with citrus trees, cedars and cypresses, mimosa and magnolia, the grounds are home to vivid parrots and bold white peacocks which strut through the azaleas and rhododendrons. The villa itself is slightly stifling, with its ornate interior, inlaid or dark cedar-wood ceilings, and uninspiring collection of dolls.

Baveno ⓬, set in the lee of a pink granite mountain, is a more subdued version of Stresa. The resort, which once drew such honoured guests as Queen Victoria and Winston Churchill, remains a favourite with the British. In the historic centre, the church of Santi Gervasio e San Protaso is graced with a Romanesque façade and belltower; flanking it is an octagonal baptistry. From

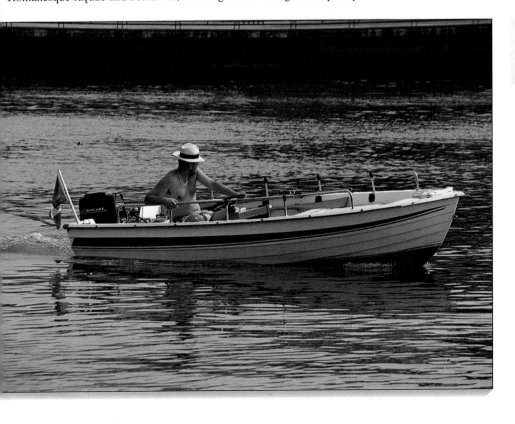

Map on pages 280–281

BELOW: cruising Lake Iseo.

Map
on pages
280–281

The copper colossus of Carlo Borromeo at Arona.

BELOW: a waterside caffé in Lake Como's port.

the waterfront there are views of lakeside villas and over to Isola dei Pescatori. At the end of the bay, between Baveno and Pallanza, lies the **Riserva Naturale di Fondo Toce** ㊸, a nature reserve and bird sanctuary.

Pallanza ㊹, set on the headland, has a lovely waterside lined by magnolias and oleanders, with porticoed ochre and pink houses merging into a maze of alleys. The lakeside towns of Pallanza and **Verbania** ㊺ fade into one another, with the latter best known as the stop for **Villa Taranto** (open daily, 9am–7.30pm) and its impressive gardens, designed in the 1930s by a Scot, Neil McEacharn. Although theoretically botanical gardens, this is not a scientific collection but an exotic composition featuring fountains and waterfalls, Amazonian water lilies and lotus blossoms. Apart from the water gardens, azaleas, rhododendrons and camellias compete with Japanese maples, English herbaceous borders, Kashmiri cypresses and Egyptian papyrus.

Cannobio ㊻, a small resort near the Swiss border, is often neglected since it is set some way up the northwestern side of the lake. The centre of this erstwhile market town is wound around tight alleys, a pleasant harbour and the Renaissance church of Madonna della Pietà. From Cannobio a road leads west to Val Cannobina and the dramatic gorge of Santa Anna, with its tumbling waterfall and an adjoining church. Just south is the quiet resort of Cannero Riviera, set amid vineyards, olives and citrus groves. **Locarno** ㊼, commanding a sheltered bay on the Swiss shore, is a crisp, well-ordered resort with a tree-lined lakeside promenade. Gamblers and browsers are drawn to the casino and shopping arcades. In the upper city stands Castello Visconti, a fort converted into an archeological museum. A cable car climbs up to Madonna del Sasso.

Luino ㊽, lying on the Lombardy shore to the east, is a lively border town, but its historic centre remains appealing. Piazza Garibaldi contains a statue to the revolutionary fighter, for it was here, in 1848, after his defeat at Custoza, that Garibaldi mustered an army to continue the struggle against the Austrians.

Further south is **Angera** ㊾, dominated by the Rocca Borromeo, a fortified castle which has belonged to the Borromeos since 1450. **Arona** ㊿, facing Angera from the Piedmont shore, possessed a twin castle, which was demolished by Napoleon. The castle ruins surmount the town, but Arona is better known for its copper colossus of Carlo Borromeo, who asserted his authority during the plague of 1576.

Lago d'Orta �MN, a mere 13km (8 miles) long, lies in the province of Novara in Piedmont. On the west bank, above Pella, Madonna del Sasso is a mountain sanctuary and forms the core of a pleasant group of hamlets. The lush promontory of Orta San Giulio, on the east bank, has island views, winding alleys and Baroque houses. A path leads through woods, past 20 chapels dedicated to St Francis, to **Sacro Monte**. Next door stands the Gothic Palazzo dei Vescovi, housing a Benedictine monastery. But the lake's main attraction (reached from the east bank) is the **Isola San Giulio**, a tiny island with passing steamers, a pretty harbour, porticoes, pergolas and slate-roofed houses. The centrepiece is the Romanesque Basilica of San Giulio, built on the site of a hermitage. ❑

Superman and superkitsch

Il Vittoriale, on the shores of Lake Garda, is a shrine to Gabriele D'Annunzio (1863–1938), maverick, poet, megalomaniac, pantheist, aviator, aesthete and nationalist, who lived there from 1921 until his death. A bizarre amalgam of founding Fascist and soldier-poet, only half convinced by his own myth-making, D'Annunzio was enamoured of Nietzsche's concept of the Superman, which was misused by the Fascists to bolster their beliefs.

A right-wing nationalist who posed as the saviour of his country, he favoured Italy's entry into the war in 1915 and plunged into the fighting, carrying out several operations, such as flying over Trieste in 1915 and Vienna in 1918. Believing that Italy had been cheated by the 1919 Treaty of Versailles, he led an unauthorised invasion of the Dalmatian port of Fiume, which he ruled until 1921, on the basis that it had been promised to Italy before the war.

Such activities convinced Mussolini that the dangerous maverick should be pensioned off to Lake Garda. D'Annunzio accepted the house as a monument to his massive ego, and called it Il Vittoriale, probably in memory of Italy's victory over Austria in 1918. Wanting the house to be a grandiose national monument, he donated it to the state in 1923, in return for further funds and in recognition of his role as "the father of the fatherland".

The villa has two waiting rooms, a relatively cheerful one for favoured guests, and a gloomy temple for those D'Annunzio disliked. Throughout the house, walls and ceilings are studded with crests, arcane symbols, mottoes and secret messages. "I have what I have given" is carved over a doorway. The entrance to his study was intentionally low so visitors had to stoop, presumably to bow to the poet's genius. The solemn "leper's room" has a "cradle-coffin" bed where the poet mused on major deaths and commemorated war anniversaries, and the blue bathroom is a gilded cage for a *fin-de-siècle* aesthete. The funereal music room is a prelude to a cluttered map room and a monastic study, all three filled with exotic bric-à-brac, from Murano glass bottles to Islamic plates and Austrian machine guns.

The furniture, swathed in silks, chinoiserie, leopard skin and Italian flags, embraces Renaissance reproductions and fake Parthenon friezes. So that it should not prove a distraction, the bust of his lover, the actress Eleanora Duse, was covered with a cloth while the poet worked. Not that D'Annunzio was without a warped sense of humour: the dining room contains the poet's embalmed pet tortoise, which died of indigestion, placed on display as a warning against the dangers of overeating. As an overview of D'Annunzio and his delusions of grandeur, Il Vittoriale leaves visitors amused and a little wiser. Curiously, it is treated with a mixture of reverence and impassivity by many Italians. ❑

RIGHT: the maverick soldier-poet Gabriele D'Annunzio (1863–1938).

GENOA

Map on page 292

In marked contrast to some of the softer, safer Ligurian resorts, historic Genoa is a challenging, cosmopolitan port city which rewards exploration

Novelist Italo Calvino called Genoa one of his "invisible cities", a place of secret alleys and sunless courtyards, of banded façades in striped marble, of private squares and jewel-box interiors. The *caruggi*, the classic city alleys, are often buried under medieval tenements and linked by myriad passages. Sandwiched between the mountains and the sea, the capital of Liguria suffers from lack of space, but once one is inside the minute medieval courtyards or across the threshold of a narrow Renaissance palace, hidden spaces seem to multiply amidst the mirrored interiors. Critics tend to connect the city's lack of space with its sense of reserve. In a city without a central piazza the mood is one of wariness, underscored by a suspicion of outsiders common to all ports.

Maritime might

Founded in the 5th century, **Genoa (Genova)** swiftly became a trading city and rose to prominence as a maritime power. By the end of the 12th century it had defeated its arch rival, Pisa, and possessed ports and colonies from the Aegean to the Black Sea. However, mighty Venice posed a greater threat to Genoa's trading empire. During its 14th-century golden age Genoa was a factional city, albeit one controlled by shrewd oligarchs; bankers, merchants, nobles and rival brotherhoods possessed private armies and separate political agendas. Whereas Venetians were loyal to their Republic, the Genoese were faithful only to their faction and fortunes: the merchant bank was trusted more than the municipal government. The mercantile character of the city and the citizens' skill at money-lending have given the Genoese an undeserved reputation for meanness. As befits an erstwhile Republic that pioneered such modern devices as bills of credit, cheques and insurance, Genoese banking and business skills continue to be held in high regard.

The city has cultivated a patrician crust of enlightened patronage ever since Andrea Doria, admiral of the Genoese fleet and founder of the Doria dynasty, won independence from France in 1528. He negotiated a sound city constitution that remained in force until 1797, enshrining Genoese values and protecting the city's financial status. During the Risorgimento Genoa was a leading centre of republican ideas and counted as a native son Giuseppe Mazzini (1805–72), the far-sighted patriot who put a united Italy on the political map.

With its reputation for obdurate independence and rugged individualism, Genoa was a centre of resistance against both Fascism and Nazism. Its industrial past, large working-class population and red-blooded refusal to submit have forged a political climate more attuned to left-wing administrations. Only in 1998

PRECEDING PAGES: Genoa is still a major port. **LEFT:** statue of Christopher Columbus, born in Genoa. **BELOW:** Genoa's old port.

was the dominance of the left seriously challenged. However, as Italy's sixth largest city and a member of the Milan-Turin industrial triangle, Genoa is not about to give up its traditional loyalties so readily.

The historic heart

The celebrated contemporary architect Renzo Piano calls Genoa "a secretive, inward-looking city, reflecting the prudent nature of the Genovese", whereas in 1846 Charles Dickens dismissed the city's "disheartening dirt, discomfort and decay".

As a historic port, Genoa cannot avoid dilapidation or the faint whiff of danger suspended in the salty air, especially at night. However, compensations lie in the hard-edged excitement generated by the waywardness of a real port. The intriguing *centro storico* (historic centre) stretches from the old port to Piazza de Ferrari and Via Garibaldi. The Genoese middle classes recommend that this maze of alleys be ignored after nightfall, and follow this practice themselves.

This is an attitude born of natural caution, tinged with a touch of racism since the port happens to be home to African immigrants as well as working-class Genoese. However, a modicum of street sense is enough to make an evening stroll a pleasurable affair, especially since most of the city's best restaurants are tucked into the old town.

The labyrinth of squares and palaces is testament to Genoa's medieval wealth and urban density: it was one of the largest cities in 14th-century Europe. Noble family homes were designed with several exits, covered passages linking different levels or houses; even a simple inn may have had a warren of rooms. A number of palaces are still inhabited by the original families. At night, beyond the Renaissance portals and façades of white marble and black slate, there are glimpses of simple family dinners taking place under grandly frescoed ceilings. One of the pleasures of strolling through the *centro storico* is the profusion of informative panels tracing the history of the area in various languages.

BELOW: Piazza Mazzini, Chiavari.

Via XX Settembre , a severe arcaded street, is a shop window on the elegant, classical quarter: the smartest shops, snootiest cafés and the old-world Bristol Palace Hotel. An air of safety and smugness pervades the street despite the discreet nightly presence of Russian prostitutes. Given the secrecy of the Genoese, it is only to be expected that, with the exception of **Zeffirano**, the best restaurants are invisible, tucked into the back streets. The cool, slightly soulless air of monumental Genoa is sustained by the grand **Palazzo Ducale** Ⓑ, set on neighbouring Piazza de Ferrari. This hollow shell of a palace once symbolised the power of "La Superba", the ancient Republic. However, the palace feels a bit of a sham, with a Neoclassical façade looming over Piazza Matteotti and an over-restored interior remodelled after wartime bomb damage. This former seat of the Republic is reduced to staging art exhibitions and antiques fairs.

Just downhill, **Piazza San Matteo** Ⓒ offers the first glimmer of authentic medieval Genoa. The church of San Matteo dates back to the 12th century but has a Gothic façade in the characteristic grey-and-white stripes that are Genoa's response to Pisan Romanesque. As well as the appealing cloisters (1308), the square is flanked by medieval palaces, decorated in Romanesque, Gothic and Renaissance styles.

Salita Arcivescovado leads to **San Lorenzo** Ⓓ, the Cathedral. In the 9th century the threat of pirate incursions prompted city rulers to transfer the Cathedral to the heart of the city. San Lorenzo was begun in 1200, but its eclectic design incorporates Romanesque, Gothic, Renaissance and Baroque elements.

From here, follow Canneto il Lungo, a narrow alley lined with crumbling palaces, to the medieval city's eastern limits. **Porta Soprana** Ⓔ, the twin-towered gateway, is the best-preserved section of the fortifications. The towers

Map on page 292

Lion guarding San Lorenzo.

BELOW: an artist's view of Genoa, 1493.

Casa di Colombo, where Christopher Columbus grew up.

dominate **Casa di Colombo**, the reconstructed boyhood home of Christopher Columbus (1451–1506). The son of a local weaver, the city's celebrated navigator was destined for a career as a cloth merchant until fate intervened. Salita Prione leads through the atmospheric Piazza delle Erbe to the 12th-century church of **San Donato** with its octagonal belltower. Just south stands **Sant'Agostino (Museo di Architettura)** (open Tues–Sat, 9am–7pm; entrance charge), marooned in a bleak quarter which suffered heavy wartime bombardment. This deconsecrated Gothic monastery has been turned into a museum of Ligurian sculpture and frescoes, and works salvaged from Genoa's demolished city churches are displayed in the Gothic and Baroque cloisters.

Set in the original Roman *castrum*, closer to the port, **Santa Maria di Castello** can also claim to be at the heart of the medieval city. Built on ancient foundations, this early Christian church has a Romanesque façade. The building was modified by the Dominicans in Renaissance times, but the interior still contains Roman columns and Romanesque sculpture. Nearby stands the **Torre degli Embriaci**, one of the few surviving medieval towers. Just beyond lie the bustling quayside and the porticoes of **Sottoripa**, with shops and stalls selling everything from fruit to fishing tackle. **Palazzo San Giorgio**, the port authority headquarters, commands a prominent position. Despite its harmoniously frescoed façade, this is a fusion of two palaces from different periods. From 1408 it was the seat of the Banco di San Giorgio, a banking syndicate and symbol of Genoa's financial might. It is also a reminder that while the city declined after the discovery of America, the wealth of the New World was channelled through its slick money markets. The Genoese were Europe's foremost bankers until they were supplanted by the Portuguese in the 17th century.

BELOW:
local wildlife.

The City Port and surrounding area

Porto Antico ❶, the old city port, had fallen into disuse and was neglected by visitors nervous of exploring this rough-and-ready area until architect Renzo Piano restructured it for the Columbus celebrations in 1992. The former cotton warehouses have also been restored, as have certain quayside buildings. The approach has a certain charm, even if it is based on a loose interpretation of medieval Genoa bordering on pastiche. The siting of the main **tourist office** in the old port has also helped regenerate the area, but the biggest impact came with the creation of the **Acquario** (Aquarium) ❸. The largest one in Europe, it includes special routes that allow visitors to view the fish from surface and sea-bed levels. Among the 500 species are grey sharks and dolphins, in habitats ranging from coral reefs to the Sardinian coast and South American seas. To the west, **Porto Nuovo**, the modern port, is fringed by an industrial zone.

A stone's throw from the old port, bustling **Piazza Banchi** is in the heart of a friendly neighbourhood noted for its small market, varied shops and typical *trattorie*. This is an opportunity to try a fishy pasta dish or *focaccia*, Genoese fast food, prepared with onions, salvia, potatoes or olives. The Renaissance **Loggia dei Mercanti ❶**, set on the square, is the last in a line of evolving banking facilities; the nobles operated banking services under the loggia, which then became the seat of Italy's first stock exchange in 1839. From here **Via San Luca**, one of the loveliest medieval streets, leads to Palazzo Spinola. Alternatively, Caffè Klainguti, a historic *pasticceria* on **Piazza Soziglia ⓜ**, provides a welcome coffee break in dignified surroundings.

Palazzo Spinola ⓝ (open Tues–Sat, 9am–5pm, Sun, 9am–1pm; entrance charge), set on Piazza Pellicceria, is tucked away in the former furriers' district but repays the effort to seek it out. The 16th-century palace, graced with frescoed ceilings and monumental staircases, has been turned into a gallery. On display are works by leading Italian and Flemish artists, from Van Dyck to the Sicilian Antonella da Messina and the Emilian Guido Reni.

Via Garibaldi ⓞ is considered the noblest of streets, lined with sumptuous 16th-century palaces, the grandest of which have been converted into galleries. Palazzo Doria Tursi has a splendid arcaded courtyard. **Palazzo Bianco ⓟ** (open Tues, Thurs, Fri 9am–1pm; Wed and Sat 9am–7pm; entrance charge) is a fine gallery displaying Flemish and Dutch paintings by Van der Goes, Van Dyck and Rubens as well as French and Spanish artists; the wealth of the city made it a magnet for foreign artists, especially the Flemish.

Palazzo Rosso ⓠ (open as above), opposite, holds works from the Venetian, Tuscan and Genoese schools. Venetian art, a celebration of colour and light, is represented by Titian, Tintoretto and Veronese, while Genoese art is characterised by drama, intensity and muted colours, as in the work of Bernardo Strozzi.

If you are in search of dinner, take **Via Luccoli ⓡ** back into the old city. A classic city pasta dish is *trennette al pesto,* with a *pesto* sauce similar to French *pistou*: made with greeny-golden olive oil, sweeter and more delicate than the Tuscan variety. ❏

Map on page 292

TIP

If you are visiting one of the city's *pasticcerias*, try the *torta di mandorle*, a tasty almond cake made with preserved fruit.

BELOW: catching up on the gossip.

THE LIGURIAN RIVIERA

Map on pages 300–301

The Ligurian coast offers a taste of the Mediterranean and the mountains, with hilltop castles, citrus groves, fishing villages transformed into chic resorts, and robust local cuisine

The vogue for sea-bathing on the Riviera did not become established until the 1930s. Until then a pampered foreign elite was more interested in winter cures and the therapeutic effects of the mild climate. The Italians had been swimming at San Remo since the 1850s, but the British, Germans and Russians regarded this as Italian perversity. The British, who were happy to swim at home, regarded the Mediterranean as suitable only for seaweed and anemone-hunting. However, for repressed northerners drawn to the winter resorts, the Riviera also represented a place to express smothered sensibilities.

Rugged individualists

The sea has determined Liguria's destiny as a trading region. As befits a former maritime state, Genoa *(see pages 291–5)* is cosmopolitan and raffish in equal measures. Its tough hinterland, Liguria, has always been a land of adventurous fishermen-sailors and shrewd merchant-wayfarers. In the 16th century its inhabitants, afraid of raids by marauding Turks and Venetians, built a series of coastal defences, which still survive. The Ligurians are an enterprising, pugnacious people, with the ingenuity to exploit the humblest of resources. Not that they lack subtlety; local excavations reveal their civilisation to be among the oldest and most sopisticated in Europe. Some complexity even pervades the language: French was the courtly language until the mid-19th century, and Ligurian dialects reflect French and Tuscan influences.

Yet a symbiotic relationship with the sea is not synonymous with an affection for the coastal environment. Roberto della Seta, a spokesperson for the Legambiente environmental group, says: "Italians are city-dwellers; they have no real love for the sea." Ecologists go further, accusing the Ligurians of indulging in disposable tourism, of turning sections of the coast into a concrete jungle. However, the steepness of the cliffs and the creation of protected zones have spared much of the area. Concrete jungles certainly exist, but so too do ravishing and balmy lemon-scented surroundings.

The landscape embraces the dramatic wine-growing coast, the remote mountainous hinterland and the millionaires' playground of Portofino. The lush vegetation ranges from agaves and oleanders to citrus fruits, umbrella pines and tamarisks. A Mediterranean mantle of greenery survives, in coastal pine groves and palm-fringed avenues. The jagged coastline harbours a wealth of architectural treasures, from bold Genoese-style churches to *belle époque* villas. As for agriculture, the cultivation of flowers might have broken the economic dependence on olives but grapes, peaches, oranges and olives still grow in abundance.

PRECEDING PAGES: the harbour at Vernazza. **LEFT:** lazy days on Alassio beach. **BELOW:** casting off.

Posing – but not for the camera.

Liguria, confident of its local cuisine, expects visitors to eat until they burst (*manja a crepa pansa*). Yet Liguria also has the highest life expectancy of any region in Italy: a healthy, homely Mediterranean diet helps foster such longevity, second only to that of the Japanese and Icelanders. Liguria has made a virtue of necessity since the region has yielded little in the way of grain, meat, dairy products, or even fish. Instead, the cuisine focuses on freshly made pasta, gnocchi and stuffed vegetable dishes.

Food is often dressed with vintage olive oil from Taggia and cooked with herbs such as thyme, oregano, basil and sage. *Focaccia – fugassa* in local dialect – is the fast food of the poor, a crispy bread snack smothered or stuffed with olives and sometimes anchovies or tomatoes. Fish also makes an impact, from fish soup to seafood risotto. The terraced slopes provide ideal territory for vines and olives. "The fact that the cuisine owes more to the country than the sea is because it grew out of the hankerings of sailors who yearned for fresh green vegetables … and fragrance, and during their time ashore this is what their women made to please them," is cookery writer Claudia Roden's interpretation.

Riviera di Ponente

The **western coast** stretches from the French border to Genoa, taking in San Remo, Imperia, Albenga and Savona, as well as a host of attractive villages in the rugged hinterland. As the centre of Italy's cut-flower industry, this coast is often dubbed "Riviera dei Fiori". Certainly the terraced hills around Ventimiglia and San Remo are dedicated to the growing of roses, carnations and anemones. Even outside the greenhouses the hothouse climate ensures that this coast is well endowed with exotic gardens and palm-lined promenades. The Via Aure-

BELOW: La Mortola.

lia, successor to the ancient Roman road, offers the most engaging coastal scenery, only rivalled by views from the hillside villages in the wild hinterland. Compared with polished Menton over the French border, **Ventimiglia ❶** appears scruffy and bedraggled, especially if one arrives by train. However, the approach by the coastal route is far more picturesque, with a carpet of flowers covering the terraced slopes. The June Battle of Flowers festival pays homage to the town's best-known industry. After being swallowed up by Genoa in 1261, Ventimiglia became a border town surrounded by fortifications, vestiges of which survive. The medieval city, tucked into the left bank of the river Roia, is centred on the Romanesque Cathedral and a cluster of dourly handsome civic buildings. The neighbouring church of **San Michele**, dating from the 8th century to the 10th, has an impressive crypt and Romanesque columns. The city has been inhabited since Roman times, but the Roman amphitheatre and other remains are engulfed by the modern lower city. However, for most people the city's greatest attraction is the **Friday market**, which invades the river bank, public gardens and part of Via Roma. The array of bags, shoes, clothes, fabrics, fruit and vegetables draws French residents from across the frontier and allows the canny Italians to have the last laugh on the chic French.

Map on pages 300–301

Flowers are Ventimiglia's best-known industry.

Prehistoric caves

Virtually on the French frontier, west of Ventimiglia, are the **Balzi Rossi ❷** prehistoric caves (tel: 0181-38113 for opening hours). Set at the foot of red cliffs in **Grimaldi**, these caves contain fossils, human skeletons and Paleolithic wall drawings. A study of these elaborate burials proves that the ancient Ligurians lived in one of Europe's most sophisticated societies. Apart from skeletons dating from 100,000 years ago, there are tools, weapons, fertility figures and a sketch of a breed of horse hitherto only found on the Russian Steppes. The museum was established in 1898 by Sir Thomas Hanbury, an English botanist and merchant who is best known for his gardens.

Commanding a headland just east of the Balzi Rossi is his home, **Villa Hanbury** ❸ (open daily, 9am–6pm; entrance charge). Struck by the cape's beauty and climate, Sir Thomas transformed the grounds into a botanical paradise between 1867 and his death. Hanbury's legacy was typical of his race, class and times: on the Riviera, the British often succumbed to the creative urge to make a lasting mark. Hanbury created Japanese and Australian gardens as well as the newly-restored perfume garden, full of scented pelargoniums, lavender and herbs. Today, exotic plants that Hanbury imported from Africa and Asia co-exist with native Mediterranean vegetation. The exotic species include papyrus and eucalyptus, cacti and rubber trees. Among the temples and follies are agaves, aloes, palms, yuccas, old roses and citrus groves.

Further along the coast is the resort of **Bordighera**, linking Ventimiglia and San Remo. There is a contrast between the historic hillside town of Bordighera Alta, with its defensive walls and maze of medieval alleys, and the elegant sea-side resort, with its palm-lined avenues. In the Bordighera hinterland is the well-tended wine-producing village of **Dolceacqua** ❹, a picturesque village set amid vineyards and crowned by a ruined medieval castle. Other delights in Dolceacqua include a humpbacked stone bridge, quaint covered passageways, and a rose-coloured parish church graced by a Baroque belltower. This stone village has its share of foreign residents, who are apparently charmed by the atmosphere as well as by the quality of the olive oil and full-bodied ruby-red wine.

On Hanbury's death his daughter-in-law Dorothy continued his work, but concentrated on landscaping rather than planting, creating paths, fountains, arbours and novel perspectives.

BELOW: the gentle waters of Dolceacqua.

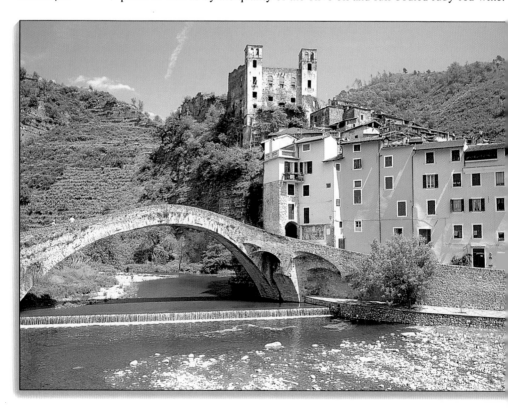

Sumptuous San Remo

Map on pages 300–301

Like Menton on the Côte d'Azur, **San Remo** ❺ made its name in the 1840s as an elitist winter resort. The mild climate, genteel atmosphere and beautiful surroundings attracted a foreign clientele, especially Russian and British aristocrats. Tourism received a further boost with the creation of sumptuous *belle époque* hotels and the arrival of the railway in 1871. San Remo, sheltered by mountains, still enjoys the lush vegetation that once drew these visitors. Lying in the lee of the Ligurian Alps, the capital of the Riviera dei Fiori cultivates the flowers for which it is known. The mild climate also means that the palm groves are more reminiscent of Sicily or North Africa. The early morning flower market on Corso Garibaldi is a chance to appreciate the fragrant local blooms.

San Remo has two centres: La Pigna, the original medieval hilltop village, is now outshone by the chic seaside resort. The palm-lined promenade of Corso Imperatrice is named after the Russian Czarina Maria Alexandrovna, a San Remo resident who filled the local gardens with palms in the 1870s.

In the same street is another legacy of the Russian community: the eclectic **Chiesa Russa** (1913), an onion-domed fantasy of an Orthodox church. The 19th century saw the creation of sweeping avenues, a setting for healthy but gentle promenades. Corso Imperatrice and its extensions, Corso Matteotti and Corso Nino Bixio, form the city drawing-room, with the Art Nouveau **Casino** (1906) at its heart. Tchaikovsky lived in this street of stuccoed mansions, as did Edward Lear, the nonsense poet, and Alfred Nobel, the father of modern explosives and prestigious prizes. As the queen of the Riviera, San Remo may have glittered during the *belle époque* but is a slightly shabby dowager now, even if splendid Art Nouveau villas are tucked into the surrounding slopes.

The Russian Orthodox Church, San Remo.

BELOW: win a car – or lose your shirt – at San Remo's casino.

TIP

If you are feeling
adventurous you can
take the funicular
railway from La Pigna
to Monte Bignone,
with its panoramic
views and nature
trails.

La Pigna, the higher, historic heart of San Remo, was once the fiefdom of Ventimiglia's feudal barons. The bastion was designed to offer protection against Turkish marauders, who regularly sacked the coast for water supplies and slaves. The walled village later flourished, surrounded by vineyards and olive groves. In time, however, La Pigna became more isolated from the chic seafront settlement. Today's old quarter curls around the vestiges of the former castle, with a succession of dark alleys and tunnels, sculpted portals and pastel-shuttered houses. At its heart stands **San Siro**, the Romanesque-Gothic Cathedral, partly remodelled in Baroque style. From here one can stroll to the small fishing harbour to inspect the catches of crayfish, swordfish and whitebait which end up on the tables of local *trattorie*.

In the hinterland, ancient olive groves give way to hills of sweet-smelling lavender, rosemary, laurel and thyme. Hiking trips into the hills may give sightings of marmots, chamois and porcupines, or owls and rock partridges. Just inland from San Remo stands the curious ghost town of **Bussana Vecchia ❻**. Abandoned after an earthquake in 1887, the village was repopulated by a bohemian artists' colony in the 1960s, and Italian and foreign artists have turned the least damaged houses into arts and crafts shops to promote their wares.

Towards Genoa

Cervo ❼ is an engaging hilltop village set on a spur sloping down to the sea. Dominated by a castle, the well-preserved medieval centre clings vertiginously to the slopes. The upper part of the village is particularly pleasing, with its distinctive porticoes, medieval walls and white houses huddled against the hillside. The majestic Baroque church of **San Giovanni Battista** has a concave façade,

BELOW: the
beach at Alassio.

a theatrical parvis and sweeping sea views. Nearby stands the austere 10th-century Romanesque Oratorio di Santa Caterina.

Albenga ❽ was founded by the Romans and flourished between the 10th and 13th centuries, but when the sea moved further out the Romanesque city was marooned by the river. The medieval centre fans out from the piazzas of San Michele, IV Novembre and dei Leoni. The latter, named after its three stone lions, is flanked by historic buildings, from the Comune Vecchio, the old town hall, to the Cathedral of **San Michele**, graced with a Romanesque belltower cast in green and white marble. Inside are the remains of the original early Christian church, including the apse of the crypt and vestiges of a 4th-century floor. Beside the Cathedral stands an octagonal baptistry with fine early Christian mosaics reminiscent of those at Ravenna. The **Museo Navale Romano** (tel: 0182-51215) traces Albenga's maritime heritage and displays the cargo of a Roman ship that sank offshore around 100–90 BC.

Savona, lying between Albenga and Genoa, is a former Florentine port overshadowed by its industrial present: the busy port handles crude oil and Italian cars for export to Britain and the United States. As the oldest nucleus of the city the port is dominated by a naval fortress and opens onto a Cathedral, Renaissance palaces and an art gallery displaying works by Ligurian painters. **The Grotte di Toirano** ❾ (tel: 0182-98062) lie beneath the hilltown of Toirano. This series of caves testifies to the importance of the Paleolithic period in the region. Among the relics dating back to 80,000 BC are traces of human and bear footprints, the remains of other wild animals, and mud balls probably used as missiles; the chambers are festooned with dramatic stalagmites and stalactites.

Pegli ❿, the faded haunt of the Genoese aristocracy, lies on the coast just before Genoa. Although now little more than a grand city suburb, it stands out for its collection of noble villas and gardens. **Villa Doria**, the naval museum, is noted for its collection of pines, while the grounds of **Villa Pallavicini** (tel: 010-6981048) include waterfalls, lakes, temples, follies, oriental pagodas and battlemented castles. Refined Pegli is now closer than it would like to be to the teeming port city of **Genoa (Genova)** ⓫ (*see pages 291–5*).

Riviera di Levante

The **eastern coast** stretches from Genoa to La Spezia, taking in Camogli, Portofino and Rapallo as well as Chiavari, Sestri Levanti, the Cinque Terre villages and Lerici. For those who wish to take daytrips to the coast, the Riviera di Levante – except for Portofino – is easily accessible by train from Genoa. Portofino, Portovenere and the Cinque Terre villages can also be reached on organised boat trips from Rapallo or Genoa.

Nervi ⓬, just east of Genoa, rose to prominence as a smart winter resort. Today this refined and hilly suburb is home to a trio of faded Genoese villas landscaped in English Romantic style, complete with lakes, avenues, rose gardens and a belvedere.

Camogli ⓭, the scenic gateway to the Portofino Peninsula, nestles at the foot of a pine-wooded slope. In the 18th century Camogli's maritime reputation

Map on pages 300–301

Charles Dickens (1812–70) called the fishing village of Camogli "the saltiest, roughest, most piratical little place".

BELOW: topping up the tan.

was such that it was known as "the port of a thousand white sails". Today the sailing fleet is gone, and this quaint fishing village symbolises the chicness of this stretch of coast.

For all its posturing, however, Camogli is more genuine than Portofino. The *porticciolo*, the tiny port at the foot of the promontory, is stacked with *case-torre*, the tall thin medieval houses that are typical of this coast; edged with dark-green shutters, they are painted in various shades, from ochre and rose to brick and burnt sienna. The village, riddled with steep stairways and vertiginous views, contains good seafood restaurants and stylish bars, and the medieval **Castel Dragone** houses the maritime museum and an aquarium. The celebrated *sagra del pesce* festival takes place on the second Sunday in May, when the country's largest frying pan is used to cook sardines.

Portofino owes its salvation to a foreigner: in April 1945 German resident Baroness von Mumm pleaded with the Nazis to spare her beloved home from bombing; the commander complied over a fish lunch.

San Fruttuoso , in the next bay, is a tiny fishing hamlet built around the abbey of the same name. Although San Fruttuoso can be reached by boat, the long trek from Camogli is as exhilarating as it is exhausting. A steep path traverses silvery olive groves, chestnut plantations and ruins in a patchwork of juniper, myrtle and wild asparagus. When not covered in mist, the cupola of the Benedictine abbey stands out against the Mediterranean landscape. The 11th-century complex embraces Romanesque cloisters and a crypt containing the noble Doria tombs. In the 16th century the Genoese Doria dynasty added a defensive tower to protect the coast from Venetian or Turkish marauders.

Portofino and Rapallo

BELOW: the abbey at San Fruttuoso.

Portofino , the most exclusive spot on the Riviera, can be reached by boat from neighbouring resorts; by foot, it is a two-hour trek from San Fruttuoso. Set on a picturesque promontory, this *faux* fishing village is adored by the stars who arrive incognito to sample its atmosphere. After an intimate tryst in the world-famous Hotel Splendido, or a studiously simple supper in a rustic inn, preferably shared with a fisherman, it is back to the yacht and the next movie deal. Since its discovery by the British in the 19th century, Portofino has been the preserve of artists, film directors and the yachting set.

Portofino's illustrious past visitors include Edward VIII, Duke of Windsor, Clark Gable and Frank Sinatra; the contemporary roll call features actors Harrison Ford, John Malkovich and Sophie Marceau, who have shot films here. Yet, even for the elite, seclusion only lasts from evening to first light: when the day-trippers arrive, the spell is broken. During the day the medieval lanes studded with bijou boutiques are frequented by yachties in designer nautical wear. But with a suspension of cynicism it is easy to fall for the sailing boats at sunset, the portside *piazzetta* framed by picturesque *case-torre*, the lanes dotted with terraces and cute cats. The hillside beyond, surmounted by a castle, is studded with villas hidden by cypresses and chestnuts, palms and umbrella pines.

As a lush coastal nature reserve the **Promontory of Portofino** is satisfying walking country, with rock, bush and pine tumbling to the sea. From San Rocco di Camogli a pleasant path leads to the cape of **Punta**

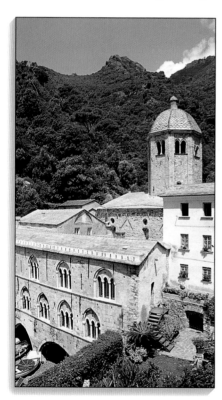

Chiappa, past the Romanesque church of San Nicolo di Capodimonte. The luxuriant scrub provides a forest of heather, myrtle, broom, thyme and saxifrage, a perfect habitat for lizards, skylarks, barn owls and nightingales.

A panoramic route connects Portofino with the neighbouring resort of **Santa Margherita Ligure**. Sandwiched between Portofino and Rapallo, Santa Margherita makes a lively touring base. The attractions include a sandy beach, ruined castle and, perched on the headland, the lovely Villa Durazzo (tel: 0185-282449) surrounded by Italianate gardens. Beyond are Classical or Art Nouveau villas nestling in the hills.

Rapallo ⓰, framed by attractive hills, is deservedly one of the most popular resorts in the Riviera, with a low-key yet lively atmosphere that satisfies old and young alike. The cultural and historical sights are quickly disposed of, leaving one time to appreciate the balmy atmosphere and gentle strolls along the seafront. If boredom sets in there are boat trips to other fishing villages on the coast, notably to the Cinque Terre. The genteel town is best explored in the early morning, when the food markets are enticing, or in the early evening when the shops and relaxed bars come into their own. Rapallo's chief sight is the seafront **Castello**, which once served as a prison. Although built in 1550 to defend the port against pirate raids, it was remodelled in the 17th century when the foundations were raised and the castle was endowed with a private chapel.

The **lace museum** is a reminder of the way in which women traditionally occupied themselves while their fishermen husbands were at sea. The museum displays everything from chaste underwear to pillow cases for wedding trousseaux or a baby's baptismal best. From Rapallo a cable car leads up to **Montallegro**, a Marian sanctuary with panoramic views over the gulf.

Map on pages 300–301

Villa Durazzo at Santa Margherita Ligure.

BELOW: picturesque Portofino.

*The Fortezza di
Sarzello in Sarzana
is characterised by
deep moats and
austere curtain walls.*

Sestri Levante, further east, enjoys a charming setting on a peninsula. As yet another fishing village that has mutated into a resort, it has made a smoother transition than most. Between here and La Spezia the road becomes distinctly mountainous. From Sestri Levante, Genoa or Rapallo one can reach the Cinque Terre villages by train, by boat or on foot.

The famous five

At this stage the prospect of exploring the **Cinque Terre** ⑰ by foot holds far more appeal. As five stunning villages surrounded by steep hills and vineyards, the Cinque Terre ('Five Lands') present concentrated essence-of-Liguria. The classic route follows panoramic coastal footpaths to lofty sanctuaries, homely restaurants, Genoese-style striped churches and tiny ports. En route there are views of jagged coasts, pastel-coloured cottages, fishing nets drying in the sun and vineyards built using dry stone walls. The walk is Liguria in miniature, a pilgrimage for the spirit and the stomach. Via dell'Amore, a lovers' path wending along the coast linking Riomaggiore and Manarola, provides a typical flavour of the route. However, summer visitors in search of solitude may find these cliffside hamlets overrated; in August, stupendous views are little compensation for the crowds. A visit out of season reveals a wilder side, particularly on the rougher trails to the sanctuaries above the villages. A popular way of doing the route is to leave your car at Riomaggiore and take the short train journey to Monterosso, where the walk back begins.

Monterosso ⑱, the western gateway to this celebrated cluster of villages, is best reached by train. The village, which is slightly more commercialised than the others, overlooks a popular sandy beach. The main sights are the Convento dei Cappuccini, with a majestic view, and the parish church of San Giovanni Battista with its crenellated belltower. Many morning walks end in the Ristorante degli Amici, set just off the beach on Via Buranco and noted for grilled fish and seafood *antipasti*. From Monterosso one can also reach the other Cinque Terre villages by train, by boat or on foot. The **Sentiero Azzurro** follows the coast, linking the main villages in vertiginous views; the stretch to Vernazza is one of the more demanding sections, climbing through vineyards high above the sea and traversing narrow valleys on old foot-bridges before descending to Vernazza about two hours later. Alternatively, to lose the crowds, take the steep climb up to the remote 9th-century sanctuary of Madonna di Soviore.

Vernazza ⑲, the most picturesque village, is also the most crowded, particularly on summer weekends. The winding back streets, dotted with wine and craft shops, make for a satisfying stroll, particularly if followed by a clam soup or lobster lunch on a charming terrace. However, the scene-stealer is the port itself, with its painted houses clustered at the head of a well-sheltered cove. The port, overrun by giggling, diving children in summer, is overlooked by an atmospheric parish church in Genoese style. Vernazza's role as a trusted ally during the Genoese Republic means that the village has a more refined aspect than the others. The stretch from Vernazza to the unspoilt village

BELOW:
Riomaggiore,
seen from the sea.

of **Corniglia** ⓴ is slightly shorter than the previous one. As a farming and wine-growing community built atop a lofty promontory, Corniglia has always had a more inland character than the other Cinque Terre ports. **Manarola** ㉑, roughly an hour from Corniglia on foot, is a colourful fishing village set amid geometric patterns of terraced vineyards. After admiring the 14th-century church of San Lorenzo, follow the celebrated Via dell'Amore (Lovers' Lane) to **Riomaggiore** ㉒, a village carved into a narrow valley. The journey ends with a visit to the 14th-century church of San Giovanni Battista and a sight of the harbour, set against strata of the strange black rock that typifies the region. Walkers in a celebratory mood can toast the towering cli[f]s with dry Cinque Terre wine or Sciacchetra sweet dessert fizz.

Portovenere ㉓, easily reached by boat from Rapallo or Genoa, makes a delightful day out and is usually far less crowded than the Cinque Terre villages. The port sprawls along a promontory, with fish restaurants lining the harbour, sunbathers on the rocks, and fishing nets cast over the sea walls. In medieval times Portovenere was a fortified outpost of the Republic of Genoa, but the Genoese bastion was largely dismantled in 1453, and the present citadel is Baroque. In the upper part of the village beguiling backstreets lead to the Romanesque parish church of San Lorenzo, which has Gothic and Renaissance additions. From Piazza Spallanzani a gentle climb leads to **San Pietro**, a Gothic church in striped bands of black and white. From the terrace, a popular setting for open-air concerts, there are stunning views towards the Cinque Terre and Lerici. A staircase leads up to **Grotta Arpaia**, known as Byron's Grotto. This stretch of coast will forever be linked to the fateful musings of the English Romantic poets. Lord Byron, a strong swimmer then living in a villa in neighbouring La Spezia, loved the wildness of the waters around Portovenere. However, in 1822 his friend Shelley was drowned while attempting to sail from Livorno to Lerici, where he had a small house.

From Portovenere there are boat trips to the **Isole Palmaria**, colonised by Benedictine monks in medieval times. Dominating the next bay is **La Spezia** with its sprawling naval shipyards, former arsenal and naval museum. The town and seaside promenades are overlooked by a medieval castle. **Lerici** ㉔, set on the other side of the so-called "gulf of poets", is illuminated by a picturesque castle that enchanted Byron, Keats and Shelley. This towering Pisan stronghold was enlarged by the Genoese, who remodelled it in Gothic style, adding a chapel. From Lerici a beguiling descent leads down to Fiascherino, a luminous bay.

Sarzana ㉕ once guarded the eastern frontier of the Republic of Genoa against Pisa, its neighbour and arch-rival. The hub of this fortified town is the Fortezza di Sarzello, a 15th-century Florentine citadel which was remodelled after the Tuscans had defeated the Genoese. Climb up for a splendid view over the town and the foothills. Other attractions in the town include the Gothic Cathedral and the Renaissance palaces flanking Piazza Matteotti. From here, however, even landlubbers will probably be tempted to return to the Ligurian coast, with its soft interplay of sky and sea. ❏

Map on pages 300–301

Shelley was working on his last great poem, The Triumph of Life, *when he was drowned on his way back to Lerici after visiting another English expatriate poet, James Leigh Hunt.*

BELOW: if you love seafood, you'll love Portovenere.

BOLOGNA

Bologna's galleries and museums are engrossing, but it is the red-brick city itself that is the central work of art. Follow this route to discover its network of porticoes and its friendly taverns

Map on page 314

Bologna is one of the most civilised cities in Europe, a monument to bourgeois bliss, personal pragmatism and public efficiency. As a stylish tribute to the beauty of urban life, Bologna unfurls a warm red-brick cityscape of arcaded streets and elegant palaces. It is also a paradigm of the good life, with its superb cuisine and cultured outlook, vibrant arts scene and youthful population, honest public administration and efficient public transport. The citizens are sociable, affable, open and cosmopolitan, proud of but not precious about their urban heritage.

Fat, learned and red

Bologna abounds in nicknames: *la Dotta*, "the learned", referring to its role as an ancient university city; *la Rossa*, "the red", in relation to its politics rather than its red-brick buildings; and, finally, *la Grassa*, "the fat", an epithet linked to its reputation as a gourmandising city, the temple of Italian cuisine. Thanks to its passion for education, Bologna also remains a city committed to museums, with a new museum of Jewish culture and a new library, the largest one in Italy, for the Millennium. Politically, the pragmatic city administration ensures that Bologna remains one of the best-run cities in Italy's political "red belt".

As for cuisine, sceptics need only stroll into delicatessens lining Via Caprairie: mountains of *tortelloni*, salami and cheeses are stacked beside spit-roasted chickens, rice croquettes, *marrons glacés* and rolls of pepper stuffed with meats.

The city has been a centre of learning since the 7th century, when scholars from Ravenna settled nearby. This academic tradition culminated in the foundation in 1088 of the city's famous law school, the nucleus of one of the first universities in Europe. Bologna, bound by 14th-century walls and entered via 12 fine gates, developed as a coherent commercial city, with wealth created by merchants who developed the gold, clothing, silk and hemp industries.

Like most major northern cities, medieval Bologna experienced power struggles between the church, the *comune* (civic council) and the guilds, represented by the lawyers and bankers. In the 16th century it became part of the Papal States but continued to follow a communal, civic-minded path; this became a conscious philosophical stance, with the common good placed before personal glory. In modern times Bologna's civic record has emphasised its hostility to Fascism and right-wing government. The region turned to Communism after leading the resistance against the Nazi occupation towards the end of World War II.

Today Bologna's political affiliations are clear in streets blessed with such names as Salvatore Allende

PRECEDING PAGES: Bolognese banter. **LEFT:** Bologna is a foodie's paradise. **BELOW:** the 16th-century bronze statue of Neptune in the Piazza del Nettuno.

and Martin Luther King. However, political ideology is tempered with pragmatism. As the mayor, Walter Vitali, says: "Bologna is not the last bastion of Communism; we simply have a good, left-wing, social democrat administration." Bologna is a pioneering city: the first to introduce pedestrian precincts, to privatise certain social services, to permit gay couples to apply for communal housing, and to impose key environmental and health measures. With its population of only 600,000, its homogeneous urban design and lack of ugly suburbs, Bologna is *una città a misura dell'uomo*, a city built on a human scale, in which people still live and work in the well-preserved historic heart (even if some workers might actually live in the countryside and commute).

Andiamo in piazza

For a Bolognese, *andiamo in piazza* ("let's go to the square") can only mean a visit to **Piazza Maggiore A**. The main square stands at the heart of this monocentric city; it forms a majestic architectural ensemble, complete with open-air cafés, palaces and public buildings. One of the grandest is the **Palazzo del Podestà**, formerly the Governor's Palace, graced with a Renaissance façade, which is being converted into a conference and exhibition centre. Despite the elegant cafés, on most mornings the square is the preserve of old men in fusty clothes putting the world to rights; the afternoon sees the arrival of some of Bologna's 100,000 students, who cycle over for coffee and conversation.

Piazza del Nettuno B, skirting the northern end of the main square, is centred on the muscular bronze statue of Neptune (*see page 316*). Facing the Palazzo del Podestà is the looming bulk of **San Petronio C**, one of the largest churches in Christendom. Founded in 1390, it is dedicated to the city's patron

Bologna

saint, a 5th-century bishop beloved for the urban planning projects he master-minded. The Gothic Basilica testifies to the seemingly limitless wealth of the medieval city, although grandiose plans to make the Basilica bigger than St Peter's came to nothing, and work on the unfinished façade was abandoned in 1650. The financial profligacy of the project was said to have helped turn Martin Luther against the Church. Visually the Basilica influenced Michelangelo, presenting an exotic expanse of pink marble in a sea of red brick. Particularly outstanding are Jacopo della Quercia's bas-reliefs over the main portal, and the marble decoration on the lower part of the façade. Della Quercia was Sienese; the alien nature of marble in this red-brick city meant that marble sculptors were rarely natives of Bologna. Inside, the highlights are Giovanni da Modena's frescoed 15th-century Madonna, and the pulpit where St Bernard of Siena and Savonarola preached. The basilica provided a splendid setting for the coronation of the Holy Roman Emperor Charles V in 1530.

Behind San Petronio is the **Museo Civico Archeologico** ⓓ (open Tues–Sat, 9am–2pm; weekends 9am–1pm, 3.30–7pm). This well-designed archeological museum paints a picture of Etruscan and Roman Emilia Romagna. Etruscan and Roman artefacts range from funerary urns and stele to mosaics and a bust of the Emperor Nero. The collection is complemented by Egyptian artefacts as well as Celtic hemets and 6th-century bronze buckles.

Nearby stands the **Palazzo Archiginnasio** ⓔ (open Mon–Fri, 9am–7pm; Sat 9am–2pm), now home to the municipal library but once the seat of the university. Set on Piazza Galvani, it occupies the site intended for the left transept of San Petronio; funds were diverted to the palace instead. Built in 1563, it was intended as a home for all faculties, from philosophy and civil law to medicine

Map on page 314

The writer and traveller Freya Stark remarked that San Petronio looked as if it had sunset built into its walls.

BELOW: Piazza Maggiore, Bologna's main square.

Neptune on top of his fountain.

and mathematics. Upstairs is the Teatro Anatomico, a compelling dissection theatre and a reminder that the world's first lessons in human anatomy were conducted in Bologna. This chamber, superbly restored after bomb damage in World War II, dates from the 17th century, but public medieval dissections were performed in similar surroundings. It is dominated by an operating table eerily supervised by statues of famous professors and dissected corpses.

To banish morbid thoughts it is enough to retrace one's steps to Piazza del Nettuno and the **Fontana di Nettuno** , the Fountain of Neptune (1563–66) by Giambologna, the Flemish artist who made his name in Florence. Neptune, unashamedly naked, trident in hand, commands four voluptuous sirens, each riding a dolphin. In the Baroque period the statue's erotic charge was considered so disturbing that bronze breeches were cast on the god and only removed in more liberated times.

On the west side of the square is the **Palazzo Comunale** , more correctly known as Palazzo d'Accursio, the town hall since the early 13th century. The palace walls are covered in photographs of Bolognese intellectuals and partisans shot by the Nazis in 1944. Part of the palace houses the **tourist office** (open Mon–Sat, 9am–7pm) and a series of splendid public rooms. Pride of place is given to the **Museo Giorgio Morandi** (open Tues–Sun, 10am–6pm), dedicated to the city's pre-eminent still-life painter. Morandi (1890–1964) had a predilection for painting bottles and bowls with great subtlety in sludgy colours.

According to Umberto Eco, Bologna-based professor and best-selling author of *The Name of the Rose*: "Morandi can only be understood after one has trailed the arcaded streets of his city and understood how a seemingly uniform brick-red tint can define different houses and alleys."

BELOW: the fountains near the town hall – the Palazzo d'Accursio.

The **Museo Civico Medievale** , set on Via Manzoni (open Mon, Wed–Fri, 9am–2pm; weekends, 9am–1pm, 3.30–7pm), occupies a delightful palace. This charming and compact museum covers the period from the Middle Ages to the Renaissance. Highlights include collections of arms, ivory and glassware as well as Gothic sculptures and bronze statues.

Lofty views

The gate of **Porta Ravegnana** ❶ is dominated by the two relatively intact leaning towers **(Torri Pendenti)** that escaped demolition at the turn of the century. Such lofty towers characterised the medieval city skyline and testified to the power of the resident feudal families. The Asinelli, the taller tower, is visible from most spots in the city; the Garisenda, its squatter companion, is half the size but leans three times as much. To work up an appetite, visitors can climb the 100 metres (330 ft) to the top of the Asinelli and be rewarded by a terracotta cityscape stretching into the villa-studded Apennine hills. As a counterpoint to these historic towers in the city centre, there are contemporary Japanese-designed towers in the new business district.

San Bartolomeo ❶, set beside the two towers, is a Baroque church with a lovely highly-decorated portico. In the north transept is a colourful Madonna by Guido Reni. **Strada Maggiore** ❶ runs east from the towers and follows the original line of the Roman Via Emilia, making a gentle introduction to the terracotta-hued shopping streets. **Santa Maria dei Servi** ❶, set further down the street, is a 14th-century church graced with Gothic and Renaissance porticoes. It is rich in works of art, with frescoes by Vitale da Bologna and a Madonna and Child panel painting by Cimabue. **Case Isolani** ❶, overlooking the same street,

Bologna-based professor and author Umberto Eco.

BELOW: Bologna is a city of piazzas and porticoes.

PORTICOES

Porticoes are a hallmark of Bologna: picturesque marble or brick affairs radiating from the city centre. These seemingly endless arcades stretch for 35 km (22 miles) and shelter shoppers and sightseers from inclement weather. The porticoes were a response to a housing crisis caused by the influx of students, migrants and merchants who flocked to Bologna in the 15th century. The first floors of houses were extended to form extra rooms suspended over the street. As well as providing space and shelter, these overhanging adjuncts were found to promote trade and social life, connect private and public areas, and even protect pedestrians from traffic. As a result the city has continued to build, rebuild or restore its porticoes until modern times.

The arcades from Porta Maggiore to Via Mazzini, the old Roman road, are the most impressive in the city, an early 17th-century affair forming a "sacred way" to the church of Santa Maria Lacrimosa. The early 18th-century saw the completion of the world's longest porticoes, built to connect the city with a hilltop sanctuary. Composed of 666 arcades, the route winds up Colle della Guardia to Santuario della Madonna di San Luca, a distance of several miles.

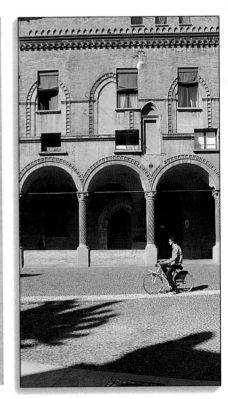

is an arts, commercial and residential complex carved out of traditional city palaces. Also known as Corte Isolani, this palatial affair has Romanesque-Gothic porticoes supported by 12th-century beams. The complex, a warren of chic boutiques and cafés, connects with Via Santo Stefano, an agreeable street lined with churches and palaces.

Abbazia di Santo Stefano Ⓝ (open daily, 9am–2pm; entrance charge) is the most bewildering of the city churches. Essentially a religious complex clustered around Santo Stefano, it's a surprisingly harmonious ensemble formed from four Romanesque churches, two chapels and two cloisters which date back to the 5th century but are predominantly Romanesque. San Sepolcro, dating from the 11th century, houses the elaborate tomb of St Petronius, built in imitation of the Holy Sepulchre in Jerusalem. **Via Castiglione** Ⓞ, which runs virtually parallel to Via Santo Stefano, is an equally typical Bolognese street.

The oldest university?

Further north, the **Università (Palazzo Poggi)** Ⓟ on Via Zamboni has been a seat of learning since the 16th century, when the campus transferred from the Archiginnasio. As one of the first universities in Europe, the law school was born out of a need to bring Roman law up to date, and resulted in Bologna becoming the pre-eminent European centre for civil law. At its height in the 13th century the university numbered 10,000 students from all over Europe. Scholars included Petrarch, Copernicus, Dante Alighieri and Thomas Becket, subsequently martyred in Canterbury. As well as law, the university has specialised in the sciences, especially in medicine and physics, a reputation underlined by the pioneering radio experiments carried out by local boy Guglielmo Marconi

BELOW: Bologna's ancient university remains a centre of scholarship – and sometimes protest. **RIGHT:** students take a break.

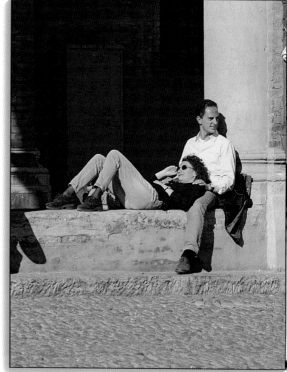

(1874–1937). Bologna remains a centre of scholarship, a role confirmed by the number of international universities with campuses in the city. The university's frescoed interior houses several minor museums, including the naval museum.

Map on page 314

The **Pinacoteca Nazionale** ❶ (open Tues–Sat, 9am–1.30pm; Sun 9am–1pm), on Via delle Belle Arti, has one of the most appealing art collections in the country. The core collection embraces Emilian painters from the 14th century. Emilian painting is traditionally overshadowed by Tuscan and Roman art but is currently being revalued. As a reaction to the formalism of Tuscan Mannerism, the Bolognese School favoured simplicity and greater realism. These elements feature in the work of artists such as Annibale Carraci, Guercino and Guido Reni, who painted during the Counter-Reformation. A few works by Giotto and Raphael help bring a less regional perspective to the collection.

To the west of Piazza Maggiore, the delightful **Piazza Malpighi** ❶ is a colourful spot surrounded by a frescoed portico. On the same square is the romantic Gothic church of San Francesco, complete with cloisters and a fine belltower. Further south, on Via d'Azeglio, **Palazzo Bevilacqua** ❶ is the boldest of Bologna's senatorial palaces. Built in Florentine rusticated style in 1474, this superb Renaissance building displays a sandstone facade, wrought-iron balconies and a courtyard surrounded by a loggia.

San Domenico ❶ dominates Piazza San Domenico, a square lined with monumental tombs. It was designed to house the body of St Dominic, the founder of the Dominican order. Dating from 1228, it was remodelled in Baroque style but incorporated existing Romanesque walls. The interior displays St Dominic's tomb, decorated with sculptures by Nicola Pisano and Arnolfo di Cambio of the Pisan school as well as by two by the young Michelangelo. ❑

Art critic Roberto Longhi praises Emilian painting as sincere, earthy and impulsive, "open to sin but also to redemption"; and local writer Renzo Renzi says: "It is openly human and therefore popular art in the best sense."

BELOW: exquisite carvings on St Dominic's tomb.

OSTERIE: TRADITIONAL TAVERNS

Bologna's *osterie* focus on genuine food and a cosy family atmosphere. They have their roots in proletarian wine shops, a cross between a tap room and a tavern. In 19th-century Bologna or Milan the typical tavern offered a daily diet of fried polenta and salt cod, steaming macaroni or left-over offal, washed down with rough wine. By the end of the century politics had prevailed over food: taverns were considered dens of iniquity. Under Fascism, these inns became notorious as focuses for subversion and seditious demonstrations. After the war they succumbed to fashion, with most surviving by emphasising their regional roots and traditional recipes.

Today, these family-run *osterie* attempt to promote Emilian hospitality and specialise in home-made food. In Bologna they often serve such standards as *bollito misto*, an abundance of mixed meats, from *cotechino* or *zampone* to tongue, shin, chicken on the bone, or stuffed *porchetta*. Recently, their cause has been championed by the influential *Slow Food* (*see page 105*), a combined culinary campaign and international journal which aims to promotes the pleasures of eating. An evening stroll along Bologna's Via del Pratello is an introduction to several inviting *osterie*.

EMILIA ROMAGNA

*The medieval and the Renaissance mingle in the cities, museums
and castles of Emilia Romagna, a smugly sensuous land of
plenty which also offers the best cuisine in the country*

Map
on pages
324–325

The broad river plain stretches languorously southwards from the sluggish River Po to the Apennines. There are cities, from Ferrara to Piacenza, which are treasure troves of galleries, churches and castles, and others, from Parma to Modena and Bologna, which are associated with gastronomy and good living.

Historically the region has been dominated by ducal dynasties and tiny fiefdoms run by huge egos. The glory days of feudalism culminated in the claims of the d'Este, rulers of Ferrara, and the Farnese, who controlled Parma and Piacenza. Before 1860, Bologna and Ferrara were governed by Papal legates; the land to the northeast belonged to the Duke of Parma; and the Duke of Modena's possessions stretched across the mountains to Carrara and the Gulf of Genoa. Politically the region has been socialist since the 19th century, and it suffered in the struggle against Fascism and Nazism. In April 1945 the Allies launched an offensive from Ravenna, which led to the liberation of the region, supported by the partisans. However, Emilia's left-wing politics have more to do with the region's traditional anti-clericalism than with belief in a Communist utopia.

The Emilian model

The post-war period witnessed the development of small and medium-sized companies, an economic success story which came to be known as "the Emilian model". Above all it is noted for the survival of city-specific industries, from tiles in Sassuolo to glassworks in Fidenza; Modena styles sleek Ferraris and Maseratis, while Parma produces ham and cheese. Emilia is the gastronomic heart of Italy, feeding the north with superb salami and sausages as well as cheeses. The region produces much of Italy's wheat and sugar beet as well as barley, tomatoes, rice, peaches and plums. It also produces almost a quarter of the country's beef and veal.

Piacenza ❶ marks the border between Lombardy and Emilia Romagna, a frontier clearly carved by the yellowing River Po. As a bridge between two cultures, this dignified and unassuming city makes a low-key introduction to the region. Piacenza has the dubious distinction of being the coldest city in Italy, the price paid for its riverside setting on the Pianura Padana, the inhospitable Po Valley.

When Pope Paul III, a powerful member of the Farnese dynasty, wished to create a buffer zone between the Papal States to the south and Spanish domination in Lombardy to the north, he granted the new Duchy of Parma and Piacenza to his son, Pier Luigi Farnese, in 1545, with territory that originally fell within the jurisdiction of the Papal States. Piacenza became the

PRECEDING PAGES:
the beautiful
frescoed ceiling of
Parma's Baptistry.
LEFT: Parma is
famous for its
Parmigiano cheese.
BELOW: Piazza dei
Cavalli, Piacenza.

first capital of the Duchy of Parma, graced with Renaissance walls, although the dynasty's greatest legacy was in Parma itself.

The historic centre is clustered around **Piazza dei Cavalli**, named after the *cavalli*, two early-Baroque bronze horses (1620–25) ridden by members of the Farnese dynasty. Flanking the square are the Gothic church of **San Francesco** and the **Palazzo del Comune** (1280), the Gothic town hall, noted for its mullioned windows and swallowtail crenellations. The Lombard-Romanesque **Duomo** (1122–1244) stands at the end of Via XX Settembre, the main street. The lacklustre façade is cast in Verona marble and stone and enlivened by Romanesque capitals and sculptures. The impressive 14th-century belltower is surmounted by an iron cage installed in 1495 as a means of public punishment: offenders were suspended above the square and subjected to public ridicule.

Emilia is prime pasta country and also produces the country's finest charcuterie, perfect food for a convivial, pampered people.

From here Via Chiapponi leads to **Sant'Antonio**, founded in the 4th century. This severe brick building served as the cathedral until the 9th century. As well as an exceptional 11th-century octagonal lantern and a Gothic vestibule, the highlights include a rich interior featuring 9th-century frescoes. The **Museo Civico** (open Tues–Sun, 9am–noon, 3–6pm; entrance charge) on Piazza Citadella occupies the unfinished Palazzo Farnese, the first seat of the dynasty. The museum holds a quirky collection of exhibits, from a Botticelli Madonna to a curious Etruscan bronze sheep's liver, used for reading the runes.

Panoramas, pilgrims and the birthplace of Verdi

Castel l'Arquato ❷ is a harmonious village with panoramic views, nestling in the hills of Piacenza province. Set between Piacenza and Fidenza, this feudal settlement was dominated by the Visconti and Sforza dynasties, who remained until 1707 when the territory became absorbed by the Duchy of Parma. Piazza Alta, at the hub of the village, is lined with appealing inns and flanked by the Romanesque church of Santa Maria and the fortified Gothic **Palazzo Pretorio**, once the governor's palace, now the town hall. Nearby is the **Rocca Viscontea**, the daunting Visconti fortress, a 14th-century complex bounded by ramparts and topped by pentagonal towers.

Fidenza ❸ is a historic halt on the Via Francigena, the main pilgrimage route to Rome. The Cathedral of **San Donnino** is adorned by friezes depicting weary pilgrims, and is dedicated to a pilgrim martyr who, after being decapitated by the Romans, managed to carry his severed head to the far side of the river. The bones and skull of the saint are displayed inside.

The feudal castle of **Fontanellato ❹**, set 20 km/12 miles west of Parma, seems to rise majestically from a glassy green moat. The castle belonged to the Sanvitale family from the mid-14th century until 1948, when the last count sold it to the town as a museum. The centrepiece is a mysterious chamber, either a boudoir or an alchemist's study. This inner sanctum, adorned with frescoes, mirrors and gilt, depicts the myth of Acteon and the huntress Diana. In Parmigianino's captivating frescoes the goddess punishes the mortal who sees her bathing by transforming him into a hunted stag encircled by hounds.

Roncole Verdi ❺ has an indisputable claim to fame as the birthplace of Italy's most famous composer. In Italy, Giuseppe Verdi (1813–1901) is revered as a genius who expressed the national spirit in his music. Although Verdi was the son of a grocer and tavern-keeper, his humble origins are thought to be exaggerated; recent studies seem to suggest that the family were also small landowners. His birthplace has been turned into a museum (tel: 0524-84047).

Map on pages 324–325

Detail on Fidenza's Cathedral.

BELOW: Castel l'Arquato.

Just north of Busseto is **Villa Verdi**, bought by the composer with the proceeds from *Rigoletto* and filled with Verdi memorabilia (open Tues–Sun, 9am–noon, 3–6.30pm). In Busseto itself the city castle accommodates the **Teatro Verdi**, dedicated to performing his works.

"I was, am and always will be a peasant from Roncole," wrote Giuseppe Verdi, Italy's best-known composer.

The city of cheese and ham

Parma ⑥, sandwiched between Milan and Bologna, was fought over by France, the Papacy and the northern feudal dynasties; the Farnese dynasty made the greatest mark, ruling the city during its heyday in the 16th and 17th centuries. When the Farnese line died out in 1731 the Duchy of Parma passed into the hands of the Bourbons. The 1815 Congress of Vienna assigned the duchy and Piacenza to the Habsburg ex-Empress Marie Louise (1791–1847), Napoleon's estranged second wife. A cultured liberal ruler, she is credited with transforming Parma into a bourgeois capital with an imperial air.

Modern-day Parmigiani have a reputation for bravery: Parma was the last Italian city to succumb to Fascism in 1922. Allied bombing raids destroyed a fifth of the city in 1944, but most of the medieval heart remains, matched by Renaissance frescoes and Neoclassical façades. Today Parma is a byword for fine living, with an urbane, prosperous population devoted to making and spending money. This chic yet understated city abounds in civic pride and splendid architecture, yet it tends to be neglected by foreigners in favour of Florence and Siena. The locals blame the climate as much as the lure of Tuscany: stifling hot in summer, snowy or foggy in winter, Parma is an acquired taste, as is the local accent. (In the French-influenced local dialect, artichoke, *carciofi* in Italian, is *artichaut*.)

BELOW: *Parmigiano Reggiano* – king of cheeses.

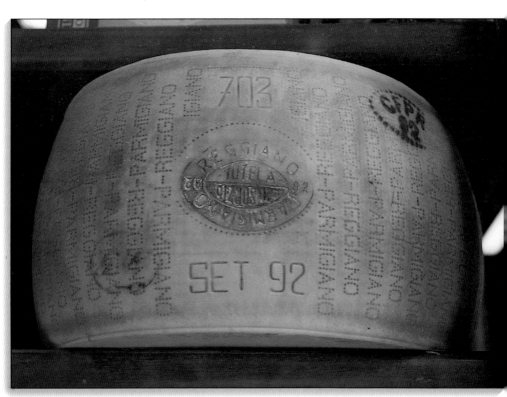

Piazza del Duomo is a cobbled square bounded by the Cathedral, belltower and baptistry as well as the bishop's palace, guarded by red and white marble lions. The **Duomo**, built between 1060 and 1073, displays a stepped façade in Lombard style as well as a Gothic belltower and a pink portal framed by lions. The Romanesque interior, damaged by an earthquake in 1117, was restored in 1130. Among the treasures within are a Deposition by Benedetto Antelami, one of the greatest medieval sculptors, and a Baroque pulpit. The dome, frescoed by Correggio in 1526, is awash with ethereal pyramids of frothy clouds and wispy saints. In this Assumption, Mary, borne by angels, is swept heavenwards in a swirling white cloak. Correggio (1489–1534) was influenced by the school of Mantegna but was largely self-taught. Noted for his sensuous style and *sfumato* technique, he also influenced Parmigianino.

Map on pages 324–325

The adjacent **Baptistry** (open daily; closed 12.30–3pm) is an octagonal five-storey Romanesque affair cast in festive pink marble. It was begun in 1196 by Benedetto Antelami, who also sculpted the three external portals and the stone reliefs depicting the labours of the months within. The building, finished in 1270 in transitional Romanesque-Gothic style, has recently been superbly restored. The galleried interior is embellished with one of the most awe-inspiring cycles of frescoes in northern Italy.

The galleried interior of the Baptistry.

San Giovanni Evangelista is a fine Renaissance abbey rising behind the Cathedral apse. Beyond the Baroque façade and belltower is a Renaissance dome with sensuous Correggio frescoes. Nearby are Renaissance cloisters, a refectory and a library still used by the resident Benedictine community; close by is a Benedictine Dispensary, complete with 16th-century apothecary's jars.

The palace-lined Piazza Garibaldi leads to Parma's plush **Teatro Regio**, the

BELOW: in the Po Valley, no part of the pig is wasted.

premier opera house for the Verdian repertoire. Inaugurated in 1829 by Marie-Louise, who appointed Paganini as director of her orchestra, this much-loved Neoclassical shell glitters in gold and white.

The **Palazzo della Pilotta** (open daily, until 1.45pm), an unfinished and bomb-damaged brick barn of a building, broods over the city centre. This maze of corridors and courtyards was a Farnese palace for almost 150 years until the death of the eighth prince spelt the end of the line in 1731. It is now the Archeological Museum; the core of the collection comes from finds in Velleia, a Roman settlement between Parma and Piacenza. The **Galleria Nazionale**, in the same palace, houses an impressive art collection, with works by such great regional artists as Correggio and Parmigianino as well as by Fra Angelico, Leonardo da Vinci and Canaletto.

Also within the palace is the **Teatro Farnese**, a wood-and-stucco theatre modelled on Palladio's Teatro Olimpico in Vicenza. Commissioned in 1619 by Rannucio I, the Farnese ruler, this was one of the grandest theatres in Europe in its 17th-century heyday and could seat 3,000 people. The interior is decorated with mythological figures and equestrian statues of the Farnese dynasty. Although severely damaged during Allied bombing raids, it has been magnificently restored.

Just off the neighbouring Via Meloni is the former convent of St Paul, containing the **Camera di San Paolo** (open daily, 9am–1.45pm). Also known as the Correggio Chamber, this dining hall in the abbess's apartments acts as a display case for Correggio's art where High Renaissance tricks of perspective and *chiaroscuro* compete with *trompe-l'oeil* pillars and monochrome figures. The worldly abbess commissioned Correggio to decorate her room in a poetic

The Teatro Regio was also the setting for the first public performance by Toscanini, the celebrated conductor, who was born in Parma. He conducted Aida entirely from memory.

BELOW: hanging the ham.

THE PARMA HAM

Since Hannibal reputedly supped on Parma ham in 217 BC, the local meat industry has grown as fast as the pigs themselves. For around 2000 years pigs in the Po Valley have provided the raw material for a thriving industry. Parma ham *(prosciutto di parma)*, the favourite Italian *antipasto*, comes from pigs bred for cured meats. The best Parma ham is sweet and succulent, marbled with pure white fat, while the mass-produced *prosciutto crudo* can be stringy, fatty or greasy. The pigs are a cross between an English and a Danish breed. Bred purely for their salami, and branded with the ducal crown of Parma, these are the only pigs permitted in the production of Parma ham. They are fattened on chestnuts and whey, the milk left over from making Parmesan cheese. After being slightly salted, the raw hind thighs are hung in drying sheds to mature for about a year. Parma hams are even hand-massaged to improve the texture. With 6,000 pig breeders and 220 slaughterers, this is a profitable industry governed by vigorous controls regarding slicing and packaging monopolies. However, the Consorzio del Prosciutto di Parma, the local ham consortium, recently failed to stop a British supermarket slicing, packaging and selling the ham for its own markets.

and richly symbolic style. It is adorned with allegorical frescoes of the four elements, fruit, foliage, cherubs and mythological creatures.

Across the river from the Palazzo della Pilote is the **Palazzo Ducale**, a 16th-century Farnese palace. It was restored in 1690 by Ranuccio II, who landscaped the grounds to feature a lake and an island, and remodelled in French style in the 18th century, with statues and a Classical temple constructed in the park.

Given Parma's culinary prowess, visitors would do well to sample the local ham and cheese, with snacks washed down with a flinty Sauvignon or a fizzy Lambrusco from just north of Modena. Meat-lovers can sample a speciality from Zibello: *culatello* salami, a choice slice of pig's bottom which the poet d'Annunzio *(see page 287)*, in a cannibalistic rapture, compared to the sweetness of his lover's breasts.

Castle country

Much of Parma province is flat, but the locals discern hidden beauty in this somewhat bleak terrain. However, now and again the crested profiles of fortified *castelli* cast shadows over the plains, for over a hundred ruined or intact castles are dotted throughout the province. While many were abandoned in Renaissance times, others were converted into palatial country mansions. Centred on Parma, a rambling castle route can take in Torrechiara, a masterpiece of military engineering, and Bardi, a bulwark built atop a rock of red jasper.

The most prestigious is undoubtedly **Colorno ❼**, more like a French château or German *schloss* than an Italianate castle. First designed as a medieval fortress, Colorno gained its present appearance after being remodelled by Ranuccio Farnese in 1660. In its heyday it was dubbed "the Versailles of Parma". Colorno

In Parma, no organ of any creature is ever dismissed as inedible. As the local expression has it: "Pork is like Verdi's music, every piece has its place".

BELOW: Pizza Garibaldi in Parma.

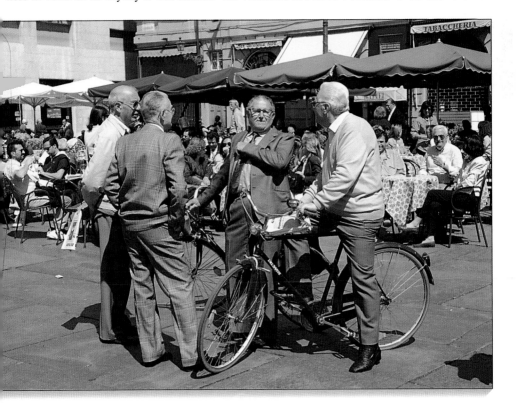

became a splendid stage-set for festivities, with frescoed ceilings, 18th-century marble fireplaces and Neoclassical stucco work. The recently restored interior is a blend of styles, but the Ducal apartments are impressive. In the grounds Colorno's warm façades are reflected in the water, encircled by English-style parkland. After 1860 the royal House of Savoy appropriated Colorno's best statuary and furniture to adorn palaces in Turin, Florence and Rome.

"The best Ferrari? It's the one we haven't made yet," says Enzo Ferrari, *the founder of the famous car firm, who personifies the ambitious character of the Modenese and their passion for one-upmanship.*

BELOW: children playing outside Modena's Romanesque Duomo.

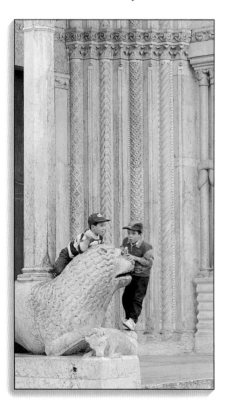

Modena: materialism and museums

Modena ❽, the historical rival to Bologna, is a place of comfort and prosperity set amid fertile countryside. To most Italians, it means materialism, fast cars and big appetites: Ferrari, Maserati and Pavarotti are all local products. Enzo Ferrari founded his firm in 1939, with the company, now Fiat-owned, still producing cars at the Marinello factories in the industrial outskirts. In recent years Luciano Pavarotti has raised the profile of his home town by staging annual charity concerts. Modena is one of the country's richest cities, yoked to a consumer-oriented culture devoted to designer boutiques and shoe shops. In addition it is the centre of the region's important livestock industry and has a healthy wine trade.

Yet commerce in Modena is always allied to a finely-honed aesthetic sense; even the shops must be tucked into the graceful arcaded spider's web of streets. Looking good is a passion epitomised by the ritual *passeggiata* in the warren of historic alleys and along the airy boulevards to the south, built over the fortified ramparts demolished a century ago. At first sight it is hard to believe that medieval Modena resembled an inland Venice, lined with canals; the waterways have been filled in, but the curved streets and porticoes trace the swirl of the erstwhile canals.

Even without a theatrical setting, and with no really stunning *piazza*, this faded ochre city presents a harmonious face to the world with its elegant arcades and kaleidoscope of red roofs. The skyline is dominated by the **Ghirlandina**, the leaning belltower that attempts to soar upwards from close to the apse of the Cathedral. The ravishing **Duomo** on Piazza Grande is one of the earliest Romanesque cathedrals in Italy. Founded by Countess Matilda of Tuscany, ruler of Modena, in 1099, and finished in the 14th century by the Campionese Masters, the pink Verona marble structure can be seen as a mirror of the medieval mind: friezes of saints and monsters, pilgrims and knights, griffons and doves, dragons and deer, fruit and vines parade before one's eyes.

First seen across the cobbled square, the Cathedral with its conical turrets and blind arcading is more than a match for the handsome **Palazzo Comunale** (Town Hall) challenging its authority from the far side of the square. Its austere interior is graced by a superb rood screen, a Romanesque masterpiece depicting scenes from the Passion and supported by Lombardy lions. The **Museo del Duomo** contains impressive 12th-century metopes, low reliefs which once surmounted the flying buttresses.

Modena's other museums are housed together in an ex-arsenal northwest of the Duomo. **Galleria Estense** (open Tues–Fri, Sun) on Piazzale Sant'Agostino houses a rewarding collection of Emilian and Venetian works. Emilia is represented by works of Parmigianino, Carracci and Guido Reni (14th–17th centuries), while the 15th- and 16th-century Venetian masters include Tintoretto, Veronese and the school of Canaletto. In the same palace is the **Biblioteca Estense** (open Mon–Sat), one of the richest libraries in Italy, containing splendid medieval codices, a 1481 edition of Dante's *Divine Comedy* and the *Bible of Borso d'Este*, a 15th-century illuminated work.

The **Palazzo Ducale** is proof that the Modenese are as passionate about military life as they are about cars, clothes and food. This severe building was built for Francesco I d'Este in 1634, but since 1862, it has been the country's most prestigious military academy.

Hiking country and foggy Ferrara

Bologna ❾, the capital of Emilia-Romagna, lies south of Modena and Ferrara, and has a chapter of its own (*see pages 313–19*). The landscapes of **L'Appennino Tosco-Emiliano** (the **Emilian Apennines**) ❿, spanning the Emilian–Tuscan border, range from gentle green slopes to deep woods and alpine crags. With traditional Apennine villages, lakes and mountain crests, it makes for ideal hiking country as well as hang-gliding, skiing and riding. From the Modena area the Passo delle Radici follows the crest of the hills to Abetone, a noted ski and hiking resort on the Emilian–Tuscan border.

Fiumalbo ⓫, set in the shadow of Monte Cimone in the Modena section of the Apennines, is an inviting base for a rural holiday, in winter or summer. Despite the cluster of historic churches, the appeal of this traditional village

Map
on pages
324–325

*Theatrical flourish
in Modena.*

BELOW: a farm
near Vignola, in
Bologna's rural
hinterland.

resides in its steep, picturesque alleys, flanked by mountain streams. Fiumalbo's quaint setting and rustic alpine houses provide an antidote to the more commercial charms of bigger neighbouring resorts such as Abetone.

Ferrara , dominated by the d'Este fortress, often erased by the winter mists, takes pride in its indefinability. Few agree on a definition of *ferraresità*, the condition of being from Ferrara. To some it is summed up by the frescoed palaces, cobbled streets, fortifications, stone halls and echoing stairways; for others it is allegories and alchemical symbols, black magic and jaded appetites. (Ferrara, supposedly built on major ley lines, vies with Turin as Italy's capital of black magic.) Giorgio de Chirico, the metaphysical artist who immortalised Ferrara castle, called his city the most mysterious and metaphysical of places.

The cradle of the Renaissance

The d'Este dynasty gained power in the late 13th century but enjoyed a cultural heyday in the Renaissance, when Ferrara became a splendid humanist court served by Pisanello, Mantegna and Piero della Francesca. Ercole I (1407–1505) remodelled the city on open lines, with broad palace-lined avenues complemented by a public park, an innovation for the period. Ferrara is often called the first planned Renaissance city, an accolade it shares with tiny Pienza in Tuscany.

The sparkling court at Ferrara came to an end in 1598 when the seat moved to Modena, and the last d'Este duke was deposed by the French in 1796. Yet the legacy lives on in the cuisine: *cappellacci con la zucca*, Parmesan and pumpkin-stuffed ravioli, dates back to the days of the noble court. The Renaissance city also flickers into life in the May *palio*, a race on horseback carried out by the competing *contrade*, the eight historic city districts.

BELOW: the cobbled piazzas of Ferrara are often shrouded in winter mists.

To avoid the perils of deadly cyclists, survey the Cathedral from a café terrace on **Piazza del Duomo**. The **Duomo**, a pink-and-white Romanesque-Gothic edifice, was founded in 1135 and dedicated to St George, the city's patron saint. The highlights are the lilting rhythms of the façade, the Romanesque sculptures over the main portal, and the Renaissance campanile.

Map on pages 324–325

The **Castello Estense** (open daily, 9.30am–5pm), the d'Este dynastic seat until 1598, is surrounded by a milky-green moat. The bastion was begun in 1385 and built on a square plan with corner towers and battlements. A sober Gothic courtyard leads to a Renaissance staircase and frescoed rooms.

Palatial living

The **Palazzo dei Diamanti** (open Tues–Sun, 9am–2pm; entrance charge), which commands Corso d'Ercole I d'Este, is named after its blistering marble façade, with its surface cut as sharply as diamonds. *Chiaroscuro* effects and changes in colour occur as the light shifts throughout the day. The palace was begun in 1493 as a private d'Este home, and finished in 1565. Inside, a picture gallery focuses on the Ferrara and Bolognese schools (13th–18th centuries).

Via delle Volte, Ferrara's most characteristic medieval alley.

Palazzo Schifanoia (open daily, 9.30am–7pm), set on Via Scandiana, celebrates the ostentation and carefree extravagance of 15th-century Ferrara. The d'Este designed the palace as a *"delizia"*, devoted to every whim. The Salone dei Mesi, the room of the months, is frescoed with allegorical tales; the scenes of court life show the Renaissance relish in depicting the pleasures of the senses. The Renaissance **Case Romei** (open Tues–Sun, 8am–2pm), on Via Savonarola, has been the seat of the university since 1963. (Ferrara's university was founded by the d'Este in 1393 and drew such illustrious students as Paracelsus and Copernicus.) **Palazzina Marfisa** (open daily, 9am–1pm, 3–6pm), on Corso Giovecca, the former home of a d'Este noblewoman, houses a mixture of authentic and pastiche frescoes.

BELOW: Ferrara's 14th-century Castello Estense.

Few cities provide such a clear contrast between medieval and Renaissance urban planning. **Via delle Volte**, one of the most characteristic medieval alleys, is a vaulted affair curved into the urban fabric. By contrast, **Corso Ercole I d'Este**, which runs northwards from the castle, is a stern straight Renaissance avenue. A walk along the city walls and tree-lined earthworks offers an invigorating overview of the 16th-century fortifications.

The ghetto

Ferrara once had one of the most flourishing Jewish communities in Italy. Unlike the Venetian rulers, the d'Este were noted for their religious tolerance and invited the Jews expelled from Spain in 1492 to settle here. But tolerance came to an abrupt end in 1627 when the Papal States imposed a ghetto, which survived until 1848.

You can take a Jewish trail which includes the ghetto, the synagogue and the Jewish cemetery in Via delle Vigne. On Via Mazzini is a 700-year-old synagogue, one of the oldest surviving in Italy and home to the **Museo Ebraico** (entrance charge). By the door there is a list of members of the congrega-

Map on pages 324–325

The fishing villages of Comacchio, Gorino, Goro and Mesola are the springboards for boat trips through the narrow canals to explore the mouth of the Po di Goro and the Valle di Gorino.

BELOW: the Tre/pponti bridge in Comacchio.

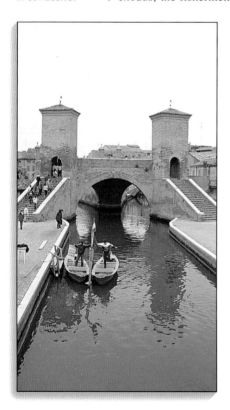

tion who were murdered by the Nazis. The Jewish ghetto embraced both Via Mazzini and Via Vignatagliata, an atmospheric street with several frescoed 14th-century houses.

The **Abbazia di Pomposa** (open daily, 7am–noon, 2–7pm) is an uninhabited Benedictine foundation in a dreamily remote location, strategically placed to allow the monks to control the Ravenna–Pavia route. The prosperous estate embraced medieval forests, salt pans and fishing lagoons. The complex, centred on an 8th-century Byzantine-Romanesque church, is graced by a slender belltower (1063), and the monastery, rebuilt in the 14th century but abandoned 200 years later, has a fine refectory and chapter house decorated with School of Giotto frescoes. Nearby stands the 11th-century **Palazzo della Ragione**, where the monks once meted out justice to the entire region.

The abbey is part of the mosaic of wetlands known as the **Delta del Po (Po Delta)**, a marshy wilderness extending north to Venice and south to Ravenna. **Comacchio**, a miniature Venice built over linked islands, lies deep in the Po Delta and frequently disappears into the mists. For centuries this distinctive fishing village, its fortunes founded on the local salt industry, was isolated from surrounding towns by treacherous marshland. It spans 13 tiny islands, criss-crossed by canals and connected by bridges, and is best explored by boat, easily booked at the quayside.

Comacchio's grandest sight is **Trepponti**, the monumental triple humpbacked bridge spanning three canals. Beside the quay is the old fish market, a reminder that Comacchio is the Po's capital of eel-fishing. During the autumn, when the mature female eels attempt to rejoin the males in a mass exodus, the fishermen are waiting, as are the water-gates that have been in place since Roman times.

Imola is synonymous with racing. As the setting for the **San Marino Grand Prix** the Imola track is the focus of national hopes, particularly if the local Ferrari team is performing well. However, this medieval and Renaissance town also has subtler pleasures in store. South of Via Emilia, the medieval **Rocca** is the most impressive Imola castle. The 18th-century **Duomo** is dedicated to St Cassian, Imola's patron saint, an early victim of student rage: he was cruelly stabbed to death with the pens of his students.

Dozza, a medieval village set in vineyards near Imola, provides an opportunity to sample the best Emilian wines in a historic castle or local inn. Dozza is celebrated for its Enoteca, a regional wine-tasting centre, carved out of a Sforza fortress, known as the **Rocca** (open Tues–Sun, 10am–noon, 3–6pm). The village is also known for its riotously painted contemporary façades which adorn its gates, doorways and walls.

Faenza, the origin of the word *faience*, spells ceramics in any language. For over 500 years this town has produced the blue and yellow designs that have brought it international renown. The **Museo delle Ceramiche** (open Tues–Sun, 9am–6pm) on Viale Baccarini contains local majolica as well as Roman, medieval and contemporary designs from around the world. ❑

Pavarotti: Tenor of Tenors

The greatest tenor of his generation has homes in New York, Monte Carlo and Pesaro, on the Adriatic coast, but his heart is in Modena, his home town, where he has a rambling estate. Luciano Pavarotti's humble origins are reflected in his name, which means "weaver of straw" in Modenese dialect. Music and football were his passions, as they are still.

As a child he recalls the suffering experienced during World War II by his family, who fled to the countryside to escape the bombing. He vividly remembers seeing in Modena the bodies of Italian partisans, murdered by the Nazis: "Every night masked men would come to your house to look for food, and to see if you harboured partisans. For every German killed, 10 Italians were hanged."

Pavarotti, renowned for his *bel canto* voice, regularly sings with José Carreras and Plácido Domingo as one of "The Three Tenors". Startlingly, he attributes his singing technique to his wet-nurse, who breast-fed both him and the accomplished soprano Mirella Freni. As a 5-year-old he was singing "*La donna è mobile*" for sweets, but his career was only launched with the winning of a Welsh choral competition. Pavarotti attributes the lenth of his career to his father, who is still singing and recording in his eighties, and his musical gift to the female members of his family: "I probably owe my way of singing to them – the lyricism, the softness, the affection." His agent describes his appeal differently: "When you leave a Pavarotti performance, he's given you something... he doesn't leave you unaffected; and in addition to his artistry, he's fearless."

One of the highlights of Pavarotti's career was singing in Verdi's *Requiem* at La Scala in 1967 in honour of the centenary of Toscanini's birth. The conductor Herbert von Karajan declared that Pavarotti's vocal chords had been touched by God. Yet Pavarotti, a blatant populist, is as happy singing Neapolitan love duets or crooning with international rock stars such as Sting and Tina Turner.

In 1998 Pavarotti staged his usual charity concert in Modena, to raise funds for the Bosnian city of Mostar: "My roots are in Modena, so that's why I wanted to create a big international event there." He recruited sympathetic fellow stars, resorting to emotional blackmail when Bono of U2 refused his request for a specially written song: "I am a rich man because I have love and because the music is in me. But you make me feel like a poor man, you make me beg you to come and help the children of Bosnia."

A connection is often made between the bulkiness of "Big Lucy" and the cuisine in his home region of Emilia Romagna, considered the best cuisine in Italy. Certainly he remains close to the earthy cuisine of Modena and adores feeding the visitors who flock to his charity concerts. Critics complain that his vocal powers are diminishing, but Pavarotti is sanguine about the future: "They say I'll sing until 2001, when I celebrate 40 years of my career, but it's not true – I'll sing while I have the voice." ❑

RIGHT: Modena-born Luciano Pavarotti.

THE ADRIATIC COAST

Map on page 340

Beach culture meets Byzantine ruins in
this curious and eclectic coastal region of smart resorts
and secretive lagoons

The Adriatic may be in Emilia Romagna but the people are robust Romagnoli rather than smooth Emiliani, with a different history, culture and cuisine. They embody classic Italian attributes: Mediterranean values and an Oriental past grafted onto a northern European culture. Culturally, a sense of ancient glory lingers on in Ravenna, the point of entry for the eastern Roman empire. Here and elsewhere linger echoes of Greek, Roman and Byzantine civilisations. Ravenna and Rimini, the main cities, are both of Roman foundation, if buried under layers of medieval brick. Romagna, too, had its great medieval and Renaissance dynasties: the Malatesta in Rimini once rivalled the d'Este in Ferrara. While Rimini was the first chic bathing establishment, the mass-tourism boom of the 1960s and 1970s put an end to any pretence that the coast was for the privileged few: the Adriatic was confirmed as one of Europe's most popular summer spots. Nowadays it is fashionable to dismiss the Adriatic resorts as depositories for tasteless Euro-trash, yet just as the local cuisine blends bourgeois and peasant styles, so the resorts appeal to aficionados of Byzantine art and to package holiday-makers, who are often one and the same.

The Adriatic coast caters to all tastes, with sprawling, mass-market resorts concentrated in the south, and smaller, more exclusive ones sheltered by pine groves in the north. Yet if Rimini and Cattolica conform to the popular idea of a full-frontal beach holiday, the northerly Lido di Jesolo is proof that even the prim Venetians can provide down-market fun, from trashy souvenir shops to family beach games and riotous clubs. However, more typical of the north coast are small, discreet bays fringed by pines and bounded by lagoons.

In the same way, the south is not without its sophisticated resorts: Riccione prides itself on being "the rendezvous of the international elite", if only because its marble-clad pedestrian zone is packed with designer shops. This chapter covers the Adriatic coast from Chioggia to Rimini, although a few of the most northerly resorts are technically in the Veneto.

The Venetian coast

Eraclea Mare ❶, north of Venice, is set amid pine groves beside the Piave estuary. A peaceful family-oriented resort, it provides pale sandy beaches and the opportunity for riding trips deep into the estuary and lagoon area. Set just off the road to Jesolo, Venice and Padua, Eraclea could also be a base for more cultural tourism.

Lido di Jesolo ❷, marking the northern entrance to the Venetian lagoon, is the largest seaside resort in the Veneto. Dominated by package tourism, Jesolo satisfies the ice cream, pizza and parasol brigades. In

PRECEDING PAGES: the Adriatic coast has a certain brash charm. **LEFT:** lazy days. **BELOW:** Rimini is famous for its lively nightlife.

addition the resort provides a good range of sports facilities, from riding to golf and tennis. Although bland, it makes an acceptable base for visitors wishing to combine a family beach holiday with cultural day trips to Venice. But among younger Italians, Jesolo is synonymous with summer nightlife.

On sultry evenings the roads between Jesolo and Venice are full of young Venetians fleeing their claustrophobic culture for the vibrant coastal clubs.

Lido di Venezia ❸, better-known as Il Lido, is Venice's access to the beach. The long sandy shores are easily reached by boat from the historic heart of the city. The Lido has been a fashionable resort since the 1840s, when the cult for sea-bathing first arrived. Today the Lido makes an ideal base for family holidays; hotels generally have access to a private beach, and rooms are more spacious and less expensive than in historic Venice.

Pellestrina ❹, which protects Venice from the sea, is a narrow sliver of land stretching into the silvery-grey lagoon, forming a natural barrier enforced by the *Murazzi*, the giant sea walls, and thus saving Venice from periodic flooding. The island is a haunt of sunbathing Venetians or solitary walkers, with a quaint fishing village, gossipy bars and brightly coloured cottages. As part of the dike which preserves Venice for the generations to come, Pellestrina plays an essential role in the Adriatic sea defences. (From Venice, the island is best reached from the Lido, with bus 11 to Alberoni connecting with the ferry for a five-minute boat ride to Pellestrina.)

Chioggia ❺, a bustling workaday fishing port, closes the Venetian lagoon to the south. The port is easily accessible from the lagoon city, or even by bicycle from the Lido. Chioggia covers two parallel islands and is often called a Venice in miniature, thanks to its historic heart criss-crossed by canals. The Roman port rose to prominence as the guardian of the river route to Padua, and as a self-governing medieval city it developed a lucrative salt-extraction industry. After this industry collapsed, Chioggia concentrated on fishing, a vocation it retains today. The port is noted for its boats: the *tartana*, an early type of trawler, and its colourful successor the flat-bottomed *bragozzo*, suitable for fishing in the shallow lagoon waters. The trapezoid sail is decorated with heraldic, religious or family devices, from lions and compasses to madonnas and nicknames.

Visiting the bustling quaysides, painted fishing boats and the Granaio fish market, followed by an inevitably fishy lunch in restaurants considerably better and more reasonably priced than their grander Venetian counterparts, is the chief enjoyment. Chioggia's beaches lie 10 km (6 miles) down the coast at **Isolaverde** and **Sottomarina**.

The north coast: discreet lagoon resorts

From Chioggia to Ravenna the coast skirts the curious landscape of lagoons and marshland that characterises the Po Delta, the **Parco del Delta del Po ⑥**. From the north the SS309, the main coastal road, follows Via Romea, the old Roman road, to the haunting Pomposa Abbey. En route, it passes the Mesola nature reserve, the **Gran Bosco della Mesola**, a thicket of holm oak, ash, elm and holly, with red deer roaming the forest glades. There were once deep forests covering the coastal strip between Ferrara and Ravenna, but these have dwindled dramatically. The forest, a d'Este hunting estate since 1490, remained in dynastic hands until 1758. Just east are the **Bosco di Mesola** botanical gardens, full of indigeneous marsh and woodland plants. Further inland is the crenellated **Castello di Mesola** (open Tues–Sat 9am–noon, 3–6pm; entrance charge), one of the few d'Este castles secreted away in the Po marshes. Built in 1583, this

Map on page 340

TIP

Despite Chioggia's fine sands you may prefer to swim further south, a fair distance from the polluted Venetian lagoon.

BELOW: risotto, a local speciality.

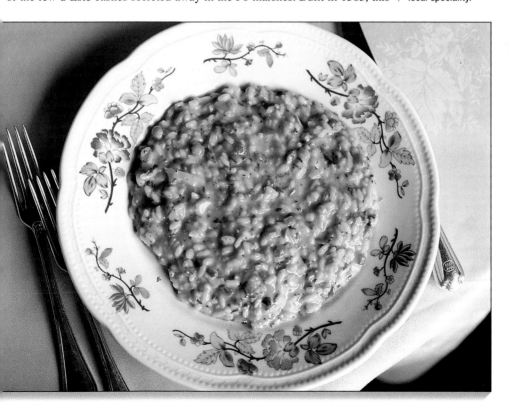

The Po Delta

The Po Delta is one of Italy's most important wetlands and a bird-watcher's paradise. This mosaic of marshes, dunes, mudflats and islands is called the Italian Camargue. Indeed, sturdy white Camargue ponies and bulls have been introduced successfully to the region. The Po, Italy's longest river, crosses Piacenza, Ferrara and Ravenna, splitting into streams and channels in the delta, with only one of its 14 mouths navigable. The delta extends 100 km (60 miles) from north to south and is dotted with nature reserves, which are easily reached from the coast or inland area.

East of Ferrara the Po gradually disappears into a labyrinth of lagoons called *valli*, fishing lakes where eels begin their migration back to the Sargasso Sea. The Valli di Comacchio were formed in the medieval period when the area around the Po Delta subsided, creating a cluster of marshy valleys. Medieval monks introduced sophisticated drainage schemes

before the d'Este Dukes of Ferrara appropriated the land and began their own reclamation schemes. Their initial success was reversed by both land subsidence and the engineering works of the Venetians, who diverted the course of the Po to prevent their own city from silting up.

With the advent of steam machinery in the early 19th century, mechanical drainage schemes led to a significant reduction in the marshland, thus shaping the present shallow salty landscape. In the 1950s parts of the marshes were again drained to satisfy the demand for farming land, and a few roads were built. Farmers are constantly pushing for more marshland to be released, but ecologists are currently winning the battle to preserve the existing wetlands.

The area acts as a magnet for migratory birds since it is a key staging post on the route from Africa to Central Europe. Parts of the delta have been declared reserves, where birds can be seen in their natural habitats. The river-lagoon setting, with its expanse of mudflats and marshes, proves a welcoming environment for waterfowl, especially the native shelduck, with their distinctive black and brown markings. Among the bird-life are bean geese, greyish geese with yellow legs and bills, and greylag geese, distinguished by their pink legs. Reed warblers, bearded tits and purple herons are also common, as are gulls and terns, with coots and black terns congregating on the marshes in winter. More persistent bird-watchers may be rewarded with sightings of white egrets and curlew sandpipers, or great crested grebes building their nests on the banks. Apart from extensive oyster beds and the local eels, fishing focuses on sea bass, carp, grey mullet, flounder, tench and pike. The distinctive tree-toad is found wherever there is a profusion of cane, shrubs or trees.

Today the salty wetlands still preserve a number of *casoni*, fishing huts on stilts, some now the private retreats of Milanese industrialists. Visitors come here for the wildlife and the solitude: one can still walk or cycle along the banks of the fishing lakes without coming across another soul. ❑

LEFT: medieval monks were the first to realise the agricutural potential of the Po delta marshes.

pleasure palace was linked to sophisticated marshland drainage works, but the advantage of the locks and irrigation channels was nullified when the Venetians created a canal to stop their city silting up, thereby causing the Mesola area to silt up instead.

Map on page 340

The villages on the sandy coast around Comacchio were formerly fishing settlements but in recent years resemble more closely simple resorts on the margins of life. Collectively known as the **Lidi di Comacchio ❼**, these resorts are strung out along the coast, stretching from Lido di Volano to the bigger and better-equipped resorts of Lido delle Nazione and Porto Garbaldi. All tend to present their public faces to the sea but turn their private faces to the lagoons that skirt the shore. The vineyards by the adjoining **Valli di Comacchio** fishing lakes were planted by Renata of France, who married into the d'Este dynasty in 1528. Her Burgundian wine is considered the only red wine suitable for accompanying local fish or eel dishes.

Lago delle Nazioni, the salt-water lake just inland from the Lido di Volano, provides extensive mullet and eel fishing. In summer the lake is also popular with sailors and water-skiers, with organised boat trips to explore the flora and fauna: the local marshes abound in swamp orchids and medicinal plants, with the reed-beds home to grebes, mallards and kingfishers. Bulls and Camargue-Delta horses are bred on a neighbouring stud farm and seem to adapt perfectly to life on the marshes.

One romantic who preferred lagoons to beaches was Giorgio Bassani, resident of Ferrara and author of the atmospheric "Garden of the Finzi-Conti". He regularly sought inspiration in the gentle water-scape of the delta.

Umbrellas and pines

Porto Garibaldi, just south of Comacchio, is the busiest, most established resort, a former fishing village now dominated by water sports and lines of beach umbrellas. The name recalls Garibaldi's foiled guerrilla exploits and his flight in 1849 from Austrian pursuit, an event that led to the death of his pregnant wife.

Gently sloping beaches, interspersed with pine woods, stretch south from Porto Garibaldi to bustling Lido degli Estensi and exclusive **Lido di Spina**, with chic villas tucked into the pinewoods. Behind the dunes of Lido di Spina lie a lagoon and a nature reserve with considerable appeal to bird-watchers: in **Vene di Bellochio**, a population of coots, curlews, teals and marsh harriers appreciates the setting of sea lavender, dunes, reeds and rushes.

The Graeco-Etruscan necropolis at **Spina**, just west of Comacchio, was discovered by chance during the drainage programmes of the 1950s. The finds, essentially funerary stele and tomb furniture dating from 6 BC to the 3rd century AD, are now on display in Ferrara's archaeology museum. Those craving solitude may decide to shun the shore in favour of the lagoons. For those who look, there are still reed-cutters, skimming the surface in flat-bottomed boats, cantilevered fishing nets and *casoni*, the green-shuttered fishing huts on stilts.

Towards Ravenna the coastline is characterised by *pinete*, waving lines of umbrella pines as neat as beach umbrellas, framing greyish-green scudding seas. **Marina di Ravenna ❽** is a well-established resort,

BELOW: locally-caught fish for sale at Comacchio.

with a wide beach, busy harbour, pine groves and sand dunes. The adjoining
Porto Cassini is a good walking destination, with its 5-km (3-mile) dam that
hugs the harbour. **Marina Romea**, just north, is one of the smartest resorts,
with a pleasant harbour and paths winding through the pine groves. However,
on sultry summer evenings, most strolls lead to *gelaterie* (ice-cream parlours)
and cosy *trattorie*.

Byzantine time capsule

Ravenna ❾ was the last enclave of the Roman Empire in the West, ruled by
exarchs, or viceroys, of the Eastern Roman Empire in Byzantium. At first sight,
it seems a provincial town which just happens to contain the world's greatest
mosaics. Like Venice, Ravenna, which dates from 2BC, was built on a series of
islands in a lagoon. The city was colonised by the Romans and, thanks to its
strategic importance, was proclaimed capital of the Western Roman Empire in
AD 402. In the 5th and 6th centuries Roman and Byzantine cultures converged
in Ravenna and bequeathed the city superb mosaics, transforming it into a luminous Western Byzantium. Ravenna was a beacon of artistic excellence at a time
when sheep were grazing in the forum of Rome.

Despite declining fortunes, and the silting up of the port, it remained prosperous during the Middle Ages and provided a refuge for Dante Alighieri, the
great 14th-century Florentine poet. The city came under Venetian domination in
the 15th century and was controlled by the Venetians or the Papacy until 1859.
Since the 1950s exploitation of offshore gas, the creation of a new port and
chemical industries and the development of the coastal resorts, Ravenna has
become a boom city once more.

BELOW: an early-
Byzantine mosaic
at Sant'Apollinare
Nuovo portrays
Christ calling the
fishermen Peter
and Andrew to be
his disciples.

Pieces of a mosaic

Ravenna's legacy is the sensuous melding of classical art and spirituality in a dazzling array of basilicas, baptistries and mausoleums. Dante described Ravenna's mosaics as the "sweet colour of Oriental sapphires". As the mainspring of early Christian art, the mosaics acted as a poor man's Bible, illuminating the Scriptures by means of iconic images and stylised figures set against a gold background. They use such images as the drinking doves, symbolising the soul sipping from the fountain of eternal life. The early mosaicists were probably Greek artists from the court of Constantinople. These lustrous interiors were partly inspired by the memory of pagan temples, partly by the sense of awe provoked by the Gospels. As with all great art, the mosaics represent man's supreme striving for the absolute. Every Friday in summer the mosaics in the basilicas are open to the public until midnight, as are the mosaic shops.

The **Basilica di San Vitale** (open daily 9am–7pm; entrance charge), Ravenna's greatest monument, dates from the first half of the 6th century, the period of Byzantine conquest. The mosaics are sometimes seen as the summation of Roman culture, the last great flowering of art in the ancient world, but they can equally be seen as the first flowering of Christian art. The octagonal basilica is itself a masterpiece, a gabled, galleried brick building surmounted by a cupola, which has been dubbed the last building born of the Roman tradition and the first of the Romanesque. The highly-decorated mosaics depict the court of Emperor Justinian I. They are characterised by a rich palette of blues and greens, from flowers and fields to sky and the glittering grandeur of the figures. The scriptural scenes illuminate Byzantine symbolism in a bold expanse of golden sky.

Map on page 340

The Basilica di San Vitale.

BELOW: a procession of virgins, Sant' Apollinare Nuovo.

Beside the basilica stands the **Mausoleo di Galla Placidia** (entrance charge), a mausoleum dedicated to Galla Placidia, the Christian half-sister of Honorius (the emperor who transferred the capital to Ravenna in AD 402), despite the fact that she is buried in Rome. Built between AD 425 and 50, it is bathed in green light which becomes aquamarine higher up the walls. The mystical atmosphere is intensified by the strikingly simple style of the mosaics, including the cobalt-blue sky sprinkled with gold stars. Despite the simple Christian iconography, the realism of the figures reflects the naturalistic Roman style as much as a nascent Christian one.

The vivid mosaics of Sant'Apollinare Nuovo inspired the Austrian artist Gustav Klimt (1862–1918).

Sant'Apollinare Nuovo (entrance charge), flanked by a cylindrical bell-tower, was built between AD 493-96. The mosaics in the palatine church depict a stately procession of martyrs and virgins. These scenes show the transition from naturalistic Hellenistic-Roman art to the more stylised tendencies of Byzantine artistry.

Opposite stands the basilica of **San Giovanni Evangelista** (entrance charge), with a sculpted marble Gothic portal. Dating from the 5th century but much altered, the basilica was built by Galla Placidia. Legend has it that she had promised to build the church in return for surviving a shipwreck on the voyage that brought her from Constantinople to Ravenna.

Further on looms **Rocca di Brancaleone** (entrance charge), a Venetian fortress and one of the captivating locations of the Ravenna Jazz Festival. Isolated in the greenery is the **Mausoleo di Teodorico**, a curious Romanesque construction with Syrian and Nordic influences. It was built in AD 520 by Theodoric the Great, who designed the tomb as his own mausoleum. Other superb buildings are the **Oratorio di Sant'Andrea**, covered in splendid mosaics, and the **Battistero Neoniani**, a 5th-century baptistry with a frescoed cupola.

BELOW: the Basilica di San Vitale dates from the first half of the 6th century.

Despite being buried under the weight of its glittering mosaics, Ravenna struggles to retain its personality as a proud provincial town. The central **Piazza del Popolo** is lined with dignified 15th-century buildings built under Venetian rule. The **Duomo** was founded in the 5th century, but the lasting impression of it is of the bold baroque facade. **Zona Dantesca**, a slightly clinical quarter, honours Dante, who lived in Ravenna between 1317 and 1321. Exiled from Florence for political reasons, Dante completed *The Divine Comedy* in the city and is buried in the adjoining church of **San Francesco**. This 5th-century building was remodelled in chilly neo-classical style and over-restored in the 1920s. In summer classical concerts enliven the Franciscan cloisters, as do readings of Dante's works. However, the city's cultural highlight is the **Ravenna Festival**, a summer jamboree of symphony concerts, opera, ballet and organ recitals which attracts top conductors, from Claudio Abbado to Riccardo Muti. A number of these concerts are held outdoors or take advantage of settings in the Byzantine basilicas.

Fans of Ravenna may want to visit **Sant'Apollinare in Classe** ❿ (entrance charge), set 5 km (3 miles) south, which is a basilica of Byzantine mosaics dating from AD 533. The striking cylindrical belltower is one of the symbols of Ravenna. Visitors wishing to learn more about the art of mosaics could try one of the many courses on offer in the city; those more interested in buying can visit the shops selling hand-crafted modern mosaics or reproductions of the greatest Byzantine masters.

Map on page 340

The southern coast: salt, sun and seafood

Although the Adriatic coast has been heavily commercialised, garden suburbs, tree-lined avenues, sandy beaches and trails through the pine groves are compensation for regrettable concrete strips. **Milano-Marittima** is a fashionable resort for young people, with packed beaches and popular cafés. By contrast, **Cervia ⓫**, just south, is a family-oriented resort, known for salt extraction since Etruscan times. As well as the salt flats, and the surviving industry, the town still retains its 18th-century salt warehouses. Known as **Maggazzini del Sale**, these include a small museum in a salt tower dedicated to the "white gold" itself.

Southwest of Cervia is the **Riserva Naturale delle Saline di Cervia**, a complex of salt works encircled by a canal. The neighbouring **Terme di Cervia** health spa treats arthritis and other complaints with mud treatments based on salty secrets.

Cesenatico ⓬ has long combined fishing and tourism, and the family-minded resort has proved particularly popular with German holiday-makers. The historic heart is centred on the harbour and canal, the **Darsena** and **Portocanale Leonardesco**. The canal was created in 1302 but redesigned by Leonardo da Vinci in 1502. Its right bank, lined with pastel-coloured merchants' houses, is a popular place for a stroll, while the left bank, dotted with fishermen's cottages, has some good seafood inns. **Piazza delle Conserve**, just off the canal, is also

TIP

As a resort, Cervia is noted for its greenery and low-key atmosphere. Its nature reserve offers opportunities for riding or cycling through the pine groves, where the landscaped paths wind through the woods to the beach.

BELOW: the historic heart of Cesenatico.

Where life's a beach.

home to a bustling fish market and seafood restaurants, but more striking are the cone-shaped underground ice chambers where fish were stored in the days before refrigeration. The **Marineria** (Maritime Museum) (entrance charge) displays a collection of Adriatic fishing boats with bold sails and hulls. The 7-km (4-mile) sandy beach provides well-organised activities, from cycling through the pine groves to boating, fishing and volley-ball.

Cesenatico's well-deserved reputation as a gastronomic centre means that the best fish restaurants are generally full. Cuttlefish, squid, lobster, sea perch and mackerel are all on offer. The seafront is lined with seafood restaurants, while the inns in the Cesenatico hinterland tend to be the preserve of country cooking and grilled meats. Regional meals are generally accompanied by Sangiovese red, straw-coloured Trebbiano or crisp white Albana wines.

Cesena ⑬, a mere 12 km (7 miles) from Cesenatico, makes a pleasant excursion into the hinterland. The profusion of seasonal fruit is a reminder that the town is one of the main exporters of strawberries and peaches. Apart from a cathedral with Romanesque traces, Cesena is proud of its 14th-century castle and magnificent Malatesta Renaissance library. In lofty Madonna del Monte, the 15th-century sanctuary overlooking the town, Benedictine monks diligently restore manuscripts and antiquarian books.

Capital of the Riviera

As Europe's biggest beach resort, **Rimini ⑭** has been dedicated to tourism since 1830, when the Italian Riviera began to be developed in response to the new fashion for sea-bathing. The vast beach is one of the safest in Europe, with motor craft banned within 500 metres (545 yards) of the shore. However, Rimini's role as unofficial capital of the Riviera has overshadowed its considerable artistic heritage. It was founded by the Romans in AD 268 and prospered as a Malatesta fiefdom from the 13th century onwards. There are distinctive Roman and Renaissance monuments, even if most visitors are only drawn to the seafront and tree-lined promenades. Rimini forms two distinct entities, contrasting the quiet historic centre with the bustling coastal strip.

Borgo di San Giuliano, set at the landward end of Porto Canale, is a fishermen's quarter of quaint cottages and medieval alleyways. There, too, stands Ponte Tiberio, the best-preserved of the Roman bridges, with a view of the park and the hills stretching into the distance. From here Corso d'Augusto leads to the historic centre and **Piazza Cavour**, which is flanked by old palaces, including the 14th-century Palazzo del Podestà, and the arcaded 18th-century fish market. With its cluster of cafés and bars, Piazza Tre Martiri, built over the old Roman forum, is a favoured city meeting-place. Just west towers the **Arco d'Augusto**, a Roman arch erected in honour of Augustus in 27 AD.

South of Piazza Tre Martiri stands the **Tempio Malatestiano**, the city's most celebrated monument. Sigismondo Malatesta (1417–68), the notorious ruler of Rimini, commissioned this Renaissance gem from Leon Battista Alberti, the great Florentine architect. The Gothic church of San Francesco was remodelled as the embodiment of Renaissance architectural values. The interior houses the Malatesta tomb as well as precious works of art by Piero della Francesca, Duccio and Giotto. Ostensibly designed as a chapel, the building became a monument to the debauched Malatesta himself. Given the man's evil reputation, combined with the bacchanalian scenes depicted within, Pope Pius II declared the place "a temple of devil-worshippers".

Map on page 340

BELOW: master film director, Federico Fellini.

FEDERICO FELLINI

Italian film directors are particularly influenced by their environments, and Federico Fellini (1920–93), who was born and raised in Rimini, was no exception. His *Amarcord* (1974), one of the seminal films of the 1970s and perhaps his most popular and accessible work, turned Rimini into a virtual reality world. It was sweet revenge on the "inert, provincial, opaque, dull" Adriatic seaside resort he left in search of Roman chic.

Through his central character in *Amarcord*, a young boy called Titta, Felllini explored his own youth and rites of passage in a small close-knit society during the Fascist dictatorship.

Fellini first gained popular and critical acclaim in Britain and the United States in 1959 with *La Dolce Vita*, which starred Marcello Mastroianni, Italy's leading actor. He described his films as "a marriage of innocence and experience", but they were also portrayals of fantasy and loss, tinged with irony, mischief and sadness. His characters were larger than life, often grotesque, yet sympathetically portrayed.

The Adriatic was always a reference point for Fellini: in a sense it was his canvas, even if he recreated his boyhood city far away, in the Cinecittà studios in Rome.

Map on page 340

TIP

In summer a shuttle bus connects all the Rimini nightclubs, while the Treno Azzurro ferries clubbers between Rimini and Cattolica.

The beaches, which stretch for almost 15 kms (9 miles), are crowded but well-groomed and clean, with the sea regularly monitored for pollution. Facilities include beach volley-ball, paddle-boats, a wind-surfing school and the Rovazzurra theme park. A seafront *passeggiata* around the marina and down Viale Vespucci is a nightly ritual for many visitors. Diners can sample clams or sea snails *(lumache di mare)*, two of the local specialities. Fans of Federico Fellini may call in on the **Grand Hotel** (1908), the Adriatic's most historic hostelry . Fellini used the place as a backdrop for various films, including *Amarcord (see previous page)*. This eclectic hotel is one of the few along the coast that can equal the grandest on the French Riviera.

Around Rimini

Santarcangelo di Romagna ⓕ, west of Rimini, is a walled hilltop town with a historic castle, curious caves and a welcoming atmosphere. This erstwhile Roman settlement became a Malatesta fiefdom in the 13th century, only to be ceded to the Montefeltro clan in 1462, and to pass swiftly from Borgia and Venetian rule to the Papal States in 1505. The pretty medieval nucleus is a warren of alleys, steeply raked steps and picturesque window boxes framed against weather beaten walls. The core of the town is the **Rocca**, the medieval fortress remodelled by Malatesta in 1447 and protected by medieval gates. Carved into the rock are ancient grottoes once used as refuges, wine cellars and possibly even tombs.

Once back on the coastal strip south of Rimini, sophisticated beach-lovers are drawn to the distinguished resort of **Riccione** ⓖ. Built on a chessboard pattern, the resort combines pleasant garden suburbs and villas with beach life. Riccione, formerly a smart Edwardian resort, likes to reinvent itself. Traditionally at the forefront of fashion, it was the first Italian city to popularise the mini-skirt and topless bathing, the first to welcome gay couples, the first to promote water parks. Certainly Riccione has little interest in attracting mainstream package tourism, preferring to cultivate a faithful Italian clientele, many of whom are second-home owners from Bologna. The upmarket pedestrian zone of Viale Ceccarini cossets visitors with designer shops, background music, fresh flowers and invitations to stop for leisurely seafood suppers.

Cattolica ⓗ enjoys a sheltered climate, with the resort set in the lee of the hills. As the fastest-expanding resort it prides itself on its pragmatic approach to tourism, specialising in inexpensive package holidays for young couples or families. Cattolica is also the Adriatic resort that attracts the highest number of non-Italian visitors, primarily Germans, Britons and Scandinavians.

Despite its somewhat bland image, the resort provides an acceptable base for exploring the art cities of southern Emilia Romagna. Its attractions include the lively summer nightlife, the pier of Punto Verde, and the medieval villages tucked into the hinterland. Cattolica is a border town, serving as a gateway to the Marche region and to the quaint principality of San Marino *(see facing page)*. ❏

BELOW: Rimini's Grand Hotel – one of the finest on the coast.

San Marino, Toytown State

On the motorway outside Europe's oldest and smallest city a sign says: "Welcome to the Republic of San Marino, land of freedom." Founded by St Marinus, patron saint of freedom, **San Marino** encompasses 60 sq. km (23 sq. miles) of tax-free terrain. The 25,000 inhabitants of this independent city state survive on the proceeds of sales from perfumes, stamps, ceramics and duty-free wine.

According to legend, the Republic was founded by a Dalmatian stone-cutter who had fled persecution from Emperor Diocletian in AD 301, only to end up establishing a duty-free haven on the inhospitable slopes of Monte Titano. Thanks to San Marino's tax-free status the state coffers are suitably full, with stamp-collecting representing 10 per cent of all revenues. The state prides itself on having given the world its first postal service, in 1607, but, as with all such mini-states, the stamps are grander than the territory.

Although paranoia is rife in this antiquated 700-year-old political system, tyranny is unlikely. The Republic is governed by two regents from opposing parties so that they can keep an eye on one another; these joint heads of state are only in office for six months, so they have no time to build up personal power bases. Moreover, any citizen is legally entitled to make an official complaint about a regent's conduct, and judicial proceedings may be instigated as a result. Citizens are fully involved in political life and have the most assiduous voting record in Europe.

On 3 September the Sammarinesi citizens celebrate the foundation of the Republic with a crossbow competition and a game of bingo. The Museo delle Armi Moderne in Contrada della Pieve has a plethora of crossbows.

San Marino fields a "national" football team, conducts its own foreign policy, and has a seat at the United Nations and a centuries-old tradition of neutrality. Peace was only recently declared with Sweden; until then San Marino had officially been on a war footing after neglecting to sign the Peace of Westphalia in 1648. However, according to a Swedish diplomat, Scandinavian citizens in San Marino need not be concerned: "There are only six or eight of them left, mostly ladies married to locals. They're certainly not prisoners of war." San Marino insists that it has not been to war since 1462, when it did battle with the Malatesta dynasty in Rimini. But for such a pacific state San Marino is inordinately keen on arms. The republic sells such arcane weaponry as muskets, halberds and arquebuses, although simple Korean bayonets are also on sale in the shops.

The Sammarinesi equate personal profit with the prosperity of the state; even the Franciscan monks sell a sickly liqueur to the unsuspecting public. Most visitors to San Marino succumb to a sheet of stamps or sweet Moscato wine. The more adventurous can buy arquebuses and crossbows or even Korean bayonets, if they can face the furore at international departures. ❏

RIGHT: the citadel of San Marino.
OVERLEAF: Portofino.

INSIGHT GUIDES 👁

Travel Tips

Insight Guides *portray destinations in depth, providing the complete picture and the top photography*

Insight Pocket Guides *focus on the best choices for places to see and things to do and include large fold-out maps*

Insight Compact Guides *portability makes them the perfect books to carry with you for on-the-spot reference*

Three types of guide for all types of travel

INSIGHT GUIDES Different people need different kinds of information. Some want *background information* to help them prepare for the trip. Others seek *personal recommendations* from someone who knows the destination well. And others look for *compactly presented data* for on-the-spot reference. With three carefully designed series, Insight Guides offer readers the perfect choice. Insight Guides will turn your visit into an experience.

The world's largest collection of visual travel guides

CONTENTS

Getting Acquainted

The Place

Area: Italy: 301,308 sq. km/116,335 sq. miles
Capital: Rome
Highest Mountain: Montblanc (4,807 metres/15,772 ft)
Principal River: Po
Population: Italy: 57 million; Milan (second largest city in Italy): 1,480,000; Turin (fourth largest): 1,025,000; Genoa: 676,000; Bologna: 403,000; Venice: 328,000; Trieste: 237,000.
Language: Italian, with some French (Aosta), German (Trentino Alto-Adige) and mountain dialects near the borders; Venetian dialect.
Religion: Roman Catholic
Time Zone: Central European Time (GMT plus 1 hour, EST plus 6hrs; summer time adds one hour).
Currency: Lira
Weights and Measures: Metric
Electricity: 220 volts. You will need an adaptor to operate British three-pin appliances and a transformer to

Climate

There are three main kinds of climate affecting northern Italy:
● In the mountainous areas (Alps and Apennines), the winter is long and cold and the summer is short and cool. Even for summer visits, you are advised to bring sweaters and light boots.
● In the Pianura Padana (region around Milan), the climate is characterised by foggy winters and hot, humid summers.
● In the rest of the region, the winters are fairly mild and the hot, dry summers are tempered by sea-breezes.

use 100–120 volt appliances.
International Dialling Code: Italy 39. Bologna +51; Genoa +10; Milan +2; Trieste +40; Turin +11; Venice +41.
National Airline: Alitalia
National Flag: three vertical stripes of green, white and red
National Anthem: *Fratelli d'Italia* (by M. Novaro, words by G. Mameli, 1847).

Geography

The Alps form a natural boundary between Italy and neighbouring countries France, Switzerland and Austria, and the limestone Dolomites provide a second tier of mountains above Venetia and Trentino-Alto Adige.

A little further south, running at a right-angle to the Alps and extending right down the country, are the Apennines, which produce the rocky western coast of the Riviera. Between the two is the fertile Po valley, where most of the country's cereals are grown. The coastal plains of the Adriatic produce long, sandy beaches. Below the Alps are the Italian Lakes – notably Maggiore, Lugano and Como.

Government

Italy's president is elected for a term of seven years by Parliament, which is composed of two houses. These are the Senate (with 315 members) and the Chamber of Deputies (comprising 630 members). The president nominates the prime minister and, on the prime minister's recommendations, the Cabinet.

Recently, after a period of constitutional corruption in the early 1990s, Italy reduced its dependence on proportional representation and moved towards a "first-past-the-post" system, more in line with the British or French electoral systems. Under the new system, the country elected its first left-wing government, a loose centre-left coalition, in 1996.

Mayors are elected and, as in the United States, wield considerable power.

The individual regions tend to have strong political affiliations, and special autonomous status has been granted to five of them. Northern Italy is influenced by federalist tendencies. A separatist party, the Northern League, campaigns for an independent Northern Italy, which it has named Padania. It polls about 10 percent of the vote.

Economy

Industry (motor and electrical goods manufacturing, chemicals, sulphur, mercury, iron and steel) is concentrated in Northern Italy, where the Alps provide a source of hydro-electric power. There are some iron mines in Aosta. Italy is the world's largest producer of wine and olive oil and Europe's foremost producer of silk, which comes mainly from Lombardy.

Milan is the economic capital of the country and is also the centre of the Italian design industry, rivalling Paris as the fashion capital of Europe. Italy's economic strength lies in the creativity and industry of its small and medium-sized companies, especially those in Lombardy, Piedmont, the Veneto and Emilia-Romagna.

Planning the Trip

Visas and Passports

EU citizens do not need a visa or a passport to enter Italy: an identification card valid for foreign travel is sufficient.

Visitors from the following countries need a passport but not a visa providing they do not stay for more than three months: Australia, Austria, Barbados, Canada, Iceland, Jamaica, Japan, Kenya, South Korea, Kuwait, Malaysia, Maldives, Malta, Mexico, Monaco, New Zealand, Niger, Norway, Paraguay, Poland (for a stay up to 30 days), Singapore, Switzerland, Trinidad and Tobago, United States, Uruguay, Venezuela (up to 60 days). Other nationalities should contact their nearest Italian consulate.

You are supposed to register with the police within three days of arriving in Italy. In fact, this procedure will be taken care of by your hotel, whatever the level of accommodation. If you are not staying in a hotel, contact the local police station.

Money Matters

The monetary unit is the *lira* (plural *lire*). Travellers' cheques are recommended as they can be replaced if stolen or lost. However, commission will be charged for changing them. Most shopkeepers and restaurateurs will not change money, so it is best to change a limited amount at the airport when you arrive, especially if it is the weekend, when banks are closed. Try to avoid changing money in hotels, where the commission tends to be higher than in banks.

Banks are generally open from 8 or 8.30am–1.30pm and for 1½ hours in the afternoon (usually 2.30–4pm).

You can also change money at airports and main railway stations.

You will find current exchange rates are published in the press and posted in banks. Rates fluctuate considerably.

Credit cards and cash machines: In cities, many restaurants, hotels, shops and stores will take major credit cards (Visa, American Express, MasterCard, Diner's Club and Carte Blanche), but most petrol stations require cash. Don't rely on being able to use credit cards in country areas.

What to Wear

The Italians are known for their sense of style. This does not mean that one has to dress formally, but you may be barred from entering some churches if dressed in shorts (or short skirts in the case of women) or you have uncovered shoulders.

Unless you are going to visit mountain areas, the moderate climate makes heavy clothing unnecessary in summer. A light jacket will be adequate for summer evenings. In winter (November–March), the climate can be cold and wet throughout Northern Italy.

Tourist Offices

Australia: Italian Government Travel Office (ENIT), 123 Clarence Street, Sydney, tel: 02 9299 4574.
Canada: Italian Government Travel Office (ENIT), Montréal – Québec H3B 2C3 1, Place Ville Marie, Suite 1914, tel: 514-

Customs Regulations

Used personal effects may be imported and exported without formality. The import of narcotics, weapons and pirated materials is forbidden.

Alcoholic drinks, tobacco and perfume can be imported in limited quantities, depending on your nationality.

Duty-free shopping for EU citizens within Europe ended on 1 July 1999. Goods on which duty

Animal Quarantine

Pets must be vaccinated against rabies and you should obtain an officially stamped document stating that your animal is healthy. This should be done no more than a month before you arrive in Italy.

8667667, fax: 514-3921429.
UK: Italian State Tourist Board (ENIT), 1 Princes Street, London W1R 8AY, tel: 020-7408 1254, fax: 020-7493 6695.
US: Italian Government Travel Office (ENIT), Suite 1565, 630 Fifth Avenue, New York, NY 10111, tel: 212-2454822, fax: 212-5869249.
ENIT, Suite 2240, 500 North Michigan Avenue, Chicago 1 – Illinois 60611, tel: 312-6440996, fax: 312-6443019.
ENIT, Suite 550, 12400 Wilshire Blvd, Los Angeles, CA 90025-12400, tel: 310-8201898, fax: 310-8206357.

Getting There

By Air

In addition to the national airline, Alitalia, most airlines run direct flights to Italy, including many charter flights offering bargain tickets.
Intercontinental: Italy has 29 main airports, but only two of them are for intercontinental flights: Roma Leonardo da Vinci (known as Fiumicino) and Milano Malpensa.

has already been paid in another EU country may be freely imported, provided the amount falls within what might be reasonably described as "for personal use".

For US citizens, the duty-free allowance is: 200 cigarettes, 50 cigars or 3 lb tobacco; 1 US quart of alcoholic beverages and duty-free gifts worth up to $100.

The airports at Genoa, Milan, Turin and Venice all have duty-free shops.

European and charter: For cut-price tickets (scheduled and charter) all year round, Milan and Rome airports offer the best bargains.

Marco Polo Airport, Venice is located at Tessera on the mainland 10 km (6 miles) north of Venice. To reach Venice there is a choice of public bus to Piazzale Roma (30 minutes); private land taxi (20–25 minutes); the Cooperativa San Marco water launch which crosses the lagoon to Piazza San Marco via the Lido (45 minutes); or a water-taxi, which costs six times as much as the public launch.

Treviso Airport is an alternative for travellers to Venice or the Lakes. Charter flights are available from London Gatwick, and a coach service runs to Venice.

Verona Airport is probably the most convenient for reaching the Lakes or the Veneto region. Charter flights arrive from London, Frankfurt, Paris and some other cities.

Milano Malpensa Airport, Milan's intercontinental airport, is 45 km (28 miles) from the centre of Milan. An Air Pullman bus ferries passengers between the airport and the Air Pullman office outside the Central Railway Station. You can buy a ticket for this shuttle service up to a few minutes before departure from the Air Pullman office.

Milano Linate, Milan's other airport, is about 10 km (6 miles) from the centre. ATM bus 73 travels regularly (5.30am–midnight) from the front of the airport (Piazzale del Aeroporto) to its terminus on Piazza S. Babila at the corner of Corso Europa.

By Car

When calculating the cost of travelling to Italy by car, allow for motorway tolls as well as accommodation en route and petrol. Motorists driving through Switzerland will need to purchase a *vignette*, an annual road pass which costs around £17 and can be bought either at the border or at any national tourist office. If you want to travel by toll-free roads in Italy, get hold of the Italian State Tourist Office's *Traveller's Handbook*, which lists them.

Public Holidays

- **January** New Year's Day (1)
- **March/April** Good Friday, Easter Monday
- **April** Liberation Day – *Anniversario della Liberazione* (25)
- **May** Labour Day – *Festa del Lavoro* (1)
- **August** Assumption of the Blessed Virgin Mary – *Ferragosto* (15)
- **November** All Saints – *Ognissanti* (1)
- **December** Immaculate Conception of the Blessed Virgin Mary – *Immacolata Concezione* (8), Christmas Day (25), St Stephen's Day (26)

In addition to these national holidays, almost all cities have a holiday to celebrate their own patron saint, for example St John the Baptist 24 June (for Turin and Genoa); St Ambrose, 7 September (for Milan); St Mark, 25 April (Venice); St Petronius, 4 October (Bologna).

The usual route from France to Italy is via the Mont Blanc Tunnel (between Chamonix and Courmayeur) or from Switzerland through the Gran San Bernardo Tunnel (between Bourg St Pierre and Aosta). Some of the many alpine passes are seasonal, so it is best to check the viability of your route with the tourist board or a motoring organisation before setting off. Alternatively, motorists can head down the French autoroute to Nice and cross the border at Ventemiglia on the Riviera.

To take your car into Italy, you will need your current driving licence (with

an Italian translation unless it is the standard EU licence), your vehicle registration document (which must be in the driver's name or supported by the owner's written permission for the driver to use the vehicle) and Green Card insurance. You are also required to carry a warning triangle in case of breakdown.

By Coach

The cost of travelling to Italy from Great Britain by scheduled coach is not much cheaper than travelling by air. National Express Eurolines runs coaches from London Victoria, via Paris and Mont Blanc, to Aosta, Turin, Genoa, Milan, Venice and Bologna. To book from London, contact: National Express Eurolines, Victoria Coach Station, Buckingham Palace Road, London SW1, tel: 0990-808080.

By Rail

This is not a particularly cheap option unless you are travelling as part of the Inter-Rail or Eurail schemes. These provide a month's unlimited train travel in Europe for anyone under the age of 26 at a very reasonable price. They can be an attractive option, especially if you are planning to stop off en route.

For details of rail travel contact the following:
Australia: CIT, 123 Clarence Street, Sydney.
Tel: 02 9299 4574.
UK: European Rail Ltd
Tel: 020-7387 0444.
Italian State Railway, Marco Polo House, 3–5 Landsdowne Road, Croydon, Surrey.
Tel: 020-8686 0677.

The Orient Express

This is a wonderful way to reach Venice in style – certainly the most romantic. The service operates from March to November. From London, the train stops in Paris, Düsseldorf, Cologne, Frankfurt, Zurich, Innsbruck and Verona.

If you wish – and if you can afford it – you can travel both ways on the Orient Express, but you must

stay a minimum of five days in Venice. Sybarites can check into the luxurious Cipriani Hotel *(see Where to Stay)*, which is owned by the same group as the Orient Express.

Alternatively, buy a single either to or from Venice, and Alitalia will throw in a single ticket to allow you to complete your journey. For reservations, tel: 020-7805 5100.

Car Trains

The following rail services will transport cars to Italy:
- Paris–Milan
- Boulogne–Lille–Milan
- Schaerbbeek (Brussels)–Milan
- Hertogenbosch (The Netherlands)–Domodossola–Genoa–Milan
- Hertogenbosch–Chiasso–Milan
- Düsseldorf–Cologne–Milan–Genoa
- Hamburg–Hanover–Verona
- Munich–Rimini
- Düsseldorf–Cologne–Bolzano
- Vienna–Venice
- Boulogne–Alessandria

USA: CIT Tours, 342 Madison Avenue, Suite 207, New York, NY 190173. Tel: 1-800 223 7987/212 697 1482.

When travelling from Great Britain via Paris, it is necessary to change in Paris (from Gare du Nord to Gare de Lyon). EC (Eurocity) and TEE (Trans Europe Express) trains are luxury first-class only trains running between the main European cities. A special supplement is charged and seat reservation is obligatory. The Eurostar connects up with the TGV to Lille from where there are connections to Turin.

Package Tours

From the UK, Ireland, or the USA, this is usually the easiest and most economical way to visit historic centres such as Venice and the Lakes. It can be an advantage to travel with a company that has good local representation. Current brochures are generally available from your travel agent. The following are among the most reputable UK companies now specialising in travel to Venice and other parts of Italy.

Citalia
8 Lansdowne Rd, Croydon CR9 1LL. Tel: 020-8686 5533.
Magic of Italy
227 Shepherd's Bush Road, London W6. Tel: 020-8748 2661.
Italian Escapades
227 Shepherd's Bush Road, London W6. Tel: 020-8748 7575.

Practical Tips

Business Hours

Shops are open for business 9am–12.30pm and 3.30 or 4pm–7.30 or 8pm. In areas serving tourists, hours are generally longer than these. Shops often close on Monday (or Monday morning only). Some close on Saturday. Almost everything closes on Sunday.

Tipping

Unless otherwise indicated on the menu, service is included. Therefore it is not necessary to tip your waiter. A modest amount of change left on the table is sufficient to express appreciation for good service. Although *pane e coperto*, an outdated cover and bread charge, has been officially eliminated in most cities, some restaurants have been slow in phasing it out. Only in the finest hotels, and for lengthy stays, is a tip for the maids/head waiters necessary.

Media

The Italian press is concentrated in Milan and Rome. The biggest papers are *La Repubblica* and *Il Corriere della Sera,* which publish regional editions. Most major cities publish weekly listings magazines which are worth getting, even for visitors with basic Italian.

The local tourist office will have information on current happenings. Television stations include RAI (the national network with three channels), the Vatican network, plus seven national and more than 450 local commercial stations.

Postal Services

Post office hours are usually 8am–1.30pm, but many towns have a main post office which is open throughout the day.

Stamps may also be purchased from tobacco shops (*tabacchi*).

The post office can provide such services as *raccomandata* (registered) and *espresso* (express). You can receive mail addressed to *Posta Restante*, held at the *Fermo Posta* window of the main post office in every town, picking it up personally with identification.

Remember that you do not have to line up to post your mail: you can simply post it in the red letter-boxes near tobacconists or at the station.

Telephone

Public telephones are often found in bars and on main squares. From some bars, but mostly from post offices, you can call *scatti* (ring first, pay later). Most accept phonecards (*carte telefoniche* or *schede telefoniche*) and these are available from tobacconists or post offices for L5,000, L10,000 or L15,000. Alternatively, you can buy a *gettone* token which costs L200 (these are sometimes given as change when buying goods). Few telephones accept coins, but those that do take L100, L200 and L500. Directory enquiries is available by dialling 12, at a charge of roughly L1,000.

The cost of long-distance calls depends on the distance and the time of day. Within Italy, the cheapest time to call is 6.30pm– 8am, after 1pm on Saturday or all day Sunday.

If you are telephoning to outside Italy, it costs least 10pm–8am and all day Sunday. Off-peak rates are affected by whether it is the peak or off-peak period in the country you are calling.

Area Codes in Italy

For numbers outside your area and for all local calls, dialling must be preceded by "0" and then the area code, which you can obtain free from Information (dial 12). The area codes (including the initial "0") of main cities are: **Rome** (06), **Milan** (02), **Bologna** (051), **Genoa** (010), **Florence** (055), **Pisa** (050), **Venice** (041), **Turin** (011), **Como** (031).

Local Tourist Offices

Every major town has an **Azienda di Promozione Turistica** (APT) or **Informazione e Accoglienza Turistica** (IAT). For addresses and phone numbers, check the directory or the *Yellow Pages* under "ENIT". Together with helpful information, main APT offices offer a free city map, a list of hotels, and museum hours and addresses. APT offices in the main areas are listed below.

Almost every town in Italy has a **Touring Club Italiano** (TCI) office, which provides free information about points of interest. Telephone numbers are listed in the local telephone book. The club also produces some of the best maps and food – and wine – guides in Italy.

Turin

Turismo Turino (APT) has two information offices: Piazza Castello 161, tel: 011-535182/535901; and Stazione di Porta Nuova (railway station), tel: 011-531327, fax: 011: 5617095.

The Riviera

Contact **APT Genova**, Via Roma 11/3, 16121 Genova, tel: 010-576791, fax: 010-581408.

Milan

IAT offices are located at: Stazione Centrale, Galleria Partenze, tel: 02-72524360/ 370. Open Monday–Saturday 8am–7pm, Sunday 9am–12.30pm and 1.30–6pm.
Also Via Marconi 1 (Piazza del Duomo), tel: 02-72524300, fax: 02-72524350. Open Monday– Friday 8.30am–8pm (to 7pm in winter), Saturday 9am–1pm and 2–7pm (to 6pm in winter), Sunday 9am–1pm and 2–5pm.

The Lakes

APT Verona, Via Montanari 14, 37100 Verona, tel: 045-8006997.
APT Lago di Garda/Trentino, Giardini di Porta Orientale 8, 38066 Riva del Garda, tel: 0464-554444, fax: 0464-520308.
APT Como, Piazza Cavour 17, 22100 Como, tel: 031-269712/ 3300111, fax: 031-261152.
APT Varese, Viale Ippodromo 9,

Calling Home

To call abroad from Italy, dial 00, followed by:
Australia 61
Canada 1
Ireland 353
New Zealand 64
UK 44
USA 1
Then dial the number, omitting the initial "0" if there is one.
● European Directory Enquiries: 176
● European operator assistance: 15
● Intercontinental operator assistance: 170
● Telegrams and cables: 186

21100 Varese, tel: 0332-284624, fax: 0332-238093.
APTL Lago Maggiore & Lago di Mergozzo (Agenzia di Accoglienza e Promozione Turistica Locale), Piazza Cadorna 22, 28838 Stresa, tel: 0323-30416, fax: 0323-934335. Open Monday–Friday 8.45am–12.30pm and 2.30–6pm, Saturday 8.45am–12.30pm.
APT Bergamo, Viale Vittorio Emanuele 20, 24121 Bergamo, tel: 035-210204, fax: 035-230184. Open Monday–Friday 9am–12.30pm and 2–5.30pm. Vicolo Aquila Nera 2, tel: 035-212226, fax: 035-242994. Open daily 9am–12.30pm and 2–5.30pm.

Venice and Veneto

APT offices in **Venice**:
San Marco, Palazzina del Santi, tel: 041-5226356, fax: 041-5298730, under the arcades of the piazza. Open Monday– Saturday 9am–12.30pm and 3–7pm. Ferrovia Santa Lucia (train station), tel: 041-5298727, fax: 041-719078. Open daily 8am–7pm.
The APT provincial headquarters is at Castello 4421, tel: 041-5298711, fax: 041-5230399. Open daily 8am–7pm.
IAT Verona is at Cortile del Tribunale (Scavi Scaligeri), 37121 Verona, tel: 045-8068680, fax: 045-8003638.

Medical Services

In cases of real need, such as medical aid or ambulances, call the

Public Emergency Assistance number, **113**. This service operates on a 24-hour basis, and, in the principal cities, response will be in the main foreign languages. Dial 112 for the *Carabinieri* immediate action service. Certain tourist cities offer medical interpreting services.

To receive free treatment in cases of illness, accident or even childbirth, EU citizens (and citizens of countries with other ties to Italy, such as Brazil, Monaco, and the former Yugoslavia), must obtain (in their country of residence before arriving in Italy) the E-111 form. This form is to state that the bearers are registered with their national health service and therefore have the right to the same assistance offered to Italian citizens. (Note: it won't provide repatriation, which you may require in the case of serious illness.) Citizens of non-EU countries must pay for medical assistance and medicine.

Health insurance is recommended for travelling in Italy. Keep receipts for medical expenses if you want to claim.

Most hospitals have a 24-hour emergency department called *Pronto Soccorso*, but a stay in an Italian hospital can be a grim experience. For more minor complaints, seek out a *farmacia*, identified by a sign displaying a red cross within a white circle. Trained pharmacists give advice and suggest over-the-counter drugs, including antibiotics. Normal opening hours are 9am–1pm and 4–7.30 or 8pm, but outside these hours the address of the nearest *farmacia* on duty is posted in the window.

Security and Crime

The main problems for tourists are pick-pocketing, bag-snatching and robbery. It is advisable to have insurance coverage against these. If you are the victim of a crime (or suffer a loss) and wish to claim against your insurance, it is essential to make a report at the nearest police station and get documentation to support your claim. When you need a policeman, dial **113** (or 112 for the *Carabinieri*,

Consulates

There is the following limited local consular representation in Northern Italy:

Milan
- British Consulate,Via San Paolo 7, tel: 02-723001.
- US Consulate, Via Principe Amedeo 2/10, tel: 02-290351.

Venice
- British Consulate, Dorsoduro 1051, tel: 041 522 7207.

Other nationalities will need to contact their **embassies in Rome:**
- Australia: Via Alessandria 215, Rome, tel: 06-852721.
- Canada: Via G.B. Rossi, Rome, tel: 06-445981.
- Ireland: Piazza Campitelli 3, Rome, tel: 06-6782541/ 6979121.
- New Zealand: Via Zara 28, Rome, tel: 06-4404035/ 4402928.

a national police force which is technically a branch of the army).

If driving, lock your car and never leave luggage, cameras or other valuables inside. This applies particularly in major cities and in the South.

Women Travellers

The difficulties encountered by women travelling alone in Italy are often overstated. Women often have to put up with much male attention, but it is rarely dangerous. Ignoring whistles and questions is the best way to get rid of unwanted attention.

Personal Security

- Don't linger in non-commercial areas after dark
- Don't carry all your cash
- Use travellers' cheques or Eurocheques rather than large quantities of cash
- Never leave your luggage unattended
- Keep valuables in the hotel safe (most hotels provide a storage service)
- Deposit your room key at the desk before going out

Getting Around

Public Transport

BY AIR

The major centres and towns of touristic interest are connected by flights provided mostly by Alitalia. Smaller airlines are ATI, Alisarda (to and from Sardinia) and Aligiulia. Flying in Italy is expensive compared to taking the train, but it can be useful for long distances. Discount flights are often available if you are prepared to arrive and return on certain days, but such fares must be booked in Italy. For detailed information, contact your nearest travel agent or Alitalia office.

Infants under two years accompanied by an adult have a 90 percent discount; children over two years and under 12 have a 50 percent discount, and young travellers of 12–21 years have a 25 percent discount.

BY RAIL

The cheapest, fastest and most convenient way to travel is by train. Train information is available from the *Uffici Informazioni* at most major stations, listed in the telephone directory under *Ferrovie dello Stato*.

Local trains are called *Locale, Diretto, Interregionale* and *Espresso*. When travelling considerable distances or along major lines, the faster *InterCity* and *EuroCity* services are the best bet – the supplemental charge being well worth the time saved and the comfort. The *Pendolino* is the fastest and most comfortable train, and requires a supplemental charge and a reservation. It is a good idea to buy tickets and make reservations for the *IC/EC* and *Pendolino* in

advance, and this can be done at any travel agency as well as at the station.

If you are planning to make more than several train journeys, it is worth buying the inexpensive official train timetable book from any station kiosk. If travelling a fair distance, it is worth reserving a seat as trains tend to be crowded.

Trains are generally cheaper and more convenient than buses on main routes.

Significant fare reductions and special offers are available for groups and young travellers, and it is worth making enquiries about these when you arrive in Italy. Train tickets are valid for two months. Passengers must stamp their tickets in the station before boarding. If for some reason that is not possible, you must find the conductor before he finds you.

BY COACH

Each province in Italy has its own inter-city bus company and each company has its own lines. It is worth taking buses, especially when you are going to the mountainous interior, where they are generally faster than the train. Some of the principal coach companies operating long-distance travel from the main cities are listed below.

Milan
Autostradale, Piazzale Castello 1, tel: 166845010. Services throughout Lombardy and the Lakes. The company also runs guided tours, which can be booked through the tourist office.

Trentino-Alto Adige
SAD, Via Conciapelli 60, Bolzano, tel: 0471-5582414. Services along the coast from Genoa to Varazze (Riviera di Ponente) or Recco (Riviera di Levante).

Genoa
AMT, Piazza della Vittoria 88, tel: 010-5997414. Services from Genoa to Alassio, Rapallo and Milan.
Pesci, Piazza della Vittoria 94/R, tel: 010-564936/ 591625. Services to many parts of Italy.

TRAVEL WITHIN MILAN

The bus and tram service (ATM) is fast and efficient. Tickets must be purchased in advance at tobacconists (*tabacchi*) or news-stands and are good for 70 minutes of travel.

The Metropolitana Milanese (MM) is the best subway in Italy. MM has three lines (1, 2 and 3) which serve almost all the city and the hinterland. Usually tourists get on line 3, which runs south from near Stazione Centrale to Piazza del Duomo.

Tickets are sold at machines in stations, in most *tabacchi* and at newsstands. Tickets allow 75 minutes of travel. A day ticket is valid on all forms of transport. Other good value tickets are the 24-hour ticket, the 2-day ticket, or the book of 10 tickets.

TRAVEL/TRANSPORT WITHIN VENICE

The city is small enough to be covered on foot and a good map is essential for exploring the maze of small streets and squares. Pick one up from the tourist office.

The main form of public transport is the *vaporetto* or water bus. The most scenic line is the No. 1 Accelerato, which takes you slowly down the Grand Canal. Line 82 provides a faster service down the Grand Canal, making only six stops and going west as far as Tronchetto (the car park island) and east to San Zaccaria (and the Lido in summer). The circular line No. 52 provides an enjoyable ride around the periphery of Venice and takes in the island of Murano.

Passengers who have not bought a ticket before boarding will be surcharged; tourists have to pay more than residents, who get reduced rates. Twenty-four-hour or three-day passes are available. Children under 1 metre (3 ft) high travel free, but a suitcase costs as much as an adult passenger.

A private and more costly water-taxi service can be hired from most hotels in the city. If arriving at your hotel with luggage, you will need to tip someone to help carry it up to the building.

Water-Taxis and Gondolas

The alternatives to water buses are water-taxis and, of course, gondolas. The former take up to four people and, like regular taxis, display meters. You can find taxi "ranks" at main points in the city. To understand the complex system of charges for water transport, pick up a free copy of *A Guest in Venice* from any major hotel.

The flat rate for hiring a gondola is about L120,000 (six persons) for 50 minutes and L60,000 for each 25 minutes thereafter during the day, and L150,000 at night, though it is advisable to haggle. A singing gondolier costs extra. Gondolas booked as a group convoy may be cheaper – if you can face it! A recommended route is Bridge of Sighs, Santa Maria Formosa and Rialto Bridge, returning via the Grand Canal.

Very much cheaper, for those who want a quick taste, are the *traghetto* gondolas, which simply ferry people across the Grand Canal in six different places where no bridge is convenient.

TRAVEL WITHIN THE LAKES

One of the most relaxing ways of viewing the lakes is from the deck of a steamer. All major towns on the lakes have ferry connections for passengers and a number of towns are linked by car ferry as well:

Ferries and Hydrofoils

There are a great many ferryboat and hydrofoil speedboat lines that offer connections between the mainland and Italy's many large and small islands. The services run by the State Railways, Tirrenia, Grandi navi veloci, Trans Tirrenco Express, Moby Lines and SNAV companies provide all the connections with Sicily and Sardinia. Many other lines connect the peninsula with the smaller islands. Here is some basic information regarding shipping lines:

Ferrovie dello Stato (State Railways): Civitavecchia–Golfo Aranci (Sardinia): departures many times a day for passengers with cars. Crossing takes nine hours.

Tirrenia Nagigazione: This Genoa-based line operates sailings to Sardinia, Sicily and Tunis.

Naples–Palermo, Civitavecchia–Olbia or Cagliari (both direct and via Arbatax). The connections with Sardinia are daily for passengers and cars, with both day and night runs. Tirrenia also runs Genoa–Porto Torres, Genoa–Cagliari and Naples–Cagliari (all to Sardinia), with an average crossing time of 12–20 hours.

Trans Tirreno Express: Livorno–Olbia, particularly during the high season.

Grandi navi veloci: This line offers connections from Genoa to Corsica, Sicily, Sardinia and Spain (Barcelona) for passengers and cars.

Moby Lines: This line offers a ferry service from Genoa to Corsica and further to Sardinia (in summer only).

Toremar/Siremar/Caremar/ SNAV: Toremar offers connections to the Tuscan islands (Elba, Giglio) while Siremar runs to the Aeolian islands, Caremar runs from Naples to the Naples Gulf islands (Capri, Ischia), and SNAV connects Naples and Palermo.

Aliscafi: This is a hydrofoil speedboat line which connects Naples and the islands Ischia, Capri and Procida.

Adriatic: This service carries passengers and cars from Venice, Trieste, Ancona, Pescara, Bari and Brindisi both to the Adriatic and foreign ports.

To obtain further information about fares and schedules, call in at any of the many travel agencies or the APT offices.

Verbania– Laveno on Lake Maggiore; Menaggoio–Bellagio– Varenna on Lake Como; and Maderno–Torri del Benaco on Lake Garda.

The Maggiore and Lugano steamers cross the border between Italy and Switzerland. so the usual border procedures apply. The larger vessels have on-board restaurants. For a trip along the full length of Lake Garda, from Desenzano to Riva. allow around 4½ hours.

Cruises are regular features during summer, and disco ships are also common. Real, old-fashioned paddle steamers are still used.

Calling a Taxi

You can call for a taxi by dialling one of the following numbers:
Bologna: 372727 or 534141
Milan: 6767, 5353, 8585, 8383 or 5251
Turin: 5737 or 5730
Venice: see *Water-Taxis and Gondolas*
● Check the *Tutto Città* (first page) or the *Yellow Pages* for other towns.

TAXIS

Cabs are found at taxi ranks or paged by telephone rather than hailed in the street. When you call, the operator will tell you the call letters of the taxi and approximately how many minutes it will take to arrive.

Fares are clocked up on meters. There is a fixed starting charge and then a charge for every kilometre (and a standing charge for traffic jams). Taxi drivers are obliged to show, if asked, the current list of additional charges. Extra charges are added for night rides (10pm–7am), luggage, journeys outside town and journeys on Sundays and public holidays. It is a general rule to leave a small tip rounding off the fare to the nearest L1,000 or 2,000.

Private Transport

BY CAR

In Italy, you must drive on the right. The motorways (*autostrade*) are

Milan ATM Metro

fast and uncrowded (except in summer), but Italians sometimes drive faster than the speed limit. Nearly all *autostrade* charge tolls and you pay as you exit.

It is compulsory to wear seat-belts at all times and infants up to nine months must occupy a baby seat. Children between nine months and four years must sit on the back seat.

Pay attention to street signs advising no parking because police are strict on illegal parking and will remove vehicles found in no parking areas. You'll need plenty of cash to reclaim your car. Try to park in a garage for the night: it will be a little expensive, but much safer.

Hitchhiking is forbidden on the *autostrade* and is not advised for

women travelling alone, especially in the South.

When travelling into the **mountain areas** during the winter months, it is advisable to call 194 for road conditions. When there is ice and snow, chains will be required.

Car Rentals

Hiring a car is expensive in Italy, as is petrol. Major car rental firms such as Avis, Hertz and Europcar are represented in most cities and at all airports, though local firms often offer better rates. Agencies are listed in the *Yellow Pages* under *Autonoleggio*. Collision damage waiver and recovery in case of breakdown are usually included in the price of hiring a vehicle, but be sure to check exclusions carefully. Additional insurance cover is usually available at fixed rates. Also, make sure that the price you are quoted includes VAT (IVA), which is levied at 19 percent.

The renter must be over 21 and must be in possession of a valid driver's licence (an EU licence, an international driving licence or a national driving licence with Italian translation). A deposit equal to the cost of hiring the vehicle is usually required, or a credit card imprint.

Driving Speeds

The following speed limits apply to cars in Italy:
Urban areas: 50 km/h (30 mph)
Roads outside urban areas: 90 km/h (55 mph)
Dual carriageways outside urban areas: 110 km/h (70 mph)
Motorways (*autostrade*): 130 km/h (80 mph); for cars less than 1,100cc: 110 km/h (70 mph)

Where to Stay

Choosing a Hotel

Italy has a wonderful variety of accommodation in all categories, from grand villas to small family-run hotels, as well as the newly-developing sector of *Agriturismo* – farm holidays. All the major international chains are represented in Italy, with Jolly and Hilton being two of the most common. However, there are also burgeoning groups of highly individualistic hotels that have banded together to present a common front. They tend to be independent hotels that are linked by their atmosphere, style and cost to others in different areas.

Be sure to call or write beforehand to verify facilities and make reservations. Smaller hotels are not always cheaper – some of the more exclusive small hotels match the grand hotels in style and expense – but even inexpensive hotels usually offer basic comforts and good service.

Hotel Listings

The following listings offer a selection of hotels at all levels. Your travel agent or the APT offices in Italy can give more complete information on these and other hotels.

VENICE

Note: Hotel rates in Venice are about 30 percent higher than those on the mainland, but the prices are worth it for the atmosphere.

Grand Hotels
Cipriani
Isola della Giudecca 10
Tel: 041-5207744
Fax: 041-5203930.
A small oasis hidden on the tip of the

island of Giudecca, the Cipriani feels far removed from the city centre. Among its comforts are lavish bedrooms furnished with Fortuny fabrics, a swimming pool (one of few private pools in Venice), gardens and tennis courts, a yacht harbour, piano bar and a launch service which whisks you, in a couple of minutes, to San Marco. **LLLL**
Danieli Ciga Hotel
Riva degli Schiavoni 4196
Castello
Tel: 041-5226480
Fax: 041-5200208.
Part of the Ciga chain of hotels, the Danieli is rich with memories of eminent guests: George Sand, Alfred de Musset, Dickens, Balzac, Wagner, kings, princes, stars. The splendid Gothic foyer, built around a courtyard, is an attraction in itself, and the rooms are very comfortable. The roof garden restaurant has a splendid view over the lagoon. **LLL–LLLL**
Europa & Regina Ciga Hotel
Corte Barozzi
San Marco 2159
Tel: 041-5200477
Fax: 041-5231533.
In front of the baroque Church of the Salute, with rooms overlooking the Grand Canal, this old hotel has been tastefully redecorated and the service is first-class. **LLL–LLLL**
Excelsior Hotel
Lungomare Marconi 41
Lido di Venezia
Tel: 041-5260201
Fax: 041-5267276.
A member of the Ciga chain, this is a huge luxury beach hotel with a facade reminiscent of a Moorish castle. Attractions include numerous sports facilities and a free launch service to Venice. **LLLL**
Grand Hotel des Bains
Lungomare Marconi 17
Tel: 041-5265921
Fax: 041-5260113.
Ciga-run, this grand old hotel is remembered for its role in Thomas Mann's *Death in Venice*. It is located across the road from its private beach. Facilities similar to those at the Excelsior (*see above*). **LLLL**
Gritti Palace Ciga Hotel
Campo Santa Maria del Giglio
San Marco 2467

Tel: 041-794611
Fax: 041-5200942.
The most elegant hotel in Venice, renowned for its formal luxury, charming setting (right on the Grand Canal) and discreet, attentive service. Doge Andrea Gritti lived here and the hotel still has the air of a private *palazzo*. Hemingway, Winston Churchill, Herbert von Karajan and Greta Garbo all stayed here. The cuisine, which you enjoy on the canalside terrace, is very refined. **LLLL**

Londra Palace
Riva degli Schiavoni 4171
Tel: 041-5200533
Fax: 041-5225032.
This elegant hotel is a flagship of the Charming Hotels group (*see Hotel Groups below*). It overlooks the lagoon and has a romantic bar and excellent restaurant. **LLL–LLLL**

Price Categories

Price categories are based on single occupancy without breakfast:
L = under L100,000
LL = L100,000–200,000
LLL = L200,000–300,000
LLLL = more than L300,000

Luna Baglioni
Calle Vallaresso
San Marco 1243
Tel: 041-5289840
Fax: 041-5287160.
Arguably the oldest hotel in Venice, dating its origins back to a Knights Templar lodge in existence in 1118, for pilgrims travelling to the Crusades. It's been operating as an inn since the 16th century. Grand public rooms decorated in noble Venetian style, with frescos, stuccowork and paintings. Recommended for its setting, close to St Mark's, and its waterside views. Refined Canova restaurant. **LLLL**

Small Hotels
Accademia Villa Maravege
Fondamenta Bollani
Dorsoduro 1058
Tel: 041-5210188
Fax: 041-5239152.
Reservations should be made

months in advance for this sought-after *pensione*. Close to the Accademia gallery, it is a 17th-century villa with delightful gardens front and back. **LL–LLL**

Agli Alboretti
Rio Terro Sant'Agnese
Dorsoduro 884
Tel: 041-5230058
Fax: 041-5210158.
Situated close to the Accademia, this reasonably priced two-star hotel is a good choice for budget travellers. It has 25 smallish rooms and is popular with American and British guests. Unlike most small hotels, it has its own perfectly acceptable gastronomic restaurant (moderate prices; open evenings only) as well as a charming little courtyard. **L–LL**

Bucintoro
Riva San Biagio 2135
Castello
Tel: 041-5223240
Fax: 041-5222424.
Simply furnished, friendly *pensione* on the waterfront with splendid views over the Basin of San Marco and the island of San Giorgio Maggiore. **LL**

Flora
Calle de la Pegola
San Marco 2283/A
Tel: 041-5205844
Fax: 041-5228217.
Charming, friendly hotel within five minutes' walk of Piazza San Marco. The garden, with fountains and flower beds, is particularly appealing. Bedrooms vary enormously and can be quite basic. **LL–LLL**

La Calcina
Zattere ai Gesuati 780
Tel: 041-5206466
Fax: 041-5227045.
This russet-coloured inn is situated along the charming quayside of the Zattere in the Dorsoduro district. John Ruskin, the aesthete and art critic, stayed here in 1876. The hotel has redecorated most of its rooms in genteel style, using muted colours and tasteful furniture. Each bedroom is different and there is a considerable price differential between them until all have been modernised. Roof terrace with appealing views over the Giudecca Canal. **LLL**

La Fenice et des Artistes
Campo San Fantin
San Marco 1936
Tel: 041-5232333
Fax: 041-5203721.
Within a stone's throw of the Fenice Opera House (presently closed), this hotel is usually popular with actors, musicians and artists. **LL–LLL**

Metropole
Riva degli Schiavoni 4149
Tel: 041-5205044
Fax: 041-5223679.
In front of St George's Island. Beautifully furnished and offering excellent service. **LLL–LLLL**

Monaco & Grand Canal
Calle Vallaresso
San Marco 1325
Tel: 041-5200211
Fax: 041-5200501.
First-category hotel located where the Grand Canal flows into the Laguna. Very intimate and comfortable, though the rooms are perhaps a little small and sometimes noisy. Good service. **LLL–LLLL**

Quattro Fontane
Via Quattro Fontane 16
Lido di Venezia
Tel: 041-5260227
Fax: 041-5260726.
This small, gabled four-star hotel lies in secluded gardens, making it one of the most charming hotels on the Lido. This is the place for visitors who are looking for comfort and pleasant surroundings without the formality of the larger luxury hotels. Courtyard for summer dining; tennis courts; close to the sea. **LLLL**

San Cassiano
Calle della Rosa 2232
Santa Croce
Tel: 041-5241768
Fax: 041-721033.
One of the few hotels actually on the Grand Canal, the San Cassiano is converted from a 14th-century *palazzo*. About half the rooms have canalside views looking across to the Ca' d'Oro. **LL–LLL**

Santo Stefano
Campo Santo Stefano
San Marco 2957
Tel: 041-5200166
Fax: 041-5224460.
This small hotel, occuppying a former palace watchtower, is a welcome

recent addition to the Venetian scene. It is set on one of the city's most spacious and stylish squares close to the Accademia. Young, friendly and efficient management. Small but tastefully furnished rooms lit by Murano glass chandeliers. Babysitting service. **LLL**

Saturnia & International
Via XXII Marzo 2398
Tel: 041-5208377
Fax: 041-5207131.
Very romantic hotel housed in a 16th-century palace close to bustling Piazza San Marco. Both intimate and comfortable. **LLL–LLLL**

Villa Pannonia
Via Doge Michiel 48
Lido di Venezia
Tel: 041-5260162
Fax: 041-5265277.
Three-star Art Nouveau hotel five minutes' walk from the Santa Elisabetta landing stages. Family-run and welcoming, with a small bar, knowledgeable receptionist and inquisitive cat; especially suitable

for families. Pleasant dining room overlooking peaceful gardens. Half or full-board is encouraged during the summer season but be warned: breakfasts are grim. Access to a private beach; trips to the Murano glass factories. **LLL**

VENETO

Verona

Due Torri Baglioni
Piazza S. Anastasia 4
Tel: 045-595044
Fax: 045-8004130.
This grand classical *palazzo* has been well converted into a luxurious hotel and has an excellent, if rather formal, restaurant with a fine wine list. **LLLL**

Victoria
Via Adua 8
Tel: 045-590566
Fax: 045-590155.
Set in the heart of the old quarter of Verona, this historic *palazzo* has

been creatively yet sensitively converted. The bedrooms are superbly inviting while the reception rooms incorporate Roman and medieval remains, including some mosaics. **LLL–LLLL**

Vicenza

Campo Marzio
Viale Roma 21
Tel: 0444-545700
Fax: 0444-320495.
A convenient hotel, though not particularly individualistic. It is near the park and within easy reach of the railway station. **LL–LLL**

FRIULI-VENEZIA GIULIA

Trieste

Grand Hotel Duchi d'Aosta
Piazza Unità d'Italia 2
Tel: 040-7600011
Fax: 040-366092.
This hotel is small but very charming, with big, well-furnished

Hotel Groups

The following is a selection of the most noteworthy hotel groups.

Charming Hotels
This delightful group of luxurious, independent Italian hotels is characterised by its impeccable taste in atmospheric locations, use of authentic antiques and excellent traditional cuisine. There are Charming Hotels in Como, Milan and Venice, amongst other places. You can book through head office in Rome: Via Pinciana 25, tel: 06-8411940, fax: 06-85210210; in the UK through Liaisons Abroad, tel: 020-7376 4020, fax: 020-7376 4442; or in the USA through European Connection, Roslyn Heights, New York, tel: 310-541 0028, fax: 310-541 1359, toll free 800 541 5412. Hotel Londra Palace (*see listing above*) is typical of the group.

Sina Hotels
This small hotel group, founded by an Italian aristocrat, runs a collection of stylish and luxurious

hotels in six major Italian cities: Milan, Parma, Viareggio, Florence, Perugia and Rome. The hotels are all different yet have a certain elegance and formality in common. You can book the hotels directly or through Sina Hotels in Rome: Piazza Barberini 23, tel: 06-4870222; fax: 06-4874778.

Turin Hotels
This group began in Turin and manages traditional, classic hotels in the regions of Piedmont and Liguria. The hotels are characterised by high Piedmontese standards of service, classical or neo-classical buildings and excellent cuisine. They are all 4-star and include the Turin Palace Hotel (*see page 367*) and the Excelsior Palace Hotel in Rapallo. Hotels can be booked through Turin Hotels International, Turin, tel: 011-5151911; fax: 011-5617191.

Logis d'Italia
This group operates on the same principles as the better-known French group, Logis de France. The

group's 90–100 hotels are found all over Italy and are listed in the *Logis d'Italia* guide, available from bookshops or the Italian tourist office. The group's principles are founded on value for money, hospitality and size (most are small, and many are family run). Hotels can be booked through a central reservations system in Milan, tel: 02-48519285, fax: 02-48519265, or booked direct. A typical hotel in the group is Hotel Select in Rome.

Abitare La Storia
This new hotel grouping operates under the banner of 'Living History', or 'Bringing History Alive'. It is an association of independently-run hotels, each of which is housed in an historic *palazzo* or villa, often with lovely grounds. The keynotes are tradition and atmosphere, often matched by a choice of good regional cuisine. This group of keenly-priced 3-, 4- and 5-star hotels has a typical representative in Hotel Ripagrande in Ferrara (*see page 368*).

rooms, and efficient service, in a convenient, central position. Be sure to try the excellent restaurant (Harry's Grill). **LL–LLL**

Jolly
Corso Cavour 7
Tel: 040-7600055
Fax: 040-362699.
Jolly-style hotel with the usual great service and comfort. **LL–LLL**

Starhotel Savoia Excelsior Palace
Riva del Mandracchio 4
Tel: 040-77941
Fax: 040-638260.
Every comfort. **LL–LLLL**

TRENTINO-ALTO ADIGE

Bolzano

Scala-Stiegl
Via Brennero 111
Tel: 0471-976222
Fax: 0471-981141.
This turn-of-the-century hotel is situated within walking distance of the old city centre. In spite of all its modern comforts, it has managed to maintain its historic ambience with a spacious garden, restaurant and swimming pool. **L–LL**

Trento

Albergo Accademia
Vicolo Colico 4–6
Tel: 0461-233600
Fax: 0461-230174.
In a historic building situated in the middle of the old town, on a tiny square near the Piazza Duomo. The charming hotel has been completely renovated. Big and spacious rooms are bright and comfortably furnished. In the former courtyard is now a garden. The restaurant is famous for its good cuisine. **LL**

Buonconsiglio
Via Romagnosi 14/16
Tel: 0461-272888
Fax: 0461-272889.
A stylish, modern hotel suitable for business and leisure travellers. Well-equipped and close to the historic centre. **LL**

Hotel America
Via Torre Verde 50
Tel: 0461-983010/239363
Fax: 0461-230603.
Long-established hotel set in the

historic heart of Trento. Good service. **LL**

Villa Madruzzo
Località Cognola
Via Ponte Alto 26 (3 km from centre)
Tel: 0461-986220
Fax: 0461-986361.
A grand hill-top villa set in charming grounds. An elegant interior is matched by pleasing service and good traditional cuisine. **LL**

MILAN

Grand Hotels

The Century Tower
Via F. Filzi 25b
Tel: 02-67504
Fax: 02-66980602.
The Century Tower is unusual in consisting entirely of identical, spacious suites, each with a large, separate office space. Good restaurant; buffet breakfasts; piano bar; small fitness centre. Friendly, efficient staff, good value. Set in a convenient, central location a stone's throw from the Stazione Centrale. **LLLL**

Price Categories

Price categories are based on single occupancy without breakfast:

L = under L100,000
LL = L100,000–200,000
LLL = L200,000–300,000
LLLL = more than L300,000

Duca di Milano
Piazza della Repubblica 13
Tel: 02-62841
Fax: 02-6555966.
Impressive hotel with spacious suites. **LLLL**

Executive Hotel
Via Don Luigi Sturzo 45
Tel: 02-6294
Fax: 02-29010238.
First-rate service and a good restaurant. **LLLL**

Four Seasons
Via Gesu 8
Tel: 02-77088
Fax: 02-77085000.
This is universally acknowledged as

Milan's best hotel, both in terms of atmosphere and unadulterated luxury. Converted from a 15th-century monastery, with lovely rooms overlooking delightful cloisters. Favoured by film/music stars and fashion personalities. Magnificent Il Teatro gourmet restaurant (open evenings only) and the less rarified La Terrazza restaurant. **LLLL**

Gallia
Piazza Duca d'Aosta 9
Tel: 02-6785
Fax: 02-68713239.
Luxury-category, historic hotel located close to Stazione Centrale, near the air terminal and business centre. Expensive, but service is perfection. **LLLL**

Grand Hotel et de Milan
Via A Manzoni 29
Tel: 02-723141
Fax: 02-86460861.
Milan's most historic hotel, founded in 1863 and containing the celebrated suite where Verdi died. Set north of the Duomo, on one of the city's most prestigious streets close to La Scala. Popular Don Carlos restaurant. Sumptuous decor and antiques. **LLLL**

Jolly President
Largo Augusto 10
Tel: 02-77416
Fax: 02-783449.
Excellent member of the Jolly chain. **LLLL**

Jolly Touring
Via Ugo Tarchetti 2.
Tel: 02-6335.
Fax: 02-6592209.
Top class comfort. **LLL–LLLL**

Milano Hilton
Via Galvani 12
Tel: 02-69831
Fax: 02-66710810.
Contemporary hotel, decorated in a provincial/modern style. Located in the new commercial centre of the city. **LLLL**

Palace Hotel
Piazza della Repubblica 20
Tel: 02-63361
Fax: 02-654485.
Close to the railway station, in front of the Principe di Savoia, this very comfortable hotel has been renovated in an ultra-modern style. Well known restaurant. **LLLL**

Principe di Savoia
Piazza della Repubblica 17
Tel: 02-62301
Fax: 02-6595838.
Located north of the cathedral, a classic luxury hotel, with superb service. Elegant reception rooms; 298 bedrooms; swimming pool and sauna. **LLLL**

Small Hotels

Antica Locanda dei Mercanti
Via San Tomaso 6
Tel: 02-8054080
Fax: 02-8054090.
Small, charming hotel set in an 18th-century palace in a pedestrianised area. Each room is individually decorated, but common features include personal "libraries", wrought-iron bedsteads, unusual rugs and marble bathrooms. **LLL**

Antica Locanda Solferino
Via Castelfidardo 2
Tel: 02-6570129
Fax: 02-6571361.
This is a delightful hotel, with old-fashioned furniture and atmosphere. From the windows, you can look out on the Brera quarter. Romantic restaurant. **LL**

Ariston
Largo Carrobbio 2
Tel: 02-72000556
Fax: 02-72000914.
This is a so-called "ecological" hotel which manages to be both comfortable and environmentally correct. Rooms are well-furnished and the atmosphere is friendly. One floor is given over to non-smokers. All guests have unlimited use of the hotel bicycles. **LLL**

Palazzo delle Stelline
Corso Magenta 61
Tel: 02-4818431
Fax: 02-48519097.
An elegant, understated hotel housed in an historic, well-restored palace. Located in a refined district just south of the Parco Sempione. A number of rooms have romantic views over the rooftops of Milan. Charming terrace. **LLL**

Radisson Bonaparte
Via Cusani 13
Tel: 02-8560
Fax: 02-8693601.
Discreet hotel by the Castello

Sforzesco, just a few minutes from the elegant Brera district. Modern and functional, suitable for both a business and leisure clientele. Good restaurant; private parking. **LLLL**

Sant'Ambroeus
Via Papiniano 14
Tel: 02-48008989
Fax: 02-48008687.
Friendly, cosy hotel near Solari Park and the Metro. **LL–LLL**

LOMBARDY

Bergamo

Agnello d'oro
Via Gombito 22
Tel: 035-249883
Fax: 035-235612.
Small inn in the upper city with 20 simple but comfortable rooms and a fine restaurant serving traditional Lombardic cuisine. **LL**

Price Categories

Price categories are based on single occupancy without breakfast:
L = under L100,000
LL = L100,000–200,000
LLL = L200,000–300,000
LLLL = more than L300,000

Excelsior San Marco
Piazza della Repubblica 6
Tel: 035-366111
Fax: 035-223201.
Impressive modern hotel with efficient service and good facilities. Roof garden. **LLL**

Mantua

San Lorenzo
Piazza Concordia 14
Tel: 0376-220500
Fax: 0376-327194.
Typical city hotel near the cathedral. The spacious rooms and beautiful salons are partly furnished with antique furniture. Good service. Pretty garden on the roof. **LL–LLL**

Pavia

Excelsior
Piazzale Stazione 25
Tel: 0382-28596

Fax: 0382-26030.
Reliable city hotel opposite the station. Although the exterior is not especially pretty, the interior is well-tended. **LL**

Pomponesco (Mantova)

Il Leone
Piazza IV Martiri 2
Tel: 0375-86077
Fax: 0375-86770.
The rather simple facade of the former house of the Gonzagas conceals this remarkable hotel with an inner courtyard and swimming pool. Cultivated lounge, big and comfortable rooms and a faultless restaurant – here, everything is just perfect. **LL**

VALLE D'AOSTA

Aosta

Europe
Piazza Narbonne 8
Tel: 0165-236363
Fax: 0165-40566.
Set in the historic centre, this is a traditional hotel, noted for its peace and quiet as well as elegance. **LL**

Hostellerie du Cheval Blanc
Via Clavité 20
Tel/fax: 0165-239140
Functional yet friendly hotel, well set up for winter sports, with a sauna and a heated pool. **LL**

Entrèves-Courmayeur

La Grange
Strada La Brenva
Tel: 0165-869733
Fax: 0165-869744.
This charming small hotel (23 rooms) is situated in the pretty mountain village of Entrèves, a hidden corner of the Aosta valley at the bottom of Montblanc. All rooms are cosy and partly furnished with old furniture. **LL**

Hotel La Brenva
Courmayeur
Tel: 0165-869780
Fax: 0165-869726.
This cosy inn has the atmosphere of a mountain chalet, with wood panelling and balconies facing Montblanc. It also boasts an exquisite restaurant, La Brenva. **LL**

PIEDMONT

Turin
City
Via F. Juvarra 25
Tel: 011-540546
Fax: 011-548188.
Small, comfortable hotel close to the station of Porta Susa, with 61 bedrooms. **LL–LLL**

Jolly Hotel Ambasciatori
Corso Vittorio Emanuele 104
Tel: 011-5752
Fax: 011-544978.
Favoured by business people. Good location and service. **LLL**

Jolly Hotel Principi di Piemonte
Via Piero Gobetti 15
Tel: 011-5629693
Fax: 011-5620270.
Most central hotel in Turin. Very comfortable, with excellent service. **LLLL**

Turin Palace Hotel
Via Sacchi 8
Tel: 011-5625511
Fax: 011-5612187.
Flagship of Turin Hotel Group (see *Hotel Groups*, page 364): a classic and elegant hotel convenient for Porta Nuova station. **LL–LLL**

Victoria
Via Nino Costa 4
Tel: 011-5611909
Fax: 011-5611806.
Modern hotel in the middle of the city, but quietly situated. Remarkable is that each room has been designed in a different style and with a lot of imagination. **LL**

Villa Sassi
Via Traforo del Pino
Tel: 011-898556
Fax: 011-8980095.
This hotel is housed in an 18th-century villa, in a great park. Only 12 bedrooms, but excellent service and comfort. Exclusive. **LLL–LLLL**

Alba (Cuneo)
Villa La Meridiana-Cascina Reine
Altavilla 9
Tel/fax: 0173-440112.
Situated high above the charming medieval small town Alba. The pretty rooms are tasteful and very comfortable. From the garden there's a wonderful view over the hills of the Piedmont (covered in vineyards) with the towers of Alba. **LL**

Canelli (Asti)
La Luna e i Falo'
Tel/fax: 0141-831643.
This likeable country inn got its name from the piedmontesic writer Cesare Pavese. *La Luna and Falo* (young moon) is one of his masterpieces. The hotel is built in the style of a villa and has spacious and comfortable rooms and an extraordinary, good restaurant. **LL**

Chiaverano d'Ivrea (Turin)
Castello San Giuseppe
Tel: 0125-424370
Fax: 0125-641278.
Comfortable country hotel with swimming pool and gorgeous garden is part of the well-preserved old Castello San Giuseppe. **LL**

THE LAKES

Bellagio (Lago di Como)
Grandhotel Villa Serbelloni
Via Roma 1
Tel: 031-950216
Fax: 031-951529.
This fabulous patrician villa has been converted into one of the finest hotels in Northern Italy. The views, grounds, facilities and service are all impeccable. **LLLL**

Como
Barchetta Excelsior
Piazza Cavour 1
Tel: 031-3221
Fax: 031-302622.
Rather anonymous modern hotel redeemed by its central location. Request a room overlooking the lake. **LL–LLL**

Isole Borromee (Lago Maggiore)
Hotel Verbano
Isola dei Pescatori
Tel: 0323-30408
Fax: 0323-33129.
The Isola dei Pescatori is one of the smallest and most romantic among the Islands in the midst of Lake Maggiore. The Verbano has 12, a bit old-fashioned but charming rooms with wonderful views over the lake. **LLL**

Sirmione (Lago di Garda)
Grand Hotel Terme
Viale Marconi 7
Tel: 030-916261
Fax: 030-916568.
Elegant, well-modernised hotel in attractive grounds. Good facilities include a pool, sauna and fitness centre. **LLL–LLLL**

Golf & Suisse
Via XXV Aprile
Tel: 030-9904590
Fax: 030-916304.
Small, family-run hotel close to the lake, with a small pool. Rather anonymous bedrooms but there's a friendly welcome and lavish breakfasts. Doesn't have its own restaurant but there are several to choose from nearby. **L–LL**

Varenna (Lecco/Lago di Como)
Hotel Olivedo
Piazza Martiri de la Libertà 4
Tel/fax: 0341-830115.
Doubtless one of the nicest hotels in this region. In spite of its simplicity everything including the restaurant is very tastefully decorated. Unfortunately, not all rooms have their own bathroom. In any case, make a reservation for a room with view over the lake. **LL**

LIGURIA & RIVIERA

Genoa
Bristol Palace
Via XX Settembre 35
Tel: 010-592541
Fax: 010-561756.
Despite its modest entrance, a well-furnished hotel – particularly the dining-room, which is decorated in the Louis XVI style. Good service. **LLL**

Jolly Hotel Plaza
Via M. Piaggio 11
Tel: 010-8393641
Fax: 010-8391850.
Small villa transformed into lodgings in an ideal location near Piazza Corvetto. **LL–LLL**

Savoia Majestic
Via Arsenale di Terra 5
Tel: 010-261641
Fax: 010-261883.
Comfortable, good service, in a central position by Principe station. **LL**

Alassio
Grand Hotel Diana
Via Garibaldi 110
Tel: 0182-642701
Fax: 0182-640304.
Open April–October, with good service, a swimming pool and a terrace garden. Half-board mandatory. **LL–LLL**

Bordighera
Grand Hotel Cap Ampelio
Via Virgilio 5
Tel: 0184-264333
Ideally located on the hill of Bordighera, this refined hotel has a splendid view over the sea and coastline. **LL–LLL**
Grand Hotel del Mare
Capo Migliarese
Tel: 0184-262201
Fax: 0184-262394.
Hotel overlooking the sea, preferred by adults for its quietness, its comfort and its beautiful rooms. **LLLL**

Camogli
Cenobio dei Dogi
Via Cuneo 34
Tel: 0185-7241
Fax: 0185-772796.
This hotel, in a wonderful spot overlooking the sea, is surrounded by a splendid park. It is well known for its beautiful rooms, restaurant, salt-water swimming pool and solarium, its private beach and its nightclub during the summer. **LL–LLL**

Portofino
Splendido
Viale Baratta 13
Tel: 0185-269551
Fax: 0185-269614.
One of Italy's finest hotels. This hotel is a peaceful oasis along a street lined with olive trees, affording a splendid view of the Portofino promontory. Every comfort and great cuisine. **LLLL**

Rapallo
Hotel Europa
Via Milite Ignoto 2
Tel: 0185-669521
Fax: 0185-669847.
Part of the Turin Hotels group, this Art Nouveau hotel was restored to its former glory in 1996. Fine restaurant, fitness centre. **LLL**

San Remo
Grand Hotel Londra
Corso Matuzia 2
Tel: 0184-668000
Fax: 0184-668073.
Set on the seafront, close to the casino. Old, quiet and pleasant. **LL**
Royal
Corso Imperatrice 80
Tel: 0184-5391
Fax: 0184-661445.
Luxury hotel surrounded by terraced gardens filled with flowers and palm trees. Big, comfortable rooms overlooking the sea or hills. **LLLL**

Santa Margherita Ligure
Imperial Palace
Via Pagana 19
Tel: 0185-288991
Fax: 0185-284223.
Luxury, big hotel in the classic tradition, surrounded by a tropical garden. Old-fashioned decor with antique furnishings, big rooms and excellent service. **LLL–LLLL**

Sestri Levante
Grand Hotel dei Castelli
Via alla Penisola 26
Tel: 0185-485780/487220
Fax: 0185-44767.
Quiet and pleasant hotel in front of the church of S. Niccolò, surrounded by a big park and overlooking the sea. An elevator descends to the hotel's private beach. Service is excellent. **LLL**

Ventimiglia
La Riserva
Castel d'Appio 71
Tel: 0184-229533
Fax: 0184-229712.
5 km outside Ventimiglia, this is a small place with a wonderful view of the Riviera dei Fiori and the Costa Azzurra. Rooms are comfortable and courteous service. **LL**

EMILIA-ROMAGNA

Bologna
Grand Hotel Elite
Via Aurelio Saffi 36
Tel: 051-6491432
Fax: 051-6492426.
Very modern and comfortable, with one of the best restaurants in Bologna.

LL–LLL
Jolly
Piazza XX Settembre 2
Tel: 051-248921
Fax: 051-249764.
Near station and the Alitalia terminal. Large and comfortable. **LL–LLL**
Royal Carlton
Via Montebello 8
Tel: 051-249361
Fax: 051-249724.
This big central hotel is extremely comfortable but a little anonymous. Excellent service. **LL–LLLL**

Ferrara
Duchessa Isabella
Via Palestro 68/70
Tel: 0532-202121
Fax: 0532-202638.
This frescoed 16th-century *palazzo* features inlaid ceilings, a lovely garden, and Renaissance dishes for dinner. **LLL–LLLL**
Hotel Ripagrande
Via Ripagrande 21
Tel: 0532-765250
Fax: 0532-764377.
This Renaissance palace forms part of Abitare La Storia (Living History), a group of historic independent hotels (*see Hotel Groups, page 364*). Fine public rooms, good cuisine and a central location. **LL–LLL**

Parma
Grand Hotel Baglioni
Viale Piacenza 12/C
Tel: 0521-292929
Fax: 0521-292828.
Sophisticated modern hotel within walking distance of the historic centre. Decorated in Liberty style, with spacious bedrooms and a good restaurant. **LLL**
Villa Ducale
Via del Popolo 35/A
Tel: 0521-272727
Fax: 0521-780756.
Charming villa set in appealing grounds; welcoming. **LL**

SAN MARINO

La Grotta
Contrada Santa Croce 17
Tel: 0549-991214
Fax: 0549-992242.

This typical small city hotel is in a quiet side street in the historic centre of San Marino. All 13 rooms are big, prettily furnished and have TV and telephones. **L**

La Rocca
Salita alla Rocca 37
Tel: 0549-99116
Fax: 0549-992430.
This small, cheap hotel in the old town has 10 small but clean rooms. A magnificent panoramic view makes up for the lack of space. **L**

Locanda dell'Artista
Via del Dragone 18
Tel/fax: 0549-996024
Situated in the old part of town, Montegiardino. Just five comfortable rooms, two of which are suites. **LL**

Titano
Contrada del Collegio 31
Tel: 0549-991006
Fax: 0549-991375.
This comfortable hotel lies in the heart of the old town of San Marino. It is one of the best hotels of the town. The Titano has a spacious panoramic terrace and a recommendable restaurant. **LL**

THE ADRIATIC

Ravenna
Bisanzio
Via Salara 30
Tel: 0544-217111
Fax: 0544-32539.
Modern and comfortable hotel, with simple rooms and good service, close to the most important monuments. **LL**

Jolly
Piazza Mameli 1
Tel: 0544-35762
Fax: 0544-216055.
Hotel with excellent standards and a restaurant. **LL**

Rimini
Duomo
Via G. Bruno 28
Tel: 0541-24215.
Very fine hotel in the old town with comfortable and elegantly furnished rooms, a small garden and garage. **LL**

Grand Hotel
Via Ramusio 1
Tel: 0541-56000
Fax: 0541-56866.
Solid hotel with beautiful garden. The rooms are tastefully furnished with antique furniture. Guests are the rich and the beautiful. **LLLL**

Santarcangelo di Romagna (Rimini)
Hotel della Porta
Via Andrea Costa 85
Tel: 0541-622152
Fax: 0541-622168.
This comfortable hotel is situated in a small village, only 15 km west of Rimini. The carefully restored building consists of two houses. Spacious rooms are very well-looked after and equipped in the traditional style of the Emilia Romagna. **LL**

Where to Eat

What to Eat

The gentle lifestyle of Italy is partly a product of its civilised eating habits: eating and drinking in tranquillity at least twice a day are the norm here.

Italian breakfast (*colazione*) is usually light and consists of *cappuccino* (espresso and steamed milk) and a *brioche* (pastry), or simply *caffè* (black and strong espresso).

Except in the industrialised cities, *pranzo* (lunch) is the big meal of the day. It consists of *antipasto* (hors d'oeuvre), a *primo* (pasta, rice or soup) and a *secondo* (meat or fish with a vegetable – *contorno* – or salad). To follow comes cheese and/or fruit. Italians usually drink coffee (*espresso*) after lunch and/or a liqueur, such as *grappa, amaro* or *sambuca*.

Traditionally, dinner is similar to lunch, but lighter. However, in the cities people are tending to eat less at lunchtime and making dinner the major meal of the day.

Every region in Italy has its own typical dishes: Piedmont specialises in pheasant, hare, truffles and *zabaglione* (a hot dessert made with whipped egg yolks and Marsala wine); Lombardy is known for *risotto alla Milanese* (saffron and onions), minestrone, veal and *panettone* (a sweet, Christmas bread with sultanas and candied fruits); Trentino-Alto Adige is the place for dumplings and thick soups to keep out the cold. *See also the chapter on Rustic and Classic Cuisine, page 103.*

Where to Eat

Italy has thousands of restaurants, *trattorie* and *osterie*. If you do not want to have a complete meal, you can have a snack at the bar or at *tavole calde* and *rosticcerie* (grills).

If you go to a restaurant, don't order just a salad: the waiters may look down on you and treat you with disdain. If you think a complete meal is too big, forego the *antipasto*, but take a *primo* and a *secondo* at least.

The restaurants listed below have been recommended by Italian food writers and/or the authors of this guide. It is difficult to generalise about prices since much depends on the choice of wine and menu selection. Even noted chefs may offer a less expensive, but restricted, menu in conjunction with the main menu.

Price Guide

The price of a three-course meal for one, with half a bottle of house wine, is:
L = about L30,000 per head
LL = L30,000–50,000 per head
LLL = L50,000–70,000 per head
LLLL = L70,000–100,000 or more per head

VENICE

Castello
Al Covo
Campiello della Pescaria 3968
Tel: 041-5223812.
Enthusiastically-run restaurant serving fish fresh from the lagoon, wild duck (seasonal) and wonderful home-made desserts. Great wine list. Lunch is less expensive than dinner. Closed: Wednesday and Thursday. **LLLL**
Antica Sacrestia
Calle Sacrestia
Campo Santi Filippo e Giacomo
Tel: 041-5230749.
Set in an alley off Campo Santi Filippo e Giacomo, this old-fashioned restaurant and pizzeria has considerable charm. Apart from pizzas, it offers a choice of well-priced menus, with one based on fish, another Venetian and a third vegetarian. Closed: Monday. **LLL**

Dorsoduro
La Furatola
Calle Lunga San Barnaba 2879
Tel: 041-5208594.

Unpretentious restaurant where local gourmets go for fish and seafood. Closed: Thursday and sometimes Monday, also January and August. **LLLL**
Riviera
Zattere 1473
Tel: 041-5227621.
Good home-made pasta and fish. Weather permitting, tables are set outside, overlooking the island of Giudecca. Closed: Sunday and Monday. **LLL**
Taverna San Trovaso
Fondamenta Priuli 1016
Tel: 041-5203703.
Cheap, cheerful *taverna* for standard Italian cuisine. Closed: Monday. **LL**

Giudecca
Harry's Dolci
Fondamenta San Biagio 773
Tel: 041-5224844.
Similar food to Harry's Bar in San Marco, but cheaper. Specialities are the *dolci* (cakes), which are served all day. A terrace for summer over-looks the Giudecca. Closed: Tuesday and November–mid-March. **LLL–LLLL**
Hotel Cipriani
Giudecca 10
Tel: 041-5207744.
One of the finest city restaurants set within the most luxurious city hotel. The elegant restaurant spills out onto a glorious summer terrace. Dishes include *carpaccio*, clams with asparagus, scampi and *calamari*, and veal with artichokes; desserts are fresh and subtle, including sorbets and home-made pastries. The setting is exquisite, the service discreet and the prices high. Closed: early November–mid-March. **LLLL**

San Marco
Al Graspo de Ua
Calle de Bombaseri 5095
Tel: 041-5200150.
Close to the Rialto Bridge. This restaurant, under its wooden roof, is centuries old, and has a long tradition of excellent cooking. It is a delight for those seeking local colour. National cuisine. Closed: Monday and Tuesday in July and August. **LLLL**
Alle Colonnete
San Marco 987
Tel: 041-5237082.

Typical Venetian cuisine. **LLLL**
Antico Martini
Campo San Fantin 1983
Tel: 041-5224121.
Close to the site of the former Fenice opera house. Elegant and intimate, serving Venetian and international cuisine. Closed: all day Tuesday and Wednesday lunch. Reserve. **LLLL**
Caffè Quadri
Procuratie Vecchie
Piazza San Marco 120
Tel: 041-5289299.
As well as the famous bar, this is the setting for a fine restaurant, the only proper one on the Piazza, serving Venetian specialities as well as creative twists on classic Italian cuisine. Refined atmosphere and punctilious service. Innovative and traditional Venetian dishes. Prices are predictably high but acceptable by Venetian standards. Closed: Monday out of season. **LLLL**
Da Arturo
Calle degli Assassini 3656
Tel: 041-5286974.
Very small, and unusual for Venice as it does not serve fish. Excellent meat, pasta and salads. Open late. Closed: Sunday and three weeks in August. **LLL**
Harry's Bar
Calle Vallaresso 1323
Tel: 041-5285777.
This bar/restaurant was a favourite haunt of Hemingway; it is now mainly patronised by very wealthy Venetians, expatriates and American tourists. Good home-made pastas at exorbitant prices. **LLLL**
Trattoria da Fiore
Calle delle Botteghe
Campo Santo Stefano
Tel: 041-5235310.
This simple Venetian *trattoria* is exceptionally good value, considering its location in a little alley off chic Campo Santo Stefano. You can order snacks or a meal in the *bacaro* (traditional bar) or choose from a wider range of dishes in the adjoining dining room. Cosy and welcoming, with a good cold buffet on display. Closed: Tuesday. **LLL**
Vecia Carbonera
San Marco 4648
Tel: 041-5225479.
Rebuilt, but maintaining its 19th-

century ambience, with good Italian cooking. Closed: Thursday and Friday lunch. **LLL**

San Polo
Alla Rivetta
Campiello dei Meloni
Tel: 041-5231481.
This restaurant, lying between Campo San Polo and Sant'Aponal, is an exception to the rough and ready inns in the district. It's a reputable canal-side *trattoria* and bar serving good Venetian fare. Closed: Monday. **LLL**
Da Fiore
Calle del Scaleter 2202
San Polo
Tel: 041-721308.
Small restaurant near Campo San Polo. Well worth seeking out for its good food, wine and elegant ambience, which also attracts Venetian celebrities. Closed: Sunday and Monday. **LLLL**
Da Leoni
Londra Palace
Riva degli Schiavoni 4171
Tel: 041-5200533.
Venetian delicacies in an elegant ambience overlooking the island of San Giorgio. **LLLL**
Poste Vecie Antica Trattoria
Mercato del Pesce di Rialto 1608
Tel: 041-721822.
Inviting rustic *trattoria* specialising in fish from the nearby market and also home-made *ravioli*. Closed: Tuesday and 20 November–20 December. Reserve. **LLLL**
Trattoria alla Madonna
Calle della Madonna 594
Tel: 041-5223824.
This is a popular fish and seafood restaurant near the Rialto. It offers good value for Venice, and hence is always crowded – the service can be brusque. Closed: Wednesday. Reserve during the week. **LLLL**

Santa Croce
Antica Bessetta
Salizzada de Ca'Zusto 1395.
Tel: 041-721687.
Near San Giacomo dell'Orio, off the beaten track. Authentic family-run *trattoria* serving regional cuisine. Good value. Closed: Tuesday, Wednesday lunch, Christmas and 15 July–16 August. **LLL**

VENETO

Padova (Padua)
Dotto
Via Squarcione 23
Tel: 049-8751490.
Classic furniture, typical cuisine. Try *pasta e fagioli* (pasta and beans) and *baccalà* (stockfish). Closed: Sunday evening, Monday and August. Reserve. **LL**
L'anfora
Via dei Soncin 13
Tel: 049-656629.
This old *osteria*, behind the Piazza delle Erbe, impresses with its constantly changing menu (according to season) and with moderate prices. Outside normal eating hours the bar does a good choice of snacks. **L**

Verona
12 Apostoli
Vicolo Corticella San Marco 3
Tel: 045-596999.
One of the best restaurants in Italy, this is located in an ancient building decorated with frescoes by Casarini. Closed: Sunday evening, Monday, Christmas and mid-June to mid-July. Reserve. **LLLL**
Locanda di Castelvecchio
Corso Cavour 49
Tel: 045-8030097.
This elegant restaurant on a beautiful corner of the old town still has the ambience of an old *osteria*. Friendly service, exquisite Veronic cuisine and an excellent wine list assure a good evening out. Closed: Tuesday and Wednesday afternoon. **LL**
Nuovo Marconi
Via Fogge 4
Tel: 045-591910.
Elegant place serving regional classic cuisine, especially fish. Closed: Sunday and August. **LLL**

FRIULI-VENEZIA GIULIA

Trieste
Al Bragozzo
Riva N. Sauro 22
Tel: 040-303001.
Traditional seafood restaurant. Closed: Monday and 3 weeks in June/July. **LLL**

Antica Trattoria Suban
Via Comici 2
Tel: 040-54368.
Friendly and simple, with a summer bower. Good regional cuisine. Closed: Monday lunch and all day Tuesday. Reserve. **LLL**
San Marco Caffè Storico
Via Battisti 18
Tel: 040-371373.
The grandest *belle époque* café in the city. Closed: Monday. **LL**

Udine
Al Passeggio
Viale Volontari della Libertà 49
Tel: 0432-46216.
Tastefully furnished *trattoria* with a family atmosphere and excellent cuisine of the region. The *fritto di verdure* is recommended. Closed: Wednesday. **LL**
Alla Vedova
Via Tavagnacco 9
Tel: 0432-470291.
Very old Friulian restaurant, with outdoor tables in summer. Good traditional cooking. Closed: Sunday evening and Monday. Reserve. **LL**

TRENTINO-ALTO ADIGE

Bolzano
Da Abramo
Grieser Platz 16
Tel: 0471-280141.
Set in the old town hall, and with a garden, serving good regional cuisine, exclusively fish. Closed: Sunday. **LLL**

Civezzano
Maso Cantanghel
Via della Madonnina 33 – Loc. Forti
Tel: 0461/858714.
This posh restaurant is situated 7 km northeast of Trento. The simple cuisine from Trident comes to full effect in this beautifully renovated and tastefully furnished farmhouse. Especially recommended is the daily changing menu and the excellent desserts. The wine list includes the best products of the region as well as wines from their own vineyard Maso Cantanghel. Closed: Saturday and Sunday. Reserve. **LLL**

Trento
Alla Grotta
Vicolo S. Marco 6
Tel: 0461/987197.
Very popular pizza place with
wooden oven. Especially busy at
lunchtime, when the locals come
here. The pizza and pasta dishes
not only taste sublime, but are also
filling. **L**
Chiesa
Via San Marco 64
Tel: 0461-238766.
On the first floor of a 17th-century
palace with a cloister. Very refined.
Closed: Sunday. **LLL**
Locanda Gius Port'Aquila
Via Cervara 66
Tel: 0461/230420.
The Port'Aquila of the family Gius is
one of the best *trattorie* of Trento.
You will mainly find dishes from
Trident on the menu. All of them are
to be recommended. Daughter Lucia
is in charge of the elegant
restaurant Maso Cantanghel (*see
above*). Closed: Sunday. **LL**
Osteria Il Cappello
Vicolo San Marco 8 – Piazzetta
Anfiteatro 3.
Tel: 0461/235850.
Only a few years old, this small
restaurant is situated opposite the
Pizzeria alla Grotta. The owners
manage it with a lot of enthusiasm.
The menu is small but exquisite, the
service excellent and the atmosphere
friendly but quiet. The regional dishes
and fish dishes are recommended. **LL**

MILAN

Al Mercante
Piazza di Mercanti 17
Tel: 02-8052198.
Friendly restaurant overlooking the
piazza. In summer you can eat out-
doors under a very old *loggia*.
Closed: Sunday and all of August.
Reserve. **LLL**
Bistro Duomi
Piazza del Duomo
Tel: 02-877120.
The temple of Italian cuisine, the
best in Italy. Modern ambience. For
the élite. Closed: all day Sunday,
Monday lunch and 3 weeks in
August. Reserve. **LLLL**

Boeucc
Piazza Belgioioso 2
Tel: 02-76020224.
A temple of Milanese gastronomy.
Closed: all day Saturday and
Sunday lunch. **LLLL**
Brasera Meneghina
Via Imperia 7
Tel: 02-89503255.
Genuine *osteria* of old Milan, dating
back to the 17th century. It features
a fireplace and a small porch painted
with frescoes, and offers outdoor
dining in summer. Closed: Saturday
lunch, Sunday and 2 weeks in
August. **LLL**
Casa Fontana
Piazza Carbonari 5
Tel: 02-6704710.
About 25 different types of *risotto*
to taste. Closed: Saturday lunch
and all day Monday. **LLL**
Dolce Vita
Via Bergamini 11
Tel: 02-583303843.
Romantic and sophisticated spot with
candles and coffered ceilings. Lom-
bard specialities, *nouvelle cuisine*
and gourmet menus (less pricey at
lunchtime). Closed: Sunday. **LLLL**
Gran San Bernardo
Via Borghese 14
Tel: 02-3319000.
Large and friendly restaurant where
some of the best regional cooking is
served. Try *casseoeula* (a stew of
pork, sausages and carrots served
with cornbread) and *polenta*. Closed:
Sunday and August. Reserve. **LLLL**
La Bella Pisana
Via Sottocorno 17
Tel: 02-76021803.
Pleasant ambience, with a garden
for summer. Padana plain cooking
and fresh fish. Closed: Tuesday and
August. Reserve. **LLL**
La Scaletta
Piazza Stazione di Porta
Genova 3
Tel: 02-58100290.
Modern ambience, with a library
and international level cuisine. Very
fashionable. Closed: Sunday,
Monday lunch. Reserve. **LLLL**.
Savini
Galleria Vittorio Emanuele 11
Tel: 02-72003433.
Exquisite decor, ultra-professional
service and typical classic Italian

cuisine. Close to Duomo. Closed:
Sunday and August. Reserve. **LLLL**
Taverna Gran Sasso
Via Principessa Clotilde 10
Tel: 02-6597578.
Kitsch restaurant, serving typical
Abruzzese cooking; live music. Closed:
Sunday and August. Reserve. **LLLL**

LOMBARDY

Bergamo
Agnello d'Oro
Via Gombito 22
Tel: 035-249883.
Good regional food in an old hotel
in the upper part of town. Closed:
Sunday evening, all day Monday and
January. Reserve. **LLL**

Price Guide

The price of a three-course meal
for one, with half a bottle of
house wine, is:
L = about L30,000 per head
LL = L30,000–50,000 per head
LLL = L50,000–70,000 per head
LLLL = L70,000–100,000 or
more per head

Lio Pellegrini
Via San Tomaso 47
Tel: 035-247813.
Atmospheric former sacristy,
serving Tuscan specialities.
Closed: Sunday lunch and all day
Monday. **LL**
Taverna Colleoni e dell'Angelo
Piazza Vecchia 7
Tel: 035-232596.
Lombard specialities. **LLLL**
Trattoria del Teatro
Piazza Mascheroni 3
Tel: 035-238862.
Nineteenth-century furniture, plus
simple, but delicious food. Closed:
Monday. **L**

Mantova (Mantua)
Cigno
Piazza Carlo d'Arco 1
Tel: 0376-327101.
In a wonderful piazza, in an ancient
building. The service is as excellent
as the regional cooking. Closed:
Monday and Tuesday. Reserve. **LLL**

Pavia
Ferrari da Tino
Via dei Mille 111
Tel: 0382-539025.
Old-fashioned, homely *trattoria*.
Closed: Sunday evening, all day
Monday and 15 July–15 August. **LL**

VALLE D'AOSTA

Aosta
Le Foyer
Corso Ivrea 146
Tel: 0165-32136.
Set just outside Aosta, this
restaurant offers excellent fish and
Italian cheeses. Closed: Monday
evening and all day Tuesday. **LLL**
Vecchia Aosta
Piazza Porte Pretoriane 4
Tel: 0165-361186.
Set within part of the old city gate-
way, this restaurant serves French
and regional specialities, *ravioli*,
various stuffed pastas and tournedos
with juniper berries. Closed:
Wednesday from October–May. **LLL**

Breuil-Cervinia
Les Neiges d'Antan
Località Cret Perrères
Statale 406
Tel: 0166-948775.
Situated on a mountain 4 km from
Breuil-Cervinia, this quiet house has
only a few rooms, and serves typical
Valdostana cuisine. Try the *fonduta*.
Closed: September–November and
May–June. Reserve. **LLL**

Gignod
Locanda La Clusaz
Località La Clusaz
Statale Gran San Bernardo
Tel: 0165-56075.
Set north of Aosta, this charming
inn has a number of rooms as well
as a frescoed, medieval interior.
Restaurant specialities include grain
soups, *polenta* and dishes made
with chestnuts or bacon. Closed:
Tuesday. In low season open
Monday–Friday only for dinner. **LLL**

Saint-Pierre
Les écureuils
Località Homené-Sainte Marguerite.
Tel: 0165-903831.

This small restaurant belongs to the
farmhouse of the Gontier family.
Nearly everything on the menu is a
product from their own farm and of
excellent quality. Some products, for
example the home-produced cheese,
jam and the preserved fruits of the
wood, are sold as well. **LL**

Valgrisenche
Perret
Località Bonne 2
Tel: 0165-97107.
In this cosy restaurant with its impres-
sive fireside, simple typical regional
meals are served; the four-course
menu changes daily. Reserve. **LL**

PIEDMONT

Turin
Del Cambio
Piazza Carignano 2
Tel: 011-546690.
Opened in 1757, one of the most
beautiful restaurants in Italy.
Nineteenth-century furniture and
atmosphere. International and
national cuisine. Closed: Sunday
and August. Reserve. **LLLL**
La Capannina
Via Donati 1
Tel: 011-545405.
The ambience is rustic, though this
restaurant is set in a fine *palazzo*.
The food is strictly cooked in the
Langarola style (the Langhe are a
part of Piemonte). The *fritto misto*
is superb. Closed: Sunday and
August. Reserve. **LLL**
Ostu Bacu
Corso Vercelli 226
Tel: 011-2464579.
Modern ambience. Come here to
taste plain, old-fashioned
Piemontese cooking. Closed:
Sunday and August. Reserve. **LLL**
Spada Reale
Via Principe Amedeo 53
Tel: 011-8171363.
Modern-style, Tuscan and Piemon-
tese cuisine. Closed: Saturday lunch
and all day Sunday. Reserve. **LLL**
Tre Galline
Via Bellezia 37
Tel: 011-546833.
Typical old-fashioned *piola* (a
meeting-place to drink wine and eat

snacks), serving regional cooking.
Closed: all day Sunday and Monday
lunch. Reserve. **LLL**
Villa Sassi
Strada Traforo del Pino 47
Tel: 011-8980556.
In a cardinal's villa, this is a
restaurant for VIPs, with an attached
hotel (only 17 rooms). Exclusive,
with superb cuisine. Closed:
Sunday. Reserve. **LLLL**

THE LAKES

Lago di Como
Antica Osteria Casa di Lucia
Via Lucia 27
Lecco
Tel: 0341-494594.
This old, established *osteria* in the
old part of the town Acquate has a
big restaurant with wooden tables
and a fireplace. In the summer, you
can enjoy your meal outside under
the beautiful pergola. Apart from
simple snacks, you will find dishes
that are typical of the region on the
menu, e.g. *polenta* with mushroom
and *gulasch*. Closed: Monday. **LL**
Santo Stefano
Piazza XI Febbraio 3, Lenno.
Tel: 0344-55434.
Restaurant with a view of one of the
most beautiful bays of Lake Como.
Known for its excellent fish dishes.
Closed: Monday. **LL**

Lago di Garda
Osteria Solferino
Via Solferino 18
Bardolino
Tel: 045-7211020.
It is not easy to find a good restaurant
at Lake Garda, which is less touristy
than the other major lakes. The
Osteria Solferino is one of the few
praiseworthy exceptions. The simple
cuisine is good and down to earth.
One of the specialities is *trippa* (tripe)
in *umido*. Closed: Tuesday. **L–LL**

Lago Maggiore
Osteria del Castello
Piazza Castello 9
Intra (Verbania)
Tel: 0323-516579.
In the historic old town, one of the
oldest restaurants in Intra. On the

menu, you will find tasty snacks and also a small selection of delicious traditional dishes. **L–LL**
Osteria dell'angolo
Via Garibaldi 35
Pallanza (Verbania)
Tel: 0323-556362.
Cosy restaurant with simple wooden tables and uncovered bricks. Recommended is the fish and always the freshly prepared desserts. **LL**

LIGURIA & RIVIERA

Genoa
Antica Osteria del Bari
Via Quarto 12
Tel: 010-387478.
Historic restaurant where Garibaldi once ate, inside a fortress over-looking the sea. Typical Genoese cuisine. Closed: Monday. **LLLL**
Da Rina
Mura delle Grazie 3R
Tel: 010-2466475.
Traditional *trattoria* with good cooking. Closed: Monday, Christmas, Easter and August. Reserve. **LL**
Gran Gotto
Viale Brigata Bisagno 69
Tel: 010-564344.
Near Stazione Brignole. Classic and elegant, with a rustic atmosphere and regional cooking. Try the *trenette al pesto*. Closed: Saturday lunch and all day Sunday. Reserve. **LLLL**
La Britta nella Pergola
Via Casaregis 52R
Tel: 010-588543.
Comfortable atmosphere, regional cooking. Closed: Monday and August. **LLLL**
Panson
Piazza delle Erbe 5
Tel: 010-2468903.
This charming Genoese restaurant is situated in a safe but slightly dilapidated square close to Via XX Settembre. All Genoese dishes are on offer, including *pansoti al sugo di noci* (pasta with walnuts), and the famous *pesto alla genovese* (pasta with basil sauce). Closed: Sunday evening and August. **LLL**
Piro
Salita Bertora 5/R
Tel: 010-802304.
Elevated restaurant offering views of

Genoa. This is a typical simple *trattoria*, with pretty good Genoese cooking. Closed: Sunday evening, all day Monday and 15 August–15 September. **LL**
Zeffirino
Via XX Settembre 20.
Tel: 010-591990.
In the centre of the city, with modern furniture and mixed cuisine. Reserve. **LLL**

Lerici
Conchiglia
Via Mazzini 2
Tel: 0187-967334.
Along the seafront, with especially fresh fish. Closed: Wednesday and 2 weeks in November. **LLL**

Portofino
Il Pitosforo
Molo Umberto I 9
Tel: 0185-269020.
Meeting place for yachtspeople. Ligurian specialities as well as international cooking. Closed: Sunday and 1 January–28 February. Reserve. **LLLL**
Stella
Molo Umberto I 3
Tel: 0185-269007.
Marine atmosphere; regional cooking. Closed: Wednesday and 6 January–3 March. Reserve. **LLL**

San Remo
Bacchus
Via Roma 65
Tel: 0184-530990.
Well looked after *enoteca* with simple delicious dishes from Liguria. Recommended are the pasta and the fish dishes, such as cuttlefish. Closed: Sunday. **LL**
Da Giannino
Corso Trento e Trieste 23
Tel: 0184-504014.
Comfortable establishment offering high-class cooking. Closed: Sunday evening and Monday. Reserve. **LLLL**

Vernazza
Gambero Rosso
Piazza Marconi 7
Tel: 0187-812265.
Close to the port: a small *osteria* noted for its seafood. Closed: Monday and mid-Dec–Feb. **LLL**

Vicenza
Cinzia e Valerio
Piazzetta Porta Padova 65/67
Tel: 0444-505213.
Set on the ancient city walls, an elegant restaurant with fish specialities. **LL–LLL**

EMILIA ROMAGNA

Bologna
Antica Osteria Romagnola
Via Rialto 13
Tel: 051-263699.
Hearty cuisine in a lively atmosphere, with live music in the evenings. Courtyard open in the summer. Closed: Monday. **LLL**
Cantina Bentivoglio
Via Mascarella 4/b
Tel: 051-265416.
Set in the cellars of a *palazzo*, this boisterous restaurant attracts a young crowd. Emilian specialities; live music. Closed: Monday. **LL**
Da Bertino e Figlio
Via delle Lame 55
Tel: 051-522230.
Quirky Emilian *trattoria*, with good cooking, especially the *gnocchi*. Closed: Monday evening and 1–15 August. **LL**
Villa Orsi
Località Funo di Argelato (13 km from Bologna)
Tel: 051-861855.
In an 18th-century villa with a beautiful porch. Both regional and international dishes are available. Try the roasted meat specialities. Closed: Saturday, Sunday and August. Reserve. **LL**

Ferrara
Romantica
Via Ripagrande 36
Tel: 0532-765975.
Classic Italian cuisine with Ferrarese dishes, too. Set in the historic quarter. Closed: Wednesday and two weeks in July. **LL**

Modena
Da Enzo
Via Coltellini 17
Tel: 059-225177.
Dating back to 1912, this place has been tastefully renovated. Typical

Modenese cooking. Closed: Monday and August. **LL**

Fini
Piazzetta San Francesco
Tel: 059-223314.
Classic, elegant, but homely, with traditional regional cuisine. Try *bolliti* (boiled meat). Closed: Monday, Tuesday and August. Reserve. **LLLL**

Parma
La Filoma
Via Marzo 20
Tel: 0521-206181.
Refined, with 17th-century furniture, offering traditional food and service. Closed: Tuesday and August. **LLL**

SAN MARINO

Grotta dei Nani
Contrada dei Magazzeni.
Tel: 0549-992636/990312.
The "gnomes grotto" dabbles with kitsch furniture and pictures of Snow White and pals. Traditional regional dishes are served here. Closed: Thursday in winter. **LL**

Price Guide

The price of a three-course meal for one, with half a bottle of house wine, is:
L = about L30,000 per head
LL = L30,000–50,000 per head
LLL = L50,000–70,000 per head
LLLL = L70,000–100,000 or more per head

Righi La Taverna
Piazza della Libertà.
Tel: 0549-991196/991970.
Rustic, but good, food. Closed: Wednesday in winter. **LL**

THE ADRIATIC

Ravenna
Al Gallo
Via Maggiore 87
Tel: 0544-213775.
Wonderful pergola in summer. Good (not exceptional) local food. Closed: Monday, Tuesday and Sunday evening. **L–LL**

Rimini
Acero Rosso
Viale Tiberio 11
Tel: 0541-53577.
Refined and elegant fish restaurant with excellent traditional cuisine enlivened by innovative influences. **LLLL**

Osteria de Borg
Via dei Forzieri 12
Tel: 0541-56071.
Situated in the heart of Rimini, in San Giuliano, the old part of the city. The menu changes according to the season. The home-made pasta with vegetable sauce is delicious, as are the main course stew dishes which include traditional favourites suchas *trippa* (tripe) and *baccalà*. Closed: Monday. **LL**

Osteria di Santa Colomba
Via A. di Duccio 2/4
Tel: 0541-780048.
This cosy *osteria* is situated in the medieval belltower of the Santa Colomba church. Not only is the historic atmosphere authentic but also the excellent cuisine of Emilia Romagna and Tuscany. Recommended are vegetables of the season, home-made pastas and the varied meat dishes. **LL**

Culture

Music

The very famous La Scala in Milan is a must for every opera fan. Ballets and concerts are also held there. During the summer, parks are crowded with people enjoying a variety of outdoor cultural events sponsored by the city.

In Turin, classical music is at its peak from late August until the end of September, when Settembre Musica, an international music festival, featuring the best national and international performers, takes over the town.

For information on opera in Milan, see the box on La Scala.

VERONA

For more than 80 years, a world-famous opera festival has been held every year – in July and August – in the big **Roman arena** (Piazza Bra). The marvellous open-air acoustics and great lighting always make it a memorable occasion. Classics like *Madame Butterfly*, *Tosca and Turandot*, Bizet's *Carmen von Bizet* and Verdi's *Aida* are performed.

An evening at the opera in Verona is not only for opera lovers, but is one of the major musical events in the world. But everything has its price: L42,000 for an unreserved stone step, right at the back and high up (*Gradinata*); L180,000 for a numbered seat on the step (*Gradinata numerata*); L210,000 for a second sector stall (*Poltrona*); L290,000 for a first sector stall (*Poltronissima*).

The information office is at: Arena di Verona, Piazza Bra 28, 37121 Verona, tel: 045-8051811, fax: 045-8011566.

The box office is in Via Dietro

La Scala

La Scala, in Milan, is one of the most famous opera houses in the world. For more than two centuries – it celebrated its 200th anniversary in 1978 – La Scala has dominated the European opera scene. It was here that the music of some of the great composers, including Verdi, Bellini, Rossini and Donizetti, was first played.

From the outside, this world-famous opera house looks rather small and insignificant. The inside, however, impresses, with its heavy chandeliers in the foyer and a splendid concert hall which is known for its excellent accustics. The opening evening of the season (usually 7 December) is the city's main cultural event.

● The La Scala information office (*biglietteria*) is at Teatro alla Scala, Via Filodrammatici 2, tel: 02-72003744. Open 10am–6pm. It is hidden in a side entrance. Here you will get information on the programme, the prices, where and when to obtain tickets, and how to pay.

● For 24-hour recorded ticket reservations, tel: 02-860787. Within 48 hours of making the reservation by telephone, you need to send a confirmation by fax. The tickets will then be sent to you by recorded mail. Payment is by credit card or cheque.

Theatres

For information on theatre performances, ask the city's APT (Azienda Promozione Turistica) or check the local newspaper. Ticket prices vary depending on the show and venue.

In Milan, you can go to the **Piccolo Teatro**, Via Rovello 2, and its off-shoot, the **Teatro Studio**, Via Rivoli 6, as well as the new **Nuovo Piccolo Teatro** next door (booking number for all three theatres: 02-77333222).

Anfiteatro 6/B (in front of the Arena wing), tel: 045-8005151, fax: 045-8013287. Open for ticket reservations and sales Monday–Friday 9am–midday and 3.15–5.45pm, Saturday 9am–midday; on performance days open to 9pm. Ticket reservations can also be made by mail, enclosing a bank draft or Eurocheque with the corresponding amount, marking the date of the performance, seat sector and number of tickets desired. It's also possible to book by phone. Major credit cards are accepted.

VENICE

Venice's **La Fenice** opera house is unfortunately closed at present, following a devastating fire in 1996. It is being rebuilt and is due to reopen during 2000. However, a dispute between rival building firms may delay the project. You should check locally for current status.

Nightlife

Late Spots

Nightlife in Italy follows the American and English fashions. There are many nightclubs, pubs and discos where young people gather to listen to music, dance and talk. Many of these places go in and out of popularity (or in and out of business) in the space of a few months, so check details in local newspapers or listings magazines.

In recent years, Milan has been tops for hip nightlife, with its rock and discos. Venice is less of a city for nightlife and many people prefer sitting in cafés and walking through the beautiful, labyrinthine streets.

Below is a list of only the more up-to-date clubs:

Milan

Nightlife, of the hot, youthful variety, is centred on the Navigli district, the canal quarter. It is enough to turn up at night and see what is on offer, from restaurants with live music to outré clubs.

Acqua Sporca
Performances of 1940s-style big bands, every night. In the Navigli area.
Beau Geste
Piazza Velasca 4.
Tel: 02-8900692.
Part-club, part-disco, with music for most tastes.
Café Teatro Nobel
Via Asciano Sforza 81.
Tel: 02-89511746.
Shows, jazz and cabaret.
Capolinea
Via Lodovico Il Moro 119.
Tel: 02-89122024.
All big-name be-bop bands meet here. It is possible to eat while listening to the music.
El Brellin
Via Alzaia.
Tel: 02-58101351.

Sophisticated piano bar and restaurant in the Navigli area.
Le Scimmie
Via Asciano Sforza 49.
Traditional good jazz in the Navigli area.

Turin
The Big Club
Corso Brescia 28.
New wave disco, rock and jazz concerts.

Turin Cafés

In Turin, the best nightlife from a visitor's point of view lies in the seductive 19th-century cafés. The most famous are **Baratti Milano** in Piazza Castello, and **Caffè Torino** in Piazza San Carlo (well-known for its cocktails).

Venice
Al Teatro
San Marco 1916,
Campo San Fantin.
This bar is situated right next to the Gran Teatro La Fenice and is open until deep in the night. You can end the evening here after a visit to the theatre.
Vino Vino
San Marco 2007/a, Calle del Caffetier.
A cut above the competition, this elegant wine bar offers an exquisite selection of wines from all over Italy.

Festivals

Special Events

The year is packed with special events, some linked to festivals of the Catholic church, others to the changing seasons. Every little village in Italy has its own wonderful festivals, so take every opportunity to attend. Many are associated with the harvest (especially wine) or to local products (*polenta*, *prosciutto*). The remainder tend to be historical re-enactments linked to jousting or to costumed cavalcades.

Calendar

Here are some of the highlights in the festival calendar:

Carnevale:
This period of festivities preceding Lent (February and March) is celebrated everywhere, particularly in Venice.

Biennale:
A major exhibition of international modern art, held in Venice every June–October in even-numbered years.

Festa del Redentore:
Also staged in Venice, on the evening of the third Saturday in July. A bridge of boats is built across the Giudecca Canal to the Redentore – the church which was built in gratitude for deliverance from plague in 1567. People row out to picnic on the water and watch wonderful firework displays set off from Giudecca island.

International Film Festival:
Once again in Venice, this is held at the Lido, at the end of August each year.

Hiking and Camping

National Parks

Italy has some stunningly beautiful national parks, including:

Parco Nazionale del Gran Paradiso
Home of the last steinbocks and chamois in Italy, this Alpine park is the oldest in the country and covers 72,000 hectares (178,000 acres). Spreading over parts of Valle d'Aosta and Piedmont, it has plenty of refuges and trekking facilities, and is a magnet for nature lovers. Tel: 0124-901070.

Parco Nazionale dello Stelvio
This is the biggest park in Italy (135,000 hectares/333,600 acres). It lies close to Switzerland and is rich in forests and animals. The mountains are wonderful and there are plenty of hotels. Tel: 0342-910100.

Parco Nazionale dell'Abruzzo
Here the last brown bear in Italy lives in remote splendour in one of the highest sections of the Apennines. Tel: 0863-91955.

The Alps

If you would like to go hiking in the mountains, pick up a map showing the network of walking paths with more than 80 overnight areas with shelters. Paths are marked with numerous red signs and distinctive small flags. Every stage calls for 5–7 hours of hiking time at an average of about 1,000 metres (3,300 ft) in altitude.

At the overnight rest areas there are shelters with double-decker bunks, essential services and a kitchen. The shelters are generally situated in inhabited localities, where it is possible to buy food, phone home, rest for a day, visit historical/ethnographic museums, chat with the inhabitants and, last but not least, eat a good meal at an inn.

An itinerary can last a month, a week or a day. From the Maritime Alps in the west to Lake Maggiore, on a route stretching for 650km (400 miles) that spans five provinces, the hiker crosses many splendid parks, such as the Gran Paradiso, the Orsiera-Rocciavrè, the Alta Val Pesio and the Argentera.

All the areas are open to the public July–September. For detailed information, call the GTA **Information Office**, Via Barbaroux 1, Turin, tel: 011-5624477.

Sport

Spectator Sports

Soccer

The national sport in Italy is soccer. Almost every city and village has its own team. The most important national championship is the **"Serie A"** (First Division). The winner of this competition is eligible to play in a kind of European championship, the "Champions' League", against the top teams of other European nations.

The "Serie A" championship is played September–May, and each of the 16 teams has to play the other teams twice.

The most successful Italian soccer team is **Juventus FC** from Turin, followed by **Internazionale** ("Inter") from Milan. But many other cities are blessed with successful sides, including Verona, Parma, Florence and Rome (which, like Milan, has two teams – in this case Lazio and Roma).

If you would like to see a game, check the newspaper to find out which team is playing, and where. Remember that it is very difficult to get tickets if the match is an important one. Ticket prices vary according to the importance of the team, the game, and the location of the seat you want. Unlike in some other European countries, matches tend to be safe, family affairs.

Motor Racing

The second passion of the Italians is represented by cars and speed. Formula One races attract people interested in the sophisticated technology and the coupling of man and car. This sport attracts mostly a TV audience because it is expensive to go around the world to see the races.

In Italy citizens support the red cars built by Ferrari. There is always a large crowd at the circuits in **Imola** (where the San Marino Grand Prix is held) and **Monza** (Italian Grand Prix). Although the car industry is centred on Turin, motor racing is based in the regions of Lombardy and Emilia-Romagna.

Other Sports

Almost all other sport is enjoyed in Italy, including basketball, golf, water polo, horse racing, rugby union, rowing and sailing. In addition, the Alps, Dolomites and the Apennines provide plenty of skiing opportunities.

May is an important month for sport in Italy. The *Giro d'Italia* cycle race, a major event on the cycling circuit, is staged; the Italian Open tennis tournament is held at the Foro Italico in Rome; and equestrian sports followers enjoy their major competition of the year, which takes place in Rome's Villa Borghese gardens.

If you are interested in buying tickets for any match or event, buy the pink *Gazzetta dello Sport* newspaper, where everything under the sun about sports is listed.

Shopping

Murano glass, hand-blown in Venice, is distinctly gaudy but a popular buy. Also look out for colourful carnival masks, to wear or to hang up.

Bologna
Bologna is one of the leading shopping centres in Italy and is, after Milan, the second city for clothes and shoes. The classic shopping areas in the city centre are **Via Rizzoli, Via dell' Independenza, Via Ugo Bassi, Via Farini, Via Santo Stefano, Via Massimo d'Azeglio** and under the arcade of the **Pavaglione**.

Turin
Turin offers excellent opportunities for shopping, especially for fashion and antiquities. The most exclusive boutiques and finest shops are to be found under the arcades of **Piazza San Carlo**, in the **Galleria San Frederico** and along **Via Roma**. Moderate priced shops as well as a big department store are situated in **Via Lagrange**, which runs parallel to Via Roma. Lovers of antiquities will want to explore the streets between Piazza Cavour and Via della Rocca, an especially attractive area of Turin.

Language

Shopping Areas

Milan
Milan is Italy's premier centre for international fashion and the nation's manufactured products. For those with expensive tastes, the most chic and elegant streets for shopping are: **Via Montenapoleone, Via Spiga** and **Via S Andrea**, all near the Duomo and La Scala. These streets feature such fine stores as Krizia, Giò Moretti, Trussardi, Kenzo, Sanlorenzo, Giorgio Armani and Ferragamo, as well as Versace, Gucci, Ermenegildo Zegna, Comme des Garçons, Valentino, Dolce e Gabbana, Hermès, Chanel, Moschino, Prada, Ferre and Fendi.

Venice
The most exclusive shopping area in Venice is the **Via XXII Marzo** and the streets around **St Mark's Square**. The best local shopping areas are the Rialto Bridge and San Polo. A market is held on the **Lido** on Tuesday morning.

Bargains to shop for include shoes, clothes, gifts and fur coats.

Language Tips

Italian is supplemented by regional dialects. In large cities and tourist centres you will find many people who speak English, French or German. In fact, due to the massive emigration over the last 100 years, you may encounter fluent speakers of foreign languages. Do not be surprised if you are addressed in a New York, Melbourne, Brussels or Bavarian accent: the speaker may have spent time working abroad.

It is well worth buying a good phrase book or dictionary, but the following will help you get started. Since this glossary is aimed at non-linguists, we have opted for the simplest options rather than the most elegant Italian.

Basic Communication

Yes *Sì*
No *No*
Thank you *Grazie*
Many thanks *Mille grazie/tante grazie/molte grazie*
You're welcome *Prego*
Alright/Okay/That's fine *Va bene*
Please *Per favore* or *per cortesia.*
Excuse me (to get attention) *Scusi* (singular), *Scusate* (plural)
Excuse me (to get through a crowd) *Permesso*
Excuse me (to attract attention, e.g. of a waiter) *Senta!*
Excuse me (sorry) *Mi scusi*
Wait a minute! *Aspetta!*
Could you help me? (formal) *Potrebbe aiutarmi?*
Certainly *Ma certo*
Can I help you? (formal) *Posso aiutarLa?*
Can you show me...? *Può indicarmi...?*

Clothing Size Chart

Women's dresses:

Italian	UK	US
38	8	6
40	10	8
42	12	10
44	14	12

Men's shirts:

Italian	UK	US
36	14	14
38	15	15
41	16	16
43	17	17

Can you help me? *Può aiutarmi, per cortesia?*
I need ... *Ho bisogno di ...*
I'm lost *Mi sono perso*
I'm sorry *Mi dispiace*
I don't know *Non lo so*
I don't understand *Non capisco*
Do you speak English/French/ German? *Parla inglese/francese/ tedesco?*
Could you speak more slowly, please? *Può parlare piú lentamente, per favore?*
Could you repeat that please? *Può ripetere, per piacere?*
slowly/quietly *piano*
here/there *qui/lá*
What? *Cosa?*
When/why/where? *Quando/perchè/dove?*
Where is the lavatory? *Dov'è il bagno?*

Greetings

Hello (Good day) *Buon giorno*
Good afternoon/evening *Buona sera*
Good night *Buona notte*
Goodbye *Arrivederci*
Hello/Hi/Goodbye (familiar) *Ciao*
Mr/Mrs/Miss *Signor/Signora/Signorina*
Pleased to meet you (formal) *Piacere di conoscerLa*
I am English/American *Sono inglese/americano*
Irish/Scottish/Welsh *irlandese/scozzese/gallese*
Canadian/Australian *canadese/australiano*
I'm here on holiday *Sono qui in vacanza*

Is it your first trip to Milan/Rome? *É il Suo primo viaggio a Milano/Roma?*
Do you like it here? (formal) *Si trova bene qui?*
How are you (formal/informal)? *Come sta/come stai?*
Fine thanks *Bene, grazie*
See you later *A più tardi*
See you soon *A presto*
Take care *Stia bene*
New acquaintances are likely to ask you:
Do you like Italy/Florence/ Rome/Venice/my city? *Le piace Italia/Firenze/Roma/ Venezia/la mia città?*
I like it a lot (is the correct answer) *Mi piace moltissimo.*
It's wonderful (an alternative answer) *È meravigliosa/favolosa.* (Both responses can be applied to food, beaches, the view, etc.)

Telephone Calls

the area code *il prefisso telefonico*
I'd like to make a reverse charges call *Vorrei fare una telefonata a carico del destinatario*
May I use your telephone, please? *Posso usare il telefono?*
Hello (on the telephone) *Pronto*
My name's *Mi chiamo/Sono*
Could I speak to...? *Posso parlare con...?*
Sorry, he/she isn't in *Mi dispiace, è fuori*
Can he call you back? *Può richiamarla?*
I'll try again later *Riproverò più tardi*
Can I leave a message? *Posso*

lasciare un messaggio?
Please tell him I called *Gli dica, per favore, che ho telefonato*
Hold on *Un attimo, per favore*
A local call *una telefonata locale*
Can you speak up please? *Può parlare più forte, per favore?*

In the Hotel

Do you have any vacant rooms? *Avete camere libere?*
I have a reservation *Ho fatto una prenotazione*
I'd like... *Vorrei...*
a single/double room (with a double bed) *una camera singola/doppia (con letto matrimoniale)*
a room with twin beds *una camera a due letti*
a room with a bath/shower *una camera con bagno/doccia*
for one night *per una notte*
for two nights *per due notti*
We have one with a double bed *Ne abbiamo una matrimoniale.*
Could you show me another room please? *Potrebbe mostrarmi un'altra camera?*
How much is it? *Quanto costa?*
on the first floor *al primo piano*
Is breakfast included? *É compresa la prima colazione?*
Is everything included? *É tutto compreso?*
half/full board *mezza pensione/ pensione completa*
It's expensive *É caro*
Do you have a room with a balcony/ view of the sea? *C'è una camera con balcone/con vista sul mare?*

Pronunciation and Grammar Tips

Italian speakers claim that pronunciation is straight-forward: you pronounce it as it is written. This is approximately true but there are a couple of important rules for English speakers to bear in mind: *c* before *e* or *i* is pronounced "ch", e.g. *ciao, mi dispiace, la coincidenza. Ch* before *i* or *e* is pronounced as "k", e.g. *la chiesa.* Likewise, *sci* or *sce* are pronounced as in "sheep" or "shed" respectively. *Gn* in Italian is rather like the sound in "onion", while *gl* is softened to resemble the

sound in "bullion".
Nouns are either masculine (*il*, plural *i*) or feminine (*la*, plural *le*). Plurals of nouns are most often formed by changing an *o* to an *i* and an *a* to an *e*, e.g. *il panino, i panini*; *la chiesa, le chiese.*
Words are stressed on the penultimate syllable unless an accent indicates otherwise.
Like many languages, Italian has formal and informal words for "You". In the singular, *Tu* is informal while *Lei* is more polite. Confusingly, in

some parts of Italy or in some circumstances, you will also hear *Voi* used as a singular polite form. (In general, *Voi* is reserved for "You" plural, however.) For visitors, it is simplest and most respectful to use the formal form unless invited to do otherwise.
There is, of course, rather more to the language than that, but you can get a surprisingly long way towards making friends by learning how to pronounce a few basic phrases.

a room overlooking the park/the street/the back *una camera con vista sul parco/che dà sulla strada/sul retro*
Is it a quiet room? *É una stanza tranquilla?*
The room is too hot/cold/noisy/small *La camera è troppo calda/fredda/rumorosa/piccola*
Can I see the room? *Posso vedere la camera?*
What time does the hotel close? *A che ora chiude l'albergo?*
I'll take it *La prendo*
big/small *grande/piccola*
What time is breakfast? *A che ora è la prima colazione?*
Please give me a call at... *Mi può chiamare alle...*
Come in! *Avanti!*
Can I have the bill, please? *Posso avere il conto, per favore.*
Can you call me a taxi please? *Può chiamarmi un taxi, per favore?*
dining room *la sala da pranzo*
key *la chiave*
lift *l'ascensore*
towel *l'asciugamano*
toilet paper *la carta igienica*
pull/push *tirare/spingere*

Eating Out

DRINKS & BAR SNACKS

I'd like... *Vorrei...*
coffee *un caffè* (espresso: small, strong and black)
un cappuccino (with hot, frothy milk)
un caffelatte (like *café au lait* in

Bar Notices

Prezzo al tavolo/in terrazza
Price at a table/terrace
(often double what you pay standing at the bar)
Si paga alla cassa **Pay at the cash desk**
Si prende lo scontrino alla cassa **Pay at the cash desk, then take the receipt** (*lo scontrino*) **to the bar to be served.** This is common procedure.
Signori/Uomini **Gentlemen** (lavatories)
Signore/Donne **Ladies** (lavatories)

France)
un caffè lungo (weak, often served in a tall glass)
un corretto (laced with alcohol, usually brandy or grappa)
tea *un tè*
lemon tea *un tè al limone*
herbal tea *una tisana*
hot chocolate *una cioccolata calda*
orange/lemon juice (bottled) *un succo d'arancia/di limone*
fresh orange/lemon juice *una spremuta di arancia/di limone*
orangeade *un'aranciata*
water (mineral) *acqua (minerale)*
fizzy/still mineral water *acqua minerale gasata/naturale*
a glass of mineral water *un bicchiere di minerale*
with/without ice *con/senza ghiaccio*
red/white wine *vino rosso/bianco*
beer (draught) *una birra (alla spina)*
a gin and tonic *un gin tonic*
a bitter (Vermouth, etc.) *un amaro*
milk *latte*
a (half) litre *un (mezzo) litro*
bottle *una bottiglia*
ice cream *un gelato*
cone *un cono*
pastry *una pasta*
sandwich *un tramezzino*
roll *un panino*
Anything else? *Desidera qualcos'altro?*
Cheers *Salute*
Let me pay *Offro io*
That's very kind of you *Grazie, molto gentile*

IN A RESTAURANT

I'd like to book a table *Vorrei riservare un tavolo*
Have you got a table for... *Avete un tavolo per ...*
I have a reservation *Ho fatto una prenotazione*
lunch/supper *il pranzo/la cena*
We do not want a full meal *Non desideriamo un pasto completo*
Could we have another table? *Potremmo spostarci?*
I'm a vegetarian *Sono vegetariano/a*
Is there a vegetarian dish? *C'è un piatto vegetariano?*
May we have the menu? *Ci dà il menu, per favore?*
wine list *la lista dei vini*

Numbers

1	Uno	17	Diciassette
2	Due	18	Diciotto
3	Tre	19	Diciannove
4	Quattro	20	Venti
5	Cinque	30	Trenta
6	Sei	40	Quaranta
7	Sette	50	Cinquanta
8	Otto	60	Sessanta
9	Nove	70	Settanta
10	Dieci	80	Ottanta
11	Undici	90	Novanta
12	Dodici	100	Cento
13	Tredici	200	Duecento
14	Quattordici	500	Cinquecento
15	Quindici	1,000	Mille
16	Sedici	2,000	Duemila
		5,000	Cinquemila
		50,000	Cinquantamila
		1 Million	Un milione

What would you like? *Che cosa prende?*
What would you recommend? *Che cosa ci raccomanda?*
home-made *fatto in casa*
What would you like as a main course/dessert? *Che cosa prende di secondo/di dolce?*
What would you like to drink? *Che cosa desidera da bere?*
a carafe of red/white wine *una caraffa di vino rosso/bianco*
fixed price menu *il menu a prezzo fisso*
the dish of the day *il piatto del giorno*
VAT (sales tax) *IVA*
cover charge *il coperto/pane e coperto*
That's enough; no more, thanks *Basta (così)*
The bill, please *Il conto per favore*
Is service included? *Il servizio è incluso?*
Where is the lavatory? *Dov'è il bagno?*
Keep the change *Va bene così*
I've enjoyed the meal *Mi è piaciuto molto*

Menu Decoder

ANTIPASTI (HORS D'OEUVRES)

antipasto misto **mixed hors d'oeuvres** (may include cold cuts, cheeses and roast vegetables– ask, however)
buffet freddo **cold buffet**

caponata **mixed aubergine, olives and tomatoes**
insalata caprese **tomato and mozzarella salad**
insalata di mare **seafood salad**
insalata mista/verde **mixed/ green salad**
melanzane alla parmigiana **fried or baked aubergine (with Parmesan cheese and tomato)**
mortadella/salame **salami**
pancetta **bacon**
peperonata **vegetable stew with peppers, onions and tomatoes**

PRIMI (FIRST COURSES)

Typical first courses include soup, *risotto*, *gnocchi* or numerous varieties of pasta in a wide range of sauces. *Risotto* and *gnocchi* are more commonly served in the North than in Central Italy.
il brodetto **fish soup**
il brodo **consommé**
i crespolini **savoury pancakes**
gli gnocchi **potato dumplings**
la minestra **soup**
il minestrone **thick vegetable soup**
pasta e fagioli **pasta and bean soup**
il prosciutto (cotto/crudo) **ham** (cooked/cured)
i supplí **rice croquettes**
i tartufi **truffles**
la zuppa **soup**

SECONDI (MAIN COURSES)

Typical main courses are fish-, seafood- or meat-based, with accompaniments *(contorni)* that vary greatly from region to region.

La carne (meat)
allo spiedo **on the spit**
arrosto **roast meat**
i ferri **grilled**
al forno **baked**
al girarrosto **spit-roasted**
alla griglia **grilled**
involtini **skewered veal, ham, etc.**
stagionato **hung, well-aged**
stufato **braised, stewed**
ben cotto **well-done** (steak, etc.)
al puntino **medium** (steak, etc.)
al sangue **rare** (steak, etc.)

Pasta Dishes

Common Pasta Shapes:
cannelloni (large stuffed tubes of pasta); *farfalle* (bow- or butterfly-shaped pasta); *tagliatelle* (flat noodles, similar to *fettuccine*); *tortellini* and *ravioli* (different types of stuffed pasta packets); *penne* (quill-shaped tubes, smaller than *rigatoni*).
Typical Pasta Sauces: *pomodoro* (tomato); *pesto* (with basil and pine nuts); *matriciana* (bacon and tomato); *arrabbiata* (spicy tomato); *panna* (cream); *ragù* (meat sauce); *aglio e olio* (garlic and olive oil); *burro e salvia* (butter and sage).

l'agnello **lamb**
la bresaola **dried salted beef**
la bistecca **steak**
il capriolo/cervo **venison**
il carpaccio **lean beef fillet**
il cinghiale **wild boar**
il coniglio **rabbit**
il controfiletto **sirloin steak**
le cotolette **cutlets**
il fagiano **pheasant**
il fegato **liver**
il filetto **fillet**
la lepre **hare**
il maiale **pork**
il manzo **beef**
l'ossobuco **shin of veal**
la porchetta **roast suckling pig**
il pollo **chicken**
le polpette **meatballs**
il polpettone **meat loaf**
la salsiccia **sausage**
saltimbocca (alla romana) **veal escalopes with ham**
le scaloppine **escalopes**
lo stufato **stew**
il sugo **sauce**
il tacchino **turkey**
la trippa **tripe**
il vitello **veal**

Frutti di mare (seafood)
Beware the word "*surgelati*", meaning frozen rather than fresh.
affumicato **smoked**
alle brace **charcoal grilled/barbecued**
alla griglia **grilled**
fritto **fried**
ripieno **stuffed**

al vapore **steamed**
le acciughe **anchovies**
l'anguilla **eel**
l'aragosta **lobster**
il baccalà **dried salted cod**
i bianchetti **whitebait**
il branzino **sea bass**
i calamari **squid**
i calamaretti **baby squid**
la carpa **carp**
i crostacei **shellfish**
le cozze **mussels**
il fritto misto **mixed fried fish**
i gamberi **prawns**
i gamberetti **shrimps**
il granchio **crab**
il merluzzo **cod**
le moleche **soft-shelled crabs**
le ostriche **oysters**
il pesce **fish**
il pesce spada **swordfish**
il polipo **octopus**
il risotto di mare **seafood risotto**
le sarde **sardines**
la sogliola **sole**
le seppie **cuttlefish**
la triglia **red mullet**
la trota **trout**
il tonno **tuna**
le vongole **clams**

I legumi/la verdura (vegetables)
a scelta **of your choice**
i contorni **accompaniments**
ripieno **stuffed**
gli asparagi **asparagus**
la bietola **similar to spinach**
il carciofo **artichoke**
le carote **carrots**
i carciofini **artichoke hearts**
il cavolo **cabbage**
la cicoria **chicory**
la cipolla **onion**
i funghi **mushrooms**
i fagioli **beans**
i fagiolini **French (green) beans**
le fave **broad beans**
il finocchio **fennel**
l'indivia **endive/chicory**
l'insalata mista **mixed salad**
l'insalata verde **green salad**
la melanzana **aubergine**
le patate **potatoes**
le patatine fritte **chips/French fries**
i peperoni **peppers**
i piselli **peas**
i pomodori **tomatoes**
le primizie **spring vegetables**
il radicchio **red, slightly bitter lettuce**

la rughetta **rocket**
i ravanelli **radishes**
gli spinaci **spinach**
la verdura **green vegetables**
la zucca **pumpkin/squash**
gli zucchini **courgettes**

I DOLCI (DESSERTS)

al carrello **(desserts) from the trolley**
un semifreddo **semi-frozen dessert**
(many types)
la bavarese **mousse**
la cassata **Sicilian ice cream with**
candied peel
le frittelle **fritters**
un gelato (di lampone/limone)
(raspberry/lemon) ice cream
una granita **water ice**
una macedonia di frutta **fruit salad**
il tartufo (nero) **(chocolate) ice**
cream dessert
il tiramisù **cold, creamy cheese**
and coffee liqueur dessert
la torta **cake/tart**
lo zabaglione **sweet dessert made**
with eggs and Marsala wine
lo zuccotto **ice cream liqueur**
la zuppa inglese **trifle**

La frutta (fruit)
le albicocche **apricots**
le arance **oranges**
le banane **bananas**
il cocomero **watermelon**
le ciliegie **cherries**
i fichi **figs**
le fragole **strawberries**
i frutti di bosco **forest fruits**
i lamponi **raspberries**
la mela **apple**
il melone **melon**
la pesca **peach**
la pera **pear**
il pompelmo **grapefruit**
le uve **grapes**

BASIC FOODS

l'aceto **vinegar**
l'aglio **garlic**
il burro **butter**
il formaggio **cheese**
la focaccia **oven-baked snack**
la frittata **omelette**
il grana **like parmesan cheese**
i grissini **bread sticks**

l'olio **oil**
la marmellata **jam**
il pane **bread**
il pane integrale **wholemeal bread**
il parmegiano **parmesan cheese**
il pepe **pepper**
il riso **rice**
il sale **salt**
la senape **mustard**
le uova **eggs**
lo yogurt **yoghurt**
lo zucchero **sugar**

Sightseeing

Can one visit? Si può visitare?
il custode **custodian**
il sacrestano **sacristan**
Suonare il campanello **ring the bell**
aperto/a **open**
chiuso/a **closed**
chiuso per la festa **closed for the**
festival
chiuso per ferie **closed for the holidays**
chiuso per restauro **closed for**
restoration
Is it possible to see the church?
É possibile visitare la chiesa?
Entrata/uscita **Entrance/exit**
Where can I find the custodian/
sacristan/key? Dove posso trovare
il custode/il sacrestano/la chiave?
We have come a long way just to
see ... Siamo venuti da lontano
proprio per visitare ...
It is really a pity it is closed
É veramente peccato che sia chiuso
(The last two should be tried in
desperation – pleas for sympathy
open some doors.)

Tourist Signs

Most regions in Italy have handy
signs indicating the key tourist
sights in any given area:

Abbazia (Badia) **Abbey**
Basilica **Church**
Belvedere **Viewpoint**
Biblioteca **Library**
Castello **Castle**
Centro storico **Old town/**
　historic centre
Chiesa **Church**
Duomo/Cattedrale **Cathedral**
Fiume **River**
Giardino **Garden**

At the Shops

What time do you open/close?
A che ora apre/chiude?
Chiuso per ferie (typical sign)
Closed for the holidays
Tirare/spingere (sign on doors)
Pull/push
Entrance/exit Entrata/uscita
Can I help you? Posso aiutarLa?
(formal)
What would you like? Che cosa
desidera?
I'm just looking Sto soltanto
guardando
How much does it cost? Quant'è,
per favore?
How much is this? Quanto viene?
Do you take credit cards?
Accettate carte di credito?
I'd like... Vorrei...
this one/that one questo/quello
I'd like that one, please Vorrei
quello lì, per cortesia
Have you got ...? Avete ...?
We haven't got (any) ... Non (ne)
abbiamo...
Can I try it on? Posso provare?
the size (for clothes) la taglia
What size do you take? Qual'é a
sua taglia?
the size (for shoes) il numero
Is there/do you have ...? C'è ...?
Yes, of course Sì, certo
No, we don't (there isn't) No, non
c'è
That's too expensive É troppo caro
Please write it down for me Me lo
scriva, per favore
cheap economico

Lago **Lake**
Mercato **Market**
Monastero **Monastery**
Monumenti **Monuments**
Museo **Museum**
Parco **Park**
Pinacoteca **Art gallery**
Ponte **Bridge**
Ruderi **Ruins**
Scavi **Excavations/**
　archaeological site
Spiaggia **Beach**
Tempio **Temple**
Torre **Tower**
Ufficio turistico **Tourist office**

Days and Dates

morning/afternoon/evening *la mattina, il pomeriggio, la sera*
yesterday/today/tomorrow *ieri/oggi/domani*
the day after tomorrow *dopodomani*
now/early/late *adesso/presto/ritardo*
a minute *un minuto*
an hour *un'ora*
half an hour *un mezz'ora*
a day *un giorno*
a week *una settimana*
Monday *lunedì*
Tuesday *martedì*
Wednesday *mercoledì*
Thursday *giovedì*
Friday *venerdì*
Saturday *sabato*
Sunday *domenica*
first *il primo/la prima*
second *il secondo/la seconda*
third *il terzo/la terza*

Don't you have anything cheaper? *Ha niente che costa di meno?*
It's too small/big *É troppo piccolo/grande*
brown/blue/black *marrone/blu/nero*
green/red/white/yellow *verde/rosso/bianco/giallo*
pink/grey/gold/silver *rosa/grigio/oro/argento*
No thank you, I don't like it *Grazie, ma non è di mio gusto*
I (don't) **like it** *(Non) mi piace*
I'll take it/I'll leave it *Lo prendo/ Lo lascio*
It's a rip-off (impolite) *Sono una ruberia*
This is faulty. Can I have a replacement/refund? *C'è un difetto. Me lo potrebbe cambiare/rimborsare?*
Anything else? *Altro?*
The cash desk is over there *Si accomodi alla cassa*
Give me some of those *Mi dia alcuni di quelli lì*
a (half) kilo *un (mezzo) chilo*
100 grams *un etto*
200 grams *due etti*
more/less *più/meno*
with/without *con/senza*
a little *un pochino*
That's enough/No more *Basta così*

TYPES OF SHOPS

antique dealer *l'antiquario*
bakery/cake shop *la panetteria/pasticceria*
bank *la banca*
bookshop *la libreria*
boutique/clothes shop *il negozio di moda*
bureau de change *il cambio*
butcher's *la macelleria*
chemist's *la farmacia*
delicatessen *la salumeria*
department store *il grande magazzino*
dry cleaner's *la tintoria*
fishmonger's *la pescheria*
food shop *l'alimentari*
florist *il fioraio*
grocer's *l'alimentari*
greengrocer's *il fruttivendolo*
hairdresser's (women) *il parrucchiere*
ice cream parlour *la gelateria*
jeweller's *il gioielliere*
leather shop *la pelletteria*
market *il mercato*
newsstand *l'edicola*
post office *l'ufficio postale*
shoe shop *il negozio di scarpe*
stationer's *la cartoleria*
supermarket *il supermercato*
tobacconist *il tabaccaio* (also usually sells travel tickets, stamps, phone cards)
travel agency *l'agenzia di viaggi* (also usually books domestic and international train tickets for customers).

Travelling

airport *l'aeroporto*
arrivals/departures *arrivi/partenze*
boat *la barca*
bus *l'autobus/il pullman*
bus station *l'autostazione*
car *la macchina*
connection *la coincidenza*
ferry *il traghetto*
ferry terminal *la stazione marittima*
first/second class *la prima/ seconda classe*
flight *il volo*
left luggage office *il deposito bagagli*
motorway *l'autostrada*
no smoking *vietato fumare*
platform *il binario*
porter *il facchino*
railway station *la stazione (ferroviaria)*

return ticket *un biglietto di andata e ritorno*
single ticket *un biglietto di sola andata*
sleeping car *la carrozza letti/ il vagone letto*
smokers/non-smokers *fumatori/ non-fumatori*
stop *la fermata*
taxi *il taxi*
ticket office *la biglietteria*
train *il treno*
WC *la toilette*

AT THE AIRPORT

Where's the office of BA/ Alitalia? *Dov'è l'ufficio della British Airways/dell'Alitalia?*
I'd like to book a flight to Venice *Vorrei prenotare un volo per Venezia*
When is the next flight to ...? *Quando parte il prossimo aereo per...?*
Are there any seats available? *Ci sono ancora posti liberi?*
Ha bagagli a mano? **Have you got any hand luggage?**
I'll take this hand luggage with me *Questo lo tengo come bagaglio a mano*
My suitcase has got lost *La mia valigia è andata persa*
My suitcase has been damaged *La mia valigia è rovinata*
Il volo è rimandato **The flight has been delayed**
Il volo è stato cancellato **The flight has been cancelled**
Posso metterLa sulla lista d'attesa **I can put you on the waiting list**

Conversion Charts

Metric–Imperial:
1 centimetre = 0.4 inch
1 metre = 3 ft 3 ins
1 kilometre = 0.62 mile
1 gram = 0.04 ounce
1 kilogram = 2.2 pounds
1 litre = 1.76 UK pints
Imperial–Metric:
1 inch = 2.54 centimetres
1 foot = 30 centimetres
1 ounce = 28 grams
1 pound = 0.45 kilogram
1 pint = 0.57 litre
1 UK gallon = 4.55 litres
1 US gallon = 3.78 litres

AT THE STATION

Can you help me please? *Mi può aiutare, per favore?*
Where can I buy tickets? *Dove posso fare i biglietti?*
at the ticket office/at the counter *alla biglietteria/allo sportello*
What time does the train leave? *A che ora parte il treno?*
What time does the train arrive? *A che ora arriva il treno?*
Can I book a seat? *Posso prenotare un posto?*
Are there any seats available? *Ci sono ancora posti liberi?*
Is this seat free/taken? *É libero/occupato questo posto?*
I'm afraid this is my seat *É il mio posto, mi dispiace*
Deve pagare un supplemento You'll have to pay a supplement
Do I have to change? *Devo cambiare?*
Where does it stop? *Dove si ferma?*
Bisogna cambiare a Roma **You need to change in Rome**
Which platform does the train leave from? *Da quale binario parte il treno?*
Il treno parte dal binario uno **The train leaves from platform one**
When is the next train/bus/ferry for Naples? *Quando parte il prossimo treno/pullman/traghetto per Napoli?*
How long does the crossing take? *Quanto dura la traversata?*
What time does the bus leave for Siena? *Quando parte l'autobus per Siena?*
How long will it take to get there?

Quanto tempo ci vuole per arrivare? Will we arrive on time? *Arriveremo puntuali?*
Next stop please *La prossima fermata per favore*
Is this the right stop? *É la fermata giusta?*
Il treno è in ritardo **The train is late**
Can you tell me where to get off? *Mi può dire dove devo scendere?*

DIRECTIONS

right/left *a destra/a sinistra*
first left/second right *la prima a sinistra/la seconda a destra*
Turn to the right/left *Gira a destra/sinistra*
Go straight on *Va sempre diritto*
Go straight on until the traffic lights *Va sempre diritto fino al semaforo*
Is it far away/nearby? *É lontano/vicino?*
It's five minutes' walk *Cinque minuti a piedi*
It's 10 minutes by car *Dieci minuti con la macchina*
You can't miss it *Non può non vederlo*
opposite/next to *di fronte/accanto a*
up/down *su/giú*
traffic lights *il semaforo*
junction *l'incrocio, il bivio*
building *il palazzo*
Where is ...? *Dov'è ...?*
Where are ...? *Dove sono ...?*
Where is the nearest bank/petrol station/bus stop/hotel/garage? *Dov'è la banca/la*

stazione di servizio/la fermata di autobus/l'albergo/ l'officina più vicino/a?
How do I get there? *Come si può andare? (or: Come faccio per arrivare a ...?)*
How long does it take to get to ...? *Quanto tempo ci vuole per andare a ...?*
Can you show me where I am on the map? *Può indicarmi sulla cartina dove mi trovo?*
You're on the wrong road *Lei è sulla strada sbagliata*

ON THE ROAD

Where can I rent a car? *Dove posso noleggiare una macchina?*
Is comprehensive insurance included? *É completamente assicurata?*
Is it insured for another driver? *É assicurata per un altro guidatore?*
By what time must I return it? *A che ora devo consegnarla?*
underground car park *il garage sotterraneo*
driving licence *la patente (di guida)*
petrol *la benzina*
petrol station/garage *la stazione di servizio*
oil *l'olio*
Fill it up please *Faccia il pieno, per favore*
lead free/unleaded/diesel *senza piombo/benzina verde/diesel*
My car won't start *La mia macchina non s'accende*

Road Signs

Accendere le luci in galleria **Lights on in tunnel**
Alt **Stop**
Autostrada **Motorway**
Attenzione **Caution**
Avanti **Go/walk**
Caduta massi **Danger of falling rocks**
Casello **Toll gate**
Dare la precedenza **Give way**
Deviazione **Diversion**
Divieto di campeggio **No camping allowed**
Divieto di sosta/Sosta vietata **No parking**
Divieto di passaggio/Senso vietato

No entry
Dogana **Customs**
Entrata **Entrance**
Galleria **Tunnel**
Guasto **Out of order** (e.g. phone box)
Incrocio **Crossroads**
Limite di velocità **Speed limit**
Non toccare **Don't touch**
Passaggio a livello **Railway crossing**
Parcheggio **Parking**
Pedaggio **Toll road**
Pericolo **Danger**
Pronto Soccorso **First aid**
Rallentare **Slow down**
Rimozione forzata **Parked cars**

will be towed away
Semaforo **Traffic lights**
Senso unico **One way street**
Sentiero **Footpath**
Solo uscita **No entry**
Strada interrotta **Road blocked**
Strada chiusa **Road closed**
Strada senza uscita/Vicolo cieco **Dead end**
Tangenziale **Ring road/bypass**
Traffico di transito **Through traffic**
Uscita **Exit**
Uscita (autocarri) **Exit for lorries**
Vietato il sorpasso **No overtaking**
Vietato il transito **No thoroughfare**

My car has broken down *La mia macchina è guasta*
How long will it take to repair? *Quanto tempo ci vorrà per la riparazione?*
The engine is overheating *Il motore si surriscalda*
Can you check the ...? *Può controllare ...?*
There's something wrong (with/in the) ... *C'è un difetto (nel/nella/nei/nelle) ...*
... **accelerator** *l'acceleratore*
... **brakes** *i freni*
... **engine** *il motore*
... **exhaust** *lo scarico/scappamento*
... **fanbelt** *la cinghia del ventilatore*
... **gearbox** *la scatola del cambio*
... **headlights** *le luci*
... **radiator** *il radiatore*
... **spark plugs** *le candele*
... **tyre(s)** *la gomma (le gomme)*
... **windscreen** *il parabrezza*

Health

Is there a chemist's nearby? *C'è una farmacia qui vicino?*
Which chemist is open at night? *Quale farmacia fa il turno di notte?*
I don't feel well *Non mi sento bene*
I feel ill *Sto male/Mi sento male*
Where does it hurt? *Dove Le fa male?*
It hurts here *Ho dolore qui*
I suffer from ... *Soffro di ...*
I have a headache *Ho mal di testa*

Emergencies

Help! *Aiuto!*
Stop! *Fermate!*
I've had an accident *Ho avuto un incidente*
Watch out! *Attenzione!*
Call a doctor *Per favore, chiami un medico*
... **an ambulance** ... *un'ambulanza*
... **the police** ... *la Polizia*
... **the fire brigade** ... *i pompieri*
Where is the telephone? *Dov'è il telefono?*
Where is the nearest hospital? *Dov'è l'ospedale più vicino?*
I would like to report a theft *Vorrei denunciare un furto*
Thank you very much for your help *Grazie dell'aiuto*

I have a sore throat *Ho mal di gola*
I have a stomach ache *Ho mal di pancia*
Have you got something for air sickness? *Ha/Avete qualcosa contro il mal d'aria?*
Have you got something for sea sickness? *Ha/Avete qualcosa contro il mal di mare?*
antiseptic cream *la crema antisettica*
sunburn *scottatura da sole*
sunburn cream *la crema antisolare*
sticking plaster *il cerotto*
tissues *i fazzoletti di carta*
toothpaste *il dentifricio*
upset stomach pills *le pillole per male di stomaco*
insect repellent *l'insettifugo*
mosquitoes *le zanzare*
wasps *le vespe*

Further Reading

General

Across the River and into the Trees, by Ernest Hemingway.
Andreas, by Hugo von Hoffmannsthal. 1930.
The Architecture of the Italian Renaissance, by Peter Murray.
The Aspern Papers, by Henry James.
Autobiography, by Benvenuto Cellini.
Christ Stopped at Eboli, by Carlo Levi.
Le Città Invisibili, Italo Calvino. Translated as *Invisible Cities*.
The Civilization of the Renaissance in Italy. Jacob Burckhardt.
Death at La Fenice and other crime thrillers set in Venice. Donna Leon.
Death in Venice. Thomas Mann. (Originally *Der Tod in Venedig*.)
The Decameron, by Boccaccio.
D.H. Lawrence and Italy, by D.H. Lawrence.
The Doge, by A. Palazzeschi.
Etruscan Places, by D.H. Lawrence.
The Gallery, by John Horne Burns.
Graziella, by Alphonse de Lamartine (AC Mclurg, Chicago).
Il Fuoco, by Gabriele d'Annuncio. Translated as *The Flame of Life*.
Italian Hours, by Henry James.
Italian Journey, by Johann Wolfgang Goethe.
The Italian Painters of the Renaissance, by Bernard Berenson.
The Italians, by Luigi Barzini.
The Italian World, by John Julius Norwich.
The Last Medici, by Harold Acton.
Lives of the Artists, Vol. 1 & 2, by Giorgio Vasari.
Love and War in the Apennines, by Eric Newby.
The Love of Italy, by Jonathan Keates.
The Mafia, by Clare Sterling.
The Mediterranean Passion, by John Pemble.
Memoirs, by Giacomo Casanova. Translated into many languages.
Pictures from Italy, by Charles Dickens.

Renaissance Venice, edited by J.R. Hale.

The Rise and Fall of the House of Medici, by Christopher Hibbert.

The Stones of Florence and Venice Observed, by Mary McCarthy.

The Stones of Venice (1851–3), by John Ruskin.

The Story of San Michele, by Axel Munthe.

Those Who Walk Away, by Patricia Highsmith.

Thus Spake Bellavista, by Luciano de Crescenzo.

A Tramp Abroad, by Mark Twain.

A Venetian Bestiary, by Jan Morris.

Venetian Life, by William Dean Howells. 1866.

Venetian Red, by P.M. Passinetti.

Venice, by Jan Morris.

Venice: A Thousand Years of Culture and Civilisation, by Peter Lauritzen.

Venice and its Lagoon, Giulio Lorenzetti.

Venice for Pleasure, by J.G. Links.

Venice: The Greatness and the Fall, by Mark Twain.

Venice: The Rise to Empire, by John Julius Norwich.

The Wings of the Dove, by Henry James.

Other Insight Guides

Other Insight Guides to Italian destinations are: Italy, Rome, Venice, Florence, Umbria, Tuscany, The Bay of Naples, Sicily, Sardinia and South Tyrol.

Thoroughly updated and expanded, the best-selling Insight Guide: Rome lifts the lid on Italy's capital.

Insight Guide: Venice is a detailed guide to this top Italian destination. Practical as well as visually stunning, it includes extensive hotel and restaurant listings.

Complementing the Insight Guides series is Insight's range of Pocket Guides. Intended for short-stay visitors, the books are itinerary based and supported by large pull-out maps. Italian destinations in the series are Venice, Rome, Florence, Milan, Sicily, Sardinia and Tuscany.

Insight Pocket Guide: Rome is the ideal guidebook to Italy's capital. Perfect for a short break, it links all the main sights in easy-to-follow itineraries, which are clearly plotted on a pull-out map.

Insight's third series, Insight Compact Guides, is excellent for on-the-spot information. Titles include Tuscany, Florence, Milan, Venice, the Italian Riviera, the Italian Lakes and Rome. Supported by cross-referenced maps and photography, Insight Compact Guides are excellent and easily portable travel companions.

ART & PHOTO CREDITS

The Insight Approach

The book you are holding is part of the world's largest range of guidebooks. Its purpose is to help you have the most valuable travel experience possible, and we try to achieve this by providing not only information about countries, regions and cities but also genuine insight into their history, culture, institutions and people.

Since the first Insight Guide – to Bali – was published in 1970, the series has been dedicated to the proposition that, with insight into a country's people and culture, visitors can both enhance their own experience and be accepted more easily by their hosts. Now, in a world where ethnic hostilities and nationalist conflicts are all too common, such attempts to increase understanding between peoples are more important than ever.

Insight Guides:
Essentials for understanding

Because a nation's past holds the key to its present, each Insight Guide kicks off with lively history chapters. These are followed by magazine-style essays on culture and daily life. This essential background information gives readers the necessary context for using the main Places section, with its comprehensive run-down on things worth seeing and doing.

Finally, a listings section contains all the information you'll need on travel, hotels, restaurants and opening times.

As far as possible, we rely on local writers and specialists to ensure that information is authoritative. The pictures, for which Insight Guides have become so celebrated, are just as important. Our photojournalistic approach aims not only to illustrate a destination but also to communicate visually and directly to readers life as it is lived by the locals. The series has grown to almost 200 titles.

Compact Guides:
The "great little guides"

As invaluable as such background information is, it isn't always fun to carry an Insight Guide through a crowded souk or up a church tower. Could we, readers asked, distil the key reference material into a slim volume for on-the-spot use?

Our response was to design Compact Guides as an entirely new series, with original text carefully cross-referenced to detailed maps and more than 200 photographs. In essence, they're miniature encyclopedias, concise and comprehensive, displaying reliable and up-to-date information in an accessible way. There are almost 100 titles.

Pocket Guides:
A local host in book form

However wide-ranging the information in a book, human beings still value the personal touch. Our editors are often asked the same questions. Where do *you* go to eat? What do *you* think is the best beach? What would *you* recommend if I have only three days? We invited our local correspondents to act as "substitute hosts" by revealing their preferred walks and trips, listing the restaurants they go to and structuring a visit into a series of timed itineraries.

The result: our Pocket Guides, complete with full-size fold-out maps. These 100-plus titles help readers plan a trip precisely, particularly if their time is short.

Exploring with Insight:
A valuable travel experience

In conjunction with co-publishers all over the world, we print in up to 10 languages, from German to Chinese, from Danish to Russian. But our aim remains simple: to enhance your travel experience by combining our expertise in guidebook publishing with the on-the-spot knowledge of our correspondents.

66 I was first drawn to the Insight Guides by the excellent "Nepal" volume. I can think of no book which so effectively captures the essence of a country. Out of these pages leaped the Nepal I know – the captivating charm of a people and their culture. I've since discovered and enjoyed the entire Insight Guide series. Each volume deals with a country in the same sensitive depth, which is nowhere more evident than in the superb photography. 99

Sir Edmund Hillary

The World of Insight Guides

400 books in three complementary series cover every major destination in every continent.

Insight Guides

Alaska · Alsace · Amazon Wildlife · American Southwest · Amsterdam · Argentina · Atlanta · Athens · Australia · Austria · Bahamas · Bali · Baltic States · Bangkok · Barbados · Barcelona · Bay of Naples · Beijing · Belgium · Belize · Berlin · Bermuda · Boston · Brazil · Brittany · Brussels · Budapest · Buenos Aires · Burgundy · Burma (Myanmar) · Cairo · Calcutta · California · Canada · Caribbean · Catalonia · Channel Islands · Chicago · Chile · China · Cologne · Continental Europe · Corsica · Costa Rica · Crete · Crossing America · Cuba · Cyprus · Czech & Slovak Republics · Delhi, Jaipur, Agra · Denmark · Dresden · Dublin · Düsseldorf · East African Wildlife · East Asia · Eastern Europe · Ecuador · Edinburgh · Egypt · Finland · Florence · Florida · France · Frankfurt · French Riviera · Gambia & Senegal · Germany · Glasgow

Gran Canaria · Great Barrier Reef · Great Britain · Greece · Greek Islands · Hamburg · Hawaii · Hong Kong · Hungary · Iceland · India · India's Western Himalaya · Indian Wildlife · Indonesia · Ireland · Israel · Istanbul · Italy · Jamaica · Japan · Java · Jerusalem · Jordan · Kathmandu · Kenya · Korea · Lisbon · Loire Valley · London · Los Angeles · Madeira · Madrid · Malaysia · Mallorca & Ibiza · Malta · Marine Life in the South China Sea · Melbourne · Mexico · Mexico City · Miami · Montreal · Morocco · Moscow · Munich · Namibia · Native America · Nepal · Netherlands · New England · New Orleans · New York City · New York State · New Zealand · Nile · Normandy · Northern California · Northern Spain · Norway · Oman & the UAE · Oxford · Old South · Pacific Northwest · Pakistan · Paris · Peru · Philadelphia · Philippines · Poland · Portugal · Prague

Provence · Puerto Rico · Rajasthan · Rhine · Rio de Janeiro · Rockies · Rome · Russia · St Petersburg · San Francisco · Sardinia · Scotland · Seattle · Sicily · Singapore · South Africa · South America · South Asia · South India · South Tyrol · Southeast Asia · Southeast Asia Wildlife · Southern California · Southern Spain · Spain · Sri Lanka · Sweden · Switzerland · Sydney · Taiwan · Tenerife · Texas · Thailand · Tokyo · Trinidad & Tobago · Tunisia · Turkey · Turkish Coast · Tuscany · Umbria · US National Parks East · US National Parks West · Vancouver · Venezuela · Venice · Vienna · Vietnam · Wales · Washington DC · Waterways of Europe · Wild West · Yemen

Insight Pocket Guides

Aegean Islands★ · Algarve★ · Alsace · Amsterdam★ · Athens★ · Atlanta★ · Bahamas★ · Baja Peninsula★ · Bali★ · Bali Bird Walks · Bangkok★ · Barbados★ · Barcelona★ · Bavaria★ · Beijing★ · Berlin★

Bermuda★ · Bhutan★ · Boston★ · British Columbia★ · Brittany★ · Brussels★ · Budapest & Surroundings★ · Canton★ · Chiang Mai★ · Chicago★ · Corsica★ · Costa Blanca★ · Costa Brava★ · Costa del Sol/Marbella★ · Costa Rica★ · Crete★ · Denmark★ · Fiji★ · Florence★ · Florida★ · Florida Keys★ · French Riviera★ · Gran Canaria★ · Hawaii★ · Hong Kong★ · Hungary · Ibiza★ · Ireland★ · Ireland's Southwest★ · Israel★ · Istanbul★ · Jakarta★ · Jamaica★ · Kathmandu Bikes & Hikes★ · Kenya★ · Kuala Lumpur★ · Lisbon★ · Loire Valley★ · London★ · Macau★ · Madrid★ · Malacca · Maldives · Mallorca★ · Malta★ · Mexico City★ · Miami★ · Milan★ · Montreal★ · Morocco★ · Moscow · Munich★ · Nepal★ · New Delhi · New Orleans★ · New York City★ · New Zealand★ · Northern California★ · Oslo/Bergen★ · Paris★ · Penang★ · Phuket★ · Prague★ · Provence★ · Puerto Rico★ · Quebec★ · Rhodes★ · Rome★ · Sabah★

St Petersburg★ · San Francisco★ · Sardinia · Scotland★ · Seville★ · Seychelles★ · Sicily★ · Sikkim · Singapore★ · Southeast England · Southern California★ · Southern Spain★ · Sri Lanka★ · Sydney★ · Tenerife★ · Thailand★ · Tibet★ · Toronto★ · Tunisia★ · Turkish Coast★ · Tuscany★ · Venice★ · Vienna★ · Vietnam★ · Yogyakarta · Yucatan Peninsula★

★ = Insight Pocket Guides with Pull out Maps

Insight Compact Guides

Algarve · Amsterdam · Bahamas · Bali · Bangkok · Barbados · Barcelona · Beijing · Belgium · Berlin · Brittany · Brussels · Budapest · Burgundy · Copenhagen · Costa Brava · Costa Rica · Crete · Cyprus · Czech Republic · Denmark · Dominican Republic · Dublin · Egypt · Finland · Florence · Gran Canaria · Greece · Holland · Hong Kong · Ireland · Israel · Italian Lakes · Italian Riviera · Jamaica · Jerusalem · Lisbon · Madeira · Mallorca · Malta

Milan · Moscow · Munich · Normandy · Norway · Paris · Poland · Portugal · Prague · Provence · Rhodes · Rome · St Petersburg · Salzburg · Singapore · Switzerland · Sydney · Tenerife · Thailand · Turkey · Turkish Coast · Tuscany

UK regional titles:
Bath & Surroundings · Cambridge & East Anglia · Cornwall · Cotswolds · Devon & Exmoor · Edinburgh · Lake District · London · New Forest · North York Moors · Northumbria · Oxford · Peak District · Scotland · Scottish Highlands · Shakespeare Country · Snowdonia · South Downs · York · Yorkshire Dales

USA regional titles:
Boston · Cape Cod · Chicago · Florida · Florida Keys · Hawaii: Maui · Hawaii: Oahu · Las Vegas · Los Angeles · Martha's Vineyard & Nantucket · New York · San Francisco · Washington D.C. · Venice · Vienna · West of Ireland